T0384354

Praise for

CONSPIRITUALITY

"No one knows the explosive intersection of spirituality and extremism better than the authors of *Conspirituality*, who have been inside these groups and lived to tell about it. In their strongly argued new book, the authors look at the charlatans, conspiracy theorists, and con men of the wellness world—and what we can do to stop them."

—Will Sommer, author of *Trust the Plan*

"*Conspirituality* brilliantly exposes the fusion between conspiracy theories and wellness while emphasizing the 'con' aspect at the heart of both. Truly, there are grifters and scammers everywhere in this world, and the authors have their number, revealing their psychological tricks and how they exploit the pain and trauma of their marks. And far from seeing themselves as too smart to fall for this nonsense, the authors mine their own experiences in cults and coercive movements having seen them from the inside."

—Mike Rothschild, author of
The Storm is Upon Us and *Jewish Space Lasers*

"Intelligent and compassionate, *Conspirituality* is full of insight rooted in direct experience and rigorous analysis. The authors are deeply familiar with and curious about their subject. An essential and unique book that captures both the yearning for and devastating effects of conspirituality as a phenomenon and way of life."

—Julian Feeld, cohost of the *QAnon Anonymous* podcast

"A thoughtful, deeply empathetic exploration of an often-disturbing convergence. As fear, paranoia, and suspicion continue to seep into the New Age health and wellness worlds, Matthew Remski, Derek Beres, and Julian Walker are uniquely well-positioned to be our guides into what they call the 'sparkling but flimsy' answers that conspirituality represents."

—Anna Merlan, author of *Republic of Lies*

"A fascinating, straightforward, well-researched, and sobering unpacking of the complex history, and present-day phenomena, of distorted beliefs within New Age yoga and wellness spaces."

—Seane Corn, yoga teacher and author of
Revolution of the Soul

"A wild and impassioned ride through the recent history of the wellness-based conspiracy movement, some of its most unsavory characters, and many of its victims and survivors. Full of heart, honesty, and immediacy."

—Dr. Theodora Wildcroft, author of
Post-Lineage Yoga

"This is a book for right now! So timely. So needed. Conspirituality takes us on a fascinating, engaging, and empathetic journey through the many ways in which harmful pseudoscience and misinformation has seeped into our world—including into a host of unexpected places like alternative schools and, yep, yoga studios. The authors provide a compelling argument as to why the toleration of conspiratorial rhetoric closes minds and erodes critical thinking. I highly recommend this book to anyone who is curious—and we all should be!—about the history and the social and cultural forces behind our current pseudoscience-filled mess."

—Timothy Caulfield, author of *Relax*

"This rigorously researched book will help future generations, or alien overlords, make sense of this bizarre and confusing moment in human civilization. Beres, Remski, and Walker have established themselves as authoritative chroniclers of conspirituality and its key figures. They are consummate tour guides, revealing all the threads of eugenics, fascism, cultism, moral panic, and magical thinking that came together to form a strange tapestry that now influences mainstream policies and institutions and fuels our culture wars."

—Jennings Brown, journalist and host of
The Gateway and *Revelations* podcasts

"An urgently needed, compelling, and accessible analysis of the deeply troubling proliferation and promotion of conspiracy theories within contemporary spirituality and wellness culture. Combining cutting-edge critique with empathetic context, the authors identify the real threats of conspirituality to societal bonds, public health, and participatory democracy."

—Ann Gleig, associate professor of religion and
cultural studies, University of Central Florida

"This is a groundbreaking and beautifully written roadmap into a topic that is so multifaceted, internally diverse, and consequential I would not have trusted anyone to write it except these authors. The book benefits from their years of immersive experience and deep research on conspirtitualist milieus. A masterful job."

—Amarnath Amarasingam, School of Religion,
Queen's University, Ontario

"An eye-opening dissection of the historical roots that gave life to this modern hybrid of grand conspiracism and spirituality, accompanied by lyrical portraits of this mad, mongrel philosophy's biggest influencers, *Conspirituality* makes sense of humanity's latest brain fart with compassion and exhaustive scholarship. Beres, Remski, and Walker have earned the mantle of torchbearers against conspirituality, illuminating the disturbing crevices of this befuddling movement and helping the rest of us understand, through impeccable prose, what is fueling the world's strangest fever dream."

—Jonathan Jarry, MSc, science communicator,
Office for Science and Society, McGill University

"Over the last several years as we doom-scrolled social media, watching the weird unraveling of the wellness community into a conspiratorial freak-out, the *Conspirituality* podcast's deep-dive analysis was a salve. In their book, they go a step further, providing important context and histories, positing maybe the great awakening was realizing these beliefs were lurking beneath the surface all along."
—Stacie Stukin, journalist

"The space of conspirituality in recent years has become an intricate and confusing web that stretches from crystal healers and vegan yoga practitioners to QAnon influencers and Silicon Valley entrepreneurs. With this book, the authors combine their years of experience and research to provide a detailed analytical map of this influential contemporary phenomenon. It is rigorously researched, deeply empathetic, and at times intensely personal."
—Chris Kavanagh, associate professor of psychology,
Rikkyo University, and cohost of the *Decoding the Gurus* podcast

"*Conspirituality* is full of personal stories, deep dives into the history of naturalist conspiracism, and an analysis of how conspirituality is shaping our modern world. It balances the need for understanding and compassion toward victims of these cult mentalities with concern for the harms of conspirituality and the need to stem its growth."
—Aaron Rabinowitz, PhD candidate, Rutgers Graduate School of
Education, and host of the *Embrace the Void* podcast

"Beres, Remski, and Walker manage something remarkable: with erudition and a wealth of experience they expose treachery and danger hiding in places few expect it. And yet *Conspirituality* is as noteworthy for its captivating storytelling and whit. The result is a book that feels like both a respondsibility and a pleasure to read."
—Benjamin R. Teitelbaum, PhD, associate professor of
ethnomusicology and international affairs,
University of Colorado Boulder

CONSPIRITUALITY

CONSPIRITUALITY

How New Age Conspiracy Theories
Became a Health Threat

DEREK BERES,
MATTHEW REMSKI,
and JULIAN WALKER

PUBLICAFFAIRS

New York

PublicAffairs
Hachette Book Group
1290 Avenue of the Americas, New York, NY 10104
www.publicaffairsbooks.com
@Public_Affairs

Printed in the United States of America

First Edition: June 2023

Published by PublicAffairs, an imprint of Perseus Books, LLC, a subsidiary of Hachette Book Group, Inc. The PublicAffairs name and logo is a trademark of the Hachette Book Group.

The Hachette Speakers Bureau provides a wide range of authors for speaking events. To find out more, go to hachettespeakersbureau.com or email HachetteSpeakers@hbgusa.com.

PublicAffairs books may be purchased in bulk for business, educational, or promotional use. For more information, please contact your local bookseller or the Hachette Book Group Special Markets Department at special.markets@hbgusa.com.

The publisher is not responsible for websites (or their content) that are not owned by the publisher.

Library of Congress Control Number: 2023931315

ISBNs: 9781541702981 (hardcover), 9781541703001 (ebook)

LSC-C

Printing 1, 2023

Derek would like to thank his parents for never refusing to buy him books, which opened (and continue to open) his mind to the world beyond his body on a daily basis. And to his wife, Callan, for challenging, supporting, and loving him at every step.

Matthew dedicates this effort to his late friend and teacher, Luciano Iacobelli: artist, sinner, mystic. To his partner Alix for her constant support, lucid feedback, and empathetic eye. And to his two young sons, that they inherit a world enchanted by emotional honesty and mutual aid.

Julian extends immeasurable gratitude and appreciation to his family and friends (you know who you are!) for their loyalty, empathy, and willingness to deal with an often too-passionate contrarianism. He also holds dear the memory of his English teacher Mr. van der Want—as brave and kind a model of authentic inquiry as a schoolboy could have had.

Thanks to the thinkers who have preceded us in the task of seeing New Age and wellness cultures clearly. Thank you to the health care professionals, disinformation researchers, and anti-extremism activists who gave us ground to stand on during the pandemic. We thank our podcast guests, who helped stretch our brains to meet a wicked problem. And we thank our listeners for stretching our empathy with their many stories of sorrow and recovery.

CONTENTS

MARCH 2020

A FRIEND OF A FRIEND is suddenly posting on Facebook several times a day. The mood is a strange blend of terror, belligerence, and sanctimony.

She isn't scared of a little virus like COVID. Fear of the virus is more dangerous than the virus itself, she says. But new 5G cell towers? These were destroying "our collective immune system."

She questions the accuracy of PCR tests, and then suggests they are actually causing the infections. One of her posts links to an article on a dodgy-looking alt-health site. You click through but then bounce when you see links in the margins to articles about vaccines and autism, and cilantro curing cancer. The comments in her feed are a dogpile of agitated folks overusing phrases that ping-pong between ominous and ecstatic: "the agenda of powers that be" and "everything is unfolding according to Source."

Who is this person? She led classes at your local yoga studio. You actually like her. Her classes were helpful during that rough patch in your life. She talked about loving your body and making peace with "what is." Her voice was soothing. She was persuasive when she criticized "conventional doctors" for not connecting physical health to emotional health.

While your family doctor didn't ask you a single question before writing you a script for Ambien, this yoga teacher connected you with an herbalist who did acupuncture. You went to two appointments, and they were great: You discussed your dreams while he stuck needles in your back. He talked about chamomile tea and valerian root tinctures, about how deep breathing resets your nervous system.

Now, her studio is shuttered by COVID-19 lockdown. Your friendly yoga teacher seems to have ditched her own breathing exercises in the scramble to keep business flowing. She's posting at all hours. It is hard to know when she sleeps. She intersperses her red alerts with livestream yoga classes. There's always a Venmo link in the top comment.

She waves sage around in front of her webcam and asks WHY THE HELL yoga isn't considered an ESSENTIAL SERVICE since there was NOTHING BETTER FOR THE IMMUNE SYSTEM. The doctors aren't telling us *that*, she complains with a knowing smile before stretching into a downward dog. Speaking of essential services, she half-jokes, essential oils were helping to keep her calm and balanced. DM her for details. Thieves oil is an amazing antiseptic, by the way.

One dude who shows up on every thread had recently left an office job to become an empowered men's life coach. He can't contain his contempt for people who are living in fear. CrossFitters lament being locked out of their boxes and share shrill articles about vitamin D and kimchi while claiming face masks are petri dishes for bacteria. Another regular is a doula who writes a mommy blog. She shares a paranoid post claiming that toddlers were all terrified of adults in masks. They were forgetting who their mothers were.

And that herbalist the yoga teacher referred you to? There he is, proudly declaring he doesn't believe in germ theory. Yes—the same guy who stuck needles in your back! "New German Medicine" is now his thing. "Viruses are essential to our evolution," he announces. "Join me on Telegram for more of the truth they don't want you to hear."

The ominous mood is periodically relieved by posts from "holistic healers" who want to reassure everyone that everything is going according to plan. All the fear and uncertainty? Just natural responses to a transformational time. A new phrase starts popping up:

The Great Awakening.

Within a few months, the ideas and memes are replicating and mutating as quickly as COVID-19 itself, infecting mutual friends, even showing up in your DMs: "MAKE SURE TO WATCH THIS BEFORE THEY TAKE IT DOWN!" followed by a YouTube link to a homemade video with a weird voice-over and tons of graphics with statistics about...something. You can't tell for sure because the uploader never linked to sources.

More DMs. Coming from randos, they're strange. From IRL friends, the messages feel claustrophobic—and coming from family members they're downright distressing. *Mom, why are you sharing this with me?*

And just when you think it can't get any more tense or weird, it becomes clear that many of these posters are either promoting or getting drawn into uncharacteristic political invective. Worse: all of it is trending hard right-wing, just as the 2020 election campaign is ramping up.

Someone you know to be gaga about organic food and ayahuasca posts a sermon from an angel channeler who had a vision that Trump was a "light-worker." A guy who leads chakra workshops for men (and who once campaigned for Bernie Sanders) is posting about Joe Biden being in the pocket of the Chinese.

The timeline is chaotic, but cryptic hashtags keep it strung together: #savethechildren, #trusttheplan, #enjoytheshow, #WWG1WGA. It's chilling, because you've heard these terms in a news report about QAnon, an online conspiracy theory that was melting brains and ruining families. "Saving the children" referred to the belief among Anons that Elites around the world existed to perpetuate child sex trafficking.

"The show" pointed to their belief that their invisible prophet, Q, was battling said Elites in lockstep with Donald Trump, according to "the plan." Victory was a foregone conclusion. The weird string of letters was for the rally cry "Where We Go One, We Go All," which they believed had been embossed on the bell of a sailboat owned by John F. Kennedy, who for some represented the last sitting president to challenge the American political orthodoxy. Other Anons came to believe he would return from the dead.

Your yoga teacher starts looking more underslept on her stream. Twitchier. She starts featuring some guy—probably dating him—who sells supplements and leads seminars on Bitcoin. They publish a couples' livestream titled "Nothing can stop what is coming."

What happened to these people, most of whom you knew to be educated, well-meaning, politically liberal (or at least moderate), and generally kind? How, with all their talk about healing and oneness, had they fallen into a rabbit hole of right-wing paranoia scented with New Age candles? Where would it all lead?

INTRODUCTION

IF YOU'VE PICKED UP THIS BOOK, there's a good chance that the landscape of our prologue feels familiar.

In early March 2020, a lot of us noticed our social media feeds starting to prickle with uneasy questions. *Is this virus thing serious? Should we be canceling that trip?* Infection rates of something called COVID-19 were spiking, somewhere. There were x- and y-axis graphs to prove it. The upward line looked like a hockey stick.

By midmonth, the clues and whispers crystallized in a world-stopping declaration from the World Health Organization. The NBA canceled its season as though turning off a light. Schools shuttered and church services were bumped to Zoom. Restaurants closed and the mail ground to a halt. The big box stores scrambled to put spacing stickers in the checkout lines. There was a weird run on toilet paper. Did you have enough flour at home? Alcohol wipes? What exactly were you supposed to wipe down, anyway? What would the children do—and what would *you* do with them at home all day?

By April, the challenge became balancing doomscrolling with the search for reliable info on what "R-naught" meant. We learned about flattening the curve and how to wash our hands long enough to sing "Happy Birthday" twice. Crafters started making masks at home from fabric ends, with pockets for coffee filters. Facebook groups formed to collate the most helpful information about keeping safe or to organize grocery runs for shut-ins. But soon, among the images of hospital chaos in Italy and cruise ships docked like floating leper colonies, an even more curdled version of social media emerged: an antisocial petri dish of rumors and accusations. *Are we being lied to, yet again? What are the Chinese up to? Was it a bioweapon targeting Western democracy? Is 5G making us sick? Why are we getting mixed messages about masks?*

To be fair: folks prone to conspiracy theories had a lot to pull on when it came to the ragged fabric of public health communications. Introverted policy wonks were suddenly in the limelight, interpreting changing and complex emergency data for a headline-hungry news cycle. They tried their best to thread the needle between *this is a dangerous time* and *we'll do just fine.* But every day, their anxious, meandering, or incomplete statements threw the red meat of controversy into the jaws of the social media beast, fueling the fire of fantasy and paranoia.

First came the warning about COVID spreading on surfaces. People spent frantic hours disinfecting grocery bags, bank cards, car keys, and door handles. But suddenly, the science changed—or rather, developed—and we learned the term "hygiene theater." It made a lot of people feel as if they had been silly or neurotic. Infectious disease expert Dr. Anthony Fauci—who'd cut his public health teeth on the AIDS crisis decades earlier—unintentionally contributed to the early confusion. At first he advised the public not to wear masks, but did not disclose that this was based on a supply concern—that vulnerable health care workers must not run out of masks. When the headlines pointed to aerosolization as the primary route of contagion, suddenly masks were essential for everyone. At first, cloth was fine. Then it was blue surgical masks. Eventually, it *had* to be N95s.

Could you catch COVID outside? At the outset, major newspapers said, "Yes, you can." Hypervigilant readers rained down a highbrow resentment on spring break beach partiers. Conservatives decried the framing of Black Lives Matter protests as acceptable—even noble—while churches or workplaces were shuttered. Were PCR tests reliable? Accessible? What did "rapid flow" mean, and who could be trusted to explain it?

On the vaccine front, history will show that the COVID response was a wonder of global innovation and adaptation. But the news fog through which it was first told was garbled with amplified panic over exceedingly rare side effects. The mayor of Detroit turned away thousands of doses of the Johnson & Johnson vaccine, appeasing his citizens' inflated fears over the rare incidence of blood clotting as a side effect. Then, Pfizer released a flawed report on vaccine injuries.

It would take many months for it to become clear that each facepalm in science communications—each vague reassurance, each bylaw that restricted employment but failed to support workers edging toward bankruptcy, each whiff of hypocrisy from public officials or opportunism from drug companies—landed on cultural wounds that crossed political boundaries. While well-meaning researchers and scientists were constantly working to keep up with the evolving science and offer the best assessments they could with the evidence at hand, social media was working in binaries to punish anything perceived as flip-flopping. This gave everyone who was already on the edge of institutional distrust a boost of validation, and a broader demographic to engage.

The official responses to the COVID-19 pandemic illuminated the opacity of medical bureaucracy. The changing rules, and the jargon they were delivered in, reminded many of every confusing and queasy doctor's office visit they'd had. Lockdowns reminded some of all the times it felt like the cure was worse than the disease. COVID exposed the craven policies of governments interested in health only as far as it could keep people working. It made many people feel, more powerfully than ever before, that they live in an age in which they are surveilled but neglected, in which they are managed but not heard.

In hindsight, this very real social precarity and sense of institutional betrayal helped to foster an urgent desire for novel answers and individual empowerment. An increasingly anti-social media began to crackle with vaguely connected phrases and memes that were both paranoid and strangely overly confident. People were posting about COVID as if they had better intel than public health officials, a better grasp of the Big Picture. They had a secret knowledge they were compelled to share, even if the details were sketchy. According to them, something far more terrible than a pandemic was unfolding. In reality, the posters argued, the pandemic was a ruse through which governments, Big Pharma, and amoral tech companies could execute ancient plans for world domination. The sacred circle of family and nature—from which health and fulfillment flow—was under attack.

At a certain point it might have clicked that some of these posts weren't coming from the usual cage-fighting political pro wrestlers. The paranoia had a Goop-y glow. The pandemic had inflamed an obsession with health.

Not the public type of health—now caricatured by tedious messages about social distancing and masks—but an impassioned, moralizing fetish for personal health that is preoccupied with low body fat, supplements, positive thinking, sugar elimination, and focus on the soul.

AS VETERANS OF WELLNESS AND YOGA practices and their volatile business climates, the three of us knew the scene and had heard the jargon—just not at this shrill pitch. In fact, conspirituality (as we named the podcast we scrambled together by May 2020) is at least a century old, and we'd been picking at its modern threads for over a decade. In its current form, we see it as an online religion that fuses two faith claims: 1) *The world is possessed by evil forces, and* 2) *those who see this clearly are called to foster, in themselves and others, a new spiritual paradigm.*

By chance, we had the chops to hack into this tangle, and quickly. Derek had been covering the pseudoscience of alternative health grifts as a journalist. Julian was a noted yogaworld skeptic. Matthew had graduated from years spent in two spiritual cults and into the world of anti-cult activism and research. All three of us loved our ragtag chosen family of yoga enthusiasts, meditators, herbalists, organic farmers, and plant-medicine psychonauts. We'd seen the clear benefits of nonconventional and personalized wellness practices in our lives, how nontraditional spiritualities could help mend the wounds left by Big Religion and fill the space where conventional medicine had failed its patients. But we also knew that this culture emerged in an ideological and economic landscape that churned out spiritual junk food, emotional manipulation, and pseudopolitical demagoguery.

We knew of vulnerable people who went to Reiki "masters," believing that warm hands hovering over their abdomens could heal their diabetes or endometriosis. We knew of drug addicts who had used yoga practice to help create new lives, only to find themselves ensnared in yoga cults. We heard stories about cancer patients on pilgrimage to rural Brazil to undergo "psychic surgery" by John of God, who, by the way, now sits in jail, convicted of multiple rapes.

We also had our own stories.

WHEN DEREK WAS THIRTY he was having anxiety and panic attacks; over time, they became intolerable. He tried yoga and meditation, and even spent six months on a benzodiazepine. Then he found "Edgar" (not his real name), a homeopath for Manhattan's jet set. The initial consultation was long and probing, and it involved a series of very personal questions. He would later wonder about the point of this line of questioning—how could it possibly relate to the treatment?—given that most homeopathic products have no active ingredient, and therefore no possible physiological benefit. But he was desperate for relief. He received a series of costly prescriptions for sugar pills with Latinate names. After four failed attempts at finding the right formulation, he lost faith in the treatment and stopped seeing Edgar. His anxiety attacks never stopped.

When Derek was diagnosed with testicular cancer in his mid-thirties, his hometown New Jersey friends rallied around him. But some of his friends and colleagues in the Los Angeles yoga and wellness worlds, where he'd taught classes for years, turned cold, sanctimonious.

"Your cancer happened for a reason," they told him. They were hinting at the New Age dogma of personal spiritual responsibility, which is used both to explain aberrations that disrupt the idealized world of love and light and to blame people for remaining sick, even when they are chanting all the right mantras. The truth, of course, was that Derek's cancer had real-world causes. As a boy, he had an undescended testicle that required hormone therapy—a strong predictor for his eventual diagnosis.

Derek also grew up overweight, and the scars of being bullied lasted for decades. In his mid-twenties, working in the wellness industry as a yoga instructor, music producer, and health journalist tilted him toward developing orthorexia, an eating disorder centered on an obsession with "pure" or "clean" foods. It's a disorder that can lead to malnutrition, chaotic weight fluctuations, and social isolation in the singular pursuit of health.

It took Derek fifteen years to leave the fad diet hamster wheel as he realized that wellness-world fat-shaming was a professionalized and socially acceptable form of bullying. It sharpened his radar for seeing how pseudoscience intersects with ableism to devastating psychological effect. A big chunk of his health journalism went on to expose how wellness influencers—most of them not certified in nutritional sciences—capitalize on bodily dysmorphia to promote certain foods and demonize others (often for profit), while overlooking the reality that many people don't have access to healthy foods in general.

* * *

JULIAN'S FIRST EXPERIENCE of the yogaworld, at twenty-three, was shaped by his relationship with Ana Forrest, a world-renowned teacher who described herself as the alpha-dog of her tightly knit group. Forrest had a gruesome backstory of abuse and addiction, which she would recount at every sharing circle and workshop. She also had an ever-changing cast of studio managers, employee teachers, friends, and lovers who would fall in and out of favor—with the door locks being changed after each dramatic new banishment. She gave Julian a job and affirmed his gifts, but she also meddled in his personal relationships, and convinced him (along with many in the community) that he must have repressed horrific family trauma memories of the sort she believed her approach to yoga could heal. Disenchanted by how pop spirituality seemed to deny suffering in the name of magical thinking, Julian was captivated by Forrest's emphasis on facing one's demons.

It turned out that Forrest had been influenced by a hypnotherapist who had guided her to her own recovered memories of awful abuse both in this life and in previous lives. Her unqualified and projective diagnosis of Julian was incorrect and subsequently devastated his relationship with his parents and younger brother for the better part of fifteen years.

In his late thirties, Julian watched a friend and fellow teacher, Psalm Isadora, grow to national prominence on the strength of claiming to have found an approach to Tantric yoga that had completely healed the trauma she sustained as a child in a fundamentalist Christian cult. Isadora had been diagnosed with bipolar disorder, and was open about believing her yoga had replaced the need for medication. As her star rose she started undergoing multiple rounds of plastic surgery, presenting herself in increasingly sexualized ways, and was cast in a reality TV show on the Playboy Channel.

Isadora was heralded as an inspiring voice for traumatized women, an exemplar of resilience, healing, and empowerment—until she tragically died from suicide at forty-two while trying to kick her Xanax and alcohol dependency. She had gone cold turkey under pressure from a close group of friends, who believed they could support her through it at home. The tragedy dovetailed with a tendency Julian had seen in yogaworld to frame mental illness as either a spiritual gift or something that could be balanced out by enough yoga, meditation, wheatgrass juice, or going gluten-free.

Yoga, meditation, and other practices of self-expression have remained important in Julian's life. But for him it was clear that the spiritual marketplace, with its charismatic figures and ungrounded philosophies, often created more suffering than salvation. As an antidote, he turned toward science and psychology, and went to therapy. When the crisis of conspirituality hit in 2020, he felt like he had some solid tools to deal with the trauma, and to protect himself from figures who might take advantage of his vulnerability.

MATTHEW CAME to the conspirituality beat through the world of cult recovery. The first group he was recruited into, in 1996, was founded and led by the American neo-Buddhist monk Michael Roach. Matthew first went to see him speak in a church when Roach swung through town, accompanied by his entourage of beaming college dropouts, who sat in a circle at his feet. At one point, it seemed that Roach looked directly into his soul (even though the place was packed) as he said: "You're going to die. What are you doing about it?" Matthew felt something crack inside. He was at a low point: a crossroads in work and personal relationships. Looking back, he was likely suffering from undiagnosed depression. But suddenly, here was somebody—a white guy like him, but in maroon robes out of the Middle Ages—who seemed to be speaking the truth amid all the ennui, cutting through the hypocrisies and dissociations of modern life. This was a person with an urgent message. That's what Matthew wanted to be.

Within months, Matthew was following Roach around the world, tasked with transcribing and editing his talks for publication. His close attention to Roach's teachings helped him see something earlier than he otherwise might have. Roach purported to teach a strictly traditional Tibetan Buddhism, rooted in the renunciation of worldly concerns in order to develop limitless compassion. His capacity to recite long passages of Tibetan scripture from memory was impressive. But before long it became clear to Matthew that Roach was also making shit up, branding a strange cocktail of Tantric worship and prosperity gospel hopium. He was clearly chasing big money, proselytizing to oligarchs from Hong Kong to Moscow about how Buddhism offered a pathway to ethical financial success. He was also exploiting his young followers, who were positioned within the group to become teachers in their own right but typically failed to launch. One woman, decades his junior, played the role of Roach's spiritual partner, which meant eating from the same plate, never standing more than fifteen feet away from him, and eventually living with him for a three-year retreat in a yurt in the Arizona desert, practicing sexual yoga.

Years after Matthew had gotten out, Ian Thorson, one of Roach's closest disciples, died of dehydration and malnutrition in that desert, just beyond the boundaries of Roach's retreat center. Helping to break this news as a former insider catapulted Matthew into cult journalism. He published a series of gonzo articles about Roach's group and his memories of Ian, including details about Ian's fragile mental health.

It took Roach only two months into the 2020s pandemic to market an online meditation program "designed to plant seeds to eradicate the virus."

After pulling himself out of Roach's cult, Matthew was recruited into another. (It's called cult-hopping, and it happens to people who can't find a social and psychological bridge back to reality.) This second group, in southern Wisconsin, was called Endeavor Academy. The group's daily activities revolved around a book called *A Course in Miracles*—a sort of post-Christian bible for New Agers, popularized by the media magnate Louise Hay and perennial presidential hopeful Marianne Williamson.

While at Endeavor, Matthew watched "Gloria," who was in her sixties, wither and die of aggressive cancer because the group's ideology valued miracles over medicine, and because Charles Anderson, the dry-drunk ex-Marine spiritual leader, pretended he could heal disciples with his "energy." Matthew never knew Gloria's real name, but he knew that the group leaders didn't even notify her children when she stopped eating, or when she collapsed for what turned out to be the final time during an ecstatic prayer session.

Matthew got out of Anderson's cult in 2003. Having strained his family connections and stalled out on his university prospects, he wound up hanging around the yoga and wellness world as a gig worker for another fifteen years. It felt safer for a while. But over time, it became clear that the dynamics that could crystallize into the brick-and-mortar cults he'd been caught up in—dynamics such as deception, hype, and charismatic leadership—were common throughout the yoga and wellness world. The industry was decentralized and baldly entrepreneurial, but it functioned as a petri dish incubating clumps of high-demand groups.

* * *

ALTHOUGH WE CAME to this project from different angles—cancer, deaths, cults—one thing we all shared was the whoosh of riding yoga's economic boom as young gig workers in the aughts. It's given us a felt sense of how the current explosion of conspirituality is wedded to the drivers of the wellness economy.

As an online religion, conspirituality today is not just a set of ideas that people come to value in their quiet and humble hearts. It is generated and circulated by virtual churches, revival meetings, and séance sessions in the form of small-group courses and mastermind Zoom meetings. How these religious networks function is inseparable from their means of support. The line between virtual worship and the e-commerce that drives it is very hard to find.

All of this comes at the tail end of a decades-long process. Up until 2005, yoga teachers and meditation instructors would market themselves by posting paper flyers around town at health food stores, coffee shops, and on notice boards of the studios they gigged at. Workshops, retreats, and weekly classes all required their own branded angle, benefits, and style. Their personal inkjet printers were working overtime, and the most online anyone got was to post workshop announcements on Myspace.

Suddenly, flyers required website addresses where people could find out more and sign up. Then came email lists, newsletters, subscriptions to newsletters. Leaders in the field were often former corporate executives who had left the rat race for the lifestyle race. They knew all about branding and customer experience. They could soft-sell their communities of loyal fans.

Top earners—or those who pretended to be—produced video courses about online marketing, email capture widgets, social media ads, Google keywords, and content-marketing in the form of blog posts and videos. And what good was all of it without selling products? DVDs, supplements, premium video courses—all of which were promised to generate oodles of passive income, while spreading the gospel of spiritual prosperity.

The movement matured to produce affiliate marketing schemes centered on free digital summits that allowed otherwise competing influencers access to shared lists and audiences.

By the time COVID hit, a well-oiled internet machinery was in place to reach millions of people across multiple platforms through massive online conferences. Conversion funnels turned consumers into members of in-groups receiving not only dangerous propaganda but also special early-access offers for online misinformation seminars. The exponential growth in these campaigns mirrored the infinite promises of the New Age, but also the growth of COVID-19 transmission rates and case numbers.

WHAT WE DIDN'T REALIZE until years later was that this whirlwind of marketing techniques and sales funnels functioned as a delivery system for the pieces of a disturbing historical puzzle we can now identify as "soft eugenics." Modern yoga and wellness, which echoed with a kind of (now-depoliticized) body fascism that was over a century old, was being laundered through aspirational consumerism so that its sexist, racist, and violent implications were almost invisible.

These were techniques by which we could constantly judge ourselves against impossible ideals of physical and moral fitness, and perform our virtues or confess our sins to dominant figures who held charismatic power. Those authorities assessed us with a warmed-over version of the nineteenth-century pseudoscience of physiognomy—the premise that the appearance and performance of one's body revealed character and social value. We didn't recognize the ableism that could easily curdle an otherwise wholesome yogic worldview—especially through the influence of American individualism. The twisted message was that if a person was injured or disabled, they were revealing the karmic punishment of their own unprocessed trauma. We didn't recognize the eugenics theme running unconsciously through all of it: that flaws in bodies should be identified, corrected, and bred out of existence so that they no longer troubled the advancement of human evolution or the conscience of the privileged.

At the time, we didn't understand that these obsessions with posture, bodily strength, and purity have always been foundational to the politics of *us vs. them* that divides the worthy from the degenerate. We didn't recognize that we were stretching and twisting in the internalized echo of cruel beliefs about the body—mixed up with evergreen prejudices against the disabled, women, and minorities.

WE'VE COVERED ONE YOGA and wellness influencer after another who have seemingly lost their minds to conspirituality. A common refrain we've heard from our podcast listeners is this: "Well, at least the pandemic has forced people to show their true colors." True enough. But there was something broader and deeper at play than personal eccentricities. What awakened in 2020 were the sleeping values of a century before. The conspirituality explosion was in part a story of bad historical ideas bursting out of their hidey-holes in the gentrified yoga studios of the Global North. These studios—along with their studio-type adjacent businesses that offer bodywork and life-coaching—provided an infrastructure that was ready for the conspirituality moment.

The bar for achieving conspirituality influence lowered at the same moment the stakes were rising. The monetization of the supposed "Great Awakening"—the familiar prophecy of a world-enlightening spiritual revelation, now framed through the promise of freedom from a trance state induced by the evil Cabal behind the "COVID-19 hoax"—no longer required lifelong investments from a small number of dedicated enthusiasts. In a moment of peak cultural anxiety, COVID-contrarian gurus could throw off their brick-and-mortar limitations, re-create themselves on Instagram, and get paid through subscriptions as they learned how to use the algorithms of these platforms to spread misinformation.

The three of us have collaborated on yogaworld cultural criticism since meeting as bloggers in 2011. We read each other's work, discussed and sometimes debated the labyrinths of religious vs. spiritual, cultural appropriation, "spiritual bypassing," and the problem of cults. At the end of April 2020, Derek published an explainer piece on a new term he'd come across: "conspirituality." A month later, the New Age–inflected anti-vax documentary *Plandemic* went viral, prompting Julian to publish a viral piece titled "The Red Pill Overlap," tracking the incursions of far-right ideology into yogaland. Within a week we were on Zoom, resuming an old and now more urgent conversation.

Since then, through our podcast, we've mapped this movement and its winding journey through anti-vax fervor, anxieties over 5G technology, trumped-up child trafficking panics, the violence of January 6, the rise of Omicron and the #okgroomer trend, the Occupation of Ottawa, the war in Ukraine, and whatever else is happening as this book goes to print. Hopefully, beginning this examination with a little of our own journeys gives our readers hope that, yes, the fog can lift.

In Part One of this book, we delve into the idea of conspirituality—what it is, how it works, and why it ensnares so many people. Part Two unearths the historical tensions and perennial brainworms that have degraded cognition in the wellness world. In Part Three, we introduce you to our rogues' gallery—the most egregious examples of influencers who instrumentalized conspirituality in the COVID era, along a spectrum of earnestness and deceit. In Part Four, we share the stories of some of those who have been impacted by conspirituality, the lessons they have learned, and what they can tell us about the future of this shared, disruptive dream. Finally, we share insights from the experts we've had on our podcast.

PART ONE

CONSPIRITUALITY 101

CHAPTER 1

CHARLOTTE'S WEB

As we scrambled to get our podcast together, we leaned heavily on a 2011 paper, "The Emergence of Conspirituality," by British independent researcher Charlotte Ward and American sociologist of religion David Voas. The paper contained the first modern-day definition of conspirituality, referring to it as a synthesis of the "female-dominated New Age (with its positive focus on self) and the male-dominated realm of conspiracy theory (with its negative focus on global politics)." It was, they wrote, a "rapidly growing web movement expressing an ideology fueled by political disillusionment and the popularity of alternative worldviews."

It goes on to say:

> [Conspirituality] offers a broad politico-spiritual philosophy based on two core convictions, the first traditional to conspiracy theory, the second rooted in the New Age:
>
> 1) a secret group covertly controls, or is trying to control, the political and social order, and
>
> 2) humanity is undergoing a 'paradigm shift' in consciousness.
>
> Proponents believe that the best strategy for dealing with the threat of a totalitarian 'new world order' is to act in accordance with an awakened 'new paradigm' worldview.

It was a chef's kiss type of academic work: unrelenting in its clarity, punch, and predictive acumen—very impressive features for research into an online phenomenon that was published before social media exploded the world.

This definition captures so much about what we understand conspirituality to be today—the handshake between hope and cynicism, and the divine accelerationist storyline—that the world is careening toward transformation, aided by political and spiritual conflict. The formula had immediate application as we tracked influencers and their followers. On the gender front, we indeed tracked female doctors, channelers, and at least two women cult leaders who presented the female-oriented positive focus on the self—echoing Ward and Voas's observation that the majority of New Age and wellness enthusiasts are women. But we also saw preacher men and bro scientists pushing a negative focus on global politics, who in some cases began to integrate arguments for gun rights into their views on natural empowerment. But, of course, there are also plenty of New Age-y men and loads of conspiracy-theorist women on our beat. Regardless of gender, conspiritualists convene at the spa, or at the MMA octagon. They indulge in self-care products, but also cloak-and-dagger political intrigue. They crave nurturance, but also dominance. They come with many identities, but vibe together to conceive an "awakened new paradigm."

Having been embedded in yoga studios and alternative health circles for decades, we began exploring the real-world impact conspirituality was having on the people in our orbit. Informed by the work of Ward and Voas, we found ourselves studying the explosion of new conspirituality themes through the interplay of COVID-denialism, the reactionary politics of Trump, anti-vaccine fearmongering, and a cultish surge of prophetic spiritual dynamics. Conspiritualist viral messaging slipped into an already seamless e-commerce delivery system that leverages social media, email marketing, and websites designed to sell books, video courses, and online conferences to passionate followers with shared fears and longings.

While we wouldn't have gotten far without this paper, we also have to report, up front, that we were duped by its lead author.

Charlotte Ward was not a dispassionate scholar of a new religious movement. She was, in her own words, an enthusiastic conspiritualist, at least until around 2015, when her online footprint vanished into thin air and became relegated to the webarchive. Prior to that, she was an active participant in the online outrage mill that churned out macabre conspiracy resources and set the stage for the explosion of QAnon, two years later.

Ward's aim in studying conspirituality was not academic. It was sectarian, even propagandistic. It appears her goal was to academically legitimize conspirituality as a politically neutral cultural orientation and practice. The bulk of her original website, conspirituality.org (now archived), records her breathless use of web analytics to track rising interest in what she termed "A Global Awakening." She giddily presented reports on the rise of web searches for keywords such as *Illuminati* in Hungary and Poland as proof that transformation was at hand. (The Illuminati is one of several names for the imaginary elite cadre of bankers, politicians, and intellectuals purported to secretly control the world.)

SINCE 1981, DAVID VOAS, Ward's collaborator on the paper, has been building a meticulous archive of research on religious movements. But he takes very little credit for the ideas that defined conspirituality.

"Charlotte deserves full credit for the paper that was ultimately published," Voas said by email. "I did my best to give it an academic gloss, and I can't now remember exactly how much I contributed, but the core content is hers."

That core content shines with what appears to be scholarly distance. Ward describes the New Age view as a natural state of spiritual wholeness, obscured by a modern loss of magic and mystery, rendering humanity out of touch with the Earth and our inner knowing of transcendent truths. By trusting the spiritual guidance of synchronicity, reading the signs, and debunking the lies of materialist science, the New Ager perceives a universe of paranormal phenomena, divine purpose, natural herbal healing, and immersive metaphysical meaning.

Against this, Ward juxtaposes the mindset of conspiracy theorists preoccupied with uncovering the hidden patterns that expose a dark and paranoid vision of the world in which nothing can be trusted. Cabals of villains with nefarious agendas manipulate current events and hypnotize innocents with lies and stratagems. Their bloodlines extend back into an ancient demonic past, and forward into a transhumanist and alien-hybrid future.

In Ward's formulation, what connects these two seemingly opposing groups—New Agers and conspiracists—is a penchant for seeking patterns, and a belief that hidden truths can be discovered through alternative methods by those who truly want to wake up. Where New Agers gravitate to conspiratorial explanations for why there is no evidence to support their favorite paranormal or alternative medicine beliefs, conspiracy theorists flirt with the idea that exposing and vanquishing evil cabals will inevitably lead to a predestined Utopia.

The impulses toward debunking, retribution, and spiritual awakening flow into each other seamlessly. As "clients seek to expose—depose—a shadow government," Ward writes, "ideas that others are becoming 'awake and aware,' or shifting in consciousness, lend encouragement. People are awakening to a new interconnected paradigm, in which they remember their infinite power."

Ward's "clients"—such a strange word for a religious studies paper—ground their views in personal spiritual epiphanies. It's a theme with a long history within the New Age and wellness worlds. Whenever a client faces pushback over implausible claims about such things as the nature of the universe, the efficacy of a meditation practice, or the value of turmeric in combating cancer, they will typically say that the Doubting Thomas simply needs to experience these things themselves. Then they will believe. In the COVID and QAnon eras, this axiom shows up in the command to "do your own research," and in the co-optation of "taking the red pill" moment from the Matrix series.

Ward's scholarship at first seems solid. But on her archived website, the enthusiasm hidden within her analysis shines through. "If you are into internet truth and conspiracy theory or alternative spirituality," Ward writes, "you will have heard about the 'global awakening'—this is what we are looking at. And if you ever feel awake and alone...well, the numbers prove that you are NOT. Feast your eyes on our data and subscribe to our blog to keep up-to-date with the numbers."

"When it came to conspirituality," Voas notes, carefully, Ward "was a participant observer. She was sufficiently detached to analyze the phenomenon, but her familiarity came from personal interest in alternative spirituality tinged with conspiracism."

A BIG RED FLAG waves over Ward's fondness for the British conspiracy mongerer David Icke, who preaches that humans are controlled by alien reptiles and who has endorsed the antisemitic urtext of twentieth-century conspiracy theories, *The Protocols of the Elders of Zion*. On her website, Ward quotes Icke to *defend* the conspirituality movement against charges of racism and antisemitism: "We need to drop the ludicrous, childish labels of Jew and Gentile and Muslim and all this illusory crap," Ward quotes Icke as saying, "and come together in the name of peace and justice for all. There is not a Jewish injustice or a Palestinian injustice, there is simply injustice."

Yikes.

This same quote appears in Ward's paper, where she launders Icke's biography with the descriptors "British author and activist." She lets his quote stand unexamined in the academic setting, and then uses that omission on her personal site to "prove" its truth. "We have had published a peer-reviewed article," Ward gloats, "which states that [conspirituality] is not about racism or anti-Semitism."

The truth is that an unchallenged quote from England's version of Alex Jones shows that conspiritualists can sound like pacifists if key facts are omitted. But as the history of conspirituality will show, it's naive to the point of negligence to argue that the movement isn't rife with antisemitic, racist, and fascist themes—and that, like Icke, it tries to present itself as centrist, rather than right-wing.

Ward's views can also be obscured by her cosmic scope. "Conspirituality is conscious conspiracy," she waxes, in a passage that links to Icke and the British conspiracy website thetruthseeker.co.uk and *Ancient Aliens* star and Illuminati tracker David Wilcock. Wilcock, a QAnon booster who hints he may be the reincarnation of famed nineteenth-century clairvoyant Edgar Cayce, believes the disclosure of secret human contact with aliens is about to usher in a global spiritual transformation.

Ward shared enough of Wilcock's concern with global pedophile networks that by 2014 she was embroiled in "researching" a moral panic in London's Hampstead neighborhood. Now known as the Hampstead Hoax, it saw 175 adults subjected to mob allegations of Satanic Ritual Abuse (SRA). The main target of the allegations was a man named Ricky Dearman. As the eventual court judgment described, Dearman's children were physically and emotionally coerced by their mother and her new partner into fabricating a lurid tale about him and fellow teachers at Christ Church Primary School. That tale involved a satanic cult, which drank babies' blood and cooked children in a secret room at the local McDonald's. The stories predicted and predated the precursor to QAnon—the Pizzagate conspiracy theory—by almost two years. And their source predicted the porous boundary between the puritanical extremism of yoga and wellness culture and the drive to spread Satanic Panic conspiracy theories. The children's mother was a Bikram Yoga teacher, and her new partner was a raw food fanatic.

Two of the rumormongers who spread the Hampstead allegations online to a global audience of an estimated four million were jailed, with the court issuing a scathing ruling against their claims. But a third online activist was never charged. In 2015, a "Jacqui Farmer" had launched an anonymous "research" and networking site committed to supporting the false allegations.

In 2017, a citizen sleuthing group supporting the falsely accused published a paper trail that unmasked Jacqui Farmer as none other than Charlotte Ward. They found her through a screenshot maze of email addresses and YouTube accounts. Ward also wrote under the name Jacqui for conspirituality .org, with the HTML link for her author's page pointing to Charlotte in the address line. In a 2018 attempt to distance herself from the Hoax, Ward emailed a journalist at ukcolumn.org to request an end to their investigation. She signed the email "Charlotte Ward aka Jacqui Farmer."

The sleuthing group also tracked down, online, a 2014 self-published book titled *Illuminati Party!—Reasons Not to Be Scared of the Illuminati*, authored by Jacqui Farmer. The promo blurb, written by Ward (as Farmer), remains online at Google Books. It reveals the gentle aim of Ward's practice of conspirituality: she wants readers to somehow gain strength as they absorb her abject tales.

> This book does not try to persuade you that the Illuminati do or do not exist. This is because they do. But it is an illusion that they have all the power; in fearing them you are under a spell they have cast. This book has been written to help you break it. . . . I've been working underground as a Warrior, subverting the Illuminati for years. I discuss a few things you can do, too—if you choose.

In the preface, Ward notes that she's written the book for ages twelve and up, then advises terrified readers to chant a protective mantra: "I release my fear and step into my power."

* * *

WE DON'T KNOW MUCH about Ward's story before conspirituality—where she came from, where she was educated, or how she acquired her interests. According to LinkedIn, she now resides in Suriname, South America. She responded to our initial email query with a cryptic comment—that there were "mistakes in the paper" she'd published with Voas, "which the reviewers could not have been expected to spot." She signed off apologetically. "If you send me a list of questions, I'd happily answer them in writing. Frankly, I probably sound a little deranged live anyway." She didn't respond to follow-up emails.

For us, the Ward/Farmer tangle is a call to caution and humility, as we go forward under a banner we unwittingly repurposed from a propagandist.

First, this story has shown us that skill at analyzing a toxic social movement does not necessarily indicate a person is safe from its seductions and excesses. Objectivity is hard. Second, it has revealed that the line between real-world conspiracies and spurious conspiracy theories—such as the reality of child trafficking vs. Satanic Ritual Abuse—can be easily blurred, especially among vulnerable populations or excitable amateur investigators. Third, it has demonstrated that exploring the world of conspirituality can provoke the unintended consequence of promoting it.

Bottom line: We spent eighteen months quoting a double agent. We used Ward's model to deconstruct the same world she was trying to build.

Charlotte's web shows how conspirituality unfolds in the chaotic shadowland of the internet, where everyone can be the detective of their own fetishes—and feel heroic about it—where no one needs to or can be transparent, and where rumor can escalate through allegation into moral panic with blinding speed. It's anyone's guess what Ward's search history contains between 2011 and 2014, but her publications suggest more than passing familiarity with what was brewing on the underground message (chan) boards that would later give rise to Pizzagate and QAnon.

Ward's story presents research challenges we must navigate, but not get caught in ourselves. We were only a few months into our reporting when a few irritated listeners began to say that our episodes were generating a moral panic around the issue—that conspirituality was less of a deal than we were making. They argued that this could only marginalize those who follow the figures we were criticizing. We believe they are wrong—that conspirituality is a powerful and intoxicating socioreligious movement that can ruin families, disrupt public health measures, and encourage civil unrest. We believe that it must be spotlit and understood. But we hope this criticism keeps us honest and empathetic.

Finally, wherever Ward is now, and whatever her current views, her story reminds us that conspirituality, like much of the internet, is an unforgiving, delusional world that entraps highly creative and empathetic people. Everyone deserves to be welcomed back from it, should they manage to leave.

CHAPTER 2

THE MYSTIC AND PARANOID TRIFECTA

WHEN MATTHEW was in the cult of the neo-Buddhist monk Michael Roach, he was witness to a lot of bullshit and emotional coercion—themes and tactics we'll see in spades throughout our stories. But it wasn't all like that. Cults have to offer something of value, or no one would stay.

Roach had been sufficiently trained by a legitimate Tibetan *Rinpoche* (a professor-priest thought to be reincarnated) that he had a solid understanding of medieval Indo-Tibetan philosophy. The content of Roach's teachings revolved around a trifecta of powerful concepts: karma, illusion, and interdependence. The ideas made a lot of sense to Matthew—they still do, in a way—and to some extent relieved what he now believes was his own undiagnosed depression.

What he didn't realize at the time is that those same three concepts, curdled by alienation and paranoia, can merge with the three pillars of conspiratorial thinking, as laid out by the political scientist Michael Barkun. Nothing happens by accident. Nothing is as it seems. Everything is connected.

"Conspiracy," Barkun writes, "implies a world based on intentionality, from which accident and coincidence have been removed." Those who control it make sure that everything happens according to plan. But this does not mean mere commoners will understand the reality of things. "Conspirators wish to deceive."

Finally, Barkun continues, "Because the conspiracists' world has no room for accident, pattern is believed to be everywhere, albeit hidden from plain view." The calling of the conspiracy theorist, therefore, is to eternally connect the dots.

Through these three mantras, the conspiracist comes to terms with evil and anxiety, and finds a way of imagining a sensible and responsive universe. The effect, Barkun says, "is both frightening and reassuring," in that evil is magnified, but also comprehensible. The world is terrible, but the terror has a purpose.

CONSPIRITUALITY INFLUENCERS are well resourced for the ritual task of using the frightful truisms of conspiracy theory to enrich their content and heighten the promises of spiritual struggle. They have venerable traditions to draw on—and a vulnerable population to impress. If someone has spent years training themselves in the basics of modern global Buddhism, yoga, or New Age thought, they may well have calmed their minds and gained some perspective, while also building an on-ramp for the Trojan horse of conspirituality.

In the summer of 2020, more than two decades after Matthew left his group, Roach was proclaiming the power of meditation to end the pandemic with an online course called "Love in the Time of the Virus."

"We will be deeply investigating how to foster loving and profound motivations to serve others," the event copy reads, "and turn even the smallest acts of kindness into a powerful method to eradicate the virus and suffering from the world."

It was an absurd project, and if followers were to become fundamentalist about its premise, it could have led them to neglect reality-based COVID-19 mitigation practices, while believing they were remaining faithful to a respectable tradition. Roach's adopted school within Tibetan monasticism— the Gelugpa school of the Dalai Lama—views itself as intellectually elite and politically neutral. Speculating about evil governments would be tawdry. And their traditional emphasis on compassion for all living beings means that cynicism really has no place.

Roach's content predates the COVID conspirituality surge. But his eloquence about the spiritual axioms that underpin the movement has been influential. With several popular quasi-Buddhist self-help books, a global touring schedule, recruitment forays into yogaworld, and a corporate coaching business, he's one of many in a long line of New Age influencers responsible for setting the conspirituality stage.

Roach's version of "nothing happens by accident" is karma, or the mystery of cause and effect. Chanting from ancient texts in Tibetan and Sanskrit, Roach described karma as an extremely subtle phenomenon that can only be understood in deep meditation, when the mind is able to slow itself down enough to witness its own processes. To meditate on karma offers two gifts, as Roach taught it: First, karma allows a person to understand that their flow of internal thoughts and feelings is no more random than the countless factors that swell the tides or force seeds to burst into shoots and then into flowers. Second, with karma, events could be understood in a panoramic way that connects a person to the flow of time, and gathers access to the past and future in the present moment. Karma describes a world that can at times feel cruel. But if you zoom out far enough, it is a world that ultimately makes sense.

Roach's take on "nothing is as it seems" begins with the Buddhist and yogic observation that human beings are rarely zoomed out enough to understand what is really occurring. Nor are we zoomed in enough to recognize our own biases and confusions. We look at things, Roach claimed, through a vague middle distance, seeing neither forest nor trees. This sentences us to sleepwalking through lives of habit and ignorance. We are under the spell of an illusion (*maya* in Sanskrit), not only about how things work but also about who we are as actors in the world, what is really important in the end, and, most important, the nature of the self. And as long as we are dreaming, we are of little help to ourselves, and even less to others.

In Roach's world, "everything is connected" is the sublime reality that we miss as we lurch through our lives, blind to infinite causes and effects. Behind the veil of *maya*, we deprive ourselves of the mystery and joy of realizing our interdependence with the world and all beings. We imagine and feel ourselves to be lonely, atomized, condemned to act out of self-interest.

The answer Roach offered was more or less in line with the Buddhist views in which he'd been trained. If we are able to feel the world mingle with our senses, to contemplate how simple acts like breathing and eating break down the seemingly clear distinction between what is inside and outside of our bodies, we might relax into the peace of empty space. If we can understand that in every part of our lives the entire web of existence supports us, we will be more fulfilled. "Nothing happens by accident" promises a responsive universe. "Nothing is as it seems," promises the possibility of always learning something new. And "everything is connected" means there is never any reason to feel alone.

This was the bright side.

THERE WAS ALWAYS a tension in Roach's brand of Buddhist teaching. That tension weaves its way through many New Age doctrines where seekers speak of the oneness of things and the importance of seemingly random events. In the most supportive circumstances—perhaps where Buddhism has not been separated from its living practice communities in South Asia to become a global commodity—the ideas of causation, dreaming, and interconnection should grant serenity and connectedness. But because the pathway to realization is one of lonely meditation, that serenity can feel distant, and the connectedness abstract. Like the internet.

And, as all cult leaders do, Roach made ample use of the shadow side of his content. His method mobilized punitive versions of all three rules. One of his instructions was to have followers confess their shortcomings in relation to a long list of Buddhist vows he'd given out. There were prohibitions against having negative thoughts about others, criticizing Buddhist teachers, or causing division with a Buddhist group. Matthew was taught to write self-critiques six times a day into a personal journal. With each anxious confession, his awareness of karma transformed into horror over how a vengeful world was reflecting his inner failings. First: Was there violence in the world? It must be the result of his own hateful thoughts. *Nothing happens by accident*, after all. Second: What did he truly understand about anything? The idea that *nothing is as it seems*—that he was sleepwalking through his life ignorant of reality—became claustrophobic. Last: The notion that *everything is connected* quickly lost its calm glow, giving way to constant, low-level paranoia. In pop-culture quantum physics, the saying was that a butterfly fluttering its wings in New York might cause a hurricane in Tahiti. In Roach's universe, a brief feeling of lust might trigger an oil war in the Middle East.

For Matthew, self-awareness within a responsive world had given way to self-surveillance within a threatening world. Had social media existed and had a pandemic erupted in 1998, this pivot within Roach's sphere from nurturance to vigilance might well have been Matthew's gateway into conspirituality, in which the anxiety about the health of his inner being expanded into paranoia about the fate of the world.

As it happened, he was also lucky to see the contrast so clearly, writ large in the dynamics of an abusive cult. Two years into living in the shadow of Michael Roach, it was clear to Matthew that Roach's content was contrived and his mission was about himself. In the wild, conspirituality relies on making the exploitation subliminal, making it harder to identify, and more exciting.

IN 2017, THE BARKUN–NEW Age paradox reached a fever pitch of intensity in the doctrines of QAnon, expressing a form of peak, accelerationist conspirituality. For Anons (followers of "Q"), "nothing happens by accident" translated to "trust the plan"—meaning the plan that Q was revealing in cryptic fashion. Anons interpreted every detail of Donald Trump's public appearances—from the presence or absence of gold fringe on US flags in the White House to his verbal tics—as signs that his war with the Deep State was accelerating in tandem with the mad pace of his tweets.

The idea of "nothing is as it seems" carries a double message for Anons. On the macabre side, they believe that buttoned-down managers in the Democratic Party worship Satan and harvest babies for their blood. And then for giddy contrast, they also encourage each other to make popcorn and enjoy the show, as if it were all an illusion, as if they were watching an action movie, assured of a triumphant ending.

Nothing expresses "everything is connected" more viscerally than two graphic-design broadsides depicting the infinite web of conspiracy theories that keep Anon brains deep in mystic contemplation. The "QAnon Map" by Dylan Louis Monroe, and the "Great Awakening Map" by Champ Parinya, carry all the complexity and allusiveness of Buddhist and Hindu icons, used by meditators to grasp deep truths, or the meticulously constructed mandalas that Tibetan monks make out of brightly colored lines of sand.

Trained from childhood in the lessons of impermanence, the monks work on their sand paintings for months, and then, at the auspicious moment, they brush them away. It's an ancient lesson about generosity and nonattachment: to build something and then watch it disappear. But when conspiritualists build their ritual sand paintings to show that everything is connected, they're not doing it to nurture wisdom, but to conjure a new world into existence, one in which they're the self-appointed hero saving civilization from an ultimate evil. A world that will take care of them forever, and never be swept away.

CHAPTER 3

SECRET PRETEND KNOWLEDGE, FOR SURVIVAL AND COMMUNITY

WE'VE SEEN A TRIFECTA of spiritual beliefs that can curdle into paranoia, especially in situations where a person is drawn into a new community with a tightly scripted ideology—like Michael Roach's. Conspirituality is an output of this process, and its explosion in March 2020 was aided by another trifecta: a series of human needs that both spiritual communities and conspiracy theories attempt—and often fail—to meet. People are drawn to both marginal spiritual communities and conspiracism because 1) they are attracted to the idea of knowing something necessary for survival, 2) that no one else knows, and 3) that they can share with other kindred spirits.

Over the seven years, beginning in 1992, that Julian spent in the thrall of the yoga charismatic Ana Forrest, her Santa Monica studio offered all three. Secret knowledge. Protection against the effects of personal and collective trauma. And a community woven of shared values and anxieties on the dreamcatcher of Forrest's life story and doctrine. As with Roach, Forrest's vibe was predictive of the conspirituality era. The ways in which her message and community functioned illuminated how the New Age elevates values that conspiracism can easily hijack.

According to Forrest, her secret knowledge was primarily innate. She claimed to possess a type of clairvoyance that allowed her to "see" the energy patterns flowing through a student's body. Several of Forrest's students believed she could "see energy" and could pinpoint both physical and metaphysical diseases from across a crowded and sweaty yoga room. In most

32

cases, Forrest diagnosed a story of trauma mingled with the ways in which the person had attempted to numb themselves.

"Many people come to Forrest Yoga," Forrest wrote about her eponymous brand, "because they have a storm brewing inside them." Julian found her role as weather forecaster and hurricane charmer a relief from the superficial and banal New Age messages choking the air of LA yoga. Forrest had Jungian gravitas. Tragically, she also had an outsized belief in her powers of intuition, which is how she came to convince Julian of a dark sexual violence in his family—which simply wasn't true. But this was no open-ended healing relationship in which the student could make sense of their own experience over time. Every interaction was stamped with the authority of Ana's intuitive gifts of the Spirit paying out in the form of truth-speaking. Objection was usually framed as denial. "I won't talk to your sickness" were often her last words when a student disagreed with the oracular pronouncements about the contents of their unconscious minds, as revealed on the yoga mat to her clairvoyant eye.

As political scientist Michael Barkun puts it, in the land of conspiracies, secret knowledge is powerful in part because it's stigmatized. It has no home in the university, the medical lab, or the mainstream church. It has been rejected by the normies, and this proves it must be revolutionary. It has been forgotten by the sheeple, or falsely debunked by soulless scientists. Above all, it has been suppressed by the State, or Big Pharma—or now, Big Tech.

It's a theme we'll see throughout our study: Conspiritualists can never quite define their nameless and untestable inner wisdom. No book can contain it and no school can teach it. But this is no deficit: the influencer seizes upon this outsider mystique as proof of their brilliant uniqueness.

Forrest marches in a century-long parade of modern charismatic teachers offering secret knowledge. In Barkun's terms, they offer something forgotten by a fickle modern world. Their wisdom has been falsely superseded by upstart materialists with newfangled gadgets. They are ignored and rejected by institutional authorities. And in the darkest times, their brilliance is suppressed by the hypocrites it threatens. Often, these attitudes foster the powerful moral high ground of the persecution complex. Almost every conspiritualist influencer we profile in Part Three of this book positions themselves as a stigmatized outsider.

* * *

THE STIGMATIZED KNOWLEDGE OF yoga wasn't enough for Forrest. Julian remembers her also being an avid student of "energy medicine" and mentoring with practitioners of Native American ceremony. According to him and other former students, Forrest is not an overt "pretendian"—a non-Indigenous person who openly claims Indigenous heritage to exploit a dubious identity of survivorship. But it appears her main mentor might be. Heyoka Merrifield is a Montana jeweler who describes himself as a Medicine Man and counts George Harrison, Bob Dylan, Elton John, and Cher as clients for his rings and medallions. His public biographies state that he was adopted into the Crow Tribe in 1980, but the biographies offer no official evidence of tribal status. And his social channels offer no evidence of Indigenous community participation.

Forrest's brand leans heavily on her own self-appointment as a "Medicine Woman," on her drumming circles, and on Native American song and ceremony in her classes. She quotes Black Elk of the Lakota Sioux as she writes that her method is her contribution to "Mending the Hoop of the People." Her company logo is lifted from the sun symbol sacred to the Zia Pueblo of New Mexico. In recent years, former Forrest students have asked her to clarify whether she secured consent from the Zia or paid them for the use of the symbol, and whether she has permission to use Native American ceremonial songs. Forrest has not responded to them, nor to us when contacted for comment.

The question of whether Forrest has honestly earned the right to monetize Native American cultural artifacts is not a digression. From plastic shamanism in Southeast Asia to claiming authority in ayahuasca ceremonies via tourist relationships with Peruvian *curanderos*, one of the key ways in which New Age subcultures create and validate their fictitious versions of stigmatized knowledge is by performing solidarity with Indigenous peoples. Unfortunately, that solidarity rarely has anything to do with knowing about or aiding current material conditions faced by actual Indigenous people. The New Age influencer is often content to merely identify with the ideas of ancient wisdom and resilience—ironically made secret or invisible through the same colonial processes they resist. Conspiritualists can benefit if they can appropriate the moral dignity of the marginalized.

Anthropologist Renato Rosaldo excoriates this veneer of respect as a form of imperialist nostalgia, which he writes revolves around a paradox: a person kills somebody and then mourns his or her victim. In more attenuated form, someone deliberately alters a form of life and then regrets that things have not remained as they were prior to his or her intervention. At one more remove, people destroy their environment and then worship nature. In any of its versions, imperialist nostalgia uses a pose of "innocent yearning" both to capture people's imaginations and to conceal its complicity with often brutal domination.

Forrest's nostalgia is far from unique in yogaworld. Julian doesn't feel that she developed it with any malice, nor certainly any personal feelings of animosity toward Native Americans. Quite the opposite. The likely human story is of a naive person who simply devoted herself to something she stumbled upon early in life—something that moved her soul, and that her culture allowed her to monetize.

While the chintzy appropriation waves a red flag over the integrity of Forrest's project, there's something else going on. A closer examination helps us to understand the origins and volatilities of conspirituality. Forrest's mash-up of yoga and Native American ceremony culture, with its focus on ancient wisdom and resilience, getting back to the land, and a return to natural sovereignty, is catnip in the conspirituality world. There's nothing that conspiritualists would like more than to recolonize the nineteenth century. As we'll see in subsequent chapters, it's a form of nostalgia that speaks to their romanticism of the past, a longing for a renewed superego to discipline them, their love for early fascism and premodern medical theories, and their distrust of vaccines.

But because these obsessions float free of the cultural networks and contexts that would promote pro-social values, there is nothing to prevent them from fueling dangerous ideologies. If we want to know why Jacob Chansley (the QAnon Shaman) was cosplaying in Native American garb when he stormed the Capitol on January 6, 2021, we have to understand that when people like Ana Forrest—and every New Age influencer who plays the same game—spend decades denuding Native American ritual of its cultural origins and economies, it can be used for anything at all. Appropriation can be used against the marginalized people it lionizes, and to hide cynical fantasies beneath a veneer of New Age serenity and all-organic living.

Chansley's lawyer, Albert Watkins, in a pretrial press conference in which he suggested that Trump should pardon Chansley, described him as being "devoted to shamanism."

"He is a lover of nature," Watkins said, hoping to paper over the obvious— that Chansley's version of shamanism bore almost no resemblance to actual shamanism. "He routinely practices meditation, is an active practitioner of yoga, and eats only organic food."

WITH REGARD TO THE existential needs of her followers, Julian remembers Forrest helping people make sense of why they weren't living as their best selves. The energy she could see with her sublime vision told her where a follower was holding trauma, where they were stiff with defensiveness. She created an intense ritual space in which she could both diagnose "blockages" and clear them.

Forrest called it "spirit hunting," and it constituted another form of secret knowledge. She was the expert in it, and the stakes were high. Those drawn to her studio, Forrest believed, were likely to have repressed memories of abuse. They had come to heal from that trauma—whether they knew it or not. The mission was endless, because, according to Forrest, the world is filled with traumatized people who have repressed their memories and can become more animated by courage, integrity, and spirit through her techniques. Julian's group bonded around this shared mission, their admiration for Forrest's clairvoyance, and the notion that they had a safe haven to do the deep and courageous work of transforming themselves.

A community organized around an authoritarian leader who pretends to have secret knowledge that cannot be questioned will never truly meet the epistemic, existential, and social needs of its members. In fact, a cult operates like an embodied conspiracy theory: promising to change the world while delivering nothing beyond broken dreams and its own social reproduction.

CHAPTER 4

DISASTER SPIRITUALITY

Only a crisis—actual or perceived—produces real change. When that crisis occurs, the actions that are taken depend on the ideas that are lying around. That, I believe, is our basic function: to develop alternatives to existing policies, to keep them alive and available until the politically impossible becomes politically inevitable.

—Milton Friedman, *Capitalism and Freedom*

ON THE MORNING of September 11, 2001, Matthew was almost exactly a year into his residence at Endeavor Academy, a New Age cult in the Wisconsin Dells. Just after 9:30 a.m., his cult bestie phoned.

"Did you hear about New York? It's on fire. You gotta come to the common room." Matthew raced from his apartment to the main building to find about a hundred group members crowded around the television. He could see the black smoke and read some of the CNN ticker, but couldn't grasp what had happened.

The responses from the group didn't help. As in their daily prayer sessions, some members held their arms aloft, gospel revival style. Some sighed deeply, sometimes whistling, to show or facilitate the processing of energy. Some sat in stony silence. Some laughed uncontrollably, or wept. Some leaped up to kundalini jitterbug across the floor.

There were shouts of "This is it!," "The world is over!," "Nothing is real!," "It's an illusion!," "Nobody really dies!," and other non sequiturs, all echoes of the cult's bible, *A Course in Miracles*.

It took about an hour for Matthew to take in the basics of what happened. Those into geopolitics said anything and everything. It was Muslims! It was white nationalists! It was Maoists! It was the Lizard People! It was an inside job! But for the majority present, it wasn't about facts at all. It was all about confirming that the semi-coherent apocalyptic ramblings of the Academy's leader, Charles Anderson, were prophetic.

Charles Anderson lumbered into the room, waving a Bible in one hand and *A Course in Miracles* in the other. He bellowed, spittle flying through his dentures, "What did you ekshpect? This world is inshane, and there's only one anshwer!" Then he opened up the Book of Revelation and read from it like it was the daily news. He said he'd seen it all before when he'd entered Nagasaki with the Marines in September 1945. He said that looking at the impossible devastation of an atomic blast zone catapulted him into the mystic realization that only God could be real.

Within a month, Endeavor swung into full 9/11 rebranding and content production. In the audiovisual propaganda department they used the Twin Tower collapse footage as backgrounds for scrolling *A Course in Miracles* quotes. They sent squads to Manhattan by bus to proselytize and recruit. No one had money, cell phones, or even New York friends to stay with. No matter: they had the Truth that would mend this rift in reality. But Matthew felt vaguely nauseated, knowing he was getting in the way of the traumatized locals—people like Derek, who worked in Manhattan and had actually been in the North Tower less than an hour before the first plane struck.

To this day Matthew wonders how many people saw him standing in the autumn rain in the cult's ridiculous prayer circle in Washington Square Park, and what they thought about these pious emotional parasites, co-opting catastrophe for their religion.

ENDEAVOR ACADEMY was a hotbed for what transpersonal psychologist John Welwood called "spiritual bypassing," or "the tendency to use spiritual ideas and practices as a way to sidestep or avoid facing unresolved emotional issues, psychological wounds, and unfinished developmental tasks." Welwood noticed the phenomenon among American spiritual seekers—boomers especially.

Bypassing is a staple of the conspirituality world. Adherents declare that the world is dangerous, but ultimately an illusion. They claim to be unattached to family relationships. They claim to be living beyond fear. They value an idealized sense of enlightenment over the supposed divisiveness of an engaged intellectual life. "Transcend the limitations of the rational mind," goes the mantra.

Certainly, Charles Anderson was not entirely well. The conspiritualist who claims to be hearing the voice of Jesus, or the voices of aliens, or ascended masters—or alien ascended masters—may be exhibiting either unresolved trauma or undiagnosed mental illness. Or, they may have cultivated the ability to live in a detailed fantasy reality—or convincingly pretend to, as a career opportunity.

Spiritual bypassing can also flatten and erase the nuance and tension of sociopolitical awareness. We see this when an influencer's prophetic narrative sees current events as signs of cosmic religious meaning—rather than a result of political and policy decisions. Conspiritualist influencers bypass academic credentials, professional expertise, scientific evidence, and standards of logical reasoning. In lieu of qualifications, they default to alternative sources of authority. Many will claim to have undergone a spiritual revelation. Some describe an initiatory process of devastating trauma or catastrophic injury. Some will claim to have access to forbidden and/or stigmatized knowledge, or to divine, out-of-this-world intelligence.

Spiritual bypassing was the basic MO at Endeavor, and is arguably the baseline strategy of most New Age fascinations. But when those planes hit the towers that morning of September 11, something more volatile kicked in.

IN HER MAMMOTH 2010 WORK, *The Shock Doctrine*, Canadian journalist Naomi Klein coined the framework of "disaster capitalism." Her book describes the agility with which multinational corporations have exploited natural disasters, civil wars, and terrorist threats to encourage deregulation, and to appropriate public assets and utilities.

Klein opens her book by recounting how the economist Milton Friedman, at the age of ninety-three, made his last vandalizing policy suggestion: that instead of state and federal governments rebuilding public schools in the parishes of New Orleans devastated by Hurricane Katrina in 2005, they issue citizens with vouchers to pay for private school tuition. The disaster, according to Friedman, was a golden opportunity to accelerate the march toward privatizing everything. For example, Klein noted that New Orleans's public school system ran 123 schools at the time Katrina hit. By 2010, privatization had driven that number down to four, while the city went from seven charter schools to thirty-one.

Within months of COVID-19 erupting around the world, it was clear that the practices of disaster capitalism as described by Klein could be adapted to create an equally ruthless dynamic. In disaster spirituality, a real public health crisis, or a fictional moral panic like QAnon, can become the basis for an evangelical call to spiritual renewal. Whereas the captains of disaster capitalism seize distressed assets for privatization, the charismatics of disaster spirituality seize the attention and emotional commitment of their followers. That attention is then funneled into monetized networks that sell spiritual and wellness products focused on individual well-being (or smugness) as opposed to the common good. As a result, the consumer is left even more isolated and unprepared for social stress.

Pierre Kory is a critical care physician who made headlines in December 2020 by testifying before the Senate that the antiparasitic drug ivermectin was a "wonder drug with miraculous effectiveness" against COVID. As the pandemic raged, he used the contrarian social media sphere to sow doubt about vaccine data, while claiming, against evidence, that the efficacy of ivermectin was being suppressed by Big Pharma. His FLCCC (Front Line COVID-19 Critical Care Alliance) website then became a global hub for hundreds of doctors offering telemedicine sessions to prescribe proprietary alternative COVID-19 treatment protocols, and pharmacies willing to sell and ship these pseudomedical combinations of dodgy drugs.

Likewise, New Age propagandist Mikki Willis (profiled in Part Three) teamed up with a discredited hydroxychloroquine doctor, Vladimir Zelenko, to create and market a supplement stack as a supposed COVID-preventative to his extensive email list. Other opportunists promoted anti-5G accessories, like a $113 belly band for pregnant women to protect their unborn babies, or a $125 pet collar for your cat or dog to create a force field against the supposed dangers of 5G radiation.

Disaster capitalism and disaster spirituality rely, respectively, on an endless supply of items to commodify and minds to recruit. While both roar into high gear in times of widespread precarity and vulnerability, in disaster spirituality there is arguably more at stake on the supply side. Hedge fund managers can buy up distressed properties in post-Katrina New Orleans to gentrify and flip. They have cash on hand to pull from when opportunity strikes, whereas most spiritual figures have to use other means for acquisitions and recruitment during times of distress.

Most of the influencers operating in today's conspirituality landscape stand outside of mainstream economies and institutional support. They've been developing fringe religious ideas and making money however they can, as they battle high customer turnover. Michael Roach was an outlier due to his skill at drawing wealthy Russian and Hong Kong donors. But Charles Anderson's operation was so hopelessly in debt he had his followers max out their personal credit cards so they could make fools of themselves in post-9/11 Manhattan.

For the mega-rich disaster capitalist, a hurricane or civil war is a windfall. But for the skint disaster spiritualist, a public catastrophe like 9/11 or COVID-19 is a life raft. Many have no choice but to climb aboard and ride. Additionally, if your spiritual group has been claiming for years to have the answers to life's most desperate problems, the disaster is an irresistible dare, a chance to make good on divine promises. If the spiritual group has been selling health ideologies or products they guarantee will ensure perfect health, how can they turn away from the opportunity presented by a disease crisis?

As 2020 rolled into a maybe-forever pandemic, we saw disaster spirituality in play from many angles—including from influencers who were not economically pressured to tilt that way. Dr. Christiane Northrup, the grandmother of alt-health gynecology, recurring Oprah Winfrey guest expert, and best-selling author of 1994's *Women's Bodies, Women's Wisdom*, initiated her "The Great Awakening" video series—borrowing a phrase from QAnon—in which one video might warn about lethal poisoning from cell phone towers, and the next video might teach her half-million followers how to ease themselves through the process of ascending to a higher plane of reality.

While Northrup reached a sea of boomers, other influencers carved out more niche markets. Bernhard Guenther, a New Age influencer with a pseudointellectual vocabulary, wrote a twenty-four-thousand-word essay exploring the spiritual implications of QAnon. The essay reached 1.4 million users via Reddit.

Guenther matched his conspiracy theory mongering with an accelerated program of online spiritual teachings. One of his online courses is called

"Time of Transition: Embodied Soul Awakening: A 12-week Private Online Group Coaching Program in Psychological and Spiritual Self-Work to Activate Your Soul Potential on Multidimensional Levels."

"We are at a turning point for humanity," says the headline copy, in perfect disaster spiritualese, and it goes on to say:

> Many people feel extremely overwhelmed with what we call "the splitting of humanity" that we see happening around us and on the world stage. The chaos and polarization we see in the external world can feel confusing and destabilizing for many people, as they watch the world that they once knew change rapidly around them. Yet at the same time, the potential for awakening has never been greater.

LIKE MANY KIDS who grew up in New Jersey, New York City was Derek's second home, and he wound up living in Jersey City and Brooklyn over the course of twelve years. He'll never forget that the months after 9/11 were unique in Manhattan. Strangers weren't strangers. People made eye contact in the subways. In December of that same year, during a snowstorm, someone set off a smoke bomb in the downtown subway car he was in. There were a few moments of absolute terror before the conductor opened all the doors. Despite the chaos, everyone helped everyone else out and made sure no one got trampled.

Sooner than he'd expected, life in the city returned to its boisterous baseline. Derek found it strange that the rest of the country was still holding vigils. It was as if not being there to help with rebuilding and participating in daily life increased some collective need for symbolic action. People outside of New York City needed a fictional New York City to mourn and argue over—a snow globe Manhattan they could shake to watch the ash rain down forever.

While Matthew was on a disaster spirituality pilgrimage to an imagined Manhattan, Derek, who grew up in a nominally Catholic but predominantly agnostic family, developed a kind of pragmatic spirituality in relation to the pavement under his feet. When you're in the middle of something you can't fetishize it. What mattered was that everyone was doing okay. Not in some ultimate, soul sense—but in the sense that they were working through whatever they had to. This meant having dinner together, meeting up just to talk. Yes: taking yoga classes and meditating, and going for Reiki appointments could all be part of it. Whatever works. But not in the expectation of any miraculous transformation. New Yorkers were already transformed.

Here's what disaster spirituality doesn't—perhaps can't—do. It can't come close to matching the human strength that can emerge within the lived experience of people who share a traumatized space, and the time it takes to recover. Disaster spirituality traffics in fantasy and myth, in heroes and villains. It thrives at a distance, beyond the daily tasks of work, groceries, and checking in with each other. It's a place where rhetoric is louder than conversation, and symbols flash brighter than service. Little wonder it intensifies as our lives are increasingly lived online.

CHAPTER 5

CONSPIRITUALITY VS. QANON

As you will know, it's important for the Illuminati and the religious Satanists, our so-called elite, to reverse things, to turn things upside down—like pentagrams. Survivors recall hearing backwards talking during rituals. Their religion dictates that they turn good into bad, health into disease, life into death, education into dumbing down and so on. They do this very cleverly. And what they do has multiple purposes. For example, they lie to us that vaccination will save our children when it sickens them. So they are turning truth into lies, health into disease, and when we offer our children for vaccination, it is our karma. And when we and our children die early because of the direct or indirect effects of vaccination the planet is depopulated—and it is our karma. Or so they believe.

—Jacqui Farmer, aka Charlotte Ward, *Illuminati Party!—*
Reasons Not to Be Scared of the Illuminati

A KEY TAKEAWAY of the Jacqui Farmer / Charlotte Ward saga is that the distance between the morbid cruelty of QAnon and the pastel anxieties of conspirituality is only a matter of degree, and defined by social acceptability.

In the event you've perhaps heard of QAnon but are fuzzy on the details, it refers to an internet-spread conspiracy theory that started in October 2018. An anonymous user claiming to have the "Q" security clearance necessary to access secret government information began posting cryptic messages on the 4chan message board. 4chan incubates nasty humor, online mobbing, competitive transgressions, and a whole lot of shitposting. The "Q-drops" became a growing focus of feverish interpretation and meme production after they originally appeared under a conversation thread related to Donald Trump's use of the term the "Calm Before the Storm."

Over the next three years a cottage industry of QAnon influencers evolved. They built social media followings by decoding the meaning of Q's drops—parsing details they called breadcrumbs, through a process called baking. A number were able to monetize their offerings on YouTube or hawk merchandise on Amazon.

The mythology that emerged was part conspiracy theory—Democrat politicians and Hollywood Elites are involved in a blood-drinking satanic pedophile Cabal—and part political religious prophecy. Donald Trump was destined to win again in 2020, said the Anons. He would expose the truth about the blood-drinking Satanists, enact public executions (the Storm), and save the children sex-trafficked by the evil Cabal. The New Age spiritual angle on the story held Trump as a lightworker divinely sent by benevolent aliens to usher in humanity's ascent into a new fifth-dimensional enlightened reality.

As the pandemic unfolded, QAnon became a meme machine for macabre fantasies that have plagued humanity for centuries. It resurrected the concept of blood libel from Europe's Middle Ages, which alleged that Jews kidnapped and murdered Christian children to then use their blood for Passover rituals, such as baking matzo. By late spring of 2020, QAnon had jumped the rails from the dark recesses of the internet onto mainstream social media (where we first saw aspects of it appearing in posts from yoga and wellness figures), and appeared on shirts and banners at Trump rallies, as well as inspiring a string of strange, violent crimes.

So: THE PREEMINENT SCHOLAR and propagandizer of conspirituality wrote what reads like a QAnon recruitment manual in 2014—three years before Q made his first appearance as a fictional Deep State insider. For Charlotte Ward, conspirituality was an endless rabbit hole. Reading the book *Illuminati Party!* authored by her alter ego Jacqui Farmer is like sitting down to tea with a very British, very chatty Q.

From a professional standpoint it makes logistical sense to separate conspirituality from QAnon, because the research demands are starkly different. Understanding even a shred of what was happening in the QAnon world required mad forensic skills in mining the creepy caverns of pre-social-media internet message boards, where an antisocial subversion of human empathy defined the outsider zeitgeist. It demanded familiarity with its sordid history—Gamergate, the pickup artist and incel movements—and the hazing tactics of meme warfare and shitposting. The best researchers of QAnon are all a decade or more younger than us. Most are gamers. It's not our scene.

On an emotional level, it makes self-serving sense to draw a respectability line between the two movements. It was hard to think of the yoga and wellness world we belonged to being vulnerable to that level of grotesquerie. Anti-vax sentiments and kooky ideas about hot yoga increasing one's immunity to a virus were not new, and the fact that they were exploding during a pandemic was on-brand for an industry built on woo-woo. But was it really possible that former friends and colleagues could cross the Rubicon into believing that Democrats were harvesting the blood of children in satanic rituals? That they could be pulled across the threshold between green smoothie social media into the cesspools of anonymous message boards? Well, yes it was. And worse than that, for some influencers that threshold became a chalk line in a game of hopscotch, as they hopped between both worlds, using QAnon to spice up their online conspirituality engagement in one post, and conspirituality to launder their QAnon beliefs in the next.

Meeting the Jacqui Farmer side of Charlotte Ward was the final straw that broke the barrier. We even found in her 2014 screed a preview of the anti-trans bigotry that was rife in QAnon, and then went mainstream in conspirituality, in tandem with the #okgroomer movement. In 2014, Farmer was an early adopter of the racist and trans-bigoted fiction that Michelle Obama was born male. In a section of *Illuminati Party!* called "Gender—the ultimate Satanic Reversal," Farmer writes:

> You can watch in action these people doing a good job of appearing 'normal'. They are doing such a good job that one of them, Barack Obama, is in fact married to a man! This is a prime example of a mass mind control programme. It is also a prime example of a satanic reversal.

While some conspiritualists consider themselves to be supportive of trans people, the ideology provides little resistance to bigoted outbursts from its mainstream heroes. By 2020, alt-health comedian JP Sears (who we profile in Part Three) celebrated the birth of his son by trolling trans people, and then cracked jokes at a comedy club about how easy it would be for real men with military training to kill wokes, who have nothing but pronouns to hide behind. That same year, the "Michelle Obama is a man" meme was boosted by failed QAnon congressional candidate Deanna Lorraine, and then by Alex Jones.

It appears Ward straddled a line with her split identity. As Charlotte Ward, she was a Dr. Jekyll who wrote with a thoughtful, adventurous spirituality. But as Jacqui Farmer, she wrote like Mr. Hyde, leaving a trail of sex panic and typos. Charlotte Ward wouldn't risk the benign image of conspirituality by sermonizing unironically about Satanists and pedophiles. She needed Farmer to do it for her.

In the summer of 2020, conspiritualist and alt-health digital marketer Sayer Ji (who we profile in Part Three) began using QAnon hashtags to promote the Telegram channel he opened in anticipation of getting booted off Facebook. He used the phrase "Take the red pill," which had become a key QAnon recruitment phrase, co-opted from The Matrix film franchise. Early in the pilot film, the hero Neo is offered a choice between taking a blue pill and waking up in his bed to continue living as if the ordinary-seeming illusory world was real, and taking the red pill and awakening to the possibility of freedom to be found in confronting a much darker revelation of reality. Being "red-pilled" later became a phrase used by MAGA influencers like Candace Owens to describe waking up out of a liberal political orientation and into a more conservative worldview. The movement was blissfully unaware that The Matrix creators, the Wachowski sisters, created the mythology of The Matrix movies partly as a metaphor for their own journey into transgender identity.

Ji also reposted a meme with the hashtag #pizzagateisreal, referring to the 2016 conspiracy theory that Washington Democrats were running a child trafficking ring out of the basement of a pizza parlor—a preposterous fiction that led to a potentially dangerous vigilante shooting.

We reached out to Ji, to ask him whether he was promoting QAnon. He dodged and weaved:

"For me, 'red pill' is simply a metaphor," Ji filibustered by email, "for being willing to take responsibility for researching and experiencing topics that either conventional authorities have presented narratively to be beyond question, or having only one official set of truths, principles, or meanings, or which are presented—as in the case of certain scientific topics—as 'settled,' and no longer open to debate, question, or revision."

Then Ji disclaimed any particular meaning for his use of #pizzagateisreal. "Forwarding memes from other channels, which may include a hashtag, does not constitute an official endorsement of those I am forwarding, nor even the content per se."

Ji deserves some credit for entertaining the question at all. Most of the yoga and wellness influencers Matthew interviewed for an investigative piece on the growth of QAnon in Canada were unwilling to even acknowledge their prior boosting of QAnon content. QAnon associations were a poisoned chalice that ginned up their engagement but risked ruining their reputations and complicating their yoga and massage gigs, especially as QAnon became a more toxic brand.

Retreating as needed from QAnon rhetoric to conspirituality marketing offers both plausible deniability—"of course I don't believe *that*!"—and economic security. Some top QAnon influencers did initiate wellness side hustles during the pandemic, selling hydroxychloroquine or magical supplements to protect against the virus they said wasn't there. But conspiritualists who were already established in monetized wellness networks had a more stable gig. They could always go radio silent on QAnon and concentrate on their alt-health or spirituality products. We saw this happen with influencers like Dr. Northrup, who in one video would be teaching followers about ascending to 5D consciousness and in the next giving advice on the best herbs to use in a vaginal douche.

The term "5D consciousness" is shorthand for the promise of higher spiritual perspectives. During the pandemic, conspiritualists framed the crisis as a prelude to this spiritual awakening. They spoke about a variety of ascension symptoms that suspiciously rhymed with COVID indicators: head or body aches, fatigue, and chills. Devotees suffering these gifts were definitely undergoing a vibrational shift.

On the douche front, Northrup tells a reader in one blog post that vaginosis can result from being "energetically 'raped.'" She then advises to cut back on sugar and dip tampons into unsweetened yogurt or diluted vinegar. She also sells a variety of herbs to help with menopause, which she writes is a phase in life in which women "have confidence, wisdom and mastery of life. You begin to experience extraordinary creativity. And you use your time wisely." Her product line of menopausal supplements include *Pueraria mirifica*, an herb from Thailand, which has not been shown to have any significant benefit for the conditions stated on her website.

IN SHORT, QAnon goes all-in on high-risk stocks, while conspirituality maintains a diversified portfolio. QAnon offers a dystopian endgame of fantasized public executions, while conspirituality radiates a world of Instagram soul journeys. QAnon is built to lurch from crisis to crisis. When its apocalyptic predictions fail to materialize, it sheds humiliated members. Conspirituality, however, is built for constant growth.

But the line between them is fluid. Extremism researcher Marc-André Argentino recognized this and gave a name to the spaces in which conspirituality becomes a gateway to the macabre. He dubbed that zone "Pastel QAnon," where high-end curation of Instagram fitness, foodie, and crystal healing influencers chastely gestures at the gory nightmares of QAnon, creating bourgeois "recruitment and radicalisation pipelines into female dominated ecosystems."

Jacqui Farmer's book *Illuminati Party!* isn't well-produced. The cover is chintzy and the typesetting is amateurish. It wouldn't stop anyone's Instagram scroll. But in her soft, wellness-oriented, almost therapeutic tone, we see an early model for Pastel QAnon, in which the terror of Satanism is soothed by mommy-blogger-style lifestyle tips. "The Illuminati has managed to invert things pretty well," writes Farmer. She continues:

> So one obvious solution is for us to start turning things back the right way up. There's a lot you can do to help right things. Start getting back into your power. Start at home. Here are a few suggestions:
>
> - Stick to the truth—weed out any lies from your life.
> - Learn something new. Get educated on the internet—reverse school and TV dumbing down.
> - Clean up your act—stop watching porn (even the free stuff earns the Illuminati billions).
> - Stop eating factory farmed meat.

- Spread love—help others where you can.
- Start praying or meditating every night.
- Plant a few wildflowers, or weeds.
- Turn off the TV. Break your addiction to computer games.
- Get healthy—replace junk food and soda with healthy foods. Avoid GMOs where you can.

In a later list of activities that she said would "scupper the Illuminati," Farmer adds "downsize your car, shop secondhand, grow cannabis, refuse vaccination."

Except for the vaccination bit, it's all a mixture of reasonable, crunchy, and dumb-but-harmless advice, which leads us to the final piece of the conspirituality definition puzzle: it's a worldview and culture with legitimate concerns and pro-social impulses. If we do not acknowledge the things conspiritualists get right, how much credibility will we have when it comes to pointing out what they get wrong?

CHAPTER 6

CONSPIRITUALISTS ARE NOT WRONG

JACQUI FARMER'S SHOPPING LIST of wholesome tips in her book *Illuminati Party!* would be right at home under magnets on the fridge doors of countless citizens around the world who sense that humanity is driving off a cliff. People who feel that their schooling gave them little preparation for all of this complexity, and that media sources, in their failure to capture reality, are opting to make it up. People who sense their political leaders are sitting on their hands, or worse—neglecting the poor, plotting to rig votes, funneling money from schoolteachers to cops, colluding with industrial polluters, getting rich on insider trading, brokering arms deals with gangster states.

Reduce the footprint of meat in your diet, Farmer counsels. Learn to meditate; plant wildflowers; turn off the TV; spread love. All very commonsense ideas. No belief in any Cabal required. Bite-sized bits of hope that don't seem unmanageable—when everything, taken all together, is overwhelming. In other sane passages of her insane book, Farmer rues police corruption and British warmongering in Syria. Fair points.

These good-faith yearnings in a burning world point to a core reason that conspirituality is so stressful to the communities it enchants—and a key reason why the three of us have been obsessed with deconstructing it. The reason is, conspiritualists are not wrong.

They are attuned to systemic problems. They have felt their existential angst insulted by lifestyle marketing, and their humanity reduced to consumer data. They have felt the cold neglect of the state, the vacant stare of the medical gaze, and the brutal rise of rents. When COVID struck, they were quick to prophesy that whether the virus was real or not, the crisis would exacerbate wealth and class inequality. They were right: the billionaire class padded their net worth by $1 trillion.

Conspiritualists know that most citizens of the Global North, and their children, are hyperurbanized, screen addled, and disconnected from rivers and forests and food sources. Yet conspiritualists feel the interconnectedness of things. Their empathy may be compromised by paranoia and bigoted blindspots, but it carries a sentimentality that lends poetry to their posts. They grasp the enormity of the human challenge, and they respond to it with an equally vast hope.

Conspirituality does not create its followers' nausea at the state, modernity, or the poisoned chalice of techno-capitalism. It does not create real-world disasters such as the Jeffrey Epstein sex trafficking network (a reality that makes QAnon reasonable on a symbolic, if not factual, level). It does not create histories of genocide, nor does it create histories of governmental cover-up.

Conspirituality does, however, exploit a pandemic of disenchantment. Disrupting that exploitation is not just a matter of debunking falsehoods, or revealing the money lust or hypocrisy of alt-health influencers who predict another Holocaust so they can cosplay Oskar Schindler–style humanitarianism. Disrupting it is a matter of reckoning with the deep anxieties about social fragmentation and ecological ruin for which conspirituality offers sparkling but flimsy answers.

WE EMPATHIZE WITH MANY of the health care complaints that conspiritualists raise. We've had our own challenges that could very easily have sent each of us down their road.

When Derek was eleven, he was hospitalized for a month with a broken femur, and then for two weeks more after the body cast came off. Being put into traction and immobilized for a total of three months—a treatment no longer practiced—left him with a shortened leg and chronic back pain. So he didn't get the best possible treatment. But he remembers the bustle of selfless doctors and nurses doing amazing work for so many people on a daily basis. It gave him a framework for understanding the necessity of good health care and how it ideally improves over time.

He ended up working for that same hospital while in college. As a patient monitor, he made sure suicidal patients didn't try to flee or make another attempt. A number of patients were so sedated that his only job was to watch them sleep. Others wanted to talk. He realized most patients really just needed an ear to listen, which was unavailable to them outside the building's walls. This could be a helping place, he learned. Amid the smell of suffering and death diluted by potent cleaning solutions, and behind the bureaucracy and statistics, he saw that medicine was practiced by real people doing their jobs to the best of their ability. Later still, as a cancer survivor, he learned that while there is no perfect treatment, this network of human knowledge has made incredible strides that have greatly extended the quality of life for many.

As for Julian and Matthew, their children wouldn't be alive without intensive natal, postnatal, and pediatric care. Julian went $16,000 into debt trying to treat Lyme disease with a battery of alternative methods, before eventually recovering quickly on standard antibiotics. Matthew almost died of pulmonary embolism following a deep vein thrombosis. In the emergency ward where he was diagnosed, he had a near-spiritual experience watching the staff care for old and young, rich and poor, with a kind of equal diligence that he never experienced in the privileged yogaworld.

All three of us have been lucky with positive medical experiences that actually drove us away from alternative medicine, after brief enchantments. That's a problem. There's no moral universe in which luck should determine whether a person is driven to seek out and buy empty promises.

PUSHING BACK AGAINST CONSPIRITUALITY also demands recognizing that it tells a far more powerful story than most public health policy wonks can dream of. In a world of streaming, memes, and hot takes, conspirituality is an online religion that strings mysteries together on a compelling narrative arc. It takes followers on a sense-making journey marked by rituals of awakening and a relentless calendar of revelations. The journey begins in the bucolic past, in which human life is married to the soil and seasons, in which sickness is a natural rite of purification best understood in spiritual terms—not meddled with by doctors, technocrats, and bankers.

The story tracks an imagined fall from organic grace, dating back to at least the nineteenth century, as folk medicines were discredited by the captains of new pharmaceutical industries, and as spiritual rites were disenchanted by academics and bureaucrats. Then, as now, vaccination is a leading plot point. As Eula Biss explains in her extraordinary book *On Immunity: An Inoculation*, the scar left by the smallpox vaccine was "the mark of the beast." Clerics at the time warned of bodies invaded by the state and materialist philosophies, comparing vaccination to being injected with sin so that the soul would eventually be overwhelmed.

These are no longer stories for passive consumption. The deeper hook of today's conspirituality narrative is that a believer can participate in it. This online religion offers a role to play. You can jump on a call, join the conversation, become a digital soldier. Posting about conspirituality generates a kind of digital Talmud of scriptural axioms and commentary. You can follow and resonate with the influencer who presents themselves as being on a hero's journey from an idyllic childhood, through a rock-bottom dark night of the soul, to a transformational triumph that's now threatened by Deep State censorship.

The conspirituality faithful are deputized as online sidekicks to ride at dawn, to wage online war against the corruption of Big Pharma, to purify themselves in the fight against impending authoritarianism, and to be rewarded with dopamine hits of engagement. All of this can lend people with trauma in their personal histories (for consumers of wellness, the percentage is high) a renewed sense of agency in a world they often feel helpless to change.

AT THE MOST INTIMATE level of bodily agency—health care—conspiritualists speak to deep cultural wounds. Disability justice activist Beatrice Adler-Bolton came on our podcast to tell us that for decades normal health care policy in liberal democracies has meant rampant neglect, exacerbated by austerity and rationing. It's meant a rise-and-grind culture that measures human worth by economic output while shrinking wages and busting unions. It's meant policy decisions dressed up as fiscal responsibility placing dollar values on the worthiness of human beings. "We are entitled to as much survival as we can purchase," Adler-Bolton says. In America—a country that spends more than any other nation in the world on health care yet has the highest chronic disease burden of the thirty-eight nations that report to the Organization of Economic Co-operation and Development—the stark brutality of Adler-Bolton's statement is essential for understanding the world that conspirituality so easily colonized. And it perhaps begins to explain why our focus has been—has had to be—on American influencers and their economies. It makes sense that an empire of predatory, for-profit health care would incubate a rebellious, religious response to it.

It also makes sense, on a visceral level, that out of hundreds of DMs, social media comments, and emails we've received from listeners over the past years, the theme that stands out most starkly is that of disillusionment with institutionalized medicine, and how that feeling casts a shadow on all relationships with institutions, from education to finance to government. For some, alienation from conventional medical care echoed another fracture: they had also been driven toward alternative spirituality by the shadows of corruption in their birth religions. They described the relief of exchanging conventional claustrophobia and hypocrisy for New Age individualism and the permission to self-explore.

Listeners often confided they were driven toward alternative medicine by the brevity and coldness of their clinical encounters. By the feeling of not being seen, or of being seen as a body with a problem instead of as a human on a journey. Research shows that in the United States, doctors interrupt their patients within eleven seconds, which adds to their frustration with a seemingly inhuman system. And if they suffer from difficult conditions, they describe bouncing from specialist to specialist—each with a narrower view on the problem than the last—none of whom seem to be speaking to each other. They describe being prescribed generic antidepressants for complex mood imbalances—with a shrug and a pat on the head. Many accounts come from women, who speak of being dismissed by a reflexive patriarchal rigidity that might not take their distress and pain seriously, or that might pressure them into childbirth interventions they do not want. Some have heartbreaking stories of seeking support for a neurodivergent child, for whom one-size-fits-all care does not suffice.

For Americans, the allure of alternative medicine unfolds against the backdrop of possible medical bankruptcy. In an economy that demands underinsured or uninsured patients keep themselves healthy, their credentialed doctors are not simply bearers of unlucky news. These medical practitioners voice the accusing question posed by the culture at large: *What have you done to yourself?*

From the 1780s clinic of Samuel Hahnemann, who spent an hour or more with new patients taking extensive personal histories before prescribing homeopathic remedies he invented from common poisons, to the 2000s seminars that taught aspiring naturopaths how to furnish and light their clinics, alternative medical practitioners have always spoken to the issues of depersonalization and disillusionment that shear the body from the spirit and treat it like a machine. One conspiritualist we followed is a leading influencer in the free-birth movement, which encourages women to give birth without medical support. Her pitch to potential clients is that with her help they can free themselves from the Industrial Obstetric Complex. At the most paranoid end, Charlotte Ward, as Jacqui Farmer, condemned the invasive and humiliating cervical cancer smear tests suggested for women in the UK every three years. She describes being traumatized by being called in for a retest that proved negative. "Whatever lies the Illuminati UK government and their medical establishment tell you," she wrote, "these tests are entirely unnecessary and may even *cause* cancer."

By framing personal health, and even a pandemic, as a spiritual crisis—as well as a sign one can break free of the rise-and-grind of the dominant culture—alternative medicine providers soften the question of *What have you done to yourself?* with *What are you capable of?* We can't underestimate the power of that reframing, nor how it obscures that the answer to clinical alienation and institutional betrayal is neither pseudoscience nor spiritual bypassing. The real answer is better clinical practice and institutional repair.

TRUE BELIEVERS OF CONSPIRITUALITY turn legitimate critiques that can be addressed through democratic policy making into apocalyptic crises that can only be solved by miracles. They've found a compelling storytelling machine that amplifies their passions. They layer and embellish their stories through online feedback loops that build trance states. Their portion of the internet is like a rosary flash mob, reciting prayers and mysteries. But they're not just dancing in step. They can be the heroes, underdogs, priests, and scribes of journeys in search of divinely inspired solutions. Their aim is not merely symptom management.

They know the territory of postmodern alienation. But the map they make of it is similar to the absurd map described in a microstory by Jorge Luis Borges. Once upon a time, an acquisitive emperor ordered his mapmakers to create for him a map to the scale of the world. But when it was laid flat, it choked the land of sun and rain. The crops failed and the empire collapsed. Soon only tattered shreds of the map sheltered the occasional beast, or person without a home. Similarly, the conspiritualist map covers over and distorts reality, betraying all good intentions: to protect the vulnerable and raise up the marginalized.

This online religion wreaked the most havoc among those who needed agency most. When QAnon broke into the online yogaworld in the spring of 2020, some of the earliest adopters of the satanic pedophilia myths were members of existing Facebook groups started by women who had survived sexual abuse in yoga schools. For them, conspirituality and QAnon were not wrong. In fact, it might have been exhilarating to see widespread interest in the topic of institutional abuse erupt into the mainstream by a popular movement, even if the details were shaky, and the sources unknown.

These are people who had come forward with their stories of abuse—often decades old—during the #MeToo wave. When the QAnon hashtags hit, some expressed an instant identification and allegiance with the fictional victims. The axiom of "believe the women" morphed into "believe the children." It made sense that true stories, suppressed for years, would find cathartic release through fictions primed to go viral. It made sense that QAnon lent a very loud symbolic language to people who had never felt heard.

In the summer of 2020, the pedophilia panic went viral through the power of the #savethechildren hashtag. In June, the Q-Tuber The Amazing Polly tweeted out the false claim that the Wayfair furniture company was shipping live children in expensive cabinetry units with girls' names to feed the appetites of the Elites. The online pileup was so bad that the legitimate Save the Children nonprofit, founded in 1919 and whose founder inspired the UN Convention on the Rights of the Child, had to release a statement distancing themselves from QAnon. A spokeswoman for Wayfair denied the absurd theory.

Regan Williams, one of our early podcast guests, runs a nonprofit dedicated to helping marginalized youth, many of whom have been sexually or emotionally abused. She told us that QAnon's false child sex-trafficking statistics—800,000 children in America supposedly go missing every year and at least 300,000 are sex trafficked—managed to red pill teenagers in her program. These clients were wary of power structures in general, having been harmed by people they trusted. The seductive messaging of QAnon, shared by wellness influencers through hashtags and Instagram posts, appealed to their distrust of authority figures. A rush of money flooded new organizations that were suddenly interested in this fake anti-trafficking circus, and this diverted resources from organizations that had spent years and decades actually combating real-world sex trafficking. Operation Underground Railroad, for instance, was accused of taking credit for rescuing a trafficking victim who escaped on her own. The nonprofit's founder, Tim Ballard, was happy to "flood the space" with QAnon talking points in his many media appearances. Critics said the organization was good at fundraising, but inept at identifying trafficking victims, and distinguishing trafficking from consensual sex work. Ballard's group also operates a CrossFit gym in Utah.

THROUGH THE LONG, hot summer, #savethechildren rallies sprang up in cities across North America led by a young LA influencer. Rapper and aspiring actor Scotty Rojas, aka Scotty the Kid, organized marches in Hollywood and beyond. At one march, Rojas, who presents as Native American on Facebook, spoke to CNN while wearing red face paint in the shape of a hand, which covered his mouth.

Scotty the Kid's red handprint, pretendian or not, pointed at another tragedy that many conspiritualists were not wrong about. It signaled solidarity with the movement supporting missing and murdered Indigenous women and girls of North America. The image was first made prominent by Jordan Marie Brings Three White Horses Daniel, who wore it as she ran the 2019 Boston Marathon. The symbol points to shameful realities. "According to Statistics Canada," writes Commissioner Michèle Audette of the National Inquiry into Missing and Murdered Indigenous Women and Girls, "between 2001 and 2015, the homicide rate for Indigenous women was nearly six times higher than that for non-Indigenous women." As for the missing, a 2018 report from the Urban Indian Health Institute in Seattle found that "in 2016, there were 5,712 reports of missing American Indian and Alaska Native women and girls, though the US Department of Justice's federal missing persons database, NamUs, only logged 116 cases."

It's unclear whether Scotty the Kid was exorcizing actual or imagined intergenerational trauma at a QAnon march as he appropriated the symbolism of a real response to a genocidal history. What is clear is that through such conflations, QAnon managed to recruit Indigenous support in pockets around the world. In 2020, for instance, the QAnon-promoting Māori musician Billy Te Kahika made a run for parliament in New Zealand as the leader of the newly minted Public Party under the battle cry "Make New Zealand Great Again."

In some cases, dodgy alliances between conspiritualists and Indigenous activists were forged before QAnon existed. Mikki Willis became a conspirituality celebrity through his COVIDsploitation short film *Plandemic*, released in May of 2020, which claimed that pandemic mitigation measures were part of a totalitarian plan. But his political backstory is complicated. He cut his pseudo-activist teeth as a videographer, first documenting the campaign of America's openly socialist presidential candidate, Bernie Sanders, and then ostensibly supporting the Standing Rock pipeline protests of 2016. By January 6, 2021, he was playing the same role for a different movement, video-documenting white nationalists breaching the Capitol as aggrieved citizens seeking to be heard.

More recently, outright white supremacists have sought to co-opt Indigenous rights language and symbology, and to stoke anti-state fears. "First Nations people's sovereignty is very desirable to white nationalists," said Morgan Yew, a video journalist who covered anti-lockdown protests in Toronto.

Yew told us that some white nationalist groups use conspiracy-theory-laden rhetoric about vaccines to co-opt Indigenous distrust of the state, thus endangering them by provoking vaccine hesitancy. In October 2021, infamous white supremacist Pat King from Alberta spread the false story that Canadian soldiers were chasing Indigenous women and children on foot into the frozen northern forests of Saskatchewan in an attempt to forcibly vaccinate them. The Black Lake Denesuline First Nation posted a condemnation of King's misinformation.

Vaccine hesitancy and conspiratorial thinking in Canadian Indigenous communities, however, can't be boiled down to the impact of QAnon memes and the disruptions of a few extremists. "It's the result of our government's legacy of not seeking reparations," Yew explained, "and not creating adequate means for marginalized people to gain access to services." After a history of callous neglect and genocidal policies, it makes sense that Indigenous people distrust settler governments. It makes sense that they may find themselves accepting help from conspiritualists, who are not wrong about state neglect and violence.

* * *

CONSPIRITUALISTS ARE RIGHT ENOUGH—AND enough of the time—to provoke emotional connection, and wield moral gravity. They get aspects of #MeToo right. They are attuned—though often through cosplay—to the oppression of Indigenous peoples. They are rightly suspicious of for-profit medicine, Big Agriculture, and governmental collusion with both.

But as the COVID science-communication (sci-comm) directors learned in a very hard way, it's not enough to be right about the world. It's not enough to have science on your side. Mythology helps, too. You need a compelling story. Conspirituality is a masterful storytelling medium.

The stories told by conspirituality influencers might be grandiose. But they also feel personal, accessible, and urgent. They can make the abstract, vaguely upbeat comms of medical professionalism seem pale in comparison: *We are always working to provide better care for you and your family. We have researchers, we deliver services, we keep tabs on the flu. And we will tell you what you need to know.*

That flatness reveals that what public health sci-comms has not done, and what conspirituality has done, with religious fervor, is mobilize what philosophy and religion scholar Alan Levinovitz calls "empowerment epistemology." Levinovitz argues that helplessness and uncertainty can be managed in New Age contexts via simply choosing to believe what feels empowering, regardless of evidence to the contrary. It could be Jesus, juice fasting, crystals, angels, or alien messages. Talismanic objects and in-group beliefs keep anxiety at bay, while the dangers being denied multiply and fester.

A FINAL ELEMENT to understand about conspirituality storytelling, and how it differs from the dry dictums of public health, is that it is not concerned with managing problems that will never end. It is about achieving salvation.

This difference plays out on a microlevel through the common refrain in conspiritualist media: that the medical-industrial complex is designed to treat *symptoms* and to ignore the *root causes* of disease. Extremists in this space go so far as to argue that medical disciplines have a vested interest in keeping populations sick. One influencer diagnosed American culture en masse as suffering from Munchausen syndrome by proxy. This is a terrible condition in which a parent pretends that their child is ill, and may go so far as to poison them in order to gain sympathy and attention, and to feel noble for offering them care—but not enough care to cure them, and allow for their independence.

The influencer who made the faux diagnosis is not entirely wrong. Late-stage capitalism is self-polluting. The surveillance state only pretends to care about its constituents. Corporations sell solutions today for the problems they sold yesterday. And this line of reasoning gets extrapolated by conspiritualists into psychosocial, and even transcendental, realms. Governments, they will say, have a vested interest in increasing social isolation via lock-down measures; doing so will make citizens more compliant. Governments have a vested interest in keeping you anxious, because anxiety will lead to even higher rates of consumerism. They want you to micromanage your hygiene so that you forget about how pure you really are, how close you are to God.

Now, we don't know about God, but it's hard not to empathize with the cynicism here, and the impatience with logic. In the conspirituality play-book, the focus on symptoms versus root causes doesn't have to be coherent. But the simple truth is that COVID will not be repelled by "enhanced immunity" or extra doses of vitamin D. The root cause of COVID infection is COVID, not a poor diet, the wrong type of turmeric, or mental weakness associated with postmodernism.

However, the very young and very old, those with preexisting illnesses, and fat people are all at higher risk for serious COVID complications. Being healthier in the first place does improve your odds of not suffering serious illness. But it is not a badge of spiritual virtue or superior character to have a favorable genetic disposition, or to come from money so that you can buy better health care. Making people feel guilty for their material conditions is cruel. People who are fat for whatever reason are not suddenly going to get ripped overnight instead of getting vaccinated. And there are plenty of cases of young and healthy people having an awful time with COVID, or even dying from it.

But the influencers don't have to make sense, or pay attention to complexity. They just have to validate the common intuition that through its micromanagement of all aspects of modern life, the state and its medical apparatus are missing something crucial. Something like a soul.

PART TWO

STRANGE ATTRACTORS

CHAPTER 7

DID NAZIS LOVE YOGA?

FINDING OUT THAT RIGHT-WING, antisemitic conspiracy theories like QAnon gained a foothold in yoga and wellness communities during the pandemic is disorienting. Why would crunchy-granola, dreadlocked and tatted, raw chocolate–eating, essential oil–diffusing neo-hippies get anywhere close to the hateful cult of Trump, let alone find common cause with it?

Well, right-wing politics have always been more deeply connected to back-to-the-earth notions of natural living, bodily purity, spiritual heroism, and intuitive prophecy than is commonly acknowledged. This doesn't mean that the majority of modern yoga and wellness people are unconsciously right-wing. Rather, it means there is an obscure pathway linking the appearance of progressivism to some very reactionary impulses. Those impulses become clearer when we take a closer look at conspiracy theories.

Becoming aware of the meanings behind conspiracy theories can feel like an acclimatization process. You become aware of a paranoid belief circulating in your milieu. For instance, the entire pharmaceutical industry, with no exceptions—tagged by New Age presidential hopeful Marianne Williamson as the "sickness care system"—has conspired to make us ill so that it can sell us medicine. If you can tolerate listening closely to the details of that belief, though, you'll find that the terms and targets are fluid. Big Pharma executives become interchangeable with bankers or techno-capitalists, and poisoned pharmaceuticals start to blend in with poisoned vaccines, bio-tracked money, and microchip implants. The perpetrators gel into Illuminati, the satanic cults of Satanic Ritual Abuse advocates, or the Cabal of QAnon.

Things get abstract, the Venn diagrams merge, and archetypes begin to take shape. The conspiracy theory works because it adheres to a pattern, and that pattern can be medieval in origin, recalling old bigotries about Jews, foreign invaders, and secularism. If you look intently enough at that pattern, a political impulse begins to reveal itself. The conspiracy theory is a paranoid fantasy about a source of disgust that haunts our lives and must be purified. It is a foreign influence. It is unnatural and repugnant. It must be purified from the body with cleansing practices, purified from the mind with prayers and chants, and purified from one's native land with anti-immigration policies, up to and including pogroms.

So it's no surprise that the politics of the conspiracy theorists we examine in this book virtually always trend right. Some will argue that the left is equally prone to conspiracism through its abstract analysis of power relations, in which another ruling elite takes center stage: the ultra rich, squeezing the underclasses for their lifeblood. But what we've seen so far among conspiritualists is that they are inconsistent at analyzing the ultra rich, or surveillance capitalism. They will impugn Bill Gates for his medical interventions and George Soros for funding various political projects, and sometimes Jeff Bezos for capitalizing on pandemic lockdowns. But at the same time they will ignore how their favorite influencers are bashing conventional medications while selling unregulated supplements or heading up huge digital pyramid schemes. They ignore the excessive wealth of their political icons, like Trump, who give them permission to focus their attention and rage on immigrants and imagined pedophiles.

The omissions and inconsistencies make sense, given the depoliticization of a demographic that tacitly aligns with whatever politics serves their self-interest. But when conspirituality does get political, under the pressure of multiple social crises, it reaches down into the right side of the historical well for its sources of energy and validation. What it finds flows from early twentieth-century fascism and its antecedents: romanticism and nationalism.

For readers who need a primer on fascism, we can offer this brief synthesis:

Fascism is a militant longing to restore the glorious mythical past of an idealized group of people. That golden age, and the land it supposedly flowered in, has been corrupted by the press, academics, immigrants, people of the wrong race, religion, or sexual orientation, or sick or disabled people. What's needed is a strongman leader who will expel the degenerates, enforce law and order, and glorify the culture, values, and historic identity of the elect.

You can see parallel elements in the modern yoga and wellness spaces if you look closely:

The body can be purified through discipline and focus, as well as dietary and devotional communion with the organic earth.

What citizen of concrete cities and fossil fuels wouldn't be attracted to this? But what exactly does purification mean, and who can do it?

The body can become a vessel for mystical experiences provoked by meditation, ritual, or psychedelics.

There's no question that disenchantment, boredom, and cynicism are epidemic. But will mystical experiences elevate the common good? Will they bolster public health? Or will they make tech-bro egomaniacs feel even more superior?

Personal mystical insight gained from astrology, exercise, breathing, meditation, or herbs can produce and nourish a resurrected golden age of supermen and superwomen.

Why are the yoga and wellness influencers of Instagram all so predictably hot? Even the ones selling nonvisual things such as mindfulness, Reiki, and chanting? Is it objectification? Yes. Unrealistic ideals of beauty? Yes. But it's also the soft eugenics of wellness: a constant drumbeat of signs that tell us who is worthy of respect and love, who has mastered the world and its fickle economy.

Supermen and superwomen can have superbabies for the dawning of a New Age, if they devote themselves to the smoothies that will nourish their special juices.

As we'll see, conspirituality draws heavily on old fascist anxieties about sexual potency and deviancy. Conspiritualists in general are obsessed with fertility and virility on a proprietary spectrum that spans from Christiane Northrup (selling followers herbs from Thailand that she blends into vaginal moisturizers) to Proud Boys (committing not to masturbate during No Nut November to store up and instrumentalize the power of their semen). Now, with Tucker Carlson boosting testicle tanning via red-light therapy to combat a crash in testosterone levels, it seems we've entered into a golden age of fascist junk science.

The uncultivated body fills up with bio-moral corruption. Without holistic discipline, the body will be poisoned by science and modernity and lose its connection to its ancestral ways of being.

In this reasoning, the corrupted body fails to protect the sacred Earth. This failure opens up society to degenerate, but more vital, forces. Those forces have always been waiting at the gates. The time to strengthen and purify is always now!

To UNDERSTAND MORE FULLY how fascism plays out in the human body, we might as well start with looking more closely at one of the most influential yet hidden aspects of modern yoga: its spiritual and shameful obsession with eugenics.

CHAPTER 8

A MAN NAMED EUGENICS

Healthier and more perfect men and women will beget children with better constitutions and more free from hereditary taint. They in their turn, if the principles and the duty of physical culture are early instilled into them, will grow up more perfect types of men and women than were their mothers and fathers. So the happy progression will go on, until, who knows, if in the days to come there will not be a race of mortals walking this earth of ours even surpassing those who, according to the old myth, were the offspring of the union of the sons of the gods with the daughters of men!
—Eugen Sandow, *Strength and How to Obtain It*, 1897

JUST IN CASE it's not entirely clear from this passage, Eugen Sandow, the father of modern bodybuilding, isn't talking about the "human" race. The year was 1893 and the strongman had disembarked from the SS *Elbe* in New York Harbor en route to performances at the World's Fair in Chicago. He arrived at this hotel and was shown to his sixteenth-floor room by a Black bellboy. (He calls the boy the N-word in his account.) Outraged when the boy lit a cigarette and told him he had to bring his shoes to the lobby to be shined, Sandow dangled him by his pants out of the window.

Sandow couldn't help himself, you see. The boy's bad manners were "really too much for white flesh and blood to bear." Sandow clutched his pearls all the way to the manager, who "fully agreed with the warning I gave the boy, and was profuse in his apologies, saying that such conduct from a bell boy was unprecedented."

What was not too much for Sandow's flesh and blood to bear were the dumbbells and damsels he hefted in his lucrative vaudeville act, and the hopes and dreams of sundowning empires that European muscularity could help flabby white people avoid "racial suicide," a foundational anxiety driving the burgeoning physical culture movement. At the root of this belief was the principle of "eugenics"—from a Greek term that means "well-bred"—which held that the health and nobility of human populations could be improved through fitness disciplines for the worthy and selective breeding toward the elimination of the disabled. Eugenicists were obsessed with racial purity in an age of colonial migrations. Many believed, following the rantings of the American eugenicist Edward Alsworth Ross about the demographic impacts of immigrant laborers in the United States, that a surge of non-white immigrants from the Global South would overcome the reproductive dominance of white women. It was an early iteration of the Great Replacement conspiracy theory promoted by today's white nationalist extremists, who worry that Europe and the United States will soon no longer be white.

Sandow was an entrepreneurial genius, selling weightlifting contraptions—Sandow's Own Combined Developer—publishing *Sandow's Magazine of Physical Culture*, getting photographed in leopard-skin loincloths, and dazzling audiences with stunts like the Roman Column, which saw him lock his feet to a metal pole so that he could stand sideways in midair, performing weightlifting feats. He was a big hit in England, where Sir Arthur Conan Doyle gushed over his perfect physique and London's National History Museum commissioned a cast of his body for posterity.

Sandow's values were as clear as his stage name. The ripped Prussian got rid of his birth name and adopted "Eugen"—for eugenics. His lectures and writings played on the racially charged fears of his age: that modern bodies were losing strength in urban technologized settings, and that office work disconnected from the soil was leading to moral lethargy and social decline. Sandow noted that in Greek and Roman times—he loved to cosplay in tunic-and-sandals glamour shots—"there were no elevators," and that men "took a pride in their bodies, while now the brain was cultivated, and the body was neglected, and life was a mere race for money."

Sandow was not wrong about the alienation of urbanized capitalism, and his barbs might have hinted at a rebuke of the excesses of gluttonous colonial lords. But his remedy targeted the people and not the machine.

Weakness, according to Sandow, was not an effect of inequality or oppression, but a hereditary taint that strong discipline and better breeding could extinguish until we all walked the Earth as gods.

It was a theme that resonated in unlikely places—including among upper-caste proto-nationalists of India, who found in the physical culture of their colonizers the inspiration to sculpt a new body politic out of an older cultural memory: yoga.

BHAVANRAO PANT PRATINIDHI, the rajah of Aundh in Pune, India—a city that later became a mecca for international yoga students—was a huge Eugen Sandow fan. He bought the books, he read the magazines, he put in reps with Sandow's Grip Dumbbells, which were spring-loaded for extra juice. But after ten years, Bhavanrao was disappointed that he had not developed Sandow's barrel chest. He ditched the weights but kept the Sandow spirit, turning his attention to reinventing an almost-forgotten exercise, the sun salutation.

But Sandow's influence in India persisted, piqued by a triumphant tour in 1905, which Indian bodybuilders, wrestlers, and yoga innovators raved about for years afterward as they rebranded the physical culture of the colonists into exercise regimes for a new nation. Aspiring Indian strongmen adopted his signature moustachios, and "Sandow" became slang for any fit man. Prominent yoga scholars today suggest that Sandow might have had more of an influence on the development of modern Indian yoga than any Indian figure.

On the surface it sounds like a typically strained cultural exchange. Some scholarship notes that non-white colonials were often encouraged to adopt ennobling aspects of occupier culture, so long as they didn't organize politically. They could build their bodies, but not nations. Accordingly, Sandow would publish articles about the physical cultures of Africans, Punjabi Sikhs, and Sri Lankans in his magazine.

The bodies of people of color were relegated to helping to lend the veneer of universalism to European physical culture while maintaining its superiority. They also were objects of mystery and entertainment. After Sandow disembarked at Dover after his India trip, his nine-year-old daughter asked him if he had brought her any "n***** boys" to play with.

* * *

SO AT THE START of the modern yoga movement—which arguably anchors the entire network of New Age and wellness ideologies we're exploring in this book—we have a bizarre colonial collision. Europeans, afraid of racial decline as the borders of empire became porous through global trade and increased long-haul travel, concocted an exercise ideology to defend and restore the once-proud national body against corruption. Indian moderniz-ers grabbed hold of this strongman aesthetic, mingled it with Scandinavian gymnastics, and then consecrated it with yoga exercises reconstructed from the medieval period. They faced east to salute the sun and sculpt a new na-tional body, purged of foreign influences and colonial shame, a body that can carry a torch of ancient wisdom onto the modern global stage.

What gets obscured in this churning transcultural whirlpool is that while European and Indian physical culturists approached their passions from op-posite sides of the colonial wound, they both tried to dress it with the salve of fascism. Their shared beliefs—which also carried and mingled religious histories from both West and East—echo forward into our own lives: that through discipline, purification, restoring virility, and weeding out all sick-ness, disability, and sexual deviance, a transcendent identity would emerge.

As the twentieth century ground on, this Euro-Indian fascist link would strengthen, with some Indian nationalists openly admiring the pride and organizational discipline of European fascist movements—especially the Germans, who were beginning to saber-rattle at a shared enemy: the British. Indian proto-nationalists also founded their own paramilitary cadre, the Rashtriya Swayamsevak Sangh (the RSS, National Volunteer Association), which worked to position yoga as India's national exercise, and continues to do so right up to the present day.

Presently, yoga is a cornerstone of Hindu nationalist social policy and religious pride, while also providing genteel cover for its fascist history and impulses. The ruling Trump-and-Putin-friendly Bharatiya Janata Party (BJP) has been heartily boosted by the billionaire yoga guru Baba Ramdev, who nurtures a frenemy relationship with Prime Minister Narendra Modi, applauding pro-yoga policies, while complaining about his enormous cor-poration not being granted a monopoly over marketing homespun clothes nationwide. (Dating back to the days of Gandhi, homespun cotton was at the root of the Indian independence movement.)

Ramdev hosts a yoga television show watched by millions where he teaches hyperventilation and stretching, and sells herbal supplements. When he's not threatening Muslims with violence for refusing to chant Hindu nationalist prayers, he's teaching that yoga can cure homosexuality. Hindu nationalism is also big on pseudoscience and pseudohistory, advancing the notions that its premodern medicine and scriptures are evidence of an advanced civilization that could have traveled to the stars, were it not for the interruption of colonialism.

Narendra Modi came to power as the unapologetic "butcher of Gujurat," so called for his role, while state governor, in enabling riots that slaughtered over a thousand Muslims in 2002. But his followers portray him as a yogic saint: celibate, teetotaling, consulting with astrologers, and rising before dawn every day to do postures and to meditate. After his first federal election win in 2014, he stood at the dais of the United Nations and intoned: "Yoga is an invaluable gift of our ancient tradition." He named as one of his goals the adoption of an International Yoga Day, claiming that by "changing our lifestyle and creating consciousness, [yoga] can help us deal with climate change."

While Modi was graciously offering yoga as India's gift to the world, his government was also weighing how to reclaim yoga texts and techniques as the IP of the motherland. For a while, bureaucrats batted around the pros and cons of whether to petition for a "geographical indication" that would tie yoga to India, as Champagne is tied to France.

By the time 2021 rolled around, Modi had pivoted from saying that yoga could help with climate change to claiming that it could help with the pandemic. "When I speak to front-line warriors," he announced on International Yoga Day, "they tell me that they have adopted yoga as a protective shield in their fight against coronavirus. Doctors have strengthened themselves with yoga and also used yoga to treat their patients." The sentiment obscured the reality for most doctors, which was that Indian public health officials had finally seized control of the disaster, with vaccination rates rising and case numbers falling.

Previously, as total COVID-19 case numbers surged toward seven million in November 2020, Modi supporters connected the modern-to-postmodern yoga fascism dots by sharing a grainy 1938 video of B. K. S. Iyengar (a towering figure in modern yoga evangelism, about whom we'll say much more later) and claiming it was Modi himself performing "high level yoga practice." Anachronistically injecting Modi into the modern yoga renaissance—and the fight against COVID—was important enough to the posters of this image to overlook the fact that Modi was born in 1950.

And the old Sandow tune of "purifying" the nation through yoga and spiritual practice delivered terrible conspirituality effects on India's COVID response. Researchers now believe that one of the world's worst superspreader events occurred at a yoga-oriented religious festival in Haridwar, in the spring of 2021.

The Kumbh Mela is a celebration of ascetic teachers and practices, and has roots going back centuries. Millions of pilgrims gather at intervals dictated by astrologers to give alms, partake in rituals, and listen to sermons. The 2021 festival was originally scheduled for 2022, but in June of 2019, new astrological insights prompted the date to be moved up. In a stunning display of institutionalized conspirituality, Modi's government ignored the pleas of epidemiologists and public health officials and forged ahead with plans, even as the pandemic surged.

After the festival ended, a region a thousand kilometers south of Haridwar reported a 99 percent infection rate among the returning pilgrims. Researchers later found that prior to the event, cases India-wide were just under 100,000 per day, but spiked sharply to over 400,000 per day by the end of the festival, then fell to 125,000 per day a month after it wrapped. While the yogis extolled the virtues of deep breathing against all illness, COVID victims suffocated on stretchers in the streets outside of bedless hospitals, as oxygen canisters sold out.

WE CAN CALL IT the Sandow Effect: no pain, no gain. The body can and should be purified. Your physique and posture are signs of your moral character and spiritual development. The enlightened person stands up straight, having freed himself from his messy history. He is a light to the nation.

That this ideology has saturated the modern yoga movement is not merely an academic fact. The three of us also felt its effects in our bodies.

In the mid-aughts, Derek was immersed in the high-intensity community of Jivamukti Yoga in New York. They told him some very strange things about his body. Teachers with a knack for intrusive eye contact would say that because he couldn't bend backward far enough to perform the wheel pose that his heart wasn't open. The psychological implication was that he was in some way frozen in his emotional life—but not in a way any mere therapy could correct.

"Jivamukti Yoga," reads the brand's grandiose mission statement, "is a path to enlightenment through compassion for all beings." Their practice is "more than mere physical exercise to keep one's body fit or to increase strength or flexibility; it becomes a way to improve one's relationship to all others and thus lead to enlightenment—the dissolution of the sense of separateness, the realization of the oneness of being, the discovery of lasting happiness." Evidently, if Derek wanted to attain spiritual freedom, he'd have to work on freeing his spine from things like cartilage and ligaments.

Derek didn't know it, but ideas like this made him practically Matthew's cult-brother. In those years, the Jivamukti brand was under the influence of Michael Roach, who had moved on to recruiting followers in the yoga market after allegations of sexual misconduct ostracized him from the broader world of Tibetan Buddhism. Inspired by Roach, the Jivamukti founders had their followers bow down before them with piously folded hands, while telling them that their physical injuries were the manifestation of karma. Derek had a long rap sheet of sports injuries, but he started to wonder whether these injuries symbolized some deeper moral failing, or spiritual meaning.

Meanwhile, in Toronto, Matthew was absorbing many of the same yoga-world pseudo-lessons about the meaning of his posture. Most of his teachers came from the highbrow school of B. K. S. Iyengar. Matthew spent years obsessing over minor adjustments in his stance and imagined micro-currents of energy that were meant to direct every cell in his body. No joke: Iyengar teachers would give hour-long lectures on the proper meeting of the ball joints of each foot with the floor. There were instructions on which way the skin on the surface of one's shin should flow, and even which way the hairs on one's calf should point. Never mind that changing any of this was impossible: transforming the constant anxiety of self-consciousness into giddy elation was the goal.

Matthew was also taught to believe that his joints were too stiff to "open up" for the enlightening flow of energy that would awaken his higher potentials. Following this path led to years of chronic pain caused by a feedback loop of micro-tears caused by stretching, and temporarily relieved by the endorphins of more…stretching.

"There should always be a certain amount of pain; then only will you see the light," Iyengar said to one of his first Western yoga students in 1959. "What is pain if it enables you to see God?" he asked. "Pain is your guru."

On the other side of the continent, Julian's guru set the morality of posture into more practical motion. Ana Forrest insisted that how a student performed yoga postures was a reflection of how they lived their life. Taking her lead, Julian began to believe that his emotional life story was written in his body. The slightly rolled forward shoulder, the disengaged abdomen, the flaccid gluteal muscle, the ungrounded foot—all were clues to where his story was "stuck." Greater healing and integration, he was led to believe, would lead to more grace, unbroken lines of energy, acrobatic freedom, and an ability to carry himself through the world and his life with strength and beauty.

But the method wasn't open source, because Forrest maintained a monopoly on body stories—specifically, of whose body was expressing what excess of trauma or maladaptation. She decided who needed more concentration, effort, discipline. The overall dynamic, Julian remembers, was that everyone felt relentlessly criticized by Forrest, which meant that getting her approval felt emotionally orgasmic. But achieving what she demanded was nearly impossible. This led to a steady rhythm of emotional breakdowns in the group. When a student would collapse in tears, Forrest's intuitive powers seemed to be confirmed. She would then pivot into the role of the comforting mother and gentle guide, leading the prodigal child toward her blessing.

In the New York, Toronto, and Los Angeles of the early aughts, the three of us had little idea of how history was coursing through our bodies. We didn't know that the German-Indian fascist pipeline created a postwar generation of yoga-loving Nazis and Nazi-loving Hindu nationalists. We did not know that for old-timey fascists, yoga was often an occult tool for purifying the individual body—as a microcosm of an exalted nation that would ultimately triumph over a conspiracy of Jews, Muslims, and other corrupt invaders. We did not know that the choreographed instructions to flow from pose to pose, given by the soft voices of our mainly women instructors, were initially barked out by ex-military men more acquainted with calisthenics drills.

We did not know that Nazis cherry-picked the superhero themes of Indian yoga gods, fantasizing about becoming invulnerable in body and spirit. We didn't know that Heinrich Himmler carried around a copy of the *Bhagavad Gita* and conceived of the SS as a yogic monastic order. We didn't know that when *Mein Kampf* was republished in India in 2003, it became a national bestseller.

We just didn't know. And the vast majority of our friends and colleagues didn't either, to say nothing of the casual yoga consumer. Why?

One key reason may be that the postwar marketing of yoga was driven by Indian charismatic entrepreneurs who saw themselves as creating a universal wellness product that would not sell if it were complicated by the politics that the world had just barely survived. Case in point: primo modern yoga guru B. K. S. Iyengar got his first big break internationally when he gave a private lesson to the violin virtuoso Yehudi Menuhin in 1952. Menuhin was suffering from insomnia in the midst of a grueling world tour. Iyengar simply laid the fried violinist out in corpse pose, instructed him to breathe deeply, and talked him into a blissful sleep. In 1954, Menuhin, now a full devotee, orchestrated Iyengar's first international demonstration and teaching tour in Switzerland, France, and England.

Menuhin, who was Jewish American, was known for his progressive politics and burning hatred for racism. Seven years before meeting Iyengar, he played a concert at the newly liberated Bergen-Belsen concentration camp and was thereafter haunted. We can find no record of whether Menuhin knew that modern yoga had fascist roots, nor can we find any indication of Menuhin and Iyengar discussing politics. But it is highly likely that the yoga master kept the conversation firmly on the topics of posture and breathing, which would serve him well in the parlors of Western Europe and the United States.

Later in life, Iyengar was tight-lipped when asked if he was or ever had been a member of the Rashtriya Swayamsevak Sangh. Occasionally he would joke that Indian yoga would "reverse colonize" the West, by inflicting the pain of stretching. Many students took this as the sardonic wit of a spiritual master who had transcended political concerns by maintaining laser-like focus on the sacred nature of the body.

The overt fascism that dominated the inception of the modern yoga movement faded into the collective unconscious, while the psychology of personal transformation came to the fore. Senior American students of Pattabhi Jois—the founder of Ashtanga Yoga and an old schoolmate of Iyengar's—were shocked to hear him complain about teaching yoga to Muslims. They respectfully pushed back, and he kept mum about it going forward. The students thought that Jois's xenophobia was unbecoming to a yoga master whose technique they wanted to market to the world for health and healing. But the truth was they knew very little about where his yoga came from. Many had been late-1960s dropouts, after all, actively trying to escape the political world.

The historical ignorance and bypassing of Jois's students was superficial in relation to a deeper state of denial many maintained in order to preserve their idealization of him. Jois sexually and physically assaulted his students on a near-daily basis, for decades, under the guise of "adjustments." The adjustments themselves—ostensibly meant to correct students' postures and improve their performance—had been pioneered largely by Jois's guru, and carried with them a hallmark of colonial-era education: corporal punishment.

Self-awareness in the yoga industry was so dim that when Mark Singleton, a British religious studies scholar, popularized his PhD thesis on the real history of modern yoga for the trade market in 2010, the ground began to shake. Singleton's meticulous research proved that modern Indian yoga was inextricable from fin-de-siècle European physical culture. The colonized had adopted the exercises—and some of the attitudes—of the colonizers. This cracked the romantic myth that yoga was somehow eternal and beyond the reach of modern cultural influences, and therefore ideally suited to heal the fractures of modernity. Singleton largely stayed away from the political implications of the Euro-Indian pipeline, but the writing was on the wall. The research step from "Modern Indian yoga innovators learned physical culture from the legacy of Sandow" to "Oh snap: this is what Sandow actually believed about bodies and races" is a small one.

THE ECHOES OF THE BODY fascism that Iyengar and Jois grew up with were theirs to bear privately—to transform all that history, all those politics, into a mystery play about the heroic, individual spiritual journey. By the time they became known to the European bourgeoisie of the 1950s, and then the American dropouts of the 1960s, they were middle-aged yoga masters, inscrutable and solitary. They seemed to have emerged out of a distant, idealized past, molded by scripture and ritual more than postcolonial struggle or postwar entrepreneurialism.

In rare moments, they shared glimpses into their internal lives that seemed to show that the politics of purity and impurity and worthiness and corruption, which had permeated the gymnasiums of their youth, had been fully sublimated into internal journeys. Fascism had become a psychodrama.

"Iyengar sat in a corner café and drank some hot chocolate," Victor Van Kooten told Matthew in an interview in 2004. Matthew was working on a research project about yoga and pain. Van Kooten had been one of Iyengar's closest students in the late 1970s and early 1980s, practicing and watching him practice for hours every day. Matthew had asked for the interview because he'd heard that Iyengar had fractured Van Kooten's spine while "adjusting" him into the correct position.

But Van Kooten told another story about his teacher. Van Kooten claimed that at the heart of the most spiritual exercise movement of the twentieth century stood a leader who was so anxious about his bodily worth that he feared God would shun him if he wasn't perfect.

> He told me about his main dreams. One of them was that he knocked on the doors of the inner room of a temple. But they were closed. He said, "God, let me in, I am B. K. S. Iyengar, and I want to be with you."
>
> And God said, 'No, you can't because you are impure.' And Iyengar said, 'I have done yoga for so long, I am pure now!' And God said, 'No, you are impure, go back, go out of the temple!' And so Iyengar saw himself going out, and he sat down on the stairs and cried.

CHAPTER 9

EVOLVING THE SOULS OF CHILDREN

DR. JENNIFER SAPIO was excited to start her job at the Austin Waldorf School. Nestled into thirty-three wooded acres on the western edge of town, AWS offered what all the thousand-plus Waldorf schools in more than sixty countries worldwide promise: a free-range, nature-based education, emphasizing whole-child development. She was drawn to the post in much the same way that the three of us were drawn into yoga teaching: through the seeming progressivism of its culture. In Sapio's case, she was also aware of the apparently serene wisdom of Waldorf's Austrian founder, Rudolf Steiner.

While the physical culture of Eugen Sandow and his contemporaries sculpted the fascist body, a parallel, older stream of mental culture and purity inspired the fascist mind of the early twentieth century. Steiner's anthroposophy played an outsized role. As Sapio discovered, anthroposophy was an early postmodern mashup of German romanticism, Norse mythology, and racist appeals to the "folk souls" of white Europe—filtered through the megalomania of Steiner's belief that he could daydream history into reality by reading the "Akashic Records."

First introduced by the Theosophists in the 1880s, who sowed the seeds of what would become New Age spirituality, the Akashic Records are purported to be a kind of energetic library that contains a spiritually truthful record of all events, thoughts, and desires that have ever existed. Those with the requisite occult gifts and training can supposedly access the hidden history of humanity, which might include the story of Atlantis, or how our ancestors were really intergalactic aliens, or the deeper meaning of current events in light of the overarching spiritual purpose of life on Earth. The unfalsifiable claim of having intuitive access to the Akashic Records is a standard trope among those adopting the professional mantle of oracular psychic, or anyone who channels unquestionable higher truths from the great beyond.

When we interviewed her for the podcast, Sapio, who has a PhD in English literature, admitted to knowing little at first about the history of Waldorf education or Steiner himself. In 2017, she signed the contract to teach second grade at Austin Waldorf School (where parents pay up to $20,000 per year in tuition) on the basis of the wholesome things she'd heard. Waldorf education was "holistic," "artistic," "healthful." There was an emphasis on outdoor play and gardening; the rustic campus sprawled like a blue refuge within the great red state of Texas. What's not to like?

Matthew had stepparented a child who went to Waldorf school in Vermont in the mid-1990s. Nestled at the end of a winding dirt road, the school was bucolic, non-technologized. Women teachers wore flowing dresses and the men wore Amish-style overalls and straw hats. The parents who volunteered at lunch supervision had a crunchy vibe, and discussed their loathing for television and the suburbs over salads of dandelion greens and steamed fiddleheads brought in stainless steel boxes. Many of them were involved in anti-war or environmental activism. In the classrooms, all the toys were wooden, all the corners were rounded, none of the crayons or paints came in loud primary colors. Transitions between activities were governed by the singing of medieval-style carols or the tooting of gentle melodies on tin whistles.

Some of the ideas were strange. The children were only allowed to draw in flowing circles: jagged scribbling wasn't allowed. They were discouraged from reading and writing until their milk teeth were all out. There was something attractive about that: the notion that the child's body would tell the teacher when they were ready to wash the garden mud off their hands and enter the abstract world of human thought. But Matthew also remembered being a really early reader. Seeds of doubt were sown: Had his brain and spirit been damaged by the printed word? Had he lost his primal connection to nature too soon?

Later, his experiences in yogaworld would haunt him with the same question.

At the time, Matthew wasn't close enough to any of the other parents to ask if they were vaccinating their children. That conversation might have told him something.

* * *

DURING HER JOB INTERVIEW, Sapio made it clear that she was very much against religious indoctrination in schools.

"Oh, I absolutely understand," said the interviewer. "All we'll have you do here is start the day with a verse."

Being an English doctorate, this suited Sapio fine. Poetry? Great. Engaging with language? Super. But within weeks of the hire, she was paired up with a mentor, a "Master" Waldorf teacher, who assigned her strange readings from the century-old oeuvre of Rudolf Steiner, who'd founded Waldorf education in 1919. The Master told her that she was teaching the students' souls. Sapio could feel that she was being drawn into something she hadn't signed up for. The paychecks and health insurance hadn't even kicked in yet.

The mentorship didn't repress her critical thinking for long. Within months, Sapio was digging through the reading, ignoring her mentor's advice to "take what is useful, and leave the rest." What she found were books crammed with racist, eugenicist, pseudoscientific ideas, wrapped up in the florid language of spiritual pretension. Steiner believed that he could astral travel, that he knew where Atlantis was, that vaccines were a satanic plot to extinguish human spirituality, and that white people had evolved, through a divine evolutionary process, out of being Black.

And Sapio was only reading materials available in English. As Peter Staudenmaier, who teaches modern German history at Marquette, points out: "One crucial stumbling block for English language readers is the anthroposophical tendency to delete racist and antisemitic passages from translated editions of Steiner's publications." For instance, Staudenmaier shows that the German text of a 1923 lecture entitled "Color and the Races of Humankind" was snipped out of the 1999 English translation of the book it appeared in.

Sapio had found herself in a fundamentalist Steiner environment. Austin Waldorf School really went all out. She was told to wear silk scarves to protect her "subtle body" from the energetic contamination of less enlightened students. Before going to bed at night, she was told to enter into meditation and commune with each of her students' souls directly. Why? Because Steiner believed that the primary role of the Waldorf teacher was to improve the karma of the child. Not through studying pedagogical research, developmental psychology, or diversity, equity, and inclusion, but by guiding their souls' progress as they purged impurities that manifested as disabilities and diseases.

LITTLE OF STEINER'S CONTENT was original. He cribbed much of it from the Theosophy of Madame Helena Blavatsky, the Russian aristocratic spiritual tourist who claimed to have spent her youth traveling the holy places of the world to discover sacred texts in languages only she could translate. She said she channeled "Ascended Masters" from Tibet as she grifted her way across Europe and New York with a tickle trunk of paranormal parlor tricks. Branches of her Theosophical Society popped up in her footsteps like mushrooms, and for a while, Steiner headed up the German franchise.

But tensions emerged over Steiner's increasing sympathy with Christianity, because one of Blavatsky's main hooks was that Theosophy represented a blessed evolution out of the infantile monotheism handed down by the Semites, whom she contrasted with the more spiritually mature Aryans.

Perhaps this is sounding familiar.

Like so many New Agers who followed her, Blavatsky functioned as a kind of post hoc colonial apologist. She concocted a hierarchy of "root races," which held that the genocide of Indigenous peoples was a "karmic necessity."

Steiner didn't rap on tables, but he remained faithful to Blavatsky's channeling with his endless stream of Akashic-inspired writing. He also doubled down on Blavatsky's racism. Translating from a 1915 Steiner lecture that's still only available in German, Staudenmaier lets Steiner speak for himself:

> People have white skin color because the spirit works within the skin when it wants to descend to the physical plane...but where the spirit is held back, where it takes on a demonic character and does not fully penetrate the flesh, then white skin color does not appear, because atavistic powers are present that do not allow the spirit to achieve complete harmony with the flesh.

Sapio left Austin Waldorf School after two and a half years teaching there—enough to save up her money to buy her time to find a new job—and has been sharing her experience since then to warn others.

THE AKASHIC RECORDS are a fantastical library, floating in the ethers, that records all events, past and future. That Steiner used it to solve the problem of his own credibility tells us something about fascist reasoning, and sets the tone for how conspiritualists of today rationalize their impossible positions.

For Steiner, it wasn't enough to just overshare his spiritual nerdery. He was also keen to undermine the basics of evidentiary research and the scientific method. His 1911 pseudohistory of *The Submerged Continents of Atlantis and Lemuria, Their History and Civilization*, opens with a self-serving attack on the legit discipline of history. He derides the idea that scholarly opinions can change when confronted with new evidence, and argues that the eternal truth of what happened can only be accessed through meditation.

According to Steiner, if knowledge accumulates in stages, or must be syncretized from different perspectives, or be updated when new evidence emerges, it can't have real value. Luckily, Steiner argues, the eternal is accessible to the man who trains himself to see beyond the husk of the mundane world and into the vibrant tableaux of oneness. And wouldn't you know it—he thinks he's just the man for the job.

When scholars argue that fascism depends on devaluing academics and glorifying anti-intellectualism, this is a great example of what they're talking about. It's a short trip between Steiner touting his pseudohistory book and Hitler coining the term *Lügenpresse* ("lying press," or in today's parlance, "fake news") to deride any legitimate journalism that would push back against the Third Reich. "The key to understanding why many Germans supported him," writes historian Benjamin Carter Hett about Hitler, "lies in the Nazis' rejection of a rational, factual world."

In a similar vein, the way in which Steiner "won" his magical power also sheds light on a crucial theme of how knowledge is authorized in New Age scenes, and in the conspirituality movement of today. Preachers in this zone typically lay claim to early life experiences of awakening, gifting them with special, often stigmatized, knowledge. Steiner explained that early studies in geometry granted him a sense that he was clairvoyant. He believed that the theorems of Pythagoras were leading him into the "occult-astral" past, where the influences of modern education would not corrupt him. He was only eight years old.

"WHEN YOU KNOW STEINER, you have the answers to the test," declared American alternative medicine practitioner Tom Cowan on March 11, 2020, the day the WHO declared COVID-19 to be a pandemic. "But you have to then figure out the details." The video was shared over 16,000 times in its first week on YouTube, and was viewed over 390,000 times in total. Singer Keri Hilson shared it with her 2.3 million Instagram followers, as did actors Woody Harrelson and John Cusack. Stats from the monitoring platform CrowdTangle show that it was shared all over the world in multiple languages.

Cowan's talk was packed with misinformation, because despite his training as a medical doctor, he thinks Rudolf Steiner knows everything—even from the grave. "After the Spanish flu pandemic of 1918," Cowan said:

> Steiner was asked, "What was this all about?" And he said, "Well, viruses are simply excretions of a toxic cell. Viruses are pieces of DNA or RNA with a few other proteins, that come out from the cell. It happens when the cell is poisoned. They are not the cause of anything.

Cowan went on to claim that the cells of alleged COVID-19 patients had been poisoned by new 5G cell tower waves. This lecture, which reached hundreds of thousands of viewers, was cited by key conspirituality influencers. The COVID-19 conspirituality arms race was on.

Cowan no longer practices medicine. His business was crippled by a five-year probationary period doled out because he prescribed an unapproved quack cancer treatment to a patient he'd never met. But his previous tenure as an anthroposophist doctor who doesn't believe in germ theory is testimony to Steiner's social acceptability. Steiner was really good at finding places in mainstream society into which he could shoehorn his cursed ideas. Through the strategic editing of offensive passages by his followers, along with Steiner's own pragmatic interests in health and agriculture—as opposed to Blavatsky's batshit-crazy fetishes—Steiner has generated a legacy of adherents with respectable careers in medicine, government, and education.

It was bad enough that Cowan quoted Steiner's ignorance about viruses. But it could have been worse. He could have quoted Steiner's views on vaccines, which sound like they could have been muttered by QAnon followers. "I have told you," Steiner blustered in 1917, as the Spanish flu raged around the world, that the spirits of darkness are going to inspire their human hosts, in whom they will be dwelling, to find a vaccine that will drive all inclination toward spirituality out of people's souls when they are still very young, and this will happen in a roundabout way through the living body. Today, bodies are vaccinated against one thing and another; in future, children will be vaccinated with a substance which it will certainly be possible to produce, and this will make them immune, so that they do not develop foolish inclinations connected with spiritual life—"foolish" here, of course, in the eyes of materialists.

According to the Texas Medical Association, which tracks vaccination uptake in the state, Austin Waldorf School scored the top conscientious objection rate in 2019, with 46.25 percent of parents refusing to vaccinate their children.

Jennifer Sapio was happy to land a new job.

CHAPTER 10

CLEANSING AND THE SACRED FIRE

IN MARCH 2020, Mak Parhar did something that both sabotaged his tiny strip mall business in Delta, British Columbia, and gained him a huge following as a protest leader in Canada's conspiracy theory community. He emailed customers of his Bikram Yoga studio with some dangerous misinformation.

> Fact—this supposed virus cannot survive in the heat.
>
> Fact—Bikram yoga is the best way to keep your immune system healthy and/or the best way to build and improve your immune system to fight flus, colds, bacteria and viruses.

The email prompted a visit from the city's bylaw officers, and the subsequent yanking of his business license. It seemingly foreshadowed Parhar's death, eighteen months later. He'd been posting videos, coughing and rambling about an illness that he professed to be treating with ivermectin, the favored cure of COVID quacks who waffled on whether they believed in COVID or not.

Both of Parhar's email claims are bullshit, in the same style of his franchiser, Bikram Choudhury, the founder of Bikram Yoga. Choudhury is worth a brief digression here, given the shadow he casts over Parhar's grave.

Currently fleeing US prosecution related to allegations of sexual assault, Choudhury is half strongman, half clownish tycoon, and all egomaniac. He built his fortune on health claims related to the 105°F heat in his practice studios—a protocol he contrived in the 1970s to mimic, he said, the temperatures in his native Calcutta, omitting for his Western customers the fact that in India, yoga is never practiced at midday, nor under the sun. As it turns out, the most researched "benefit" of the artificial heat applied in Bikram Yoga suggests that it brings participants dangerously close to heatstroke. A 2015 study by the American Council on Exercise found that participants were clocking internal temperatures of up to 104°F.

Choudhury would tell students that if they did thirty minutes of yoga per day, "it is not necessary to spend a single cent on a doctor in your whole life." He says he can cure arthritis and multiple sclerosis and help the elderly have multiple orgasms. The main evidence for his claims has always been that he can shout them at people.

All Bikram Yoga classes are taught according to Choudhury's script, which gives precise instructions for the execution of twenty-six postures over ninety minutes. Memorizing that script is the main task of the nineweek teacher trainings Choudhury hosted for years before he went on the lam. Up to six hundred hopefuls would gather in a white circus tent buttressed by industrial heating ducts to get stretched, dehydrated, and verbally abused, after paying tuition and fees of over $10,000.

On archive.org, we found a photocopy of a Bikram training manual from 1997. Across the top page there's a handwritten note: "75 years ago: Guru said mental stress and strain is the cause of all the diseases—even the infectious ones." If the document was uploaded by a training participant taking notes on Choudhury's sermons, the guru in the note likely refers to early modern Indian bodybuilder-yogi Bishnu Ghosh, who counted none other than Eugen Sandow as a primary influence.

Going by the coughing in the livestream videos Parhar released up to November 5, 2021, the day before he died, he seemed personally familiar with the virus he thought was a hoax. Shouting into his phone as he drove around Vancouver, he described taking ivermectin, Tylenol, and Advil, while denying he had "Convid." The postmortem found that Parhar did in fact have COVID, but died of ethanol, fentanyl, and cocaine poisoning.

Parhar might have thought he was sick from the stress and strain, per the wisdom of Ghosh. He had been in a spiral for a while—perhaps since 2017. In January of that year, his Facebook page took a sharp turn away from anodyne posts about favorite vegan restaurants, the dangers of GMO foods, and the benefits of enema therapy. "Time to wake up," Parhar posted. "Earth is FLAT. Not a spinning Globe hurtling through Space...NASA is nothing but liars...do the research."

Three days prior to his death, Parhar was arrested and charged with repeatedly breaking the Canadian Quarantine Act, after returning from a conference of flat-Earthers in South Carolina. He had given a fiery speech at a protest rally, where he bragged about dodging quarantine, refusing to wear a mask on the plane, and using pseudolegal sovereign citizen jargon at the border to claim he wasn't subject to Canadian law. His studio had been closed for eighteen months. In 2019, Parhar had separated from the mother of his daughter, in part because the mother had had the girl vaccinated without his knowledge. Telling the story on a podcast in between rants about Charlotte Ward's hero David Icke and pharmaceutical companies while puffing on his vaper, he sighed, saying, "My life is a mess."

After the town of Delta shut down Parhar's hot yoga studio in March 2020, he used the space for unmasked meetings, where compatriots gathered to talk conspiracy theories. The police checked in on the meetups at the request of concerned neighbors, but found no statute under which they could issue tickets.

While Parhar turned to full-time anti-lockdown propaganda, other conspiritualists took up the gospel of heat. In December 2020, the FDA sent a warning letter to Enlighten Sauna in Burlingame, California. The infrared sauna sellers had been claiming that the heat could help one's immune system fight off COVID-19. In August 2021, Austin-based "Master Coach" Preston Smiles released a selfie confession that he had contracted COVID, but had battled it heroically with ivermectin, zinc, unnamed nebulized chemicals, an awakening to Jesus, and his in-home infrared sauna—which he used twice a day. He also played the corrupted food card by claiming that the worst of his symptoms were caused by eating a teaspoon of sugar.

THE CONVICTION THAT ONE'S BODY is "impure" forms the primal terror that motivates cleansing ideology. But for cleansers in the know, this is balanced by a primal confidence: that within you lies the power to generate immunity and radiant health through a burning combination of digestive power and mental fortitude. In Ayurveda—the premodern, religiously inflected medicine of India—this inner heat is the blessing of the fire element. We're talking about the *essence* of fire, a bio-spiritual principle that governs metabolism, vision, intelligence, and capacity to perceive the divine. The fire element that heats every cell is also the individual's portion of the sun.

"In cleansing the blood (the soul's fluid in the body)," writes David Frawley, "sweating can purify the senses, emotions and mind and open us up to the powers of the spirit." Frawley, a Wisconsin-born ex-Catholic chiropractor, is now famous as a Western shill for the Hindu nationalist BJP, and his brand of Ayurveda is both hyper-religious and supportive of the xenophobic mythos of neo-Hinduism. "Sweating helps liberate the soul from its bodily limitations, taking our life-force beyond the boundaries of the skin."

To the extent that Choudhury, Parhar, Smiles, and the sauna sellers were directly or osmotically influenced by this very old idea, they were given a powerful metaphor for "building immunity" that suits their egocentric worldview. This is a fire, associated with health and inner wisdom, that they can meticulously nourish by gathering the appropriate fuel, and by watching it carefully. From there it's just a matter of adding breathwork, which in Ayurveda and other alt-health modalities is often compared to a bellows for that fire.

It makes sense that fire tending is a symbolic core of alternative health, and is appealing to conspiritualists. It will burn away toxins and delusions. It feels like you can do it yourself. It feels as ancient as a temple sacrifice, no priests required. What lab-coated bureaucrat can know, let alone manage, your inner flame?

And to the extent a person's internal fire points to the sun as its ultimate source, individuals are encouraged to identify with the center of the universe. When they were weaning themselves from the influence of cult leaders, Julian and Matthew found this identification helpful. But they feel lucky that they didn't stay at the center of the universe for long, since it's also where the self-obsessed fascist body—dedicated to expressing constant mastery over personal and social impurity—finds its strength and meaning. This may say something about why the sun, long associated with patriarchal power and divine order, is fascism's dominant symbol—and may lead us to wonder what some modern yogis are really saluting.

The right-wing yoga firebrands of today's India are definitely not confused about the meaning of the sun salutation. Yogi Adityanath, Prime Minister Narendra Modi's appointee as chief minister of Uttar Pradesh, said that those who want to avoid the sun salutation can leave India. He was addressing objections from Indian Muslims and agnostics to the religious creep of the government, which had recently dubbed Yoga Day a compulsory holiday. "My humble request to those who see communalism in [the]

Sun God," he said, dismissing the fact that yoga has religious connections, "would be to drown themselves in the sea or live in a dark room for the rest of their lives."

FOR BOTH JULIAN AND MATTHEW, a funny thing happened on the road between yoga cults and everyday freedom. As Julian moved away from Ana Forrest, and Matthew moved away from Roach and Anderson, they both reached for practices that were in the same ballpark—but that they could do themselves, with the effect of regaining some of their personal agency. They needed lifelines that would help them make a delicate transition from a culty world they could not yet entirely reject—because if they did wholly reject it, they would have to face, all at once, the terrible question of whether they had been abused and exploited in the name of utter make-believe.

The stepping-stone answer for both was to shift from the top-down authoritarianism of much of yogaworld to the self-imposed authoritarianism of "cleansing" culture in the broader wellness scene. In some ways, it was a step up. They were no longer submitting to the X-ray vision of charismatic teachers, who insisted their hearts or joints weren't open enough to be vessels of pure spirit.

But it was also a step to the side, because in order to believe in cleansing, a whole series of quasi-religious and pseudoscientific beliefs around one's internal purity have to be in play. By getting into liver cleanses and intestinal purgations, they were grabbing hold of their own innards, but with beliefs in impurity now so internalized they were willing to do some disgusting stuff to get right with the world.

Every few months, Julian would fast for up to three days on water and tart green apples. This liver flush, which is believed to clear the liver and gallbladder of gallstones, was all the rage in yogaworld at the time, rising out of the mists of folk medicine popularized by the pseudonymous Penny C Royal in the 1982 book *Herbally Yours*.

At around 5 p.m. on the appointed day, Julian, appled to the gills, would slowly chug too much of a barfy concoction of equal parts olive oil and lemon juice. The evening was spent in stomach-churning contemplation, before retiring early. Julian cannot *emphasize enough* how *important it was* to sleep *on his right side only*, to energetically *guide the holistic Drano* toward the liver and gallbladder, where it could do its sacred flushing work.

The real magic revealed itself in the morning, when his crapper filled up with crumbly shiny green river stones, expelled in slippery cathartic toots. And there it was, the proof of a cleansed liver and flushed gallbladder. Julian had rid himself of gallstones and toxic cholesterol! And no, it couldn't *possibly* have been congealed oil and applesauce, tinged green with the peels. *Of course not!*

Matthew learned similar techniques, but through the more baroque system of premodern Indian medicine called Ayurveda, which had ridden the coattails of the yoga boom to become both an adjunct industry and a side hustle for gig-working yoga teachers seeking to expand their portfolios.

He'd taken an extensive correspondence course in Ayurveda, authored by Frawley, not knowing of his politics at the time. Matthew even invited Frawley to headline the yoga festival he directed in Toronto in 2011. But when he saw dozens of white attendants—the women in white saris and the men in white kurtas—show up to scatter rose petals at Frawley's feet, he knew something was off.

To Frawley's doctrines, Matthew added a training in yoga therapy, and he learned how to self-administer a modern reconstruction of an old practice called *panchakarma* (the "five actions"), prescribed for centuries by Ayurvedic physicians for everything ranging from seasonal illnesses to cancer. The five actions, undertaken after a week or more of fasting, oil massage, and sweating, are vomiting, purgation, enema, nasal irrigation, and bloodletting. (Matthew skipped action number five.)

In his training, these ideas were mixed with ascetic practices cribbed from medieval yoga. These included passing a cotton string stiffened with beeswax and made slippery with clarified butter up your nose and through your mouth to "floss" (while crying out in agony) and swallowing two yards of sterilized cotton cloth, about two inches wide, so that you could pull it back out, coated with mucus and stomach acids, like a plumber's snake.

All of this stuff came from a different time and place, where it surely made more sense, and was more integrated with the warp and weft of daily life. To package it for sale, and buy it, and go through these torturous rituals of self-transcendence while living in a world of peer-reviewed medical research, was a defiant act. It was a real *fuck you* to modernity, to institutions, to the people in lab coats who, like the gurus of old, presumed the authority to tell you who you were. On some days, it was more metal than metal. It was *medieval* metal.

For both Julian and Matthew, the ideological premise was that their bodies had been holding on to all the environmental and foodborne toxins that permeate modern life. The logic is this: These toxins are blocking our energy flow, keeping us physically jammed. And, over time, the thickness of our internal crud impedes our transformation and healing and leads to disease. But: there was always the "polishing the turd" problem. In many Iron Age philosophies, the body itself is inescapably dirty. It exists only because the soul or spirit is deluded and enmeshed in impure desires. If your very body—in any state—is evidence of your fallen nature, how could it ever be clean enough?

Ayurveda added a complex typology to the category of toxins, where various bodily extrusions spattered in the toilet bowl were read like tea leaves for consistency and color, and assigned moral and even spiritual meanings. For instance, Matthew was taught that the end of the saltwater purgation was at hand when he was eliminating nothing but bright yellow water. This was after spending the morning drinking several gallons of salty water and twisting and turning to stimulate dozens of movements. In Ayurveda's physiological language, bright yellow indicated that you were scraping the bottom of the liver barrel, and getting close to peak cleanliness.

But there was a psycho-spiritual meaning as well. The angry color was anger itself. The salt water was like the ocean tide washing the shore of Matthew's soul, scraping free every bit of congealed rage. He didn't need a teacher to tell him he was okay. The color proved it, along with his burning rectum. The aftereffect was the mental haziness of exhaustion and low blood sugar, which was easy to confuse with serene wisdom.

We definitely had more extreme experiences than most people do in these practices. The fact we were professionalized into this scene incentivized us to go further than we might have otherwise. But having gone all-in gives us granular insight into ideas and attitudes that are ubiquitous in the yoga and wellness worlds. Every green smoothie picture on Instagram tracks back to some variation on these themes. Wellness influencers and supplement shills are obsessed with purification. Intense sweating—with the added bonus of weight loss that may actually be dangerous dehydration—is super popular.

People juice fast for days on "macronutrients" for a promised "metabolic reset." They chug the magical lemon juice, maple syrup, cayenne pepper potion of the "Master Cleanse," and, once released from the gross desire for ordinary food, are struck with light-headed reveries of quasi-spiritual freedom. Hay House author and so-called Medical Medium Anthony Williams has 3.3 million Facebook followers. His primary obsession is with the power of celery juice to "ignite healing when all odds seem against it." He also published an alt-med download to his website titled "Virus Protection," with a COVID-style microscopic viral graphic on the cover.

All of these materials are marketed with pseudoscientific panache to solve two problems. First, your body is an absorptive vector for the toxins of the world. Second, if the world doesn't fill your body with poison, your corrupt mind will, from the inside.

The answer we, Julian and Matthew, chased wasn't environmental activism, improving food access, or supporting public health. We were way too busy working on ourselves for complexities that involved things such as other people and democratic institutions. We were washing, sweating, and purging—cleansing the world through its most humble pathway: the personal poop chute.

These soft-fascist anxieties, rebranded as self-care, waste time and money and may make people overly fixated on the quality of their waste products. They can make middle-class liberals unwitting marketers of Hindu nationalism, as they promote International Yoga Day on their Facebook feeds with pictures of vast, uniformed yoga gatherings on the boulevards of Delhi. Closer to home, they can provide spiritual rationalization for disordered eating, avoiding or refusing qualified medical care, or forcing people to stay in overheated, white-cultist-run "sweat lodges" until they die.

All three of us have watched people become very sick through combinations of excessive cleansing practices and refusing to avail themselves of real treatment. We watched them move the goalposts between body and spirit as they got sicker: if the "therapy" wasn't showing good physical results, it was still a sign that the soul was purifying, and so the process should continue.

The COVID-19 conspirituality explosion added kerosene to the fire of these beliefs: hot yoga can kill the virus; the immune system can be bolstered by sweating; homeopathy can raise oxygen saturation levels. But watch out: vaccines brewed by the vampires of the Cabal will make your precious blood impure.

CHAPTER 11

ANXIETY OF THE PUREBLOODS

Quite a bit of human solidarity has been sacrificed in pursuit of preserving some kind of imagined purity.

—Eula Biss, *On Immunity: An Inoculation*, 2015

WHEN CHIROPRACTOR DAVID FRAWLEY talks about sweat "cleansing the blood," he's speaking in several tongues at once, and appealing to different but overlapping audiences. Some in his audience fancy themselves scientists. Some are dreaming they're living in a bygone age. All of them, whether they realize it or not, are engaging to some extent in a war of eugenics. When focused on the topic of blood, Frawley's rhetoric reveals deep anxieties about bodily and spiritual corruption.

Those seeking evidence-based information should know that Frawley is speaking the language of pure pseudoscience. The only detoxification treatments prescribed and backed by real studies are designed by trained toxicologists for those who have ingested poison or who are struggling with deadly substance abuse issues. For most of us, our kidneys, liver, skin, and lungs do all the detoxifying necessary to keep us alive. No wellness influencer has found a way of directly monetizing what the body already does naturally. The products and services they sell—supplements, dietary cleanses, and colonic irrigations, to name a few—are considered scams by actual qualified medical experts and nutritionists.

Another implication of Frawley's blood ideology speaks on the level of Ayurveda, which he gleaned from years of spiritual tourism in India, and then simplified for English-language yoga gig workers. To Frawley, blood as the soul's fluid in the body is both a physical and nonphysical substance, a bright river that flows toward health and enlightenment. It's essential for building muscle, fat, and all the higher tissues of the body, up to the crowning juice of reproductive fluids—especially semen.

[*Record scratch.*]

This isn't a digression. Blood purity in conspirituality health circles is tangled up with reproductive anxieties. It leads some anti-vax women to speculate on whether vaccines will sterilize them and some anti-vax men to attempt to sell unvaccinated sperm in online bazaars, and has led to the launch of dating apps that promise to connect people for sweet unvaccinated love.

Blood-and-semen anxiety is going increasingly mainstream. In April 2022, Tucker Carlson featured a "fitness professional" named Andrew Mc-Govern in a Fox News documentary called *The End of Men*. McGovern talked about how testicle tanning with red-light therapy could help restore falling testosterone levels. (It doesn't.) The vibe was self-care, but the context was the endless stream of Carlson conspiracism about how wokeness was destroying masculinity, and dog whistles at the Great Replacement theory. As the documentary aired, MAGA-inspired state legislatures across the United States were rolling back abortion rights and implementing anti-trans legislation, along with various forms of Florida's "Don't Say Gay" bill. It's no coincidence that body-fascist fears about permeable national borders and impure bodies go hand in hand with an obsession with genitals and the anxious desire to protect the right kind of semen.

But let's get back to the roots of body fluid panickry. According to Indian lore, the yogi strives to distill strong semen from his blood through a vegetarian diet, postures, breathing exercises, and strict celibacy. A real keener can then meditate this stored semen up his spine and into his head, where it sublimates into glowing nectar. He can then insert his tongue into the cavity at the back of his throat and sip it like a hummingbird.

It's a delicate process. As the yogi's storehouse of magical semen swells, an increased vitality makes him horny and distracted from meditation. (In this patriarchal context, women are typically depicted as sex-obsessed sirens, bent on dragging the upright man down into the prison of pleasure and domesticity. According to legend, for example, the awakening of the Buddha was almost derailed when a demon made a booty call at the Bodhi tree.) The horniness increases the yogi's need for celibate discipline. If he gets the balance just right, the yogi's body will overflow with bio-spiritual illumination, and, at the time of choosing his death, he'll nut his consciousness across the Milky Way.

Frawley himself is not celibate, but his friend Narendra Modi is, and all good Hindu nationalists know what this means. Modi is a lifelong RSS soapbox preacher, and the fascist paramilitary organization has long conflated sexual continence and spiritual vitality with national strength. The group advocates celibacy for its senior leaders, who are tasked with protecting the purity and vitality of the nation.

This leads to a third implication of Frawley's blood ideology, and the blood-to-semen-to-enlightenment flowchart. Given his support for Modi's anti-Islamic rhetoric, we can't ignore the possibility that in any talk about blood that Frawley indulges, some followers will hear a dog whistle in the key of ethnic purity. He's not a mobster in robes, like Yogi Adityanath, the chief minister of Uttar Pradesh, who has warned that "if they take one Hindu girl, we will take one hundred Muslim girls." Frawley prefers to disparage the "modern Hindu" who tolerates unspecified insults from Christians and Muslims within his borders. "He seems weak, in disarray, without confidence or self-esteem," Frawley writes of the liberal, Westernized Indian. "He appears to think that if he ignores these things they will go away in time, *but like an infection they continue to spread and poison the country*" [emphasis added].

To HIS CREDIT, FRAWLEY has posted some begrudging pro-vaccine tweets, while remaining careful not to conceal his pseudoscience framework. "Strengthening physical and psychological immunity through Yoga and Ayurveda is very helpful with the long term issues," he writes. Vaccines, he preaches, are good for acute conditions. This implies that he thinks people need to get vaccinated when they're acutely sick, which is false, even as it underlines a basic Hindu nationalist sentiment familiar to alt-health consumers everywhere. The claim is that the materialistic medicine of the "West" is always superficial in function. It treats symptoms, while the great wisdom of the ages carries the antidote to the root causes of all disease. In fact, actual vaccine science dismisses this hubris.

For Frawley, and many in the alt-health, New Age, and conspirituality movements, the authentic vaccine against all disease is spirituality, injected from above and incubated from within. This starts to explain why real-world medical vaccination can be framed in horror film terms by conspiritualists obsessed with being poisoned by the Deep State, tech billionaires, vampiric doctors, or modernity itself.

The bloodiest battles of conspirituality wellness are fought over what kind of authority and expertise is allowed to enter and influence the internal, vulnerable space of the body. Blood is the fluid—both immanent and transcendent—by which the inner body becomes visible.

When disturbing scenes of anti-vaxxers harassing nurses and doctors began to multiply throughout 2021, we saw a diverse movement pointing a single finger at the State, disguised in scrubs. They carried signs that told many lies: that the vaccines were deadly, part of a genocide, violations of the Nuremberg Code. But the deeper sentiment was clear, perhaps even poignant: *The State will not get inside me, where I create my reality, my relationship to God, and my health.*

It's a tragic polarization in a world in which the reality is that vaccination only works to the extent that we nurture a common trust, and recognize our interdependence as clearly as any religious devotee. As writer and poet Eula Biss writes in her science-and-empathy-soaked study:

> The unvaccinated person is protected by the bodies around her, bodies through which disease is not circulating. But a vaccinated person surrounded by bodies that host disease is left vulnerable to vaccine failure or fading immunity. We are protected not so much by our own skin, but by what is beyond it. The boundaries between our bodies begin to dissolve here. Donations of blood and organs move between us, exiting one body and entering another, and so too with immunity, which is a common trust as much as it is a private account.

SPEAKING OF PRIVATE ACCOUNTS, it's unclear at this point which TikToker kicked off the "pureblood" hashtag, used by anti-vax influencers to signal their pristine status. The likely originator first posted in early September 2021. The keyword text was laid over her mugging face animated by shifting filters: "We will No longer be referred To as Unvaxxed...We simply go by....Pure blood." In a follow-up, she explained she was making a Harry Potter joke.

The trend got a boost from right-wing influencer Lyndsey Marie, who goes by @patriot_lydnz and has over thirty-seven thousand followers. Marie describes herself as a Christian and Trump-supporting veteran. Her videos include celebrations of the Kyle Rittenhouse verdict and often use hip-hop tracks to express her hatred for Joe Biden and Democrats. Marie added the Instagram hashtag #HarryPotter to underline J. K. Rowling's identification of aspiring wizards with no Muggle (non-magic normie) blood. Marie also had plans to sell pureblood merch to compete with the multiple lines of pureblood T-shirts already for sale on Amazon.

Typical of the endless contradictions of social media, the term "pureblood" really tells on itself. The Rowling characters who call themselves pureblood are thinly veiled Nazi types who loathe and undermine Mudbloods—like the beloved character Hermione Granger—not only because they are reviled as impure, but because they win social status through intellect rather than breeding. Sound familiar? Rowling thought you might; she even said it out loud in a 2007 interview. "There are quite consciously overtones of Nazi Germany," she told *Dateline*.

TikTok was recycling themes from the spring. In mid-April 2021, Instagram alt-health star @selfhealingmama, or "Chloe Angeline," released a selfie sermon that turned the laws of epidemiology inside out by suggesting that vaccinated people were infecting unvaccinated people, especially women, with viral shedding. The logic turned the vaccine into a virus. We dubbed this brain-flip Reverse Contagion Anxiety.

Angeline advertises herself as an entrepreneur in Conscious Pregnancy+Birth+Motherhood, and a Cosmic Doula Through the Portal of Motherhood. These seem like big jobs that come with enormous responsibilities. "I'm here to birth a new earth," Angeline rhymes.

She substantiated her argument in the usual manner for medical disinformation on social media. She correlated random anecdotes of women feeling nauseated, sweaty, anxious, or having a bad period to being increasingly surrounded by vaccinated people. She offered no hard data, no publications, no control group, no consideration that the symptoms might be the psychosomatic effects of cognitive dissonance, or the social isolation of being an anti-vaxxer.

CHRISTIANE NORTHRUP DEPLOYED a similar logic just days before, falsely claiming on Instagram Live that the mRNA vaccines shed virus through sweat glands. Then she went further. In the comments under the stream, she suggested that her followers withhold sex from partners who were considering getting the vaccine.

While Angeline sermonized from home, Northrup uploaded her lecture from the warpath, preaching into her phone from an airport en route from speaking at a Health and Freedom Conference hosted at Rhema Bible Training College in the Tulsa area. The roster was a parade of MAGA, pseudoscience, and QAnon influencers, which included QAnon digital general Mike Flynn and Stop the Steal lawyer Lin Wood, who took to the stage to call for the execution of all political enemies. Wood had been instrumental in fomenting the election fraud conspiracy theory movement, which falsely claimed that Trump had won the 2020 election. Four days before the Capitol siege, he fantasized on Twitter that Vice President Mike Pence could "face execution by firing squad" for "treason." On January 6, as MAGA rioters breached the doors of the Capitol, screaming "Hang Mike Pence," Wood tweeted out "1776 again," "Time to fight for our freedom," and "Pledge your lives, your fortunes & your sacred honor."

Northrup limited her public comments at Rhema to false claims that the mRNA vaccines might prevent the formation of the placenta, make women infertile, and poison the sperm of men. But sharing the stage with Wood seemed to have yanked her out of alt-health-related social-media-infotainment conspirituality and into extremist territory. There, vaccines are not simply poisonous, but a planned spiritual attack on the blood of the righteous. On smaller stages, Northrup is less inhibited. "This is an evil agenda by bloodline families that's been going on for two thousand years," she told a QAnon podcaster in August 2021. She's referring to families purported to have royal and aristocratic blood that are sometimes believed to be part alien or to have demonic agendas.

QANON'S VIOLENT INSANITY AMPLIFIES the primal anxieties of the broader conspirituality movement. Backstage at the Tulsa event, Wood pushed his rhetoric past Northrup's focus on blood and fertility to spotlight the logical end point of her concern: children.

"To the people at home," he warned, "if you're killing little children, if you're sacrificing little children, if you're drinking the blood of little children, watch out." It was straight-out antisemitic blood-libel talk, echoing centuries of European conspiracists who claimed that Jews were kidnapping Christian babies to harvest their blood to bake into Passover matzo. In the QAnon reboot, the Jews targeted by the medieval slander are thinly disguised with terms like "Cabal," the "Elite" (or the "Hollywood Elite"), or the "Illuminati."

Whatever they're called, the villains are after innocent children, whose blood, according to the lore, contains some essence of purity and vitality. This would be the adrenochrome of the QAnon fever dream: a substance that Anons believe the Elites extract from kidnapped children to ingest as a youth elixir. QAnon memes spreading the fiction show children, post-harvest, with dark circles over their eyes. The so-called panda eyes are striking on the mostly white faces.

And so children are pure and empty vessels for adult neuroses that flow in two opposing directions. As the victims of vaccination, their innocent blood is allegedly corrupted, with made-up consequences such as autism. As the victims of QAnon blood libel, innocence is extracted from their veins, leaving a lifeless, terrified husk. Whether poisoned or bled, the violation occurs at the tip of a needle, where the state gains access to the inner person. "The natural body meets the body politic in the act of vaccination," writes Eula Biss, "where a single needle penetrates both."

IT'S NO ACCIDENT that the pseudoscience of conspirituality crystallized—and hard—around vaccines. Even deeper than the gothic cues and emotional triggers, vaccination presents a signature triumph in global public health history, backed by extensive and incontrovertible research. This is the science—government-funded and for the most part freely distributed—that eradicated smallpox, virtually eliminated polio, and reduced the morbidity and mortality rates of dozens of childhood diseases.

The collectivist logic of vaccination proves that immunity is a group effort. This truth strikes at the heart of the consumerist economy of alternative health treatments that are marketed to consumers based on individual needs. The notion that every human being in the world can benefit from the exact same 0.5mL dose of colorless vaccine is an insult to the world of bespoke treatments based on temperament, heritage, body type, or astrological sign. The vaccine tells the wellness-world consumer that they are not special, that they need no special crystals or remedies, nor special attention. It tells the alternative health practitioner who claims to be able to "boost the immune system" with herbs or acupuncture to take a seat and STFU.

Discrediting vaccine science with pseudoscientific claims about injury rates or false reports about mercury poisoning or autism is crucial for the professional conspiritualist. It's the tip of the spear, so to speak, for a world-view intent on invalidating whatever it cannot compete with, or monetize. Because if the powers that be are lying about the most commonly accepted and reportedly successful public health movement in history, well—they are probably lying about everything. If the success of vaccines can be turned into a fiction, then the Overton window of doubt can open out onto germ theory, the spherical nature of the Earth, and perhaps even climate science.

WHEN VACCINATION IS FRAMED as a pandemic, and when the doctors who give them are portrayed as vampires extracting the lifeblood of children, there's a strong possibility we're in the realm of mass projection. In this light, it's worth reflecting on the very first victim of blood libel, and his community.

Twelve-year-old William of Norwich was a tanner's apprentice who went missing on Holy Tuesday in 1144. His body, which was found on Holy Saturday, showed evidence of foul play. The townspeople initially accused their Jewish neighbors of the murder, but the local magistrate rejected the charge for lack of evidence.

The tragedy faded until a Benedictine monk named Thomas of Monmouth arrived in town six years later, and, like a QAnon researcher of today, decided to investigate the incident. His resulting 1173 book, *The Life and Miracles of St. William of Norwich*, was a tawdry propaganda piece accusing the Jews of murdering the boy in a mock-crucifixion ritual. Going further, Monmouth claimed that the murder was part of a larger plan. Not only were the guilty Jews proving their original murderous intent toward Jesus, they also believed that by ritually murdering Christian children, they would one day be restored to their homeland in Israel. Monmouth's book disappeared for centuries, until it was resurrected in 1896 and became a root text of modern antisemitism.

Accusing Jews of crucifying young William of Norwich is a good way of obscuring the story of a Christian god who sacrifices his own child and distributes his pure blood to give his followers eternal life. The projection highlights a psychological need shared between the conspiracy theorist and the fascist: to find a scapegoat for all the things that fill us with horror and shame, and to make someone else responsible for the vulnerability of our children.

In the conspirituality paradigm, children are not vulnerable because of inadequate health care access or horrible economic inequality. They're not vulnerable because of ordinary family dysfunction and abuse, alcoholism, or repressive religious attitudes. They're not vulnerable because of our tacit consent to engage in predatory capitalism, which bleeds all but the mega-wealthy dry, and is driving the human bus off the climate cliff. The enemy is not our habits and policies and confusion. It has to be someone else, someone impure who can infect us, someone we must resist.

CHAPTER 12

THE BARBARA SNOW JOB

IN THE GREAT TRADITION of cultic literature and New Age writing dating back to the Theosophists, the QAnon schtick is an entirely unoriginal remix of perennial fever dreams. Drunk on copy-and-paste shortcuts and the infinite replication of memes, this mostly online movement is rife with repetition and plagiarism. And when it comes to its morbid fantasies about satanic pedophilia, the QAnon recycling machine doesn't have to dig back very far.

The OG Satanic Panic erupted in the 1980s following the publication of *Michelle Remembers*, by Lawrence Pazder and Michelle Smith. Pazder, a trained psychiatrist, had purportedly helped Smith, his client (and future wife), recall memories of Satanic Ritual Abuse from when she grew up in 1950s Victoria, British Columbia. None of the book's outrageous, insane claims were ever corroborated, but that didn't stop Pazder from becoming a TV celebrity in what became a viral movement to identify and prosecute allegedly rampant Satanism. Crucially: Pazder's motivation was not rooted in his training as a mental health practitioner. As a devout Catholic, he looked to the Church as the final answer to the hell he imagined his wife escaping. Smith is ultimately "healed" not through psychiatric treatment, but by converting to Catholicism. Her series of fever dreams ends with a hallucination of the Virgin Mary, who asks her to become an emissary of global spiritual renewal. In this sense, *Michelle Remembers* serves as an early scripture of modern, Catholic-flavored conspirituality.

By the mid-1990s, more than twelve thousand cases involving charges of Satanic Ritual Abuse had rendered no forensic or corroborated evidence that it was a reality. Courts and investigators did, however, find ample evidence of therapists, social workers, and police officers using terrible interview techniques to pressure children into producing fictitious memories of satanic abuse at the hands of day-care workers, schoolteachers, and small-town bureaucrats.

How did it happen? The instruments to which we resort for some degree of resolution—journalism and the law—prove especially weak in the aftermath. The search for a single villain fails in the realms of structural violence and social contagion. While families of the accused try to reassemble their lives, and psychologists battle over whether "false memory syndrome" is to blame, or even exists, the most plausible explanation for why the Satanic Panic happened remained speculative. Perhaps the phantasm of Satanic Ritual Abuse is a groupthink symbolic expression of something much more painful, and difficult to look at: that child sex abuse is far more common than is typically recognized, and that it mainly occurs within families, churches, and institutions. The Satanic Panic allowed a generation coming to grips with shameful trauma to seek catharsis through a mass-media frenzy that was as lucrative as it was unresolved.

For Charlotte Ward—as Jacqui Farmer—the dangling threads were hiding in plain sight. "These poor children," she wrote in 2014, recalling SRA accusers from decades before, "would now be young people. Perhaps their minds were compartmentalized through the trauma? Perhaps they became dissociative or carry with them terrible memories that they feel they cannot face or talk about? Perhaps they are self-harming? Many thousands of young people may be unable to achieve closure about the terrible acts that were perpetrated upon them."

Ward's earnest if misguided concern for children rings deep notes in the conspirituality world that Jacqui Farmer partially created, and now haunts. In the broader yoga and wellness spheres, which, as in older religions, encouraged women to view their reproductive lives as part of their spiritual paths, children are symbols of innocence and storehouses of pure energy. One snippet of old Tantric lore says that the eyes of babies are captivating because they are connected to a wellspring of glowing divine nectar that sits in their brain centers like jelly in a donut. Tragically, according to the story, with age and moral corruption, that nectar drips down through the body to exit through the lower organs, to be lost forever. Rudolf Steiner believed that children grew further away from God the older they got, and the role of the teacher was to prevent this from happening completely. But if it did, as Farmer suggested, there would be trauma to navigate and repair.

There's a straight line from these ideas to more contemporary and online visions of children as divine but also vulnerable beings in the land of conspirituality. The Indigo children—who represent "an upgraded blueprint of humanity" that will save the world, according to the New Age clearinghouse Gaia.com—have something to tell the world, and many of their moms became bloggers to help them tell it. By the time yoga and wellness social media really took off around 2012, the innocent child was a symbol of spiritual potential in a highly charged way that almost seemed destined to implode.

The hyper-idealization cast such a foreboding shadow, it's little wonder that a key influencer who rose to extreme prominence during this time embodied a double identity of Indigo child and satanic victim. Teal Swan, born in 1984, made her name in yoga and wellness spaces through channeling—the premise that one can be a mouthpiece for disembodied spirits. From Steiner to the present day, channelers have always served as ministers of conspirituality, and their prognostications come from the same source as spiritual knowledge: not through journalism, science, or the law—but through intuition, faith, and fear. In Swan's case, channeling allowed her to speak about the future in the voice of New Age angels, but also about the past as a supposed survivor of SRA.

As we'll see, this Swan Effect helped spin a zip line from the Satanic Panic, through the yoga and wellness world, and straight into QAnon. Understanding these events helps to unearth just how close to the bone conspirituality can cut, and how it rips communities apart by co-opting unresolved histories and traumas.

LAWRENCE PAZDER TAPPED the bishop of the diocese of Victoria to endorse *Michelle Remembers* in a letter that appeared in the front matter of the book. "The Church is well aware of the existence of mysterious and evil forces in the world," wrote Bishop Remi De Roo. "Each person who has had an experience of evil imagines Satan in a slightly different way, but nobody knows precisely what this force of evil looks like." But De Roo also hedged. "I do not question that for Michelle this experience was real," he continued. "In time we will know how much of it can be validated."

The bishop's respectful skepticism proved wise. Numerous investigations over two decades failed to validate a single detail of Smith's account. In addition to journalists finding two siblings left unmentioned in the book (who, when found, denied Smith's claims) and clear impossibilities in her timeline, a scholar of psychiatry found that virtually all the claims Smith made about the cannibalistic, blood-drinking cult rhymed with stories that haunted West African media during the time in which Pazder worked there as a doctor in the early 1960s.

Facts be damned. The book and the media tour that Pazder and Smith undertook as *a newly married couple*—you might want to read that twice—sparked the viral myth that hidden within suburban, middle-class society, hundreds of Satanists were on the loose, abusing and murdering children. Intrinsic to the book's theme was the idea that the only way the abuse would be revealed and stopped was if children were treated as if they were oracles, with every utterance freighted with hidden meaning.

On May 16, 1985, Pazder was a featured talking head in the first major news report on Satanism, on ABC's *20/20*. Among breathless insinuations that heavy-metal concerts were demonic ceremonies, and horrific claims of bloody child sacrifice, Pazder laid out the telltale signs of secret ritual abuse that parents should watch out for in their kids, and framed sexual abuse as serving the purpose of destroying the children's belief in God. His professional seminars for psychologists, social workers, and psychiatrists, dating back to a first appearance at the American Psychiatric Association in 1981, led to "ritual abuse" being codified and institutionalized in their diagnostic manual. Following the *20/20* appearance, Pazder participated in seminars introducing police agencies to the phenomenon of Satanic Ritual Abuse. During the 1980s, the combination of media reports, workshops for psychological professionals, and law enforcement seminars gave Pazder's and others' claims about SRA great cultural impact. But by 1991, an FBI investigator's guide compiled by the Center for Missing and Exploited Children discussed the topic with more critical skepticism.

The panic burned through North America and the UK in the late 1980s and early 1990s, leading to thousands of families torn apart by suspicion and shame, with virtually no forensic evidence uncovered. Some researchers now argue that if a Satanic Panic reveals anything, it's the lengths a culture will go to bury the dominant context of child abuse under the fiction of "stranger danger," when, in fact, children are far more likely to suffer abuse from people they know. Forty years later, QAnon would concoct a similar nightmare of epidemic levels of child abuse committed by a shadowy Cabal. Spun from anonymous posts and misinformation, QAnon's morbid fetish obscures the shame of the less spectacular but very real problem—abuse committed by family members.

The Satanic Panic at the end of the twentieth century laid a pre-digital foundation for QAnon, in terms of its abject themes and the stoking of mis-directed social rage. According to one report, in a 1984 visit to Los Angeles to meet with enthusiastic therapists, Pazder coined the term "ritual abuse," and said that "anybody could be involved in this plot, including teachers, doctors, movie stars, merchants, even—as some parents came to believe— members of the Anaheim Angels baseball team." It's hard to conceive how QAnon could have emerged separately from this earlier, tortured era, which hovered, unresolved, in fading newsprint and internet backwaters.

A MAJOR DRIVER of the Satanic Panic of the 1980s and 1990s was a swath of hypervigilant child psychotherapists who caught the bug of believing that buried childhood sexual abuse committed by strangers was far more common than it is, and that the best way of drilling down into the truth of repressed memories was to ask children leading questions. Many went so far as to assert that a child who couldn't remember being ritually abused must be repressing a memory too traumatic to bear. Recovery techniques included daylong investigation meetings, the assertion that any disclosed information—whether offered to please the therapist or not—was always the tip of the iceberg, and what to do if a child recanted their disclosure.

The power of this movement disguised its tiny size. One survey of over 2,700 clinical psychologists found that 785 had treated one or two cases of alleged ritual abuse. But that same survey found that sixteen respondents reported having treated over one hundred cases each. One therapist who came out of this landscape was Barbara Snow, of Utah. Her 1990 coauthored paper, "Ritualistic Child Abuse in a Neighborhood Setting," became a mi-nor bible among Satanic Panic therapists. The paper cites *Michelle Remembers* as a central and credible source. Its case studies all came from either Snow's private practice or that of her coauthor.

Snow was very frank about her methods and biases. In a 1989 trial trig-gered by claims made by one of her clients, Snow admitted that she never took notes, and relied on her "own integrity" to record her sessions. The court ruled that Snow's own remarks on the stand about her techniques for eliciting dis-closures compromised her credibility. "Any claim that scientific principles," the judge wrote, "or Dr. Snow's own expertise and experience validated her conclusions and procedures is devastatingly refuted by her own statement, 'I didn't believe any of those kids when they told me it didn't happen.'"

Snow's technique extended beyond disbelieving her clients. In reporting on a 1987 trial of a man accused by one of Snow's charges, the *Salt Lake Tribune* quoted a Utah deputy county attorney who witnessed one of Snow's interviews. He described Snow pressuring children into disclosing abuse that they originally denied. One girl testified at that trial that she felt Snow would not let her leave until she made an accusation of ritual abuse. Even in her own research paper, Snow admits that "not a single child subject made such a 'purposeful' disclosure" of the abuse she was reporting. "The ma-jority of children initially denied any knowledge or involvement and many maintained silence for a significant length of time." Snow says nothing in her paper about her questioning techniques. "Disclosure became a process, not an event," she writes.

A full twenty years later, Snow was placed on probation by her licens-ing board for allegedly providing therapy to her family members, some of whom came to believe that they had experienced SRA, and had been sub-jected to secret tests by the US military. The case went before the board after Snow entered the home of a family member she had been treating, armed with a baseball bat, to confront the accused. She destroyed computer equip-ment and battered family members she accused of enabling ritual abuse.

Between the time of Snow's court infamy and her family implosion, she also influenced the figure who has popularized the pseudotherapeu-tic treatment of SRA through the media of parasocial charisma—and New Age–style channeling. Barbara Snow treated a woman in her early twenties named Mary Teal Bosworth, who would later become a crucial modern fig-ure in the conspirituality movement.

MARY BOSWORTH IS NOW known as Teal Swan, which better suits her fash-ion. Via designer clothes, oversaturated lighting, and dramatic makeup, her image leaps out of the screen like the cover of a fantasy novel. It's not a surprise that she has attracted a flurry of media attention, including a well-researched podcast series with journalist Jennings Brown, and a highly sensationalistic streaming docu series on Hulu. But the real hook for her 1.2 million followers on Facebook, 1.17 million on YouTube, and over 300,000 on Instagram, is her claim that she suffered thirteen years of abuse in a murderous Mormon satanic cult where she was routinely tortured, made to torture other children, and once spent twelve hours sewn into a corpse.

On the basis of these stories—but without training, qualifications, or oversight—Swan developed a signature method for healing deep trauma that she calls The Completion Process. Fifty practitioners trained in the method are listed on her website. She also invites followers to a $5,000 weeklong retreat at her casa in Costa Rica. Some retreatants end up never leaving, choosing instead to live there and work for Swan as unpaid volunteers. Swan also sells tarot decks, online courses for about $200 each, and frequency paintings that she claims are medicinal and will help people to manifest what they want in their lives.

Alongside promoting a dubious backstory, Swan drew fire in 2012 by describing suicide as a reset button. In 2019, Facebook shut down one of her private groups out of concern that members had attempted suicide, and one had succeeded, after exposure to Swan's views on the subject. Claiming to have attempted suicide several times herself, Swan feels she is qualified to offer advice.

In 2006, Barbara Snow filed a complaint with the North Park Police Department in North Logan, Utah, on behalf of her patient Teal Swan, alleging that a man had ritually abused her when she was between the ages of seven and nineteen. According to the police report, Snow accompanied Swan to a meeting with a detective, who interviewed Swan and received her prepared written statement, which detailed a series of abject memories.

At first, Swan asked that the detective not pursue the case. But when, a few months later, she asked for the investigation to be opened, the medical examiner could find no evidence of the injuries Swan had described as resulting from the abuse. Then the detective examined Swan's childhood diaries, which supposedly contained evidence that she was recording the crimes at the time. On Snow's suggestion, Swan had circled relevant passages in red. The detective noted that the passages referred to "dark sadness, hopelessness, and pain…disturbing for a child of 7 or 8." But he found "no specific reference to the abuse." Swan told the detective that she had been writing in a secret language.

After the deputy county attorney looked into Snow's history of false accusations, Swan's file was closed, forcing her story back into the realm of the channeled, where anything is possible.

In 2020, channelers and New Age influencers seized on the sexual abuse of innocents as a clarion call and exerted influence over a community that had just moved through the paroxysms of the #MeToo movement, in which the principle of believing victims had become sacrosanct. People who had helped women corroborate and disclose their experiences of sexual abuse were suddenly—amidst the uncertainty of the COVID-19 pandemic and while bombarded with other conspiracy theories—asked to believe and support women who told stories about SRA.

The yogaworld floodgate of #MeToo testimony had burst open in 2018, releasing decades of stories about sexual assault and abuse. One top yoga influencer received over three hundred submissions in response to a call-out. Major news outlets covered assault allegations against yoga superstars like Bikram Choudhury and Manouso Manos. Matthew's book on Pattabhi Jois's abusive practices came out in 2019; the following year, he reported on decades of sexual and emotional abuse in Sivananda Yoga, a multinational organization that claims to have trained fifty thousand yoga teachers since the late 1960s.

Parallel to this media frenzy was an explosion of Facebook support groups in which survivors could share stories, resources, and encouragement. These spaces became bastions of feminist activism—newly charged after years of yogaworld depoliticization—that seized the cultural moment to examine and challenge patriarchal systems on a larger scale.

Within that discourse, a strong historical echo emerged, voiced by people who described the #MeToo movement as a necessary first step in finally acknowledging that sexual abuse is only a superficial problem in relation to the deeper (but elusive) problem of Satanic Ritual Abuse. Supporters of the SRA theory landed on a cultural moment in which the bias of disbelief they had been faced with for decades was now reversed. Their hidden stories were suddenly bolstered by the sentiment of #believewomen.

When QAnon exploded in the early summer of 2020, one yogaworld #MeToo leader we'll call "Sophia" pivoted her focus from the verified sexual crimes of yoga gurus to her own story about being the childhood victim of sexual slavery at the hands of Europe's elite in the 1970s. She shared the QAnon recruiting film, *Out of Shadows*. Sophia began to moderate an online survivors' group, and advertised $250-per-hour private therapy sessions despite listing no therapeutic training or credentials. Interviews in which she disclosed her story, which is as extreme, contradictory, and as thin on details as Teal Swan's, are still up on QAnon-adjacent accounts, linked with hashtags like #pizzagate, #newworldorder, #911, #insidejob, #vaxxed, #moonlandinghoax, and #depopulationagenda.

Sophia had a real story of sexual abuse in yogaworld. She had done organizing work on behalf of other survivors, and she had spoken on public panels to address the issue in the yoga industry. Now, through the power of her other, unproven Satanic Ritual Abuse story, she was acting as a conduit between survivor communities and QAnon indoctrination funnels. Many who respected her work in one area felt compelled to support her claims in the other.

So the eruption of QAnon in yogaworld didn't just come from the magpie minds of influencers like Christiane Northrup who got red-pilled by Q-adjacent content and used it to spice up their feeds. In this case, it also came from people who were already established as voices for a progressive, justice-seeking movement that sought to elevate and protect women. QAnon's growth was driven not just by 4chan trolls and opportunistic influencers. It was aided by memories obscured by trauma and fantasy, and abetted by altruism and a yearning for justice.

Seane Corn is an A-list yoga teacher and a veteran leader in that same progressive faction of the yoga demographic. As cofounder of a charitable nonprofit that raises money to combat problems like poverty and real sex trafficking, her street cred as an activist is solid. In 2019, she lent high-profile support to the #MeToo movement, and made her own disclosure that she was an abuse survivor. She was disturbed when she saw the yoga scene she loved being infiltrated by QAnon content that appealed to her colleagues' sense of justice. She prepared a "We Care and We Stand Against QAnon" post with colleagues.

"They are an alt-right movement of conspiracy theorists working to spread misinformation, confusion and paranoia," the statement said. "They are deliberately and strategically targeting the wellness communities appealing to people's interest in alternative health practices and mistrust of the government." The post went viral, sparking coverage in the *New York Times* and *Rolling Stone*, and garnering Corn media appearances throughout the English-speaking world.

It was a watershed conspirituality moment. Here was a progressive leader in yogaworld who was pushing back against a conspiracy theory that had exploited the real social justice issue of sexual abuse. The backlash Corn received was intense.

By interview and email, Corn described hundreds of negative comments, but also dozens of communications threatening her with sexual violence—because she spoke out against QAnon. Corn says that it was clear that many of her trolls were not in yogaworld, given obvious clues, such as thinking she was male, given her name. Closer to home for Corn, however, was the criticism she faced from Sophia, the #MeToo movement leader who claimed to be an SRA victim. In particular, she was provoked by an interview Corn gave to the Canadian Broadcasting Corporation in which she dismissed the satanic abuse mythos at the heart of QAnon. "This isn't true," Corn said of the Cabal. "This isn't happening. Please use more discernment."

"Seane Corn," Sophia replied on Facebook, in a caption for a video that now has almost 800,000 views, "your words came at the expense of many SRA survivors and all the children who did not survive. I never thought that the worst disbelief of my story would come from yogaworld, but after your public negation, it did. Yogis who already knew my story suddenly became confused, trying to separate what happened to me from your attacks."

The shaming rebuke exemplifies a core pressure exerted within conspirituality circles aligned with progressive politics and social justice. To reject a conspiracy theory in this milieu—whether it's about the alleged poison of vaccines, or an alleged pandemic of Satanic Ritual Abuse—doesn't simply make you uninformed, or a patsy of the powers that be. It exposes your lack of empathy, your willingness to snub survivors, your callous disregard for the downtrodden.

Earlier, we detailed how conspiracy theories allow believers to gain feelings of in-group knowledge, protection, and kinship. But in a conspirituality space rife with New Age piety, endorsing a conspiracy theory can grant something even more attractive: a sense of moral superiority.

CHAPTER 13

CURSED YOGA NETWORKS

THE THREE OF US know yogaworld very well. We have all worked as faculty for teacher training programs and felt conflicted about the ubiquitous blend of professionalized pseudoscience, bad metaphysics, and entrepreneurial libertarianism. We're admittedly working through a narrow lens here, but, nonetheless, we believe that yogaworld serves as a good microcosm of the wellness industry on the whole. It has been a robust hub of normalized magical thinking, as well as a transition space for people looking for work and meaning. It's a world in which charisma trumps confidence, and always needs to expand.

Which brings us back to B. K. S. Iyengar, the obsessive yoga master who had that dream about being locked out of heaven because his body was imperfect. His life story is an important piece of the conspirituality story for two reasons.

First, without Iyengar there would be no global yoga industry in its current form, branded as equal parts spirituality and health care. There would be no props—the straps, blocks, wedges, and bolsters that make up the lucrative, pseudomedical accessory side of the economy. Iyengar invented them all. Without Iyengar, yoga studios would not have that slightly elitist feeling of zen simplicity and naturopathic tech, where a student in a lunge can imagine their front foot is in a doctor's examination room while their back foot is on a temple stone.

Second, Iyengar's encyclopedic practice manual, *Light on Yoga*, has been a required text for nearly every yoga teacher training program in the world over the past half-century. That means that as many as 500,000 people have not only read this book as a guide for personal practice, but have been exposed to a professional-level epistemology—and an archetype of charismatic leadership—that sets the stage for conspirituality chaos. If we wonder how the yoga and wellness worlds became a vector for COVID conspiracy theories, we have to look at how its most populous semi-professional class first got red-pilled by a scrambled mindset they were taught to revere as a pathway to self-awareness.

The year is 1936. It's sixteen years before Iyengar helps Yehudi Menuhin take that nap in Bombay. The eighteen-year-old Iyengar was in precarious shape. Orphaned, extremely poor, and still recovering from a childhood of chronic disease, he had been working as a house servant for his brother-in-law, the ornery and violent Tirumalai Krishnamacharya, a key leader in the modern Indian yoga renaissance. Krishnamacharya had a commission from the maharaja of Mysore, the philosopher-king Nalvadi Wodeyar, to teach yoga classes in the palace gymnasium as part of a new physical culture curriculum.

Part of Krishnamacharya's job was to train a troop of boys as yoga demonstrators who would promote the art form to the masses in village squares and town halls. After Krishnamacharya's top boy fled his beatings, the master gave Iyengar three days of intense instruction—"He broke my back," Iyengar recalled—so that the young man could himself become a lead demonstrator. Thus began a career during which Iyengar gave thousands of yoga performances, spreading the gospel of inner peace through stretching around the world.

On his first local tour of the towns north of Mysore, Iyengar's demonstrations were a hit with all the housewives. But his mostly improvised skills also caught the eye of a certain Dr. V. B. Gokhale, down from the big city of Pune.

"He was impressed by my performance," Iyengar told a *Yoga Journal* interviewer in 1997. "Though he saw I had no muscles at all. He asked, 'Why your body is not developed?' I explained to him about my poverty, my diseases. He said, 'I have not seen anything in my life as a surgeon like what I am seeing in that presentation.'"

A few months later, Dr. Gokhale sent Krishnamacharya a request that the teenager be sent to Pune to work as a yoga instructor for the Deccan Gymkhana ("South Indian Gymnastics") Club, as well as nearby engineering and industrial colleges. The Gymkhana was a hotbed of wrestling, bodybuilding, and nationalist organizing. It had been named by none other than Bal Gangadhar Tilak, the first leader of the Indian independence movement, and an early advocate of swaraj, or "self-rule," a political philosophy of self-discipline and self-governance that found expression in a robust physicalist culture that updated South Indian martial arts with European training techniques and apparati. Gokhale had recruited Iyengar for a new genre of performance, fit for the zeitgeist. Iyengar's body would serve the project of scientizing this reconstructed spiritual exercise system for a new postcolonial era.

Nonetheless, Dr. Gokhale had Iyengar perform yoga for his fellow students and university dignitaries, and they struck up a tag-team relationship. "[Gokhale] used to give talks, and I used to give the demonstrations," he told *Yoga Journal*. "Because I could not speak on yoga, and I was not knowing philosophy. He said 'The body is known to me. You leave it to me, I will explain very accurately. And you do the poses.'

"It was a really good combination; I was really happy, and while he was explaining I started getting the anatomical words, which helped me a great deal to develop my subject."

So here is a teen whose only meal ticket in the world was the performance of intricate yoga postures. He brought a fierce survivalist attitude to the task, won through childhood struggles. He never attended high school. He knew nothing about clinical medicine. But with this stroke of luck, he found himself on tour with a big-city doctor who was ignorant of yoga but was nonetheless convinced that its exercises were curative in ways that conventional medicine was not. Their collaboration is iconic of a modern wellness movement that makes pseudoscience its backbone: Iyengar learns to preach the gospel of yoga using medical terms he doesn't understand while the doctor sanctifies his worldly subject through a mystic lens.

Before long, Gokhale was referring well-heeled clients to Iyengar for improvised yoga cures. In 1937, he asked the teenager to minister to an elderly scholar suffering from dysentery.

The teen improvised techniques that over time would give him a reputation as a miracle-working physiotherapist. He had the scholar learn the postures while lying on the ground, positioning his limbs and using his walking stick to help stretch his withered legs. "So that's how I learned!" he said. "And I did one person after the other... Just by instinct."

Decades later, after his career and method had gone global, Iyengar was traveling the world teaching "medical yoga" in which he would purport to treat people with heart conditions, infertility, and cancer. Stories of miraculous healings followed him wherever he went for the rest of his life. But no systematic data has been gathered to verify any of the lore.

The stories—and there are thousands of them—are at once modern and new-world-y, but also hearken back to a more magical period. Fact is, Iyengar learned medical language from Dr. Gokhale in the same way Brahmin boys in India have learned ancient mantras for millennia from their fathers: by hearing words they couldn't understand at first and repeating them until they took on a life of their own. Iyengar's mentorship with the doctor, and his increasing confidence that he could heal students through his pastiche of postures and medical jargon, crystallized into the text that became *Light on Yoga*.

First published in 1966, Iyengar's magnum opus is written in a clinical format, and has sold three million copies worldwide on the strength of blending medical promises with spiritual ideals. It made modern readers, alienated by their urban technologized lives, feel like they could touch a mystery again.

Light on Yoga looks like a medical encyclopedia, with over six hundred images of Iyengar himself posing against a white backdrop like a specimen. But the clinical format also hints at a method reminiscent of the oldest books in Indian wisdom culture. Dating back to somewhere around 1500 BCE, the Vedas are eccentric collections (*Saṁhitā*) of aphorisms, hymns, stories, commentaries, ritual instructions, philosophical speculations, and lists of remedies, grouped by theme. There are four Vedas: one Veda focuses on mythic stories, a second contains liturgies for ceremonies, a third describes how those liturgies should be performed, and the fourth is a collection of charms and spells.

In *Light on Yoga*, Iyengar assembles his own *Saṁhitā* by grouping together "Curative Asanas for Various Diseases." The lists of Sanskrit posture names read like long threads of mantra under subtitles that mash together categories of focus and centuries of discourse. The subtitles include acidity, ankles, brain, loss of memory, chest, chill, coronary thrombosis, epilepsy, eyes, flatulence, giddiness, halitosis, hernia, impotency, kidneys, labor pain, nasal catarrh, polio, piles, pleurisy, ulcer, and dribbling urine.

There's an old saying: "If it isn't described in the Veda, it doesn't exist." By design or by accident, Iyengar reached for a similar effect in *Light on Yoga* through a combination of cultural memory and personal bombast. The result? His famous book presents a surreal jumble of subjects within a format that looks very orderly and clinical. It's a perfect blend of the rational and the irrational. It stretched the sinews of his English readers out of their scientific stiffness. This was part of Iyengar's magic: he asked people to feel and think impossible things. He medicalized ancient spirituality while breaking the spell of modern medicine.

The book has gone through more than a dozen printings, and its publisher still hasn't impressed the front leaves with a disclaimer that would inform readers that Iyengar's medical claims—which mark nearly every page—aren't actually to be taken as medical claims. This omission is a lasting tribute to the power of Iyengar's charisma, which for his publishers continues to overpower conventions like citation, peer review, legal liability, and medical ethics.

LIGHT ON YOGA is a towering achievement of pseudoscience. To be clear, pseudoscience does not just mimic scientific language and method but declares that the premise of science as practiced in clinics and labs is somehow unnatural, dead, or benighted. Iyengar's story and book show that while pseudoscience is a kind of fakery, a person can come into it through dogged work and good faith, and in their earnestness be very convincing. The kind of disinformation about COVID vaccines that spread through yogaworld in 2020 had an old and righteous passion behind it.

That passion burns as hot as Iyengar's tireless creativity, fueling what is now an over $88 billion hub for the wellness economy. Unfortunately, by following his lead and that of others in his generation, that industry has given the stamp of completely unearned medical authority to "correctly" performed and sequenced yoga poses as both diagnostic and prescriptive of a range of orthopedic, endocrine, and organ dysfunctions. More broadly, it has standardized some terrible epistemology and created a marketplace for high-brow quackery.

Iyengar surely knew that science offers a method of discovering and testing knowledge about the world. In fact, he would often present his teaching on posture in a kind of experimental language, and report back from his own practice as though reading a laboratory report. This made him vulnerable to all sorts of cognitive biases, and may have encouraged him to believe that anecdotes were data.

Abject poverty denied Iyengar more than rudimentary schooling. He just didn't have the opportunity to learn that the real strength of the scientific method lies in its systematic pathway, which ideally welcomes fellow travelers and encourages humility in collaborative work. The rules are simple and strict: Carefully construct an experiment that tests a hypothesis about how something works. Run the experiment, and record the findings. Then have other qualified people examine the methods and results. Rinse and repeat. In its best expression—in the quiet of the lab, free from personal feelings and political pressures—the method should be ruthless at exposing unseen biases and common flaws in our thinking about the world. Science should allow the honest testing of ideas and then offer accurate predictions based on the findings.

In the wild, however, the elegant symmetry between intelligent test and clear conclusion is fragile. In the COVID era, public trust in the scientific process was disrupted by mixed messaging from competing health agencies about the effectiveness of masking. Expert-level arguments about the comparative value of COVID-zero versus COVID-mitigation strategies trickled down into popular media as politicized disputes. The merits of Hail Mary treatments like ivermectin were touted in pay-to-play science journals via studies compromised by faulty methodology or outright fraud. Some pro-ivermectin studies were hyped through the release of preprint papers—studies not yet verified by other researchers. These were really meant to be circulated among experts for discussion, but they wound up in the hands of people like Joe Rogan.

Conspiracy theorists grasped at any straw of premature data that suggested the virus might not be as bad as reported, or mask efficacy was lower than originally believed. The scientific process only works when research is verified, and the practice of publishing preprint papers is a good-faith attempt to expedite the process. But, as we saw with unvetted studies on unproven COVID interventions, preprints can be weaponized—in this case by anti-vax activists with low levels of good faith.

The problem is not just communications. Conspiritualists intent on undermining the credibility of scientific institutions on COVID did not have to look far for fair evidence. They could point to the racist medical atrocity at Tuskegee, doctors in the 1950s paid to endorse cigarettes, the US military pouring Agent Orange over the jungle canopies of Vietnam, or Merck scientists hiding the cardiac risk factors of Vioxx. They could flag egregious errors committed by respected members of the medical establishment and perpetuated for generations—such as the eugenicist attitudes that generated diagnoses like feeble-mindedness in the early days of clinical psychology. They could justifiably point out that entire sectors of social science research currently suffer from the replication crisis, the rattling discovery that a lot of peer-reviewed research cannot be verified in follow-up studies, thereby throwing initial findings into doubt.

Conspiritualists who had learned enough decolonization language could argue on Facebook that conventional and corporatized COVID science erased non-Western approaches to wellness. They pointed to India's advocacy of Ayurveda and homeopathy in the fight against the pandemic (though homeopathy emerged from Germany in the eighteenth century). They argued that practitioners of Traditional Chinese Medicine who prescribed acupuncture and herbs to "support immunity" against COVID should be lauded for preserving ancestral ways—and that not doing so revealed implicit racism. (This argument avoids the complex story of how TCM was largely reconstructed by Mao Zedong for global export, and today is mostly commodified by non-Asian practitioners.) Posters who had a glancing familiarity with Foucault could argue that quarantine measures were cynical expressions of the surveillance and carceral state.

While Iyengar always counted real doctors among his closest allies (clearly wanting to be one himself), the purely spiritual sector of conspirituality is prone to wave away the power of science altogether. Many yoga devotees, along with *A Course in Miracles* enthusiasts and readers of best-selling authors like Deepak Chopra and Rupert Sheldrake, are taught that consciousness absolutely creates all reality. Built into this philosophy is a tidy preemptive defense: that arguments in favor of scientific evidence are either deluded by a materialist bias that refuses to acknowledge anecdotal evidence of the paranormal, or have failed to keep up with how quantum physics proves the power of magical thinking. It doesn't. Ultimately, among conspiritualists invested in the political economy of alternative health, the goal is not to erase the power of science, but to co-opt it by mimicking its language and hierarchies of authority.

At best, pseudoscience is a naive and creative disregard for the mechanisms of verification, undertaken in the hope that magic might be real. This is the Iyengar-level variety of pseudoscience, which unfortunately softens the ground for deeper holes. Farther down on the integrity plane, pseudoscience expresses disdain for the value of expertise, collective knowledge, and consensus reality. At worst, it allows aggressive political ideologies to be dressed up as scientific fact. In all cases, pseudoscience works by hijacking the specialized jargon of science—and sometimes its mechanisms of communication—to create a mirage of legitimacy, or an alternate universe in which viruses aren't real and vaccines make you magnetic.

Efforts to dissolve that mirage are more than a century old.

THE FLEXNER REPORT OF 1910 was a landmark publication on the state of medical education in North America. It called for higher admission rates, higher graduation standards, and strict adherence to evidence-based research and teaching. It provoked sweeping reforms that decertified modalities like homeopathy, traditional osteopathy, and the prescription of untested herbal remedies. Curricula were streamlined and standardized, with physiology and biochemistry taking center stage.

As would be expected for the age, Abraham Flexner was bigoted toward women and non-white doctors. But he was right about germ theory, and largely on the strength of that, the ideas and practices that fell outside of his reformed vision were relegated to the category of "irregular medicine." Eventually, irregular medicine was bundled together with the traditional medicines of non-Western cultures under the new name "alternative medicine"—a term that first appeared in a medical journal in 1975.

If capitalism is good at anything, it's co-opting and monetizing transgressive trends into new income opportunities. So the alternative medicine category didn't stay in the box of shame that Flexner built. Mass-marketing in the 1970s pitched alternative medicine to a counterculture distrustful of authority, hungry for natural cures as opposed to chemical fixes, and attracted to premodern wisdom.

The broad political appeal of the movement predicted the horseshoe-type scrambling of COVID-era conspirituality. In its rejection of institutional knowledge, alternative medicine allows progressives to believe they are embracing ancient, Indigenous wisdom. But that same rejection also appeals to more libertarian values such as self-reliance, freedom, and back-to-nature traditionalism. Alternative medicine allows a broad coalition of political actors to sing Kumbaya around a rejection of medical science in favor of faith, prescientific tradition, and even magical thinking about prayer or ritual.

In 1985, a new term appeared in the medical literature: "complementary medicine." The language marked a return to a mainstream resorption of what was previously "irregular." Critics have argued that this new framing, along with the term "integrative medicine," launders pseudoscience in an attempt to gain greater academic and public credibility. The marketing suggests that alternative methods can be used in conjunction with medical science to produce better results. Proving this, however, is difficult.

For as long as the three of us have been involved in the yoga and wellness worlds, we've heard a standard chorus. Alternative medicine, goes the song, has not been sufficiently tested to warrant its lowly position in the health economy. The more conspiratorial voices claim there's no incentive for researchers to study yoga, breathing, and kitchen herbs, because they don't generate the same profit margins as miracle drugs.

But that's not correct. In 1991, a US federal agency called the Office of Alternative Medicine was established to study alternative healing practices, train researchers, and disseminate information to the public and clinicians. In 1998, the agency was renamed as the National Institute for Complementary and Alternative Medicine. In 2014, it became the National Center for Complementary and Integrative Health. The name changes reflect the endless reframing of the agency's slippery topic.

Between 1991 and 2009 the agency's budget grew from $12 million to $122 million a year. During those years, it laid out a total of $2.5 billion to study irregular, alternative, complementary, or integrative treatments. The results? Ginger capsules may help for chemotherapy nausea. All other herbal remedies—including echinacea, glucosamine, black cohosh, saw palmetto, variously touted as cures for hot flashes, prostate conditions, memory, immune function, cancer, and arthritis—failed to beat the placebo.

The NCCIH also found that acupuncture may help with chemotherapy nausea, and some joint pain. However, they also found that sham acupuncture treatments—using retractable needles or ignoring traditional acupuncture points and meridian lines—worked just as well. Yoga and meditation were shown to possibly help anxiety, pain, or fatigue. And contrary to what health conspiracists might imagine, critics and former NCCIH heads describe a reluctance at the agency to ever say that treatment had been shown not to work—even when that's what the evidence showed. The NCCIH routinely gave grants to alternative therapy providers to run the testing protocols themselves.

In 2012, the *Journal of the American Medical Association* came out with a paper slamming the NCCIH for funding study after study, yet failing "to prove that CAM [Complementary and Alternative Medicine] therapies are anything more than placebos." They pointed out that the agency spent $250,000 to test the effects of energy healers on rabbits with high cholesterol, $374,000 to find out whether aromatherapy heals wounds, $406,000 on coffee enemas as a cure for pancreatic cancer, $417,000 on distance healing for HIV patients, $2 million on using magnets for arthritis, carpal tunnel syndrome, and migraine headaches, $22 million on prayer for treating diseases, and a whopping $110 million on a range of fringe methods to reduce diabetes symptoms—including the therapy of expressive writing. For the studies in which results were reported—many rendered no results at all—no treatment performed better than placebo.

The lackluster results have not slowed down the CAM economy. Why? Podcast guest Britt Hermes gave us a number of clues. Hermes is a former naturopathic doctor who resigned from the profession after working for a clinic that doled out unapproved cancer treatments. She went on to become a naturopathic apostate, and anti–alternative medicine activist. She told us that a major part of her training at Bastyr University in Washington State involved learning how to set up and furnish a welcoming alternative health space. Students were coached on lighting design, color palettes, finishes, and even how to dress in such a way as to soften the authority differential between themselves and their patients. The idea, Hermes said, was to provide a kind of anti-clinic, in which the patient felt relaxed and pampered— and also listened to, in depth. Initial consultations often lasted for an hour or more, and involved a lengthy history-taking that could feel as personal and intimate as psychotherapy. In the absence of teaching solid medicine, Hermes explained, her school offered training in creating good vibes.

Nonetheless, CAM has made great incursions into academia as well, with big-money donors setting up programs at major medical universities and CAM finding ways to keep reinventing itself linguistically so as to seem legitimate in parallel with actual medical science for those who find the idea of a more holistic integration appealing and humane. The most extravagant example of this has been the Susan & Henry Samueli College of Health Sciences at UC Irvine—made possible initially by a $200 million donation. This college is continuing to grow with the aim of establishing what is touted as the first truly integrative health sciences complex for training, research, and patient care.

As PSEUDOSCIENCE INSTITUTIONALIZED, the yoga professionalization movement Iyengar helped to inspire became its own economy, with pressures and incentives that would later drive the escalation of conspirituality as both an online religion and a monetization network, poised to make big promises and take big risks. When you are a professional yoga teacher who has been trained to believe that yoga practice holds the keys to perfect health, you might feel you have little choice but to put your faith to the test when a pandemic breaks out.

Modern yoga teacher training dates back to 1969 in the Laurentian ski town of Val-Morin, Quebec, where Kuttan Nair—dubbed Swami Vishnudevananda by his guru, Swami Sivananda—started selling "yoga vacations." Students typically stayed at the bucolic Sivananda Yoga Camp for a month, and the program of classes and lectures they received soon morphed into what is now the two-hundred-hour training blueprint of today. In their online materials, Sivananda Yoga claims to have graduated fifty thousand people from these programs around the world. Its model inspired a training industry that grew steadily over three decades.

But Kuttan Nair was a cultish leader who sexually abused many students— including his personal assistant—for decades. His wider cultural impact lives on in his brain-melted influence on yoga education. "Science is not absolute, but relative," he liked to say, as he promised that his stretches and chanting would grant the wealth of health. Nair was also fond of speculating about whether UFOs are trying to communicate with humanity—but that they're not aliens per se, but Hindu gods, riding through time in spaceships crafted in the Iron Age. Not a great start for the legacy of yoga teacher training.

Currently, the Yoga Alliance trade organization tracks the legacy of Nair's training innovation, registering over 6,600 schools worldwide, with the majority in the Global North. Some programs are large, churning out hundreds of graduates per year. Most are smaller, and some might not be hosting programs every year. Given these caveats, if we conservatively estimate that each registered school is turning out ten graduates per year, then sixty-six thousand freshly minted yoga instructors enter the wild each year. Some go on to join the gig economy of yoga teaching. Others are satisfied with the personal enrichment experience. But all of them receive the same general training. And most of them, along with the rest of the world, wind up online.

By the 2000s, the yoga teacher training program had become a transitional life ritual for liberal, wellness-oriented Gen Xers and millennials who had—or could borrow—up to $10,000. Going through tough changes? Divorce? Sickness? Death in the family? Shit economy? Has that humanities degree lost its market value? Have you crossed that five-year dry spell threshold in Los Angeles trying to make it as an actor? Maybe it's time to look within, says the marketing. Care for yourself. Consider a new career, gig-work-style, in spreading the message of yoga. Be the change you want to see in the world.

These programs are usually presented as professionalization opportunities, but they're not comparable to accredited learning processes. The curriculum is not regulated by any social or academic consensus. While *Light on Yoga* was a yoga program reading-list staple, other assigned texts could be just about anything. You might be assigned Rhonda Byrne's bestselling *The Secret*, which presents the universe as a mail-order catalog that delivers to your door whatever your mind focuses on with the power of intention. Wealth, poverty, happiness, suffering, trauma, healing, war, and peace are all, according to Byrne, manifestations of the power of the mind.

Maybe the list included *You Can Heal Your Life* by Louise Hay, which reductively assigns all physical maladies a metaphysical meaning and emotional cause. Or there might be popular titles repurposing quantum physics terminology as a language of healing and enlightenment by chiropractor Joe Dispenza or alternative medicine guru Deepak Chopra.

In the absence of curricular vision, yoga trainings are driven by the charismatic confidence of entrepreneurs, who transform a pastiche of personal anecdotes and uncited resources into a pyramid of increasingly expensive training levels. Many students flock to this structure during a vulnerable time, inspired by the possibility of self-transformation. Sound familiar?

* * *

TO SEE HOW the brain melt played out on the ground, it's worth looking briefly at materials produced by the Jivamukti Yoga School of Manhattan in 2007. Founders Sharon Gannon and David Life were known eccentrics with roots in performance art and vegan activism, but Jivamukti was no fringe operation. They represented a fully Americanized, celebrity-friendly version of global yoga, claiming authentication from multiple Indian masters. And they expanded, with franchises eventually opening in places such as Toronto, Paris, Berlin, Barcelona, and Moscow. To staff their growing empire, Jivamukti trainings were organized in the Sivananda-style intensive month format, in which students are expected to absorb piles of history and philosophy content while also spending hours every day practicing postures and sequences, and learning how to narrate yoga choreography so that they could lead a class.

The schedule was unreasonably cramped. Jivamukti Yoga had students training three hundred hours over twenty-four days. That's 12.5 contact hours per day. Almost half of those hours were taken up with low-intensity instruction topics such as meditation, chanting, breathing practice, and *satsang*, which involves listening to the leaders give a sermon about something. Therefore, almost half of the contact hours aren't really content driven. They are about being in the glow of the experience, in the charismatic radiance of what the founders have created.

On the first page of the 156-page, ring-bound photocopied manual they admit as much, in all-caps: "BE PRESENT! JUST SHOW UP! THIS IS THE PRIMARY COURSE REQUIREMENT. The development of the aspirant is from listening to being. LISTEN—HEAR—KNOW—BECOME—BE."

The rest of the manual is an exuberant jumble of uncited sources, stick-figure drawings, diagrams, and quotes. No footnotes, no bibliography.

There are quotes from someone's commentary on the *Bhagavad Gita*, followed by a quote they claim is from Noam Chomsky, but sounds wrong. Centered on the page, it says: "Don't speak your truth to power," which is a strange thing to find in the training manual of a culty group. Other quotes are from Rumi, Gandhi, Leonardo da Vinci, Helena Blavatsky, Wavy Gravy, and Carl Jung. There are long lists of anatomy terms and lots of space for diary notes on meditation and postures.

Gannon and Life were also smart enough to give themselves an out when it came to what they were ultimately delivering. The text of the closing prayer states, with impressive vagueness:

> *Tonight we are honoring accomplishment.*
> *Who has accomplished anything?*
> *Everything that happens*
> *Happens because of God.*
> *God is the only real doer.*
> *But who are we, and what do we do?*
> *This is a riddle. It is the greatest riddle*
> *Each one of us has only a small amount of time—*
> *A precious life to dedicate to the solving of that riddle.*

IN 1999, PSYCHOLOGY RESEARCHERS David Dunning and Justin Kruger published a study showing that for many people, levels of confidence on specific topics are inversely correlated with actual knowledge or education. This cognitive quirk results in experts expressing cautious opinions, while ignoramuses bluster about with great certainty.

When earnest yoga people signed up for trainings at places like Jivamukti, they weren't just entering a Dunning-Kruger machine, in which they'd be told that single lectures in diet and psychology would make them knowledgeable in both because the framework was the magic of yoga. They were unwittingly placing a bet that, as future instructors, they could find economic security within an exploding, unregulated marketplace. The love-and-light vibes of the training disguised the fact that gentrification, more than expanding consciousness, was pulling the real strings. The modern urban yoga studio has always been on the bleeding edge of rising real estate prices, especially in areas where the working class is driven out and yuppies flood in with income to burn on boutique wellness.

Studios like Jivamukti, which functioned as a hub for gig-working teachers, would always make some money for a while, but the margins would tighten as the rents went up. What saved the bacon of most urban yoga studios was the high ticket price of the yoga teacher training program. Over two decades, this created an economic cul-de-sac, in which a proliferation of trainings saturated the labor market while increasing the perception in the workforce that qualifications had to be continually upgraded. As studios raced to keep ahead of their rents, and yoga teachers searched for pathways toward influencer-dom, the entry-level training became a pipeline for 500-, 750-, and 1,000-hour upgrades.

For many schools the upgrades would happen within the span of the typical five-year commercial lease. But what kind of institution can just double its curriculum every few years, based upon aspiration and financial need? The kind that isn't really an institution at all, but rather a content mill, in which program directors are constantly scouting for more material to jazz up a gig economy threatened by constant financial pressure. This is the short story of how yogaworld became an accelerated heat sink for every New Age scheme and add-on alternative medicine modality out there. The industry always needed more content, more income streams. The more aspirational the better.

And if teaching yoga—or teaching other people to teach yoga—wasn't enough to get by, you could add Reiki training, crystal therapy, supplement sales, cacao ceremonies, sound healing rituals, meditation circles, and transformational breathing.

In tragic cases, a yoga school could try to boost its income by going further than organizing a pyramid of self-feeding trainings. They could buy into a multi-level marketing scheme. Unscrupulous yoga influencers could do it, too. In the 2010s, you couldn't swing a yoga mat in a yoga studio without knocking over a display rack of essential oils. Some of the top sellers in that category gained their status by marketing to client networks built up over years in yogaworld. Many were well practiced at reciting the pseudoscientific benefits of essential oils, because they had done the same thing with yoga for years. Then as now, the ambitious and earnest yoga teacher can intensify claims about oils with the urgency of spiritual promise.

Multi-level marketing (MLM) is an exploitative structure employed by companies that use direct sales to move product, as opposed to the retail model. In direct sales, customers earn the right to sell products—and earn commissions every month—based on buying preset levels of inventory, which they must then sell on to other customers in a fixed period of time or else face steep losses.

The structure is often called a pyramid scheme because new members are recruited to an overcrowded bottom rung with the promise they will receive a percentage of profit from the sales of those they recruit beneath them. Position in the hierarchy is based on how many members one has recruited, with decreasing numbers of sales affiliates at each step up in the organization. Inevitably, people lower down in the pyramid risk operating at a loss, while chasing the promise of one day ascending the ranks and making millions.

As in a cult, all power in an MLM flows upward. The few at the top benefit from a guaranteed monthly influx of cash from their recruits. But how few are they? The Federal Trade Commission's study of 350 MLMs over a fifteen-year period found that less than 1 percent of participants make any profit at all.

Well-known MLMs include Amway, Avon, Herbalife, Mary Kay, Young Living, doTERRA, LuLaRoe, and weight-loss herb sellers Usana—in which Christiane Northrup and her daughter Kate are top-tier sellers (as was Christiane's late mother, Edna). All offer an upgraded American dream: Be the captain of your destiny! Find a path to abundance outside of conventional 9-to-5 structures and qualifications!

That path today is almost entirely virtual, as social media provides an efficient vector for MLM recruitment, especially for new moms, empty nesters, housewives in search of a community or side hustle. Boss babe influencers with huge Instagram followings grow their downlines by performing opulent lifestyles fueled by fun times with soul sisters selling great products. High-impact motivational conferences in amphitheaters fitted with epic audiovisual systems merge entrepreneurial capitalism and the aspirational self. These New Age spaces are like prosperity gospel megachurches where sales data paves the road to the holy land.

The MLM machine carries an added sting when it exploits the New Age, yoga, and wellness worlds. When yoga teachers are recruited into an essential oil scheme, for example, the constant pressure to sell can turn every interaction with a client or student into a recruitment pitch. A yoga studio owner can easily cross-market high-priced teacher trainings with the promises of MLM participation using the same language of self-development and financial autonomy. If the yoga influencer has mobilized the term "community" to describe their ideal of shared practice and personal growth through the art of yoga, that term can quickly curdle into "sales force." Every potential friend is really a potential mark.

The layperson who sells essential oils for an MLM will build recruitment in the wild by relying on the company's claims that, for example, Thieves oil boosts the immune system. But the yoga teacher already has a captive audience and potential market that's ready to view any new promise and product through the lens of spiritual progress. At the highest levels of integration between MLMs and New Age spirituality, the business models merge. Esther Hicks, who we'll talk more about in Part Three as a key channeler of the New Age, got her start with her husband Jerry in the Amway MLM, where they both earned top dollar. Sitting at the peak of a financial pyramid that promised wealth and independence to downliners prepared Esther for marketing and running a spiritual pyramid, where she claims to channel wisdom from disembodied spirits down to consumers who buy books and courses, and are encouraged to recruit in turn.

MLMs find strong traction in the New Age wellness economy in part because the promises of limitless financial growth rhyme with promises of limitless spiritual potential. Structurally, the MLM business model is also familiar. Even since the internet revolutionized wellness, top producers have mobilized many direct sales techniques such as email marketing, engaged in algorithm-based online advertising, and monetized connections among social media accounts, email lists, and websites for selling products and digital courses.

Influencers whose content overlaps enough to benefit from cross-marketing—but not so much as to pit them against each other—can also team up through affiliate marketing: software tracks how a user first arrives at the landing page for a sales pitch, and then sends the referer a commission when the click is converted. It's a magic moneymaking machine for conspiritualists who want to network with each other and share the profits from large online events. It's a system that worked well, for instance, in promoting COVID-contrarian conferences centered on alternative wellness practices, faux-political activism, and conspiracy porn.

In one investigation we did for the podcast, we found that Elena Brower, a former fashion designer and highly successful yoga celebrity in the 2010s in New York City, had used her yoga training program to recruit students into the doTERRA essential oils MLM. But she didn't stop there. She also recruited students into an expensive life-coaching scheme called Handel Group. Students who signed up for unrelated programs wound up receiving Handel Group life-coaching questionnaires and materials, and were subjected to group therapy sessions with both Brower and the Handel CEO, Lauren Handel Zander. Brower also used student contact lists to continue marketing pricey Handel courses and coaching calls. But Brower's yoga-to-coaching pipeline didn't flow forever. Later, she turned her attention back to selling essential oils. Same yoga marketing contacts, different content.

Brower's story illustrates the yoga-teacher-training-MLM-boss-babe pipeline, slick with big charisma and bigger promises. If you slide all the way up, the sky is the limit. Today, Brower boasts over 354,000 followers on Instagram, and pulls in over $1 million yearly from oil sales.

COMPLETING A YOGA TEACHER training made a person…a yoga teacher. It granted permission to guide people in the gardening of their internal lives. It let people think they could act like a physiotherapist, a psychologist, and a theologian, if only because they had a glancing familiarity with each of these subjects. Or, it helped them benefit from the halo effect, by which their skill in one area is interpreted as proof of their skill in all areas. This is how the greats did it, after all. Iyengar was the world's greatest demonstrator of yoga poses. Therefore, there's no question he must also have been a very wise man.

If you didn't take good notes during the bizarre and scrambled training sessions, the transcendent experience of the training itself filled in all the gaps. What you couldn't absorb through study was beamed into you by the presence of your teachers during all those hours in which you were sitting there, meditating—or whatever it was you were doing. Of course, there are no meditation proficiency exams. You could have just been spacing out— but looking like you were being really pious and compliant—and your certificate would look just like everyone else's.

In March 2020, global yoga was a deflating-bubble economy teetering on the edge, with major studio chains across North America starting to lose the battle against the gentrification they once stimulated. In 2018, the industry had been rocked by a wave of #MeToo revelations that struck at the heart of its moral leadership and exposed schools that were organized very much like cults. But when the COVID conspiracies started flying, a third weakness became clear. Yogaworld was vulnerable to misinformation. Decades of aspirational marketing—rife with overreaching claims about health benefits and designed to recruit students into unregulated trainings—had provided the culture with little moral or intellectual protection against a propaganda war.

But this is also a demographic that was more than merely vulnerable. They had purpose. In the absence of concrete content and measurable skills, the yoga teacher training system gave its most enthusiastic graduates an urgent sense of mission. The programs were the promise and the delivery system for how to be a countercultural, but also legitimate, heroic figure. It was a way of dropping out without being a dropout, of being a rebellious seeker of forbidden knowledge through multiple trainings, certifications, sharing circles, and catharses. It was a place where people could openly struggle with their shadows, and where they were destined to help others do the same.

Upleveled yoga marketing said that deep down inside of you, there's a teacher and healer that's yearning to be born. *Of course* you should pay the top ticket price on the menu of options to do this teacher training. You'll put in all those hours during times when the studio has no other business going on. You're in a life transition. You're turning that divorce or job loss into a well of wisdom, learning special things that mainstream science doesn't know. You will feel like the elect.

Inevitably, the law of diminishing returns kicked in, with the industry hitting a critical mass where every successful yoga studio was turning out boatloads of graduates. It got harder for each grad to be successful as that in-real-life special medicine person and ritual leader. For good or ill, the internet exploded at just the right moment to allow brands and teachers to promote themselves in new ways. When COVID shuttered the studios in the spring of 2020, the internet became a claustrophobic lifeline for a culture that was always demanding a new world but was never equipped with the analytical, political, or cultural tools to create one.

CHAPTER 14

THAT'S US IN A HEADSTAND, LOSING OUR COGNITION

AT THIS POINT IT should be clear that conspirituality has deep historical roots, and that the strains of body fascism that arose to support and glorify the paranoid and grandiose nationalistic movements of the early twentieth century are still lingering in yoga and wellness cultures in internalized form. We've seen how the cascade of social, economic, and existential crises of 2020 pressure cooked these buried values until the gaskets blew. We've seen that body fascism can enter periods of latency, and can also roar back.

But we can't let our argument devolve into "COVID-19 flushed the yoga Nazis out of hiding," because it's not true. None of the conspirituality influencers we have studied have shown any overt knowledge of or even interest in explicit body fascism, neocolonialism, or white supremacy.

It's not surprising that they don't. To be blunt, they come from a subculture distinguished by a self-satisfied and privileged distaste for history and politics. For the three of us, professionalizing into the yoga and wellness worlds of the early aughts meant inheriting a culture in which most of our mentors had not only given up on political interests but insisted that political nonengagement was a high virtue.

According to the vibe, discussing politics anywhere near a yoga studio or wellness clinic could only increase division. And yet there was a strange allergy to collective thinking as well. To practice yoga together was to do similar things at the same time, but in separate bubbles, and for the benefit of ourselves alone. The lines of yoga mats in gentrified studios, each demarking private spaces of revelation, represented our checked-out communion of solitude.

For the three of us, this amounted to a subtle betrayal of our roots. Derek's first full-time job was as a local beat reporter in Monroe, New Jersey, where he covered zoning meetings—the ground zero of policy making. To later find himself practicing at the Jivamukti Yoga School in Manhattan, where teachers and students seemed to think that politics was accomplished through meditations for world peace, gave him a mild case of whiplash. He knew how politics worked on the granular level. It was all points of order and piles of paperwork. It had nothing to do with fabulous backbends or chanting in bad Sanskrit.

For Julian, growing up in South Africa, playing in an anti-apartheid rock band and being part of the first small group of white boys who risked heavy jail sentences for refusing mandatory police-state military service, political struggle was in his blood. To Julian, Ana Forrest seemed to be tuned in enough at first. For a while she would gather her students in a circle to meditate on healing the hole in the ozone layer. When she dropped this practice one day, Julian asked why. Forrest explained that Mother Earth had come to her in a dream and told her she was just fine—that she needed a "smokestack" after all.

Matthew grew up in a union family. He got arrested with eco-activists in the early 1990s, protesting Air Force training runs over First Nations reserves. But in one of the first lectures on Tibetan Buddhism he heard Michael Roach give, Roach announced that there was no such thing as objective news reporting, because everyone experienced things according to their personal karma. Matthew stopped reading the news, and he felt the strange, temporary relief of not having to care about the world. It took years for him to realize that Roach was not only building his brand through metaphysical depoliticization, but also actively downplaying the harsh realities of Tibetan life under Chinese rule. If Roach thought about Tibetan liberation at all, he seemed to think it would happen if he offered workshops in meditation and compassion to oligarchs in Shanghai.

Through the 1990s, we shared the core elements of a Gen X story of white, mainstream culture, getting sleepier under the blanket of neoliberalism. *Everything's fine, or as good as it can be, and hey, video games are getting cooler.* The answer to 9/11, as President George W. Bush said, was to keep the economy going by shopping. We acclimatized to the fading hope that anything approaching a social contract could exist in a union-busted, trickle-down, banking-and-technology landscape. It was up to us to "Just Do It," to "go with the flow," and to "follow our bliss." In the United States, we normalized the fading hope that universal health care was an achievable goal. It made sense that yoga and supplements became important forms of health care for many of our friends.

By the mid-aughts, we were harried gig workers in an economy even more depoliticized than the mainstream zeitgeist. Because, after all, in the yoga and wellness worlds, it wasn't just seen as déclassé or even useless to be politically engaged. Disengagement was a spiritual law tangled up in a consumer imperative. It's hard to think about—let alone make time for—the revolution when you've got to work on the world-transcending aesthetic of your personal brand.

We had somehow fallen into a river in which the only acceptable politics—or the only politics anyone had time for—was an orientalist universalism defined by good vibes and appeals to an ancient past. That riverhead snaked back to the 1893 splash made by Swami Vivekananda at the World's Parliament of Religions during the World's Fair in Chicago. The charismatic Hindu nationalist gave electric lectures that made yoga all the rage in the bourgeois salons of America. Speaking to mainly Christian audiences—already primed by the transcendentalist reveries of Emerson and Thoreau—Vivekananda proposed that his new form of homogenized and ecumenical Hinduism, sweetened by yoga, could put an end to "sectarianism, bigotry, and its horrible descendant, fanaticism." He didn't say how.

Nor did the alleged sex abuser Swami Satchidananda when he took the stage in white robes to open the Woodstock Festival in 1969. "Often we hear groups of people shouting, 'Fight for peace,'" the Swami said into a PA, ringing with feedback. He may have been referring to the anti–Vietnam War movement, or the civil rights clashes of previous years. "I still don't understand how they are going to fight and then find peace," he puzzled. "Therefore, let us not fight for peace, but let us find peace within ourselves first."

How would all the young hippies do it? By grooving to the universal sounds of consciousness in acid rock and folk music. By chanting the name of the Hindu god Ram, as though Ram transcended politics in a modern India that modeled peace. But twenty-three years after that mud party on

Max Yasgur's farm, the name of Ram was also chanted by Hindu nationalists as they destroyed a centuries-old mosque in Ayodhya, Uttar Pradesh,
with iron pipes, clubs, and their bare hands. The demolition marked the
postmodern rise of the nationalist BJP and its sun-saluting paramilitary,
the RSS.

Many North Americans who stuck with yoga after the 1960s wanted a
religion that wasn't a religion to bless a politics that wasn't political. And
they found their suppliers. Throughout the postwar era, as modern yoga
scholar Andrea Jain explains, "Indian gurus as well as European and North
American yogis began to reconstruct modern yoga systems in ways that
universalized them by attributing to them benefits that were removed from
specific Indian nationalist and mystical contexts and instead reflected the
self-developmental desires that dominated consumer culture."

CHIEF AMONG THOSE DESIRES, especially in the 1970s, was the mandate to
"get loose," to use the phrase of sociologist Sam Binkley. Getting loose meant
stretching, breathing, and relaxing from two paradigms: the tense condi-
tioning of 1950s productivity and conformity, and the rage of 1960s protest.
It meant choosing a lifestyle that transcended the old binary of conservative versus liberal, and identifying your citizenship with something greater.
The goal was to *feel* looseness in the present moment as opposed to within
history and society. One had to "loosen into one's own body," Binkley
wrote, immersed in the senses and bodily experience, aided by good food
and unrepressed sex, through physical culture and presenting yourself as
empathetic. "Loosening," he argued,

> meant becoming an active chooser of a more authentic self. To be loose was to
> be mobile in a shifting world, to free oneself of the constraining baggage of tra-
> dition, and to sail out across the sea of unmediated experience even as one trav-
> eled with one's favored companion, the lifestyle adviser whose prescriptions
> were always available in the latest journal, book, or magazine on the New Life.

In yogaworld—our perennial sample for the broader "wellness" category—
that "latest journal" and magazine was *Yoga Journal*. First published in Xe-
rox form in May 1975, it was the only publication of its kind for more than
a decade. If yoga enthusiasts in North America wanted to learn anything

about the practice, or its growing scene, *Yoga Journal* was it. As yoga gained wider mainstream popularity in the US, the magazine's influence grew, reaching 1 million readers by 2010, and 2.2 million Facebook followers today. The print edition is currently published internationally in eleven languages.

"Our intention," announced the inaugural editorial, "is to bring you material that combines the essence of classical yoga, with the latest understandings of modern science." It was a modest goal, but also a test for how a new spirituality might meet reality, and situate itself politically. If they really were going to let things like science into their breathwork and meditations, wouldn't economics and public policy be relevant as well? Or was science only interesting in relation to raising consciousness?

The first issue featured an article about keeping one's diet light so that the body could be sensitive. Another discussed yoga and the endocrine system. One health writer used the ramblings of the nineteenth-century sleepwalking channeler Edgar Cayce to show why readers should be concerned about aluminum and plastics in food.

It took two years and an upgrade in print and layout before *Yoga Journal* risked an article on politics. Sort of.

In "The Developing Political Awareness in the Growth Movement," John Amodeo, then a grad student at the California Institute of Transpersonal Psychology, laid out the problem of politics in the New Age clearly. "With the demise of political activism in the late 1960s," he wrote,

> a dynamic shift took place in our society. Dissatisfaction which had led to widespread social and political action slowly moved toward dissatisfaction with one's personal life. A shift from external activities to a more introverted, self-exploring style of life began to take place in serious minded persons who felt deeply committed to a vaguely perceived goal.

But wait! This is a good thing, claimed Amodeo, because it alerted seekers to what they could achieve internally. There was no need to fantasize about a transformed social state if personal happiness and inner growth were more relevant and realistic goals.

The keynotes of Amodeo's analysis are a parade of intellectual vulnerabilities that practically roll out a red carpet for conspirituality. He criticized the "patriarchal belief" that values evidence-based medicine over homeopathy, which he falsely related to Chinese medicine. He criticized the drive to regulate psychotherapy training, "which Buddha and Jesus, perhaps the greatest psychotherapists of all, never had or needed." He railed against the "myth of professionalism," and the "false god of science." He worried about politicians who were inhibited by dirty chakras and lack of self-growth. He argued for a redefinition of politics, based on intuitively touching the depths of our being to realize we are all One. So many things would help: self–medical care, self-education, natural childbirth.

Amodeo offered that the plight of "Blacks and Third World people" should not be ignored, but offered no analysis of power or strategy for racial or global justice. He preferred that readers relax into the sense of "naturalness" he associates with premodern Buddhist and Christian monastic communities. When the inner work is done in simple and holistic ways, he suggested, the outer work will take care of itself—if it even matters anymore.

Amodeo went on to become a contributing editor at *Yoga Journal*. The magazine kept nibbling at the edges of political issues with articles on the benefits of food purity, natural childbirth, and moderating consumption—even as it advertised a growing storehouse of New Age products and events, and a lazy Susan display of gurus.

In 1985, the magazine took a step up by running an extended interview with Buddhist peace activist Joanna Macy, beloved for her therapeutic reflections on global crises. According to Macy, the real benefits of yoga and meditation in the world are not that they make our future actions clear, but that they help us negotiate grief and reactivity. From a place of emotional openness and transparency, she argued, our choices can have more integrity.

This was a politics of lean-in Buddhism, the yoga of Brené Brown–style vulnerability. It would never analyze power; it would never discuss concrete policy issues; and it would never tell you how to vote. Where things got tense, it stayed loose, man.

If it addressed the topic at all, the *Yoga Journal* stance on politics was that it was good to vote and to be politically engaged, so long as positive intentions and mindful focus protected your inner peace and grounded center. You could use breathwork to calm your nervous system before marking your ballot, for whoever.

The open, receptive—and very naive—vibe was perfectly captured in 2008 when one well-meaning yoga nonprofit attempted to positively influence the electoral process by offering free yoga classes and chair massages at special booths set up by the *Huffington Post*—as part of the HuffPost Oasis initiative—at the Democratic leadership convention. For the 2012 cycle, they expanded their wellness services and soft political activism to the GOP convention as well, hoping to transform Republicans from within.

In 2008, Matthew thought it would be a good idea to use his growing presence in the online yogaworld to do some expat organizing for the Obama election campaign from his home office in Toronto.

He only stuck it out for about a week, because the instant and overwhelming response from his networks on Facebook and yoga blogging sites were variations of *This is NOT what true yoga is about*, or *This is not a place of DIVISION and SEPARATION*, or *Don't bring politics into yoga: I come here to experience my higher SELF.*

Sheesh. The posts had been about petitions, phone banks, Election Day rides to the polls. Basic stuff, yet suddenly everyone wanted to talk to the manager.

It felt like a watershed moment, to be shown so clearly that large chunks of yoga and wellness spaces were not just ambivalent toward the material conditions that allowed them to exist and expand; online yoga people seemed actively hostile to the pragmatics of everyday politics and calls to action. Facebook in particular allowed these subcultures to curate and protect their otherworldly values in a pseudoreality of oneness-through-posting. Large Facebook groups for students or teachers or followers of a particular brand actually enforced moderation rules like "No political topics or conversations allowed. This is a space of unity."

There were some responses to this from those unwilling to ignore politics altogether. Over time, a social justice movement—less naive than the one on display at the HuffPost Oasis in 2008—began to organize around issues such as racism and ableism in wellness, or the confusing issue of cultural appropriation in yoga. Before the pandemic shuttered a raft of studios, there was actually a yoga teachers' unionization drive gathering speed in Manhattan, organized by gig workers who were fed up with papering over terrible pay with good vibes. These movements did politicize the scene in some ways, but not to the extent that any yoga or wellness demographic—unlike Christian denominations—could ever emerge as a viable political organizing base.

Those Facebook yoga group moderators had good reason to enforce those "no politics" rules. Because the truth was that despite a culture-wide policy on valuing detachment, yoga and wellness people were continuing to live their lives in a world that could not be saged away. If they were gig workers, their precarity was increasing. If they were relying on yoga and wellness for their health needs, they were also getting older. Some were terrified by the growing evidence of ecological doom and getting antsy with the idea that meditation would stop the planet from burning. So, if by accident, a political discussion did break out on yoga and wellness Facebook, it was like a volcano of suppressed rage.

The moderators had little choice but to stand firm. They were adminning a depoliticized culture that harbored deep and growing political anxieties. But there was no consistent analysis or framework that could manage any of it. That is, until conspirituality and QAnon came along to provide a way for political angst and aggression to be disguised in the language of spiritual righteousness and transformation.

THE 2020 COVID CONSPIRITUALITY meltdown is the story of a subculture that would exert an outsized influence on social media—which its gig workers relied on for exposure. But in terms of educational, political, and moral resources, it was a subculture set up for failure. It may have wanted to run on altruism, but it really ran on vibes and consumerism.

Yoga and wellness culture presented itself as being educated by virtue of being spiritual. It confused politics with good intentions. Worst of all, it promoted the attitude that the common good could be served not through concrete activism, or by engaging with the details of public policy. People could change the world, it taught, through private practices, and by personally contemplating ancient moral edicts.

It was a proud, aspirational culture that thought it had shared values, until the shit hit the fan.

CHAPTER 15

ALIENS KILLED THE LOVE
AND LIGHT VIBE

YOGA JOURNAL MAY HAVE steered clear of national and global politics from the start, but behind the scenes they did take a serious moral stand against a deep source of industry shame. Members of their first nonprofit board drafted and approved a policy that the magazine wouldn't advertise or promote teachers accused of sexual misconduct. One source reports that this policy was effective in keeping known sex offenders out of *Yoga Journal*'s ad pages for years.

That same policy also supported an editorial stance that was willing to investigate an industry that was all about self-awareness, but not so much into self-examination. In late 1990, *Yoga Journal* published a top-notch investigative piece by Katharine Webster about the sexual abuse committed by Swami Rama, the guru-founder of the Himalayan Institute of Honesdale, Pennsylvania. Rama came to prominence through alleged mystical tricks like consciously raising his heartbeat and appearing to make one side of his hand several degrees hotter than the other. Webster's detailed and devastating account revealed that the guru abused many women students, and was then defended by his lieutenants after being sued by the family of a nineteen-year-old victim. Rama fled to India to avoid the trial.

A few months after Webster's piece dropped, Swami Rama's institute launched its own magazine, *Yoga International*. Either the no-abuser policy had barred them from advertising in *Yoga Journal* or they really did not want to promote their programs in a magazine that had just exposed their leader.

While its origins were messy, *Yoga International* went on to create a content library of considerable integrity. By the late 2010s, young, social justice–savvy editors were helping to platform interesting wellness content on accessibility, anti-ableism, trauma awareness, racial inclusivity, and how to support victims of sexual assault in yogaworld—which used to be *Yoga Journal*'s beat.

Meanwhile, *Yoga Journal*, founded as a nonprofit, was bought and privatized in 1998 by John Abbott, a money manager who liked yoga. Soon after, some of the old guard—senior women teachers in California—started to notice that the no-misconduct policy was starting to slip. They were disturbed to see that yoga celebrity Rodney Yee was now being advertised and promoted by the magazine, even after he was alleged to have violated the California Yoga Teachers Code of Ethics by having sex with two of his students. They sent a petition to Abbott demanding he reinstate the no-misconduct policy and install an ethics board. He politely dismissed them in his reply. "*Yoga Journal* is a special interest consumer magazine," he explained. "It is not our place or business to rule on moral and ethical issues."

When *Yoga Journal* CEO John Abbott responded to the women who petitioned that the magazine honor its prior commitment to not advertise those accused of sexual misconduct, he didn't stop at wiping his hands of the matter in the name of corporate neutrality. He explained that the ethics to which teachers should adhere were already plain to see in the moral codes laid down by the Iron Age yoga philosopher, Patanjali.

The problem is that the yoga ethicists of past millennia were not concerned with abortion, racism, eugenics, the environment, misogyny, or the dignity of trans people. And so a complex, late-stage capitalist culture was lulled into believing that the glow of old scriptures and the ephemeral relaxations of stretching and breathing would provide solid guidance in times of stress.

Yoga Journal's moral abdication essentially left *Yoga International* alone at the top in terms of yoga and wellness media integrity, as well as online services. In the lead-up to the COVID-19 pandemic, the platform headhunted industry leaders in biomechanics, ethics, and trauma recovery to build a robust library of online classes and courses. When COVID hit, they were ready to boost some very competitive online packages. We knew many of the instructors personally—they were evidence-based, pro–public health, and big proponents of critical thinking.

But at the end of 2021, their employer, *Yoga International*, was swallowed whole by the largest conspiracy theory and fake-documentary platform in the world, Gaia. Suddenly, a whole battalion of progressive-minded content providers—who together seemed to form a bulwark against the industry's worst instincts—had been absorbed into the Netflix of New Age bollocks.

Our personal experience of and reporting on the yoga and wellness worlds had made it clear that they were always vulnerable to the most extreme forms of delusion. We knew that legit yoga and wellness media platforms were perilously adjacent to spaces that incubated fever dreams. But this buyout, made at the very moment that vulnerable wellness consumers needed content that wouldn't melt their brains, collapsed that adjacency into a new type of oneness. Now, paywalled social justice yoga content would be cross-marketed with the drivel of David Icke, the antisemitic conspiracy theorist who believes Lizard People have infiltrated world governments.

THE STORY OF GAIA Inc., founded in 1988, is a microcosm of the technological and ideological acceleration of yoga and wellness economies across the threshold of the twenty-first century, driven by entrepreneurs who hit on a gold mine idea: the internet was an analogue for the infinite possibilities of New Age thought. Cyberspace unfolded limitlessly—just like the mind in meditation! It offered endless space for manifesting wealth! All the edgiest gurus knew it. Back in 1998, Matthew listened to Michael Roach wax on about how the internet had instantly "created billions in new wealth," which he counted as proof of good global karma paying off.

Gaia used to be called Gaiam, which the three of us remember from the 1990s as a mail order catalog selling yoga mats, Hindu rosaries, Zen alarm clocks, and incense holders. The company was founded by a Czechoslovakian immigrant and former champion hurdler named Jirka Rysavy, who came to the United States in 1984 and made a substantial fortune in Boulder, Colorado, by transforming a small office supply company he bought into a $5 billion-a-year business. In 1999, he sold the company for $1 billion and moved full-time into the New Age market.

In 2009, Gaiam went virtual, pivoting from tchotchkes to video streaming. By 2016, the rebranded Gaia left the material world behind altogether, selling the mail order side of the business for $167 million.

By 2019, Gaia was not only hosting thousands of hours of video content, but livestreaming events by preachers who rely on misleading and sometimes offensive pseudoscience claims. Shining brightest in their firmament are figures like Gregg Braden, who teaches that the elemental chemical makeup of human DNA literally spells out messages from God in numerological code associated with Jewish mysticism. Then there's Caroline Myss, who has said that AIDS was caused by "victim consciousness," and Bruce Lipton, who claims that the new science of epigenetics proves that the power of thought can change DNA and create healing without medical interventions.

Gaia also sponsored another kind of seven-day trial, hosted by beloved quantum-woo author Lynne McTaggart, a passionate anti-vaccine activist who uses the language of quantum physics to imply that we can heal illness with the power of intention. McTaggart coordinated thousands of participants in a weeklong meditation intention experiment broadcast by Gaia, with the aim of decreasing violent crime globally. It didn't.

Today, Gaia has close to 700,000 paying subscribers. At $11.99 a month, that adds up to over $100 million a year in revenue. This is before factoring *Yoga International*'s additional yield from their 2021 stock of 300,000 subscribers paying either $9.99 a month or $99 for the year. The purchases make up between $29 and $35 million of the Gaia pie. Part of Rysavy's outrageous success has come through social media domination, with Gaia apparently spending tens of millions on Facebook alone. In 2017, Facebook actually used them as a case study of success in their own pitch deck to entice more advertisers.

During the pandemic, Gaia's revenue increased by 28 percent per year. Their CFO predicts that by 2024 they could have as many as twenty-six million paying subscribers.

Yoga International prided itself on hosting programming from providers that take an evidence-based approach to yoga postures and breathing. Several key teachers on the platform were trained exercise scientists. During the #MeToo era, *Yoga International* began to expand its focus to areas beyond individual practice. A few young and social-justice-savvy editors were commissioning content on topics like anti-ableism, trauma awareness, racial inclusivity, and decolonization. They published proactive articles such as "How to Respond to Sexual Abuse Within a Yoga or Spiritual Community."

While accessing this material, earnest yoga students will also be exposed to fever dreams about Lizard People. Much of *Yoga International*'s evidence-based and progressive content will now function as a potential recruitment doorway for influencers like David Icke and Joe Dispenza.

When the takeover was announced, a statement from Gaia and *Yoga International* signaled that the magazine's editorial independence would remain intact. But within months, *Yoga International*'s top brass and editorial staff were out.

And what's at the heart of this juggernaut? In 2021, investigative journalist Rob Price interviewed thirty existing or former employees at Gaia and found that getting red-pilled on anti-vax and Q-adjacent materials at the twelve-acre campus near Boulder (festooned with enormous crystals) is a type of initiation for staff. Price reported that CEO Rysavy announced to employees the extraterrestrial "Blue Avians" were in contact with him, providing feedback on the documentary series in which they were to be featured. Some staffers organized group meditation retreats to try to contact aliens. Others would use prayer and rituals in the office to try to call down rain to extinguish wildfires in the nearby Rockies. Rysavy reportedly holds 81 percent of the company's stocks and was characterized by some employees as wielding absolute power in decision making, at times conducting sudden firings with no warning. The result is a paranoid workplace in which some staffers believe they are being surveilled electronically, while others speculate that Rysavy is listening in on their thoughts directly, or invading their dreams.

FOR BOLD NEW AGE explorers, the internet became a digital manifestation of Steiner's Akashic Records, allowing for anything to be stored, accessed, or created. Akashic space was impossibly vast and empty. And nature abhors a vacuum. Endless injections of content were needed, and Gaia built an engine for it. For spiritualists dreaming of utopian worlds and unending connectivity, the real estate was nearly free. But as the Gaia catalog reveals, a digital empire cannot be built on unicorns and rainbows only. The kids would get bored.

Gaia's success depends not only on wishes for heaven but also on the seductions of conspiracism: *nothing is as it seems, nothing happens by accident, and everything is connected.* Subscribers know that alien contact has occurred and normies will be shocked by inevitable government disclosures. In some of the shows, extraterrestrial sightings and terrorist attacks are framed as false flag events enacted by governments hiding *something*. Sasquatch might or might not be an alien life-form, and we're told that 20 percent of Bigfoot sightings are reported close to locations where UFOs have been seen. You can *Escape the Matrix* with David Icke and wonder at *The Power of the Heart* with Rhonda Byrne, author of *The Secret*. You can take a course, *Rewired*, by former chiropractor Joe Dispenza, who implies he's a neuroscientist.

While so many of us were reading and writing for *Yoga International*, Gaia was creating a parallel world for sectors of the internet that the three of us, along with many left-leaning Gen Xers, were blind to. The chan boards that launched QAnon exploded in user counts along the same timeline as Gaia's success. But these boards were populated by people who would have loathed Gaia's vibe, those who couldn't or didn't want to sublimate their anxiety with meditation and herbs.

While Rysavy was filling his aspirational sandbox with crystals and alien prophecies, that same internet vacuum sucked out into the open an endless stream of despair and cruel, disconnected nihilism from an inaugural generation of trolls and shitposters. We learned more about this world from interviewing Dale Beran, author of 2019's *It Came from Something Awful: How a Toxic Troll Army Accidentally Memed Donald Trump into Office*. He describes a universe that, similar to Gaia's, requires endless content, and finds it in the trash heap of capitalist ruin—rather than in the reading nooks of New Age bookstores.

Beran's book describes the melting pot quality of the internet, and the detritus it churned up. "With the advent of the web," Beran writes, "all the discarded pieces of pop culture, entertainment fiction, advertising, and video games that manufacturers had sold to youth to tell them who and how to be began to rise in their gorge as a spout of sliced-up, digitized chunks."

He calls 4chan.org "the number-one psychic garbage dump into which young people discarded their misery and creativity into a pile of old art, cartoons, ads, video games, movies, TV shows, comic books, and toys." The memes, in their immediate and spicy power, seemed to give users a renewed sense of agency, even if they were about the callous celebration of humiliation, suicide, self-hatred, mass-shootings, and rape. There was an inverted power in refusing to believe anything meaningful or vulnerable or hopeful about yourself or the world.

Beran describes early chan users as declassed, and lacking the social privilege that allowed them to find a positive identity. Contrast this to yoga and wellness consumers, who view their depoliticization as a source of spiritual pride. Chan users, unlike Gaia subscribers, knew they were powerless, and they sought out fierce allegiances with identifiers that might give them a culture and a meaning. "They clung to race as a means of self-definition... Degraded and superfluous, convinced life was nothing but a cruel power struggle (because they were constantly losing it), they fashioned their own context out of absurd medieval power fantasies."

ONE OF THE MOST oft-repeated aphorisms in the yoga and wellness worlds is that "a finger pointing at the moon is not the moon." The adage has been attributed to Buddhist sources, and of course Rumi (a reliable go-to). Even Bruce Lee did a bit on it. It's everywhere, and despite its pop-culture cringe, it encapsulates a core teaching of the postwar internal turn that globalized yoga and wellness industries have monetized.

On one hand, it instructs the spiritual seeker to not confuse the teacher for the teachings. The Buddha himself is not the truth. Instead, you're told to seek the radiant and eternal experience he can only gesture at. On a practical level, it warns the seeker about the difference between spiritual concepts and spiritual experience. Yoga, meditation, and natural medicine all point at a Truth available to all people: they are not the Truth in themselves, but a pathway. On the most granular level, the aphorism suggests that the experience the seeker is pursuing must be direct to be worth the effort, and to deliver the goods. Anything that merely points to a thing in the world— language, concepts, metaphors—is a corrupting mediation that will always obscure the inexpressible glory of reality.

The mode of direct experience sounds very appealing. It is a fast track to getting loose. It encapsulates the obsessions of a subculture yearning to touch grass, to be authentic, to flow in the body or in the present moment. If we were to peg a single overarching desire that animates the zeitgeist, this is it: to develop the capacity for direct, unmediated experience of a life flow so perfectly surprising and complete it could never be reduced to mere ideas, labels, concepts, or politics. But this same desire also burns in the heart of conspirituality, where believers are constantly admonished to awaken to both the true horrors in the world and their sovereign potential in the present moment, to take the red pill, to fiercely transform themselves by "doing their own research"—a phrase that carries the archetypal weight of "know thyself."

What is so mind-bending about watching yoga and wellness media spiral down the figurative and literal Gaia-hole is hearing the language of direct experience, awakening, and reality deployed to market poppycock that covers over the world that people want to touch and understand. Today, the former *Yoga International* subscriber, having clicked a new terms-of-service agreement with Gaia, will quickly find the meditation and yoga videos offered by down-to-earth teachers of mindfulness. But then the algorithm will quickly point them to other categories: Paranormal & Unexplained, Ancient Teachings, Disclosure, Alien Contact, The Secrets of Atlantis, and Secrets & Cover-Ups—a category with twelve different subcategories, including The Cabal.

Gaia is like boot camp for conspirituality. It's a map to nowhere, a hall of mirrors, a galaxy of nonsense embedded in a multiverse of crap. It's spiritual pretense, dressed up in the language of pseudoscience, strung with the gift shop baubles of enlightenment, then doused with the scent of a bad trip. It's a real illusion, presented as waking up from a false illusion, which is, er, actual reality.

Bottom line? By early 2022, one of the largest and most progressive yoga platforms in the world had been sucked into a machine that was just as chaotic and senseless as the worlds of 4chan, 8chan, and 8kun (the rebrand of 8chan following its implication in several mass-shooting tragedies carried out by 8chan users)—which together generated and sustained the madness of QAnon. But in some ways, Gaia was worse, because it was respectable and well monetized.

And also hopeful. The consumers of Gaia were still earnestly looking for meaning in the world. The Anons who generated the fever dreams of Q had, for their part, given up on meaning long before. When these zeitgeists crossed paths on COVID-era social media, conspirituality gained new urgency, and Anons found fresh blood.

CHAPTER 16

CHARISMA, BELIEF, BULLSHIT, AND LONGING

IF THERE'S A MYSTERY at the heart of conspirituality leadership—a magic powder or special sauce—charisma is it.

The word *charisma* carries more than the "pizazz" meaning of it in casual conversation—the glamor of a celebrity or the glow of someone like Barack Obama. Up until the last hundred years, charisma was mainly a theological term meaning "grace" or "gift" of divine origin. But in an essay published in 1920, modern sociology founder Max Weber secularized and generalized the term to describe a contagious charm that orbits a standout individual, and is magnified by a mirror house of social validation. Charisma is, he explained, a ring of shared perception around a person that makes them seem superhuman. Charisma explains the aura of prophets, saints, mythic warriors—and now, glowing social media influencers.

Crucially, Weber makes no claim about the *essence* of the charismatic person—what they're really like inside and whether their glow is objectively real. Charisma is in the eye of the beholder in Weber's world—a social feedback loop, in which the attribution of specialness goes viral. This description provides insight for how one person's charismatic icon can be another person's lunatic. Consider Tony Robbins. Some hear his hoarse shout for two seconds and feel like they need to take a shower. But for a critical mass of others, that same two seconds initiates a hypnotic trance that careens toward walking over hot coals and investing thousands of dollars in a self-help pyramid scheme.

Cultural anthropologist Ernest Becker wrote about cult leaders as cultivating a charisma that seems free from death anxiety, and that performatively transgresses taboos. This tracks with the influencers we followed who exhorted their followers to, like them, not buy into the fear of COVID as symbolized by masks and social distancing.

Charisma is not something a person has so much as something that swirls around them, like weather. In its benign form, it flows outward to motivate, inspire, and nourish a community. But when used as a tool of recruitment to glorify the eye of a storm, its social capital—adulation, deference, obedience, compliance—crystallizes into a self-protective economy that hoards power for its own sake. The proof is in the pudding. On the blessed end of the charismatic spectrum—taking Black liberation movement leaders as examples—Martin Luther King Jr. left behind a vibrant democratic discourse. On the cursed end, Louis Farrakhan built an antisemitic UFO cult of lackeys dedicated to carrying out his authoritarian whims.

So it's no surprise that Weber's model is used both to describe effective political leadership and to understand a cultic organization. Cult survivor and researcher Janja Lalich lists charismatic authority as one of four pillars of a cult. Following Weber, Lalich frames charisma as a social economy, not as a special property of the person. Charisma is not to be confused with personal creativity or originality. This is a key point for understanding how the old themes of conspirituality get reanimated during a social crisis. Charismatics—especially in their ultimate form as cult leaders—are like theater directors, always searching for new scripts. Without new content their magic grows old. They are notorious magpies and plagiarists, compelled to pick up any shiny thing that works to refresh the spell they cast, and the control they seek.

We're often asked who started a particular conspirituality brainworm—about vaccine shedding, or the symptoms of ascension. In some cases, super-laborious digital forensics will find an answer, but it's rarely meaningful, given how derivative the meme will be, and how it morphs as it goes viral. Similarly, this is the nature of the charismatic leader who borrows or steals existing content, mashes it together, and then claims to have uncovered some ancient knowledge authentic enough to enlighten a fallen world.

Followers are usually deceived by the idea that the leader has unique insight and intuition that have given them access to things no one else can see. In reality, the leader is much less a visionary than a DJ, sampling and mixing tight hooks and dope beats—not necessarily out of any love for or commitment to the artists or their work, but to keep everyone dancing as fast as they can.

Do charismatics believe in what they are saying? Or do they only believe in themselves?

Of all the questions we field about the characters we cover in Part Three, the most vexing relate to their internal lives. Do they *earnestly believe* in what they are saying? Are they *trying* to confuse or deceive people? Are they true believers? Are they charlatans? Grifters? Are they gaslighting us? Themselves?

The questions make a lot of emotional sense. If you are new to thinking about cults, conspiracies, propaganda, and pseudoscience charlatanry, it's natural to look for the bright line that separates bad actors from those who cause harm in good faith. The distinction matters, psychologically. But the investigation is complicated by ecosystem forces, and by the metaphysics that create interpenetrating webs of causality that don't require huge amounts of malevolence or sociopathy to spin out real damage.

If, for example, a conspirituality influencer truly believes that the COVID vaccine will change a person's DNA and make them susceptible to satanic influences, then their posts in favor of that position may be tragically misguided, but also make a kind of forgivable moral sense. On the other hand, that influencer might not be a conspiritualist at all, but merely LARPing the role (that is, live-action role playing). If this is the case, and they know full well they are lying in a way that will boost audience engagement and pad their wallets—while likely killing people—that's something else, perhaps approaching sociopathy. The most vexing category of influencer falls in between. These are people who seem to be earnestly high on their supply, but not so much that they lose their entrepreneurial instincts. We might call them messianic marketers, believers who measure virtue in dollars.

Sometimes questions about intentions carry the weight of possible spiritual betrayal or even abuse. It is very common for survivors of yoga and wellness cults, for example, to wonder aloud whether their former leader ever really did mean all the promises they made. Whether they were in fact trying to help them out of some kind of authentic compassion. To imagine that one's former cult leader was lying about all of it, consciously, in order to gain money, power, or sex—this would deepen an already grave moral injury.

But the truth is that these questions can never be answered with any closure. The only way to achieve closure would be if the charismatic provided a complete and truthful admission. Good luck with that. If the charismatic influencer or cult leader were ordered to therapy by a court—it's unlikely they'd go voluntarily—the therapist might indeed come away with insights...which then would be kept confidential.

OUR LACK OF ACCESS to the intentions of a given charismatic is complicated by the process of how those intentions might change over time, under the pressures of gamification and audience capture. The meteoric flight and burnout of trad-masculine self-help author Jordan Peterson is a perfect example. Was he always the Christofascist supervillain he now plays on Ben Shapiro's streaming TV network, or has he twisted himself up ever more tightly to suit the tensions of his followers? Peterson originally rose to viral YouTube fame as a free-speech crusader after objecting to proposed Canadian human rights legislation that sought to protect trans people as a class—falsely arguing that "compelled speech" around preferred pronouns was a slippery slope toward Marxist-inspired mass murder. Young men flocked to his video and public talks on personal responsibility and how mythological traditions held clues to self-development.

Hard-core Peterson trackers will see the continuity of his themes over years. But assessing how his greatest moral panics became hits—selected and funded by an increasingly large set of megaphones—is a more complex matter. What we can observe, in general, is how rapidly that selection for more extreme content happens, how lucrative it is, and whether the influencer in question ever backtracks in the face of criticism.

Derek coined an aphorism for this process: "Watch what they say, and then watch what they sell." It's a distillation of the fact that on one hand, the influencer is expressing beliefs, ostensibly in good faith. On the other hand, they're also making bank. An imperfect calculus of how close their beliefs jibe with their products and services allows some insight into where the influencer falls on a spectrum from true believer on the pure end to shameless booster on the opportunistic end.

As this book goes to final edits, we're watching the Alex Jones–Sandy Hook settlement trial unfold. It's not hard to speculate on Jones's mental states or addiction issues, or to loathe the man and everything he stands for. But where we start to make headway on the believer-to-booster scale is in considering the yawning gap between his stated beliefs—that most domestic terrorist acts and school shootings are false flag events in a political-spiritual war—and his income streams.

Infowars generates strong ad revenue, but Jones's main cash flow comes from online sales of his branded health supplements. Almost unbelievably, he took time to pitch these products in court, while on the stand, in front of parents of the murdered Sandy Hook children who had sued him because he claimed for years that they didn't exist. Whether the reality deficit between erasing dead children and defaming their parents as crisis actors while hawking testosterone pills in open court is a sign of a psychiatric condition is up to the doctors. Whether it is shamelessly opportunistic is there for anyone to see.

WHICH BRINGS US to Joe Rogan.

Rogan, who infamously hosted his longtime friend Alex Jones twice, is also in the booster category of conspirituality, though the difference between what he says and what he sells is less stark. While Jones merely talks (yells, really) about health and wellness, Rogan is a legit hot yoga fan, obsessed with body optimization, ice bathing, meditating in isolation tanks, psychedelics, and supplements. And when COVID hit, he played a global role in spreading conspirituality vibes.

He got there by being a nine-hundred-pound gorilla in a new information ecosystem. He smashes the stats of big cable news, because listeners from various political demographics say they trust his affable, irreverent style, and a seeming open-mindedness that allows him to talk to anyone, about anything, for hours at a time. He's smart enough to ask engaging questions of A-list authors and academics—but as a stand-up comedian, he's also fluent in the lore of rock stars and the debauchery of Hollywood, and sees laugh-wow value in crypto-archeology and UFO cover-up stories.

Rogan was a Bernie Bro. He hosted firebrand progressive Dr. Cornel West. But Rogan also hosted Gavin McInnes, the founder of the violent alt-right street gang the Proud Boys, which played a central role in the deadly

Charlottesville Unite the Right rally in 2017, and later, the Capitol insurrection on January 6, 2021.

While Rogan started off in March of 2020 hosting epidemiologist Michael Osterholm for some science-informed analysis of the emerging pandemic, by January of 2022, in addition to a range of conspiracists, snake-oil peddlers, and right-wing anti-quarantine politicians, Rogan had hosted the holy trinity of discredited doctors and anti-vaccine COVID-profiteers: Robert Malone, Peter McCullough, and Pierre Kory.

On separate episodes, they each treated Rogan's audience to a three-hour deluge of medical misinformation about the dangers of vaccines, the advantages of "natural immunity," and the supposed lifesaving efficacy of the failed treatments hydroxychloroquine and ivermectin, which they claimed were suppressed by the government in collusion with Big Pharma.

Malone also said that Americans were experiencing a "mass formation psychosis" in response to COVID-19, which was similar to what Germans went through during the rise of Nazism. McCullough said that the pandemic was premeditated. Kory (who has the biggest networked ivermectin sales website in the world) and his fellow guest Bret Weinstein classified the evidence against ivermectin as the "crime of the century" and urged Rogan to declare their visit "the first-ever emergency episode" of the podcast. Affable Joe pushed back on none of these outrageous claims.

In the months between, Rogan gave guest Sanjay Gupta of CNN a well-prepared grilling using anti-vax talking points, and called out the mainstream media for not telling fat people to get fit if they wanted to survive COVID. He went public on social media about his own short-lived bout with the illness, and detailed his alt-med COVID-cure cocktail. Sports celebrities like UFC president Dana White and defiantly unvaccinated NFL quarterback Aaron Rodgers would go on to say that they consulted Rogan for expert advice when they tested positive.

Rogan advised healthy people who were twenty-one and younger and who work out not to get vaccinated against COVID. When he got COVID himself, he told his millions of followers he recovered using an expensive cocktail of treatments that included the ineffective drug ivermectin. He provided a Wild West megaphone for disgraced doctors with apocalyptic fetishes, and with health regimes to sell. His show was like *Shark Tank* for conspirituality.

By the time this book is in print, *The Joe Rogan Experience* podcast will be nearing its two-thousandth episode. Episodes run for hours, a long-form format that its host has pioneered. The sheer volume of content resists any final word on Rogan's personal political values or worldview on reality— beyond the sense that he seems to reflect and amplify the American zeitgeist as a whole. He's a mixed-martial-arts aficionado who has punched his way out of the category of influencer to blitz the epistemological infrastructure of a nation.

To take an economic metaphor: Rogan's podcast functions like the Walmart Supercenter that opens up on the access road to a midsized town. It's enormous. It's open late. It dries up the mom-and-pop shops in town. Parking is easy. You can buy anything there in a low-cost, frictionless consumer experience. But usually, you can't tell where the product comes from, and you won't know its quality until you get it home and use it.

Here's what we can say for certain about Joe Rogan: in the same way he was prescient about his winning podcasting style and its independent business model, he was also able to sniff out the shiniest bits of content for an anxious pandemic media market. But too often, that meant boosting misinformation to millions.

To honor the open-minded aura of his brand, he did host some sober public health voices in the mix. But over time his guest list has trended not only deeper into anti-vax, COVID-denialism, and conspiracism but also further into parroting right-wing talking points about quarantine, Biden, guns, and culture war moral panics. He emphasized his values shift in an interview about moving his business from California to Austin. "I moved to Texas because I want fucking freedom."

In terms of boosters vs. believers, Rogan is a unique case of a booster who seems to have become a believer, with enormous clout. In 2022, *Forbes* estimated his net worth to be $190 million.

IN THE HEART of many conspiritualists is a longing for a heroic identity. After all, they have awakened to pierce the veil of Big Pharma and institutional corruption. They are exposing the darkest secrets of hidden power. They are saving all the innocent children from diabolical abuse.

They seem driven by Martin Luther King Jr.'s notion that the arc of history is long, but it bends toward justice. But in their minds, the villains are journalists, scientists, and public health officials. They must preach a gospel of radical skepticism toward everything except their own paranoid and poorly evidenced style of reasoning. It's an intoxicating journey that converts ordinary thinkers into evangelists.

In an online religion, the hero of an empowerment epistemology both utilizes and is captured by the machines of online influence. Facts, evidence, and coherent analysis get sacrificed on the altar of gamification—the application of game-design elements that juice up previously nongaming activities. The gamer scores points and rises through levels of progress. The poster wins likes, shares, and followers. Both feel like winning. Conspiritualists gain mojo by exploiting the algorithmic exposure that values reactive shock value over truth.

But is the pandemic a game? Not to sci-comm directors. For them, it is a material disaster with no clear heroic end point. Conspirituality, however, adds a storyline and a selection of possible outcomes. Unlike the pandemic tweets of municipal public health offices—which never went viral—a gamified spiritual battle was far easier to boost.

Video view counts, blog post reads, and podcast downloads "game" conspirituality content. They give real-time feedback—gratifying or disappointing—that motivates creators' responses. It's addictive. And when these metrics are financialized through YouTube, Substack, or Patreon, the dollars-and-cents incentive can further radicalize content.

What we saw again and again—to be detailed in Part Three—is that the gamification of audience response to conspirituality content, in terms of popularity and money streams, consistently drives influencers toward more extreme ideas and beliefs. While so many people were trapped in quarantine, we watched influencers in the COVID era become trapped in a feedback loop in which their radicalizing followers encouraged and indulged their worst instincts and most grandiose self-perceptions—in the quest to become more effective and transcendent heroes.

PART THREE

GALLERY OF ROGUES

OUT OF HUNDREDS of possible contenders, there are ten figures who define and exemplify this surge of conspirituality that hit hard in 2020 and continues today. There's an old Indian art theory that Matthew learned a little about, called *ghandarva veda*. It states that any satisfying work of literature will engage the reader with a dynamic mixture of core emotions, or *rasas*, a word that also means "flavor." We hope our ten figures offer a similarly strange carnival of confusion, sadness, humor, disgust, and ultimately, shards of understanding.

In most cases, we have limited ourselves to A-list influencers. But as is the nature of social media, every influencer with a high follower count will have dozens of minor-league imitators sacrificing their integrity for low returns. Memorializing these smaller operators in a book for posterity could unfairly obscure the fact that many are themselves victims of indoctrination, caught up in a storm far bigger than they know.

Three themes repeat themselves over and over again in these stories. Conspiritualists fetishize science, philosophy, and community, but make a mess of all three.

On the science front, they preach about viruses as if they were illusory, the immune system as if it were magical, and view vaccines as suspicious. They are skeptical of conventional medicine, often sell unproven supplements, and, when they can't cherry-pick enough studies to support their biases, some of them invent imaginary forms of evidence.

Conspiritualists philosophize in a mania of mind-over-matter hyper-idealism. They preach the cognitive fallacies of "freshman skepticism"—which seeks to blank-slate all knowledge and hold evidence suspect, save for paranoid conjecture. They soothe themselves with "spiritual bypassing"—which seeks out abstract higher truths to avoid the messy facts, details, and legitimate human concerns of the ordinary world. And when the heat is on, when mass crises demand collective responses, they default to the crudeness of personal sovereignty and I-got-mine politics.

Conspiritualists bang on about community and tribe, while some engage in tactics familiar to cult researchers. Many of those who aren't running literal cults honed their community-building tactics in multi-level marketing schemes already populated by pseudoscience entrepreneurs and life coach grifters. They brought sales psychology, social media savvy, and seamless integration of content marketing, web sales, and email funnels. Living and moving in a world in which every contact is a sales opportunity, budding conspiritualists brought a bazooka to the public health communication knife fight.

You'll see these three themes woven through the stories of our influencers, each acting as gateways into the movement at large. Investment in one can lead to investment in the other two. Recruits can enter the fog of conspirituality through the pseudoscience of Rudolf Steiner. They can enter through the spiritual bypassing of *The Secret*, or *A Course in Miracles*, or the run-of-the-mill "love and light" aphorisms of popular yoga. Or they can skip the content altogether and get roped in by cultic dynamics. And as we'll see, in the strange case of the late Guru Jagat, all three are at play as she denies COVID, preaches the salvation of Kundalini Yoga, and influences her devotees' every decision.

CHAPTER 17

UPSCALE BONNIE AND CLYDE OF COVID DENIAL

IF YOU WANTED to pitch a series to a Netflix executive on how the conspirituality movement surged into global relevance during COVID-19, we doubt you'd come up with slicker stars than "holistic psychiatrist" Dr. Kelly Brogan and her (now-ex) husband Sayer Ji. Their whirlwind story has it all: romance, yogic superpowers, three hours on Joe Rogan's podcast, Satanic Panic, and international infamy. They also punched those algorithms hard, with their main site reaching one million views per month, and an online workshop group with over two thousand members who each paid up to $1,000 to sign up.

At the height of their Bonnie and Clyde run, Brogan and Ji mixed a cocktail of legitimate and illegitimate critiques of modern medicine, spiked with enough pseudoscience to prolong a global pandemic. Their COVID denialism spree unfolded against the pastel skies of Miami while Florida's case numbers exploded.

On March 11, 2020, *the same day* that the WHO declared a global pandemic, Brogan ditched her role as an alternative health critic of conventional psychiatry to cosplay as an epidemiologist. She posted a video selfie-sermon called "A Message to Dispel Fear" to a private online therapy group. Framed by palm trees swaying against azure skies, Brogan startled followers by declaring that germ theory was false, and by citing anthroposophist Tom Cowan and alt-health charlatan Joe Mercola. Ominously, she warned that the anti-COVID protection measures that public health officials around the world were only starting to figure out were akin to the "dehumanization agendas that preceded the Holocaust."

The beta-test audience for this dire message was familiar with Brogan's holistic psychiatry content, which combined a narrowing set of pharmaceutical interventions with a widening toolbox of yoga exercises and dietary rules. Some of her online group members had been her patients, and so were familiar with her views on the evils of pharmaceuticals and the wonders of giving birth at home, clean diet, yoga, coffee enemas, and an evangelical belief in one's natural divinity. Several group members worried in interviews with Matthew that Brogan's new take—that the emerging pandemic was yet another example of the same medical overreach that pathologized and disempowered them as women—would be dangerous for those in the group with mental health conditions. The next two weeks saw that danger realized on a public scale, as Brogan released her alarming sermon to the public and basked in the ensuing firestorm.

"WHEN I WENT INTO psychiatry, attended MIT and Cornell University," Brogan explains in one of her self-help books (co-authored with writing coach and ghostwriter Nancy Marriott), "never did I imagine that I'd come to shun the primary tool of my trade—namely, pharmaceuticals."

But she did, laying down her prescription pad for good in 2010. "I now take a holistic approach to helping people overcome their most crushing struggles, including those labeled as generalized anxiety, bipolar disorder, and major depressive disorder." She refers to herself as a "doctor of the soul," pinging the Greek etymology of the word *psychiatrist*.

Women seeking this more soulful health care had flocked to her swanky Manhattan practice. They were also attracted by her stinging criticism of medical misogyny in her field. "Depression, generalized anxiety, bipolar disorder, chronic fatigue," she once wrote of the diagnostics she was trained in, "are modern-day hexes" that cast a spell of fear manipulated by Big Pharma to sell pills. Conventional psychiatry, she asserted, is rooted in patriarchal and controlling attitudes that lead to women being overmedicated and silenced.

She was not entirely wrong. But like many conspiritualists, Brogan had figured out how to blend valid critiques with simplistic politics and mind-over-matter claims that reject mere materialist Western medicine. And her bold program of female empowerment didn't come cheap: in 2018, her initial consultation fee set patients back $4,187. Subsequent forty-five-minute appointments cost $570. Needless to say, it wasn't covered by most insurance companies.

Brogan had a Madison Avenue lewk, spoke in serene paragraphs, and worked Gwyneth Paltrow's Goop platform hard, holding court at pricey events and publishing articles about depression being caused by inflammation and emotional pain being eased through Kundalini Yoga. She hobnobbed with Natalie Portman, Carrie-Anne Moss, and Ricky Lake. Today, Brogan's Goop articles languish on webarchive.org, removed from the site after she started playing armchair COVID expert. Even a platform built on couture pseudoscience canceled her.

BROGAN'S NEW GOSPEL MIGHT have stalled out on alt-health Instagram if it weren't for her husband at the time, the extremely online Sayer Ji. Ji founded the pseudoscience research clearinghouse GreenMedInfo in 2008, after earning a bachelor's degree in philosophy from Rutgers and managing a health food store in Naples, Florida. As of 2022, Ji's site—a biohacker's index of 50,000 alt-health journal articles—draws up to 440,000 visitors per month. Ji claims his sometimes twice-daily newsletters, which flog a buffet of herbal remedies, anti-vax articles, and Bitcoin pitches, reach over 300,000 subscribers.

To all appearances, their skill sets and vibes fit together like lock and key. Brogan brought high-end degrees (from Cornell and MIT) and feminizing style to Ji's cluttered, ticky-tack DIY web assets. In turn, Ji expanded Brogan's halo through the powerful network of affiliate agreements he'd forged over years throughout the alt-health world. It was a dangerous combination.

In April 2020, barely a month after Brogan's debut as a COVID contrarian, she collaborated with Ji on launching the website questioningcovid .com, a disinformation hub for COVID denialists. On launch day they sat together in front of their webcam and high-end lighting to announce that their marriage was now at the center of a medico-spiritual revolution, and also promoted some new websites, including one advertising an (anti-) 5G Summit. (In this early stage of conspirituality, one prominent meme was that symptoms of the new coronavirus were actually a reaction to new 5G mobile phone technology being rolled out around the world as the first phase of a supposed techno-authoritarian takeover.)

The video was called "Love in the Time of Covid." In it they tag-teamed through their fears of vaccines as tracking mechanisms, useless PCR tests, and the horrors of submitting to the control of the nanny state. They presented the rejection of science on COVID and public health as a sign of spiritual maturity. Brogan finished up by leading followers through a tender but ghoulish visualization of nursing one's abused child-self.

"Pull up in your mind's eye," she murmured, eyes closed, "the image of yourself walking on a mountain path. And as you're walking you begin to hear the sounds of a child crying. And you walk over to this child that you find in the brush on the side of the path."

The child, Brogan explains, should be the same gender as the follower, perhaps to better identify oneself in the child's terror—which she and Ji have just stoked with their tales of global conspiracism.

"She has cuts and bruises on her body, and she's soiled. She's full of dirt. Her clothes are tattered, her hair is totally unbrushed. She has bruises on her face and she's inconsolably crying. She can't even verbalize what's going on. You try to ask and she just keeps crying."

The QAnon-tinged visualization coaches the follower to crouch down and cover the imagined child's shivering body with their own. When the child manages to say that they are scared, Brogan instructs the follower to point to the horizon to reveal a vision of the child's friends and family dancing in a flower-strewn valley lush with gardens and filled with music.

"Look how happy everyone is," Brogan breathes, winding down, "and you can feel her entire nervous system relax into the reality that is right before her eyes."

"Kelly is the most loving person I've ever known," Ji sighs as they wrap up, "and who's ever known me." He tells the camera that she has helped him transcend his toxic masculinity and access his sacred vulnerability.

FRAMING THEIR MARRIAGE in idealized terms was baked into the Brogan-Ji brand. In a blog post about their splashy wedding in November 2019, Brogan cast their bond as a transformational journey undertaken on behalf of those around them. "All of those affected by this seeming cataclysmic love happening," she wrote,

> would attest to there being equal measure of suffering and harmony emergent in this process. Our irrepressible connection has reconfigured our families,

former marriages, and unleashed an organizing force that has seemingly liberated all of us from too-small boxes we had placed ourselves in.

She dubbed their union Our Spiral Path.

By July 2020, Brogan and Ji were expanding the supposed influence of their marriage through their Community Is Immunity campaign to drive followers toward Brogan's subscription platform. They sat together in their pastel-styled Miami home. "We're starting to have a better sense of how important community is," Ji said, as Brogan gazed lovingly at his profile, "starting with our relationship to each other and ourselves and from there moving outward with you."

If we haven't underlined it enough, it's a good time to reiterate that charisma is a relational fog machine that obscures the details of what the charismatic influencer is doing and offering. This is how the content of an influencer can be ephemeral and transitive, how the conspiritualist can jump between paranoias about vaccines, 5G technology, and satanic rituals like a child playing hopscotch. It so happens that this is also how cult leaders flip from crisis to crisis, keeping their followers off-balance in everything except their dependence.

Accordingly, Kelly Brogan's real spiral path took her from a credentialed criticism of psychiatry to bad Holocaust comparisons, COVID denialism propaganda, and affiliate marketing for workshops in vaginal kung fu, cryptocurrency, and the pseudolaw of the sovereign citizen movement. The content is never really the point in this game. It's all about the flash, the mystique, and how the charismatic bond forms between influencer and follower in the parasocial space.

As their COVID-denialism machine was ramping up, Brogan published a high-end video documentary of her wedding day with Ji in November of the previous year. It opens with a drone pan of the cypress domes of the St. Sebastian River network in Florida. The shot merges into a ground-level tour of the ChoZen eco-resort. An event design company called Ritual Experiences has festooned the tents and the Buddha Garden and the Safari Camp with paper lanterns and tropical flower arrangements, and scheduled a day and night of trance dance and deep-eye-contact workshops. There's a cacao ceremony with angel cards. There are prayer circles around the

Cosmic Fire Pit. After the garlanded ceremony, Brogan and Ji drift away from their congregation on what looks like a 1920s mahogany runabout boat with polished brass fittings.

The film is the perfect setup for turning their relationship into a symbolic microcosm of the wholesome and sensual world that will protect them in ways that clinical medicine conspires to strip away. Their intense eye contact with each other is reminiscent of a common sexual iconography at play in the background of the yoga and wellness worlds. You can see it painted on the yoga studio walls in neo-traditional or cartoon-like form: Hindu gods and goddesses entwined in contemplative ecstasy, splashing their followers with the juices of their love.

As a private affair, the wedding video presents what seems like a perfect day for wealthy organic-lifestyle Floridians. But by posting the video to her site and YouTube in the midst of a pandemic alongside her COVID-denialism materials, Brogan crosses a line into something we can call wellness pornography—a key marketing conceit in conspirituality.

Wellness pornography is the production of attractive images and beguiling ideas of personal well-being, offered to the consumer for the sake of vicarious pleasure. Wellness pornography allows Brogan and Ji's followers to engage in the pleasure of their relationship performance, to forget about the complexity of biological sciences or social determinants of health, and to forget about the negative outcomes of fashionable wellness consumption.

Projecting a faux-intimate and unrealistic soulmate relationship in which love, wealth, and holistic health are all aspects of spiritual awakening doesn't help anyone. Associating external indicators of spiritual status with personal virtue is bunk. Perpetuating the notion of a mind-over-matter relationship to money and physical health is privileged nonsense.

And yes, the money makes everything shine. The wedding is high-end. ChoZen's accommodations start with glamping tents for $400 per night. And as Ji waits for the "Community Is Immunity" livestream to start, he murmurs, while watching the audience stats climb, "My immune system is getting boosted right now, just counting the numbers."

A MONTH AFTER BROGAN spilled her Holocaust oppression fantasy in March of 2020, the same theme started turning up in Republican talking points.

On April 16, three weeks into the COVID shutdown orders issued by Idaho governor Brad Little, Idaho state representative Heather Scott told a Houston podcaster that the governor was Little Hitler, and suggested that the shelter-in-place provisions were authoritarian and genocidal.

"I mean, that's no different than Nazi Germany," Scott said, "where you had government telling people, 'You are an essential worker or a nonessential worker,' and the nonessential workers got put on a train."

Four days later, the Dallas Holocaust and Human Rights Museum issued a harsh rebuke of Scott (without naming her) and anyone else tempted to make the false comparison. "This accusation is as disgraceful as it is historically insupportable and morally reprehensible," the statement says.

If Kelly Brogan was insensitive and inflammatory about the Holocaust, she wasn't alone. Canadian anti-lockdown activist Susan Standfield gained notoriety by selling T-shirts emblazoned with the word "COVIDCAUST" over a yellow Star of David. Standfield is the cofounder of an anti-vax group, 100 Million Moms, which boasts seventeen thousand Instagram followers. They sell tote bags with their logo and baby onesies printed with the words "Freedom Fighter."

Between Rudolf Steiner's fantasies and the blood libel that haunts so many conspiracy theories, antisemitism is in the water that soaks the roots of conspirituality. But some modern conspiritualists launder the theme, and turn it on its head, appropriating the victim status, even while keeping the old tropes alive.

Do their tears lie? Stephanie Sibbio, Standfield's 100 Million Moms cofounder, wept openly at a Toronto anti-vax protest in the summer of 2021 over the delusion she was being poisoned by other people getting vaccinated. Then she went on Instagram to get in there and make that Holocaust all about her. "As a collective human race," she said,

> we have to know the history so that we can remind people. They've forgotten that the fifteen years leading up to the Holocaust looked exactly like it does today. The people who don't wear masks are the people who are the lepers, the spreaders of disease. We're not allowed to stand on the grass. We're not allowed to sit on the bench. We're not allowed to use the toilet.

Alongside the ignorance and privilege of Brogan pretending that a pogrom is coming for her in Miami, and the absurdity of Sibbio pretending she can't use the toilet, we also have to keep in mind just how asinine the internet is. Back in 1990, the American internet ethics lawyer Mike Godwin proposed Godwin's Law of Nazi Analogies, writing in *Wired*: "As an online discussion grows longer, the probability of a comparison involving Nazis or Hitler approaches one."

It's germane to note that Sayer Ji built a substantial chunk of his advertising outreach on junky memes, which currently litter his Telegram feed with an incoherent mess of tasteless jokes and random Holocaust comparisons. Beneath the slick marketing, Ji's media carries the echo and energy of the early chan boards, where LOLs trumped substantive discussion—all for clicks. Brogan's Holocaust appropriation laundered this impulse for bourgeois sale.

WITHIN MONTHS OF "Love in the Time of Covid," Ji began explicitly pushing his followers toward the macabre fantasy of rescuing abused children by using the QAnon recruitment phrase "Take the red pill." In August 2020, Ji threw the weight of his site behind *Plandemic 2*—the follow-up film to the breakthrough pseudo-documentary that catapulted the anti-vax movement to mainstream attention—with a promo video in which he lauded the director, Mikki Willis, as his very close friend and hero. Ji also noted that Willis's star subject, anti-vax activist Dr. Judy Mikovits, had served on the GreenMedInfo advisory board.

And almost exactly a year after Brogan had pressed Publish on "A Message to Dispel Fear," the couple was named by the UK-based Center for Countering Digital Hate as members of the Disinformation Dozen, which, by the Center's analysis, is responsible for up to 65 percent of all anti-vax propaganda online. That report made its way deep into the Biden administration. On July 16, 2021, the White House press secretary Jen Psaki took the podium to say that stopping the Disinformation Dozen was a life-or-death issue that tech platforms must address.

Far too late, Brogan and Ji were thrown off Twitter, Facebook, and Instagram as the platforms cracked down on anti-vax and COVID misinformation. If they are visualizing healing their abused inner children today, they're doing it on the right-wing social media haven of Telegram, where they retain a small percentage of their former Facebook follower count, but also more freedom to radicalize their rhetoric through an unending firehose of posts. More recently, and perhaps reflecting a narrowing of income streams post-deplatforming, Ji has been promoting cryptocurrency and blockchain projects, touted as beyond the reach of mainstream moderation.

In May 2021, not two months after losing his mainstream social access, Ji was interviewing the 1990s Satanic Panic celebrity Cathy O'Brien, who claims to have been sex-trafficked by a Philippines-based CIA operative to a satanic cabal that included Gerald Ford, Canadian prime ministers Pierre Elliott Trudeau and Brian Mulroney, Manuel Noriega, Lamar Alexander, Reagan's drug czar Bill Bennett, Dick Cheney, Hillary Clinton, and Bill, who she describes as constantly snorting cocaine.

Ji introduced O'Brien as a beacon of courage for both himself and Brogan.

THE SPECTACLE OF BROGAN and Ji's descent into conspirituality mayhem provides an almost perfect template for how charismatic leaders can blend New Age promises with medico-political terrors in the gamified world of social media. Nearly every story we cover in this book—whether about the producers of conspirituality or its consumers—borrows tricks from the Brogan-and-Ji playbook: They entered the theater with earned social capital—Brogan in feminist-flavored psychiatry and Ji as a "do your own research" disrupter of medical bureaucracy. They built their followings from populations alienated by clinical indifference and vulnerable to the predatory American model of for-profit care.

With charismatic flair, Brogan simply transposed her critique of psychiatry onto epidemiology, in which she has no training, setting herself up as the loyal opposition to COVID experts—as though science was conducted by parliament, and could be verified by spiritual insight.

Neither Brogan nor Ji was shy about frightening the vulnerable people who followed them, or casually letting conspiracism enter their content, or offering soothing meditations for that fright. They marketed their marriage as the center of a new enlightened society, in which community is immunity— not vaccines.

And with that spectacle of their sacred union, Brogan and Ji performed a remarkable bait and switch on what Brogan decries as the authoritarianism of daddy government and mommy medicine. Speaking to their followers as if they were children, Brogan presented as Mommy Mystic to Ji's Daddy Cyberpastor. They clearly channeled the existential stakes of conspirituality:

"We are entering a post-science world," Brogan wrote. "And like when wars were fought and blood was shed over seeming differences in religious doctrine, ideology, and faith—we are now in a spiritual war, and your body is the battlefield."

As 2021 MERGED with 2022, Brogan's social feeds indicated all was not well on their spiral path. Suddenly there were posts about the crucible of monogamy, and alchemizing pain, and then self-love. The duet sermons with Ji evaporated.

Sources close to the family confirmed the couple's estrangement. But the charisma machine, whether in union or solitude, kept chugging. Brogan posted a catchy tagline in a meme with a hot pink background: "loving you is leaving me, leaving you is loving me." She posted a video dancing suggestively, hinting at a new income stream. "I hired an Erotic Blueprints coach," said the caption, "and I turned away from the clown world of current events and tuned into my own sensual intimacy and self-pleasuring practices."

"I told myself, consciously," she wrote, "that Eros—embodied sensuality—is what could save the world...and perhaps is the only force that can." Followers should stay tuned, she suggested, for brand new content.

CHAPTER 18

NEW AGE Q

JUST A FEW DAYS after Kelly Brogan went corona-rogue, Charles Eisenstein—her good friend and New Age pundit—published an essay with a punny coronavirus title: "The Coronation." It was an epic conspirituality ballad, sung in the key of Burning Man Thought Leader. It reached over 15 million followers on Facebook, and was tweeted out to 4.5 million users by Jack Dorsey, then CEO of Twitter, with a single-word endorsement: "Remarkable."

Eisenstein argued that the pandemic offered a transformative opportunity, if only people could open themselves up to the spirit of "not knowing," and recognize that the reflex of control—as embodied by mitigation measures like social distancing—would only deny us our humanity. The essay, published just four days after the WHO declared COVID to be pandemic, was some nine thousand words long. But—lest anyone think it was an original response to a novel crisis—Eisenstein beta-tested this same critique of quarantine measures as being fascist during the 2016 Zika outbreak.

Having no scientific training didn't stop Eisenstein from cherry-picking bits of early reporting on death rates and comorbidities, which, according to him, showed that the COVID-19 pandemic was not a grave public health crisis. "Separation from normality," he argued, "followed by a dilemma, breakdown, or ordeal, followed...by reintegration and celebration," is a spiritual doorway that "follows the template of initiation."

"Now the question arises," he goes on: "Initiation into what? What is the specific nature and purpose of this initiation? The popular name for the pandemic offers a clue: coronavirus. A corona is a crown. 'Novel coronavirus pandemic' means 'a new coronation for all.'" The wordplay was popular among erstwhile progressive and science-literate demographics in the alt-health and New Age worlds.

Over the next eighteen months, Eisenstein published a string of essays that crystallized his role as a kind of COVID mystic for conspirituality intellectuals. The thrust was equanimity in the face of terror. The content was bullshit, dressed up as nuance.

He proposed that conspiracy theories are truths that haven't yet been accepted. Therefore, labeling people as conspiracy theorists was a way of marginalizing intuitives. It sounds like a reasonable argument, except that real conspiracies are discovered through evidence, and pushing theories without evidence isn't intuitive so much as publicly disruptive.

Eisenstein also argued that Indigenous ways of knowing the world and healing the body challenge the principles and technologies of modern medicine, and that his white readers should somehow adopt them. In the context of COVID, however, pitting premodern Indigenous wisdom against modern public health is more of a narcissistic fantasy than an on-the-ground reality. By September 2021, the CDC found that among racial demographics, American Indians and Alaska Natives boasted the highest vaccine uptake in the United States, after an initial period of COVID devastation in their communities. "It's embedded in our values that we don't just think about ourselves," said Navajo Nation member Leonela Nelson, of the Johns Hopkins Center for Indigenous Health. In explaining the vaccination success, researchers cited the power of actual, pragmatic bonds that some wellness influencers only point at: respect for elders, community, and a desire to maintain tribal sovereignty.

In other essays, Eisenstein suggested that QAnon stories have meaning even if they aren't true. It might be a competent argument in an undergrad seminar on myths or Bible stories, but not when applied to an antisemitic fever dream. He said that asking people to restrict their movements during the pandemic was a plot to drain them of all desire and capacity to rebel against the state. And he praised a French commune that follows the teachings of 1970s-era New Age cult leader Adi Da and *A Course in Miracles* as a model for communal living in the age of social breakdown.

Throughout, Eisenstein mobilized a facile empathy for all sides that went far beyond being sensitive to the concerns of conspiracy theorists and those hesitant to take the vaccine, to advocate for a kind of sublime relativism in which anything can happen and anything can be true. We cannot fully understand the pandemic, his logic went, but we can see that our responses to it are panicked overreactions that betray our inner authoritarianism, as well as the bankruptcy of every institution—except that of the galaxy-brained pundit. In an interview with Sayer Ji, he pointed to the medicine he does believe in. His wife Stella, he explained, does not believe that the body is a machine over which physicians should exert more control. Stella is an acupuncturist who has developed what she calls Resonant Attention. Eisenstein said that "she's simply holding a field in which healing happens. In the inner reality of wholeness, the miracles happen."

It's unclear why Eisenstein escalated his content during the COVID period. Perhaps he felt dissatisfied in remaining above the battleground. Perhaps his nuance was becoming less marketable in the carnival of COVID content. Whatever the reason, within eighteen months of publishing "The Coronation," Eisenstein helped to make a film that suggested COVID denialists were like aliens who had come to save Earth from human wickedness. And to ring in 2022, he presided over a mask-off all-night New Year's Eve party at the home of a supporter in Ithaca, New York. In his after-dinner talk, Eisenstein wondered aloud whether the pedophile elite would ever be punished.

IN THE 1950s, Eisenstein might have found his groove as a novelist or poet, tackling postwar angst and yearning for ecological renewal. But as a New Age freelance public speaker in the era of self-help retreats and listening circles, he's carved out a niche market in transformational nonfiction for educated seekers. The grandiose vibe is on full display in his book titles: *The Yoga of Eating*, *Sacred Economics*, *The Ascent of Humanity*, *The More Beautiful World Our Hearts Know Is Possible*, and *Climate: A New Story*.

Eisenstein has a bachelor's degree in math and philosophy from Yale. He's not a nutritionist, economist, anthropologist, or environmental scientist. But he can play all four roles on the workshop circuit, and can conjure enough credibility to be introduced as a "scholar" by Oprah Winfrey on her *Super Soul* podcast. And over the past two decades, he's built an audience that seems to expect him to spontaneously pontificate about anything, as long as he keeps it long. COVID-19 had created a panicked vacuum of existential dimensions, and Eisenstein was part of the New Age content-production engine that rushed in to fill the gap.

Eisenstein's technique was sophisticated enough to cross political lines as a form of public philosophy. It could plausibly deny indulging in conspiracy theories—even while hitting all the conspirituality keynotes. It used a dumbass version of postmodern thought to cheapen and reduce life-and-death issues down to problems of "narrative."

The success of "The Coronation" led to a string of podcast appearances, including one on the *QAnon FAQ* platform, run by Sean Morgan, a self-described digital soldier who hosts a battery of QAnon, evangelical, and sovereign citizen guests. Morgan prides himself on questioning "the official narrative from the mainstream media about QAnon, Covid-19, BLM, Riots, Lockdowns, Masks, Vaccines and Election Integrity." His podcast feed features interviews with top QAnon influencers, and an episode with the chilling title "How to Redpill Your Mom #QAnon."

Morgan asked Eisenstein for the 101 on his work leading up to his hit essay. His response was a conspirituality primer. "Everything that I speak and write about," he said,

> is basically an application of a conceptual tool that I use to understand the world…that we are in a time of transition from an old story of separation into a new story of interconnection, interdependency, interbeing, where we're not understanding ourselves as separate individuals in a world of others. My work basically examines how our current civilization is built on the story of separation, how that story generates crises that intensify with time, offering humanity an initiation or a birthing into a new story.

So for this writer, COVID-19 is just another crisis story among crisis stories, told by the deluded. But with a little rewriting, it can become a story of self-awareness and salvation. Eisenstein doesn't need to be interested in the pandemic *per se*. He certainly doesn't need training in epidemiology to sermonize about what the world should do about a novel coronavirus. His gig is to co-opt *discourse about* the novel coronavirus as a branding exercise.

What does that brand say, with its single tool? Eisenstein has used the "story of separation" motif to generate a lazy nondualism that pretends political conflict can be resolved through spiritual integration. This leaves him free to take any position, because it's all just stories. For example, conspiracy theories might be showing us an alternative history of the world that offers not a factual truth, but a mythological truth about the nature of human societies and the imagination.

This sounds okay, insofar as conspiracy theories tend to draw on partially revealed facts and stories tethered to shadows in the social psyche. But in a 2013 essay, Eisenstein curls this argument into a New Age manifestation feedback loop, wondering whether "our emotions and beliefs actually attract experiential data that fits them," and whether "patterns of events are drawn to history because we need them to flesh out conspiracy theories and give expression to the psychological energies driving those theories." Ironically, Eisenstein is predicting his own motivated approach to COVID-19 conspiracism, along with the pseudoscientific method of conspirituality as a whole.

There's a ton of COVID-19 conspirituality writing that's rife with pseudoscience, cognitive fallacies, and spiritual bypassing. But with Eisenstein's pandemic output—which escalated from "The Coronation" to full-blown cross-marketing with multimillionaire anti-vax influencers—there's something else going on, related to its philosophical pretense and emotional ambivalence. There's a willingness to use a global crisis to exercise one's singular conceptual tool, which just happens to dismiss the expertise of actual epidemiologists in dangerous ways. There's a willingness to write nine thousand words about a pandemic and for none of them to be "public health," to use the word "I" thirty times, and "our" sixty-six, as if the essay was speaking for everyone, and not a narrow but influential slice of white American privilege and hipsterism.

And then there's the skill to do it all with writing that's elegant enough to capture hundreds of thousands of liberals, plus Ivanka Trump. In June, the First Daughter would quote the essay in a video commencement address recorded for Wichita State University Tech (which was ultimately never played due to student backlash):

"COVID-19 is like a rehab intervention that breaks the addictive hold of normality. When the crisis subsides, we might have occasion to ask whether we want to return to normal."

Links between Eisenstein and the Trump family deepened when, after the 2016 election, Eisenstein called for empathy toward Trump voters, and quoted Kelly Brogan calling Donald Trump a "wolf in wolf's clothing"—which might be better than the Clinton alternative: the wolf of business-as-usual in the sheep's clothing of progressive pretense.

EISENSTEIN'S SIGNATURE book from 2013, *The More Beautiful World Our Hearts Know Is Possible* ends with a fable he first published in blog form in 2009. "A Gathering of the Tribe" tells the tale of a band of aliens who "lived in a state of enchantment and joy that few of us today dare to believe could exist."

One day the shaman of the tribe calls them together to let them know that Earth needs their help. Humans have fallen into confusion and corruption, and they need help from beyond. To be of service, the shaman explains, the aliens will have to take human form, and give up their natural wisdom to fully connect with human suffering. They will retain their intuition, he says, and this will enlighten the world. It will be a trial, but they will have celestial help.

The shaman allays the aliens' concerns that the task may be too difficult. "I know it will work," he tells them, "because I have done it many times before. Many have already been sent to earth, to live human lives, and to lay the groundwork for the mission you will undertake now. I've been practicing! The only difference now is that many of you will venture there at once. What is new in the time you will live in, is that the Gatherings are beginning to happen."

A few weeks before Eisenstein held court at that New Year's Eve party in Ithaca, he recorded this alien tribe story in the podcasting studio of Aubrey Marcus, the multimillionaire founder of the Onnit fitness and supplement empire. Marcus published the reading to YouTube as the soundtrack under an animation that followed the story with ethereal figures making their descent.

The visuals, created by an anime artist whose other illustration work features a lot of very young nude women, are evocative and hypnotic, designed to evoke a dreamlike trance in the viewer that plugs into an intuitive and emotional sense of revelatory significance. The viewers are encouraged to identify as the hero of the cartoon—the lost, tearful, lonely young woman longing for community and purpose, and to be reawakened to her cosmic destiny. Along the way, she must dodge technology, pills, and hypodermic syringes.

"The volunteers gathered in a circle, and the shaman went to each one." This is how the story ends. "The last thing each was aware of was the shaman blowing smoke in his face. They entered a deep trance and dreamed themselves into the world where we find ourselves today."

The animation fades to live action, revealing Marcus and Eisenstein sitting across from each other, locked in a mutual gaze. "Here we are," they say to each other, placing themselves in the story as savior aliens sent to wake up the world. The video has captured some 950,000 views.

EISENSTEIN HAS DONE REMARKABLY well as a New Age freelancer, putting out an endless stream of blog posts and podcast appearances over many years. His book sales total over eighty thousand copies. He made it to Oprah. But leaning into QAnon territory by making crass comparisons between lockdown measures and the Holocaust was a step too far for his publishing house, North Atlantic Books. Twelve days after Eisenstein dropped an essay called "Mob Morality and the Unvaxxed," North Atlantic's Tim McKee issued a rebuke, and a commitment. The essay—eventually shared over six thousand times on Facebook—was "harmful, hyperbolic and antisemitic," McKee wrote in a statement dated August 13, 2021. North Atlantic would thereafter donate 100 percent of the net profits of Eisenstein's books to three social justice organizations.

In an email, McKee told us that the incident had prompted a policy shift at his house, and that they would be vetting authors more carefully for health-related misinformation. "This also includes," he wrote, "viewing health and healing books through different justice lenses (racial, disability, class, etc.), given the way that disinformation and conspirituality impact, intersect with, and take advantage of communities in different ways."

Eisenstein losing support from North Atlantic wasn't as high stakes as Brogan getting canned from Goop. But Eisenstein must have seen his own blood in the water, and, like many contrarians, began to show an increased interest in independent monetization. Unlike Brogan, Eisenstein couldn't retreat into the digital network of Sayer Ji—but there was Substack. The week after North Atlantic posted its statement, Eisenstein declared that he had migrated all of his writing over to the subscription-based platform.

It was a move that rhymed with a general pattern we saw accelerate during the COVID era. We can call it the Broken Mirror Effect. As conspiracy theories gained mainstream traction, their theorists faced increasing pressure to break through all social media guardrails, and whatever vestiges of institutional validation they still retained. Starting in the summer of 2020, establishment news organizations ran in-depth critical profiles of many of the figures we cover in this book. But as soon as that *New York Times* or *Atlantic* or *Vanity Fair* article appeared, the influencers' followers suddenly had another reason to distrust mainstream media. Filter bubbles narrowed, and echo chambers droned with single notes, and if the media was a mirror, it continued to shatter and throw off incongruent prisms.

If a fringe anti-vax doctor got disinvited from conferences, or had their license suspended, or had their papers rejected by journals, they could always retreat to YouTube. If they violated the terms of service there, they could retreat again to platforms like BitChute—an unregulated video hosting website launched to get around YouTube's community guidelines. It's one of the right-wing alternatives to mainstream social media platforms that include Telegram, MeWe, Gab, the now-defunct Parler, and Trump's own Truth Social. Sayer Ji anticipated it all, not only by working to build Telegram streams but also by investing in a parallel internet project based on blockchain technology. All have been favored retreats for conspiritualists, when they feel the approaching heat of Facebook moderation.

Every time a follower count fragments under the mainstream ban hammer, an influencer's total reach declines—along with scrutiny from the public, and the need to be more broadly accountable. What rises, arguably, are the parasocial bonds with followers, strengthened through the economy of subscription. A self-selected audience can reflect an influencer's now-isolated status back to them as a sign of ingenious heroism that makes their work all the more important. If Facebook kicks you off for narcissistically spreading misinformation you can find a space where nothing but your narcissism will matter.

Of course, the Broken Mirror Effect doesn't always reduce reach and audiences. With luck, one of those shards can become a magnifying glass, concentrating light into a burning stream. A single bro-caster, without any expertise in medicine or public health or religious studies, with no editorial support or oversight, but a huge following through his stand-up comedy and commentarial career in cage fighting, can become a vector for conspirituality without even necessarily believing in it.

Joe Rogan, as we've outlined, isn't a conspirituality influencer per se, which is why he doesn't get a dedicated chapter in this book. His function is enabling: he provides an entrepreneurial yang to the yin of content providers like Eisenstein, and marshals a Wild West influence network into which charismatics who lose institutional support from publishers or medical colleges can fall...and hit the ground running. So it went during the pandemic that Rogan's Austin studio became a fusion cell for every major bad and dangerous idea out there, from vaccine efficacy to the nonexistent benefits of ivermectin.

Eisenstein hasn't made it onto *The Joe Rogan Experience* as of this writing, but by teaming up with Aubrey Marcus—Rogan's business partner and fellow Austin bro—he's getting awfully close. And Marcus is a good match, given that his interests and values are much more overtly New Age, and that he has some education that brings him into Eisenstein's league. Marcus even fancies himself a writer, although he limits himself to QAnon-inspired poetry slam material. As Marcus declaims in his smooth alpha-male voice, in a poetry video called "The FORGOTTEN Voices of The Pandemic Will Have You in Tears":

> For the five million trafficked slaves,
> The little boys and girls
> who don't have a voice.
> who don't have a choice.
> Bought and sold...
>
> ...because they are moist.

He holds the text of his verse open on his phone and conducts his beats with his free hand. The microphone glints before him, and the contours of his mustard-hued muscle shirt stand out against a shadowed backdrop. The video cuts from his rugged face to sad-eyed, now-starving children. The score slows down into contemplative synthesizers, but speeds up with taiko drumming when the stock footage of Martin Luther King Jr. starts to roll.

Marcus's themes in this slickly produced video from January 2021 hit all the QAnon keynotes. The world is corrupted by media, vaccines, child sex trafficking, and environmental poisons. The chosen can be saved by rising up, and saying the word "freedom" with the right intonation. But there's something off about it all. With Eisenstein, there's something earned about the content. Some kind of wizened melancholia. But it's hard to put a finger on what Marcus brings to the table, besides self-satisfaction.

He's very proud of this poem, which runs through a laundry list of modern abominations—"pay your taxes, get your vaxes"—post-political aspirations. "We are ready now for the boy to become a man, for 'United' to return to the States, for blue and red to blend together into royal purple like the kings and queens we are." It took a lot for him to lay this all out there. The day before he dropped it, he posted a vulnerable behind-the-scenes video of his wife gazing into his eyes, tapping his chest, and saying "Put it in your heart." And that's really where the poem should have stayed, because it's such garbage. You have to wonder how it didn't sink the man's brand, or send him into a shame spiral.

Marcus doesn't need to be as convincing as Eisenstein. He comes from money. Mostly oil money—around $80 million of it on his father's side. He graduated from the University of Richmond with a degree in philosophy and classics, but has no employment history outside of his own ventures. By all appearances, he can live a life free from material pressures, and with access to start-up cash for a string of lifestyle companies, peaking with his CrossFit and fitness supplement brand Onnit, cofounded with Rogan.

Onnit was sold to Unilever in 2021 for anywhere from $100 million to $400 million, leaving the forty-year-old with nothing to gain but self-actualization. And he really goes for it. Biohacking, performance optimization, ayahuasca in Costa Rica, lots of podcast episodes about polyamory, monogamy, sex magick, and masturbation. Marcus inhabits a world of entitlement conspirituality. It's a rarified place in which matters of politics and the soul can be played at like a hobby, while people—including a lot of young women—surround you to tell you how wonderful you are, and while you gather top content providers around you to make you look smarter.

Eisenstein's breakout moment as the Marcus court philosopher came in 2021 as a coach for Marcus's life coaching program, Fit for Service. The weekend featured intrusive eye-contact sessions, a ritual dance for the 150-odd participants who dressed up in pseudo-Indigenous garb and war paint, and a keynote address by Eisenstein, in which he compared participants—who pay up to $20,000 per year to attend the full program, including retreats—to the humble but "unkillable" dandelions in a field.

CHAPTER 19

THE CURSED GOLDEN GIRL

FOR ABOUT TWELVE MINUTES every day, Dr. Christiane Northrup invites you into her gracious farmhouse in Yarmouth, Maine. You sit in a wingback chair in her study. Through the Facebook video window, you can almost smell the essential oils diffusing. It feels like a refuge from the pandemic, and all the panic about it. You admire her silk scarf and chunky necklace. Glass figurines twinkle on the bookshelves. She entertains, breezily shifting between wit, worry, and grandmotherly advice. She's funny and wry and a little bawdy. She tells you about what the angel-channeling YouTubers said that day, as if it were the neighborhood gossip.

Northrup has clout. She's a retired ob-gyn and women's alternative health icon, author of the bestselling *Women's Bodies, Women's Wisdom*, first published in 1994. She's a top MLM guru as well, and as of 2011 has belonged to the "Million Dollar Club" of the Usana supplements company, meaning she earns at least $1 million in yearly sales. MLM success runs in the Northrup family, starting with Christiane's mother Edna, and continuing with her daughter Kate—a life coach whose books *Money, A Love Story* and *Do Less* teach a Marie Kondo take on the prosperity gospel, telling women how to earn more while working less through changing their thought patterns.

Northrup's mainstream media presence has been formidable. "Her rise to the stratosphere," writes ob-gyn Dr. Jen Gunter, who has tracked Northrup's pseudoscience for years, "came via Oprah, at least 12 appearances, and eight PBS specials. The dual authority of Oprah and PBS is something to behold. Oprah makes you a household name and PBS makes people believe you have been vetted by academia."

But regardless of fame and reach, this Northrup Facebook page feels cozy and intimate. Northrup hands you a cup of chamomile-lavender tea. *The world is raging out there*, goes the message. *Everything has gone mad! People think there's a pandemic on! All of the sleeping ones are paralyzed with fear, complying with a satanic vaccination agenda. But*—she arches a blotchy painted eyebrow and smiles knowingly—*you don't have to concern yourself with all of that. There are scientific papers out there that say viruses are harmless. And you don't have to watch the mainstream news.*

The most important part, she intimates, *is that we're ascending to the next dimension. All of us, light warriors together. This is what all of this women's wisdom is for. We are sovereign. We are starseeds. The local sheriffs will protect us from the mask and vaccine mandates. It's really happening!*

If all of this transformation gives you a headache, the good doctor can recommend a nice hot bath with alfalfa greens and scrubbing yourself down with Dr. Bronner's Peppermint Pure-Castile Soap. Or you can buy helpful supplements through her helpful service. Or you can listen to her play her harp.

Welcome to the *Golden Girls* LARP of Dr. Christiane Northrup, who uses her Betty White–esque charm in faux-liberal ways that Betty White herself, RIP, would have abhorred.

Northrup is one of the most endearing, horrifying, and influential conspiritualists on our timeline. Endearing as a grandmother offering hormone-balancing tinctures and relationship advice. Horrifying to the thousands of followers she's gathered over the decades who have watched her spiral as a leader in alternative women's health into a mania, pulling thousands more with her. And influential. Given the sheer scope of her reach, she has become a primary vector of QAnon and COVID-19 conspiracism into mainstream spaces.

But you would never know it, listening to her play her big golden harp on Facebook live. Usually she improvises. One time it was "Greensleeves."

BACK IN THE 1990S, there weren't very many ob-gyns talking frankly with their patients about self-care, or how to deal with the difficulty of achieving orgasm, or about how menopause was a journey of possibilities. Over Zoom, we spoke with one of our listeners, Tasha Savage, who told us what seems to be a common story about how compellingly Northrup spoke to these issues, and how rare it was at the time.

With a degree in women's history and feminist theory, Savage always had her ear to the ground for data and wisdom that would feel empowering. "We came out of the 1980s," she remembers, "we were working." Little attention was paid to one's inner life and personal journey. In the 1990s, Savage said, a new "girl power" theme gave value to the idea that women should take care of themselves, "but nobody really did."

For Savage, Northrup stood out as a new breed of feminist thinker who challenged social norms around endless busyness and productivity, and made room for a creative appreciation of pleasure, mythopoetic growth, and a healthy acceptance of change. Also, Northrup was ultra-pragmatic, and funny. Savage still laughs at one of her menopause tell-em-like-it-is gags: "Your twenty-year-old body wrote a check that your fifty-year-old body can't cash."

Savage inhaled all of Northrup's materials and followed her avidly into the social media era. She was vaguely aware of some New Age principles hovering in the background. Northrup would refer, for example, to ovulation being ruled by the moon, or the idea that "disease is not created until a woman is frustrated at effecting changes that she needs to make in her life." But Savage had grown up in and rejected the Catholic Church, and had a pretty solid reflex for deflecting tripe. Her feminism wasn't about to replace one set of religious beliefs with another. She was happy to pluck out the more solid gynecological advice, and let the rest lie.

Most of Savage's friends were of the same mindset as well. Which is why all hell broke loose in 2015 when, in a Facebook group hosting participants in an Integrative Nutrition online course, Northrup suddenly—and without any warning that anyone could glean—came out as an anti-vax activist.

"She didn't go easy," Savage recalls. "She didn't say, 'I'm starting to really think about vaccines and I'm really starting to wonder...' It was hard core." Savage was shocked by the message, which amounted to "You are a shitty parent if you vaccinate your kids."

Beyond the obvious anti-science stance, Savage and her friends remember being dismayed at the hypocrisy of someone who had built her brand on the value of self-inquiry and personal choice. "You told our inner goddesses to decide what's right for our kids," Savage remembers commenting, pointing out that suddenly, according to Northrup, a parent's choice to vaccinate their children couldn't be what the inner goddess ordered.

* * *

ON APRIL 4, 2020, Northrup began her series of over one hundred Facebook videos that she soon grouped under the tag "The Great Awakening." The phrase has a long history in American evangelicalism, denoting three distinct revivalist movements between the early eighteenth and early twentieth centuries that focused on moral renewal and generated waves of charismatic preachers and cults, united in their anticipation of the savior's imminent return. (The term was also repurposed by QAnon in 2019, if not earlier, to predict a mass conversion or red-pilling event.)

She opened her first Great Awakening installment with a reflection on the numerological significance of the date. She announced that a portal is opening up, and those who joined her for an online meditation event at 10:45 EST could walk through it with her.

"If we can get over a million people meditating at the same time," she said, "this can change the entire planet in the best possible way." Northrup tipped her hat to Aries people, starseeds (who believe they are advanced intergalactic spiritual beings with cosmic scientific knowledge), and truthers, saying that this Great Awakening was a rebirth for everybody, and advising followers to take information from "many different sources."

In the caption to the video, she linked to a newsletter from a "global decentralised group of Lightworkers working on World Peace."

The newsletter was a catalog of disinformation, slathered in QAnon and evangelical dog whistles. It falsely claimed that three million people had died from radiation poisoning in Wuhan, China. And the cause was clear: "The corrupt elite and dark forces never cease in furthering their dark agendas," it said, "which is evidenced by the recent global coronavirus scare / potential false flag to mask their 5G weaponry and attempt at mandating bio-chipping vaccines and the further enslavement and eradication of mankind."

But all was not lost! "There are Legions of Light Beings that have entered our galaxy at this time to assist us in our ascension and help direct this high dimensional light our way on that momentous day." The newsletter claimed that the "financial debt slave system" constructed by the Knights Templar seven hundred years ago can soon come to an end, due to the combined efforts of a minimum of 144,000 meditators around the world. The number appears in the Book of Revelation as a symbolic representation of all human persons, but went on to symbolize the small number of people destined to be saved from hell. The two usages encapsulate the double exceptionalism of conspiritualists: they see themselves as both representing everyone and transcending everyone.

Northrup's appeal seems archetypal. She soothes her followers with self-care tips, knowing gazes, and harp arpeggios. And soothe them she must, because she spends the balance of her time scaring the living shit out of them. She tells them—and they should trust her as a doctor—that evidence-based medicine is out to kill them. That they'll get sick or go sterile if they have sex with their vaccinated partners.

In one harp-playing Great Awakening session, Northrup says, "They want to make you afraid," referring to the unnamed Elites of all conspiratorial fantasies. The projection is painfully ironic, because in reality, it's Northrup who paints a far more terrifying picture of the world than any public health official could. Throughout the pandemic, we watched mild-mannered, very uncharismatic health ministers stand at podiums all over the world and attempt to deliver evidence-based instructions that encouraged vigilance but not panic. Meanwhile, Northrup and her colleagues served up the most morbid fantasies they could improvise among themselves.

Why was this attractive to so many people? Why did Northrup gain followers during the pandemic, even while she torched her credibility as a doctor? Psychologist and cult survivor Alexandra Stein is the pioneer in the field of applying disorganized attachment theory to cultic bonds. Her analysis holds that trauma-bonding functions as the glue of cultic movements. And certainly when Northrup flips back and forth between doomsaying and harp playing, the emotional whiplash is intense. She becomes the storm that only she can shelter her followers from.

Another thing to remember is that Northrup's New Age and purportedly feminist women's health content has always used pseudoscience to conceal a deep conservatism.

"It is no wonder *Women's Bodies, Women's Wisdom* was a bestseller," writes Dr. Jen Gunter. "Not only was she the only gynecologist speaking out publicly and railing against the patriarchy, but she has a folksy writing style that makes the reader believe she is advocating for you against medical misogyny."

But the tome was never the forward-looking manifesto Northrup and her readers claimed it was. In it, Gunter points out, Northrup asserts that women get sick because they are misaligned with their spiritual purpose, and that the fear generated by mammogram results is as dangerous as any cancer. AIDS is caused by pollution and sexual repression, and can be reversed through love. Northrup reports that she stopped performing abortions because they diminish women's self-esteem, and because people can communicate with the unborn. She recounts consulting with a medical intuitive about a patient's ovarian cyst.

SETTING ASIDE THE ALLURE of alternative medicine, it might be that Northrup is attractive to her followers in the same way that Trump is attractive to his—through a series of beguiling contradictions that reflect and amplify unresolved needs.

Trump is the authoritarian father building walls and fantasizing about assassinations and parades. But he's also the permissive father who's high on Adderall and assaulting women. Northrup is an avenging old woman predicting the end of days. But she's also the comforting matriarch serving up gluten-free cookies.

Perhaps she pulls on even deeper cultural strings, especially through her mastery of parasocial intimacy. She can rock the *Golden Girls* vibe, but then when she reads letters and postcards from supporters, there's a 1960s children's television feeling to it.

"I watched the film *Out of Shadows*," Northrup said on April 12, 2020, in her Easter Sunday Great Awakening installment, "and I found out this has been done by a Hollywood stuntman who tells you a little bit about the inner workings of Hollywood, and films as propaganda, films as mind control.... It turns out that this man was divinely guided to release it on Good Friday, and as I speak to you now, it's had nearly two million views."

Northrup was guiding her 482,000 Facebook followers to Mike Smith's nonsense documentary, which played a major role in the COVID-19 era QAnon recruitment world. It does not appear that Northrup is aware of this role.

In *Out of Shadows*, Smith describes going through a period of OxyContin dependency following a stunt accident, during which his physiotherapist—who he does not name—alleged that she had worked as a doctor for children abused by Hollywood Elites. Inspired by this encounter, Smith "researched" his industry to uncover what he alleges to be a decades-old psy-ops campaign to normalize satanic imagery and infect the public with mechanisms of mass hypnosis.

Smith's "analysis" leans on the QAnon premise that the Elites conspire with each other and humiliate the masses by communicating in occult symbols and leaving clues that can be found by those waking up. *Television* means "tell-a-vision," *channel* refers to psychic communication, and *Hollywood* is named for the poisonous holly plant, sacred to Druids.

On April 15, digital researcher Mike Donnelly published a report on the viral spread of the Smith film, focusing on 6,800 tweets mentioning #outofshadows. "This hashtag," Donnelly observes, "has already evolved into an additional in-group marker for QAnon and adjacent communities, as #wwg1wga, #qanon, #pizzagate, and #thegreatawakening are among the hashtags most often used alongside #outofshadows."

Donnelly also notes that the #outofshadows viral spread carried with it anti-vax freight, along with all the common claims that Dr. Fauci and United Nations officials were obsessed with controlling populations and minds.

It HAD TAKEN ONLY eight days for Northrup's Great Awakening series to drift, apparently rudderless, into a boomer's version of Pastel QAnon.

In Northrup's case, direct links to QAnon recruitment materials and anti-vax propaganda are interspersed with—and moderated by—posts advertising her self-care and herbalism products. It's hard to gauge the impact of most of these hidden shards of chaos and disinformation. But in one very important case, we have receipts. On May 5, Northrup shared a link to the viral anti-vax propaganda film *Plandemic* to nearly a half-million Facebook followers. Prior to that, the largest vector for its spread had been a QAnon Facebook group with twenty-five thousand members.

More than a thousand people shared it from Northrup's Facebook, "many of them to groups that oppose mandatory vaccinations," according to the *New York Times.* Just over a week after its release, the video had been viewed over eight million times, making Northrup's share a turning point in the vaccine wars.

On May 15, in among the promotions for the release of the updated edition of *Women's Bodies, Women's Wisdom*—her bestselling magnum opus on women's alternative health—she appeared on Sean Morgan's *QAnon FAQ* platform. (Charles Eisenstein would have his turn at the QAnon mic two weeks later.)

In October of 2020, after being informed about our reporting on her content, Northrup defended her appearance on *QAnon FAQ* by describing Morgan as "a young father who had questions on vaccines." She denied knowing that Morgan was a QAnon propagandist, despite the title of his platform. "Nor did I know that the term 'Great Awakening' was also associated with that movement," she said.

However, the first show note for Northrup's episode on Morgan's stream is a link that says, "Get the free QAnon ebook to educate your friends and family." The notes also advertise QAnon clothing and "personal access to me and our private group to get coaching on 'The Great Awakening' process such as sharing with family and friends, research, and emotional support."

Let's remember that one of Morgan's early episodes is called "How to Redpill Your Mom #QAnon," which brings up the question of whether he was using his techniques on Northrup, and makes it hard to parse her denial. This confusion is essential to the fog of Pastel QAnon—especially on a firehose of a feed like Northrup's. Plausible deniability swells with a large volume of content that constantly shifts topics and is delivered at a frenetic tempo. The technique is pastiche, and followers are invited to serve themselves at the buffet. And it's impossible to know whether the dishes are home-cooked or came from bags in the prepared food section at Costco.

Plausible deniability is also enforced by a point of etiquette on conspirituality social media. If a follower shows the first symptom of critical thinking—by asking, for instance, what QAnon content has to do with women's perimenopausal health—conspirituality enthusiasts have a response: "Take the information that is useful and leave the rest." But can anyone really do that? Can anyone really separate out Northrup's dodgy criticism of the HPV vaccine in her mainstream work from her Pastel QAnon take that COVID-19 vaccines are making women sterile?

In COVID-19 terms, Northrup's skill at plausible deniability is both concrete and dangerous. In her first Great Awakening video, she acknowledges hearing about a COVID-19 death, through a friend of a friend. So she admits it exists. Great. But from there, the strategy is to question germ theory, dismiss transmission data, claim that COVID-19 has never been isolated in a lab, and claim that the PCR tests are useless and that doctors are falsifying death certificates.

Northrup never has to say outright that COVID-19 doesn't exist, or doesn't have an impact. This is a maneuver that can work in favor of the conspiritualist grifter. They can acknowledge that something is dangerous, as long as that something is not what mainstream medicine says it is, and as long as they can market an alternative cure for it, from boosting immunity to ascending to 5D consciousness to offering an ultimate opportunity for transformation. Referring to COVID-19 deaths in that video, Northrup reaches peak brain scrambling by suggesting that the souls of the dead are closer to us than those of the living.

WHAT ABOUT THE GOOD doctor's politics? Prior to the 2020 election, she did not openly voice support for the Trump ticket on social media. Rather, political references in Northrup's Great Awakening video series tended toward the typical wellness-world stance that political affiliations don't matter. She did say that being a single-issue voter—on vaccines—was reasonable, along with really feeling the energy of the candidate.

As it turns out, Northrup isn't really nonpartisan. Her 2020 Federal Election Commission filings show that she made 100 contributions to Donald J. Trump for President, Inc., the National Republican Senatorial Committee (NRSC), and WinRed (a GOP fundraising platform endorsed by the Republican National Committee) in September 2020 alone.

Another 276 contributions were made between June and August 2020. During those highly active four months, Northrup often made several contributions in a single day. Amounts range from less than $2 to around $200. In some cases, the $200 mark was the total for the week; in other weeks, Northrup donated roughly $2,000.

Prior to her 2020 contributions, all of Northrup's previous donations were to Democrat, progressive, and independent organizations or candidates, including the pro-choice organizations NARAL and Emily's List. Between 2001 and 2018, Northrup donated 20 times, totaling $9,750, to liberal groups and candidates. She contributed 379 times during 2020 to right-leaning groups, totaling nearly $9,000.

Parallel to this active Trump contribution period, Northrup was soliciting (and offering thanks for) "love offerings" in the captions of her Great

Awakening video series via a direct PayPal link. The first of these solicitations to her 482,000 Facebook followers and 137,000 Instagram followers was during the week of June 20, when she donated over $1,600, with over $2,000 dropped into Trump's coffers by the time she posted a July 23 gratitude message that said "profound gratitude for your love offerings."

Northrup is a case study in the quiet slide of a red-pilled alternative medicine influencer toward the political right. The confluence of anti-vax medical contrarianism, New Age spiritual goop, and right-wing information sources, fanned by a very active social media presence, drove her content deep into conspiracy territory as the year went on.

THINGS HEATED UP FOR Northrup in the spring of 2021. In March, she got tagged by the UK think tank Center for Countering Digital Hate as one of the Disinformation Dozen. "Dissenting opinion freely and openly expressed is one of humanity's highest standards," she responded on Facebook. She called the report a smear campaign and compared it to Republicans chanting "Lock her up" at Trump rallies.

No one locked Northrup up. On April 18, she took to Instagram to broadcast paranoid disinformation about the impacts of COVID-19 vaccines on women's reproductive health, and to boost a new and crucial argument for the anti-vax demographic to mobilize. She falsely suggested that the mRNA vaccine secretes poison through the sweat glands of a vaccinated person, and could sterilize women who come into contact with it. On the podcast, we noted the brain-flipped epidemiology and tagged this argument with the phrase "Reverse Contagion Anxiety." The argument belies a commitment to personal choice as touted by the anti-vax movement, but with Reverse Contagion Anxiety the anti-vax activist is no longer limited to resisting social pressure to be vaccinated—they can now openly pretend that their health is being threatened by those who choose to be vaccinated. The argument also makes it easier to justify standing outside of vaccination clinics to harass people seeking medical care.

Northrup was streaming from the Tulsa airport en route from that mega conference, hosted at the Bible college. The speakers list was a parade of QAnon, pseudoscience, and MAGA influencers, including former Trump lawyer Lin Wood, who resurrected Q in a speech in which he called for the execution of political enemies.

In the comment thread, Northrup upped the ante further by advising her followers to tell their partners that their sexual relationships would end if the partner were to be vaccinated.

"Here's what you want to say to ANY man you're involved with who wants the jab," she wrote in the comment thread. "I will never have sex with you again."

THERE'S ONE LAST THEME in Northrup's pandemic output we have to look at. It was there from very early on, but it was easy to overlook as a curiosity—like a single silver thread glinting in a turquoise cashmere shawl. At the time of this writing, however, that thread is now a razor wire. Northrup, the cursed Betty White of conspirituality, seems to tolerate violent rhetoric, up to the point of indulging in it herself.

We first noticed it in November of 2020 via her attendance at a COVID-denialism conference called "Line in the Sand," hosted from Bali by Sacha Stone, a shouty aging Zimbabwean almost–rock star who gave up his spandex for Thai pants, and his guitar riffs for Q-drops.

"Rather than pushing back against legislators, why not get rid of them altogether?" he asked before Northrup took the stage. "When we deal with agendas, which are leading to genocide by any other name, surely it's about evisceration, it's about eradication, it's about wholesale takedown of the godless goddamn toxin in our civilizational midst. We should not be negotiating with any ambiguity. This is a leviathan. This is a Medusa and we need to take it out altogether."

Northrup didn't parrot Stone's bloodlust. But through that same fall, Northrup was building a case for resisting federal and state legislation by boosting the pseudolegal framework of the Constitutional Sheriffs and Peace Officers Association, a far-right organization headed up by a former Oath Keepers board member. The Constitutional Sheriffs are very popular among proponents of sovereign citizen conspiracism, and their small movement claims that they hold ultimate authority over their counties, and can and must meet state and federal interventions that they deem to violate the US Constitution with armed force.

The Sheriffs went on to play a pivotal role in organizing the Capitol siege of January 6, 2021. Northrup stayed quiet—or coy—on that day. After all, it fell in the middle of her water-fast retreat. She had no internet at the undisclosed retreat location, she explained, but she was getting news from her colleagues in Washington. Her Insurrection Day Great Awakening installment was called "Hold the vibration of what you want. Many things will be revealed now." She wasn't in Washington, DC. The whole installment had the vibe of Luke Skywalker projecting himself into battle against Kylo Ren, while meditating on Temple Island.

By February 2022, The Great Awakening had disappeared from Christiane Northrup's Facebook feed. Health inspiration cards alternated with affiliate invites: seminars by fellow alternative doctors, workshops on financial freedom. And, almost daily invitations to join Northrup on the unmoderated social platforms that many of her fellow Disinformation Dozen colleagues had fled to: Gab, Telegram, MeWe, CloutHub, Rumble. On Telegram, she continued to post QAnon-adjacent content.

But it was in sitting down with filmmaker Jeff Witzeman that Northrup let the bloodlust fully rip.

"Why would the Ascension process happen," Witzeman asked her, "only when the Deep State would come in and try to control everybody, use fear, use forced jabbing, forced masking? Why would the Ascension process have to happen alongside that?"

"Because to get stronger," Northrup replied, "you need to lift heavier and heavier weights. And there's this thing in the physical body. You can do way more than you think you can do, but you're not gonna do it until you're forced to do it. And we're all like that."

Witzeman nodded like a padawan.

"You and I are not afraid to drop the body and leave," Northrup said. "This whole Deep State psy-op plays on people's fear of death."

Witzeman wondered aloud whether Northrup is on a higher plateau of consciousness. Northrup dismissed the idea, and confessed to sometimes having murderous thoughts, such as "Do I get to pick the firing squad to kill these demons?" Northrup admitted that such thoughts are typically taboo in New Age circles.

"I like those thoughts," she confessed. "I am all for love and forgiveness. And if anyone comes near one of my children, I will have no problem putting a bullet in their head.

"I want people to own that part of themselves because that is righteous anger. It is a cause of health."

CHAPTER 20

NEW AGE ZELIG

THE FICTITIOUS SUBJECT of Woody Allen's 1983 mockumentary *Zelig* physically transforms himself to merge with whatever sociopolitical scene he finds himself in. In the salon, he's a Republican with a Bostonian accent. In the kitchen, a Democrat speaking Brooklynese. He can grow the beard and sidelocks of a Hasidic Jew one week, then chop it all for a Nazi undercut the next. He's a man without a center, a chameleon who survives by fading into the background of a history upon which he has no effect.

Now imagine taking this neurotic character and turning him inside out. Upgrade his willpower and self-esteem through theater school and life coaching workshops. Let him keep the ability to merge with the multiple worlds through which he travels, but also show him the power of manifestation. Teach him *The Secret*—that he can transform any scene to reflect the radiance of his self-image. If successful, he'll be able to LARP as Democrat or Republican, Indigenous rights activist or MAGA apologist. He'll be anybody for anyone, while remaining equanimous, perfectly coiffed, and always on message (at least about himself). He will have gone from a soulless husk to a spiritual Everyman, convinced that his presence alone blesses a troubled planet. Meet New Age Zelig: a shapeshifter, pulled inexorably toward history-shattering events, so that he can put them back together with love and light glue.

FOR MIKKI WILLIS, born circa 1978, a life of male modeling and Hollywood vanities ended in the rubble of 9/11. At least that's the way he tells it. One version on the bio page of the almost defunct website for Elevate Films, the company he founded in the New Age mecca of Ojai in 2004, puts it this way: "Having been inside the twin towers just hours before they fell," the copy reads, "he helped to organize a group of civilians who remained at Ground Zero for 3 days to aid in the search and rescue efforts." The experience was transformative.

But it's not clear what Willis means by "hours." Janitorial staff might have been in the towers at 6:46 a.m. on September 11, 2001, but for everyone else this was well before the workday. Other details of Willis's story are slippery. In a 2011 monologue shot to promote Elevate, he recalls watching the towers collapse from the uptown apartment of a friend, and then immediately running downtown to help. But just after the attack, on September 13, as he told the White Plains newspaper the *Journal News*, they waited until that afternoon, and then rode bikes toward the rubble. Later, he told the reporter, he slept for a few hours in an abandoned hotel. In the Elevate promo, the hotel became an abandoned apartment, and the site of a prophetic dream, in which one of the victims he'd seen crushed in the rubble appeared to him and whispered, "This could be your Vietnam."

He rose from the hotel, or the apartment, and walked out into the blaze of work lights shining on the destruction. He sank into a disaster spirituality trance. "It felt like I was just in slow motion," he says. "All I could see was just spirits crossing and spirits working and chain gangs of spirits. And it was so clear to me that everything was interconnected. And it was all one big body of God."

Willis realized that his media career had been soulless up until that point, that he had been wasting his time reproducing an empty culture to feed it back to itself. No more. He was done. He would create a new media enterprise dedicated to spreading that feeling of oneness.

"Knowing that the entire world was experiencing what it was experiencing—all the separation and fear and chaos that was going on in the world—here, I was standing there experiencing the greatest bliss and beauty of my life. And I just remember wishing that the world could see this situation through my eyes."

ON MAY 4, 2020, Willis made sure plenty of people saw the world through his eyes when he uploaded a twenty-minute video to multiple streaming services. But the vision of his brainchild, *Plandemic*, wasn't so divine. This noir and claustrophobic docsploitation revolved around the testimony of a disgraced research scientist named Judy Mikovits.

Mikovits, who is in her midsixties, unleashed a torrent of false claims about COVID-19 and vaccines. She claimed that COVID-19 had been lab-manipulated, masks made wearers sick, doctors were being paid to list COVID-19 as the cause of death on certificates, getting the flu vaccine made a person more susceptible to COVID-19, and hydroxychloroquine was an effective COVID-19 treatment. She also said that rolling around on the beach is all a person needs to do to have a healthy relationship with bacteria.

The film gathered eight million views in a week and shot Willis into pole position in the COVID-19 disinformation race. He drove that status all the way to Washington on January 6, 2021, when he went to the Capitol to speak at a "health freedom" rally. While there, he cosplayed as a journalist embedded with the rioters, bearing witness to what he called a "beautiful" event.

Willis lets Mikovits be wrong about every single thing, despite touting his three decades as a professional journalist. Subsequently, as tankers of digital ink were spilled ripping her bullshit apart, Willis remained silent. His only rebuttal was to ask who's fact-checking the fact checkers.

As we've learned so far from the intersection of charisma and misinformation, the data isn't the point. If it was, Willis's supporting materials would have included links to peer-reviewed research. If careful filmmaking were the point, Willis wouldn't mispronounce "doctorial thesis" in his opening accolades of Mikovits, and he wouldn't misspell "filmaker" under his own talking head. Willis's production, perhaps in line with his fashion industry background, is a bizarre mix of stirring spectacle and editorial who-really-cares-about-the-details.

Instead of spotlighting any evidence for his COVID claims, Willis opens the film with Mikovits's false persecution story over an issue unrelated to the pandemic. In 2011, she claims, she was arrested and jailed without warrant in a plot to punish her for discovering a retrovirus she claimed was at the root of chronic fatigue syndrome. In reality, the publication of her claim was in a 2009 *Science* article that was retracted when her trial results couldn't be replicated. While true that she was arrested and detained briefly, it was with a warrant, not by a full SWAT team. Two minutes into her story,

Willis splices in stock footage of helmeted troops pointing automatic rifles at a house while police strobes light up the night.

Not one bit of this happened. Mikovits's former employer—she'd been fired for shoddy research and insubordination—had obtained the warrant after alleging she'd stolen proprietary materials from the lab.

Within a week, Facebook and YouTube had deleted *Plandemic*. Willis later speculated that Bill Gates was personally responsible for this cancellation. Undaunted, Willis scrambled together *Plandemic 2: Indoctornation*, which was released in August 2020. The seventy-five-minute format allowed Willis to expand his misinformation portfolio and use of stock footage. But the tech platforms were ready this time: Willis's sequel gathered no viral momentum. Nonetheless, within eighteen months, Willis claimed that *Plandemic* had been streamed a billion times globally, that every data point was 100 percent accurate, and that all the critical articles in publications like *VICE*, the *New York Times*, and the *Los Angeles Times* were hit pieces driven by rage at anyone who goes against their narrative.

Throughout his pandemic shooting spree, almost every single thing that came out of Willis's mouth and video editing suite was dodgy. If it floated, it was on a backlog of good vibes and purportedly post-political empathy for a world both out of control and filled with possibility. The output of Elevate Films had been a mix of alternative and aspirational, crunchy and hipster, focusing on hemp farming, psychedelics, the festival music scene, and the theme of the heroic changemaker. The company's YouTube channel still hosts teasers for *Be Brave*, a documentary project started in 2013 to collate and edit three thousand hours of the eccentric video diaries of Daniel Northcott, a globe-trotting mystic who died of leukemia in 2009, at the age of twenty-nine. Elevate helped crowdfund $184,000 for the project, which was never released.

In 2013, Elevate crowdfunded $40,000 for a proposed-but-never-released doc called *From Neurons to Nirvana*. Willis also says he was filming the violently suppressed protests against the Keystone Pipeline at Standing Rock in 2016. He asked for PayPal donations for the project in order to replace drones that had been shot out of the sky and buy winter camping gear. But out of Willis's ostensible Standing Rock footage, only one six-minute interview shot in a studio with a lawyer advocating for the protestors is currently available.

A 2014 production reel for Elevate sums up the company vibe. A montage of counterculture inspo footage ends with a text slide: "Those who tell the stories shape society." Willis attributes the quote to Plato, as do other internet sources—unless they claim it comes from Aristotle, or the Navajo, or Hopi wisdom. No one provides an actual citation. It's a fitting denouement for Willis's postmodern New Ageism: copy and paste a probably fabricated quote to lend ancient or Indigenous authenticity to the projects of raising money and making anything true.

THERE'S A PARTICULAR WAY in which Willis listens intently to Mikovits's shaggy-dog persecution story, gazing into her eyes like a therapist with boundary issues. Released two years after the height of the #MeToo movement, the setup seems to salve an open wound. A younger male "journalist" listens carefully to the middle-aged female survivor of institutional abuse. Willis's eyes go moist as she recounts her story of being ignored and abused by the mainstream scientific community. He bears witness, forges solidarity.

In countless shares of *Plandemic*, Mikovits was lauded as a warrior and prophetess, indicating the film had quickly become a thirst trap for a key conspirituality demographic: middle-aged women who have been—or feel they have been—silenced by a patriarchal culture, especially on matters related to wisdom and the body. Willis is not a journalist beholden to skepticism. He can implicitly believe what Mikovits says, merging #believeallwomen with #believeallfringescientists. He can be her savior. "God sent me Mikki Willis," she shouted at an anti-mandate rally in Los Angeles in the spring of 2022.

There's something predictable, then, that his film would break through from QAnon Facebook groups into the mainstream through the share of Christiane Northrup, who presented her pre-pandemic work as being focused on the healing power of #MeToo in smashing the patriarchy. In her 2020 updated preface to *Women's Bodies, Women's Wisdom*, she argues that a toxic "culture of victim-shaming has finally been put under a glaring spotlight recently, as the #MeToo and #NeverAgain movements have caught fire."

The rape-culture-busting of 2018 was, according to Northrup, part of the longer historical process through which women have reclaimed power from the male-dominated medical paradigm in which she was educated.

It was part of her realizing, for example, the correlation between chronic pelvic pain and sexual abuse, and that ignoring the former was tangled up in denying the latter. Her whistleblowing, she wrote, came at a steep price, "just as it has cost every whistleblower and rape victim who has ever come forward and rocked the boat, because up until now, our society has been ruled by a belief system known as patriarchy—the rule of the fathers."

In this light, the repression of Mikovits's allegedly revolutionary research—especially into a condition like chronic fatigue syndrome, where approximately 65 percent of those diagnosed are women—would be consistent with a generalized repression of women's bodies and their wisdom. "In essence," Northrup writes, "patriarchy blares out the message that women's bodies are inferior and must be controlled. And then we women internalize this message and become our own worst enemies."

For Northrup's hundreds of thousands of female followers, believing not only what the beleaguered Mikovits has to say about COVID-19 and vaccines, but what she claims about her alleged persecution, seems to be as much about solidarity with women exposing hidden truths as it is about medical evidence. It's about conflating real histories of domination and abuse with the suppression of women's wisdom that would upend the male-dominated medical world. So it wasn't only Willis's content that drove the viral reach of *Plandemic*. It was also the casting and performances.

LESS THAN TWENTY-FOUR HOURS after *Plandemic* went viral, Willis flipped the script on the Mikovits interview to center himself as the persecuted but saintly truth teller. He took to Facebook to stream himself lit with a honey-yellow filter.

"What I want to talk to you about in this moment," Willis said, "is the cheerful subject of death. About our fear of death. Your fear of death, my fear of death, and the way that it stops us from doing the things that most need doing right now in this time and this incredibly critical, precious moment." He's locked into a rhythm and affect of vagueness, and he can't help himself. The moment recalls Willis's post-9/11 vision. It's as if he's walking out into the glare of COVID chaos, enthralled by the miraculous potential of it all. Only this time, he created the rubble.

In *Plandemic*, Willis claims to reveal an unfolding catastrophe of government corruption. But in his follow-up sermon, he promises that spiritual relief is at hand. In the film, the world is filled with sexual, emotional, medical, financial, and technological abusers who can never be trusted. In his sermon, Willis implies there are also saviors who not only understand all of these things, but whose love will save the people. The whiplash is palpable.

He includes himself in the messianic cohort. "And so the declaration that I'm making," Willis says, "is that I love this life so much that I am willing to die for it. Are you?"

We don't know whether Mikki Willis is running—or ever has run—a cult. We have no evidence that he has gathered in-person followers or is directly influencing people to alter their diets, marriages, or professions. Nonetheless, this Facebook stream made it clear that an influence technique familiar to cult researchers could be a key tool in the spread of a vaccine panic.

Willis's workflow was clear. The release of *Plandemic* provoked panic, terror, and outrage. The follow-up selfie video—a hypnotic but also menacing sermon—offered emotional oversharing, intrusive eye contact, the premise of caregiving, and soft apocalypticism. While the film provoked hypervigilance, the sermon soothed, positioning Willis as a spiritual guide. It's a rhythm of contrasts through which viewers can run for comfort to the person who terrified them. It's a feedback loop, and it's difficult to disrupt with facts.

The history of cults is largely a history of paranoid charismatics who lock followers into their description of a double world. The outside, conventional world is a place of demonic danger, while the inner world of the leader and his group offers love and safety. In the field of cultic studies, the rhythm of this double world is understood as a driver of the phenomena of disorganized attachment and trauma bonding. The cult member is actively confused by the oscillation between terror and care. The leader's main impact is not to communicate content, but to forge an exploitative relationship through that confusion, which can only be resolved by staying, committing, and investing in the leader's message and mission.

The main thesis of psychologist Alexandra Stein is that disorganized attachment, a condition first observed by child psychologists studying young children who develop erratic and high-stress responses to traumatizing caregivers, is the very model for cultic bonding, in which the group member feels contradictory impulses of terror and love that can only be resolved through devotion. As cult survivors, Matthew and Julian can confirm that it really is difficult to leave the presence of the charismatic leader because they're simultaneously the source of terror about the outside world and the source of protection from it.

How do these bonds loosen? In pre-digital, brick-and-mortar cults, they could last for decades. In the more diffuse online QAnon-networked cultosphere, the stability of the bonds is unclear. But we should note that Willis's *Plandemic* primed viewers for his longer follow-up feature, *Plandemic 2: Indoctornation*. These films together, punctuated by his sermon, ask for more than the debunking of dangerous misinformation. Science is not Willis's wheelhouse. He's from the entertainment industry and produces wellness and spirituality media content. His spectacle parasitizes the complexity and stress of the pandemic, and uses it as a front. His sermon makes this clear, as it contains almost no reference to the claims made in the film. In sum, the Willis spectacle pivots on the intense relational feedback loops that colonize emotional attention and center male charismatic leadership, offering an answer to the problem it provokes.

The real trouble is that public health communications operate in the exact opposite fashion. For obvious ethical reasons, science communicators cannot beat Willis and others at this game by becoming better manipulators. But they can begin to look at ways in which public health institutions can nurture more secure attachments with the populations they serve. This may begin at the broadest policy level of universalized health care. The success of Willis's propaganda depends on a chaotic and fraying commons. It depends on cynicism and distrust. Willis's hook is that he's saving followers from a society that doesn't care about them.

Even though *Plandemic* can now be found only in the armpits of the internet, mending the cynicism and distrust Willis exploited will be a decades-long project.

MIKKI WILLIS LIKES to say, over and over again—and especially in front of MAGA audiences—that he has always been deeply enmeshed in progressive politics. In October 2020 he spoke at a QAnon-adjacent conference called the Red Pill Expo on Georgia's Jekyll Island. Other speakers included David Icke and Oath Keepers founder Stewart Rhodes—tagged by the Southern

Poverty Law Center as a right-wing extremist, and now convicted of seditious conspiracy over his January 6 activities.

"I was a hero of the Far Left," Willis declared during a talk called "How I Became a Recovering Socialist." But he was vague on the details. He talked about following the Bernie Sanders campaign with a film crew in 2016, and filming the protests at Standing Rock. He worked on primary events for Tulsi Gabbard in 2019. It's not clear where any of this footage has wound up.

In reviewing his socials, it's hard to see any commitment to political values mixed into the New Age aspirations to transcend political divides. His love posts for Bernie Sanders, for instance, rarely mentioned platform issues, preferring to focus on populist gumption and the willingness to disrupt two-party hegemony. Willis backed Sanders, it seems, because he believed that Sanders was breaking politics-as-usual. It's a naive take on Sanders, a seasoned politician who has held office since 1981. But it's on brand for a depoliticized New Age scene fixated on how "those who tell the stories" shape society, rather than "those who draft the policies."

The fascination with disruptive stories is also predictive of a political spinelessness that pushed Willis through MAGA land toward the Capitol riot. On the evening of November 3, 2020, Willis headlined an Election Day party in Austin, attended by a who's who of wellness figures. He was there to pitch a new anti–George Soros documentary project. The party's host, a life coach named Joyous Heart, led two prayers for Donald Trump. The hour-long presentation focused on the creation of a medical freedom eco-resort called Home Ranch and Gold Star Oasis, registered that month with plans to build on Lake Travis.

Willis shouted out to co-investors Del Bigtree, an anti-vax impresario, and Trump-supporting comedian JP Sears. Marla Maples led another prayer for her ex-husband Donald Trump at the end of the festivities. According to Heart, the resort, which will supposedly include helicopter service directly from Austin-Bergstrom International Airport, is being built to help residents and guests reclaim sovereignty and will be protected by four on-site ex–Delta Force members.

Two months later, on January 6, Willis appeared on a stage set up close to the Capitol. He was a featured speaker for the MAGA Freedom Rally, alongside the COVID-denying Dr. David Martin and QAnon film recruiter

Mike Smith, and anti-vax propagandists. Roger Stone, the Trump-pardoned felon, was also on the initial billing.

Willis was introduced by one of the organizers, Charlene Bollinger, an alternative health activist who built her fame along with her husband Ty on marketing quack cancer cures. Before Willis stepped onto the stage, Bollinger said, "We are at war. This is a war between good and evil."

In his fourteen-minute speech to the small crowd, Willis said that the Capitol breach (from which he'd just returned) was "a beautiful thing to see" enacted by "our patriots." He railed against the mainstream media, praised Mike Smith as a personal friend, and referred to the coming eradication of the Cabal. He seemed to choke up when mentioning his own children, stating they deserved not to be injected with poisons, and to have childhoods in which they could ride their bikes freely. Police sirens wailed in the background.

Within hours, video footage uploaded to Reddit showed Willis at the riot, before his speech, pushing and getting pushed within a phalanx of insurrectionists breaching one of the Capitol door entrances. Willis holds a mobile phone aloft, filming into the building. Around him, the mob chants "Hang Mike Pence."

On January 8, Willis posted his account of his participation in the mob action to his Facebook page. In the post, he said he was there as a journalist, called the mob protesters, claimed some of them were Biden supporters, repeated false claims of election fraud, and quoted an insurrectionist falsely claiming that the violence was perpetrated by Antifa. He also claimed he dissuaded mob participants from attacking police and was not happy with the actions of those who entered the Capitol. In an addendum to the post, he said he didn't hear the mob he was standing in chanting "Hang Mike Pence"—he said he thought they were chanting "Where's Mike Pence" or "Hey Mike Pence."

There's an eerie resonance between Willis's minimization of COVID and how he went long on laundering the events of January 6—and his participation in them. After Facebook users started tagging Willis and the FBI together, shouting for an investigation, Willis disabled his account and retreated into radio silence for several months. But he resurfaced in June on the podcast of Paul Chek, a San Diego–based veteran fitness guru for the conspirituality set—a kind of Jordan Peterson of the gym.

Chek's professional feats include kinesiology work with the Jordan-era Chicago Bulls, followed by a stint with the championship Los Angeles

Lakers. But his esoteric roots cast a longer shadow. Chek grew up in the Self-Realization Fellowship—the yoga group founded by Paramahansa Yogananda—and is known for holding court on the spiritual dimensions of physical fitness.

"When you're working on the knee of a Hindu," Chek told an interviewer in 2006, "it might look like the knee of a Christian or a Muslim, but it isn't. The software that drives it is completely different. In order to be an effective therapist and trainer and coach, I've had to study world religion. The physical body is like a vehicle, but your spiritual beliefs are your software by which you navigate life." With regard to COVID-19, Chek hews to the common conspirituality bromide: a strengthened immune system is all the protection one needs to fend off a novel coronavirus.

Unsurprisingly, Chek was receptive to Willis's aspirational account of the riot. Willis wanted to go to the Capitol, he said, because he knew that the gathering would be portrayed by the mainstream media as being centered on white supremacy. Willis was going to see what the real story was. While planning his trip with his crew, he said, he received an invite to speak at the rally. Later, however, he balked when the flyer pegged it as a MAGA event—a demonized brand, he said, that he didn't want to associate with. The organizers soothed him, he said, saying the flyer had only gone out to a small list, and that Roger Stone wouldn't be attending. (Indeed, he didn't.) As the riot unfolded, Stone was frantically throwing his fancy suits into black garbage bags in his high-end suite at the Willard Hotel, plotting his exit.

When Willis arrived for his speech, he told Chek, he got word that the Capitol was being stormed. He ducked out of his timeslot, promising to return.

"I was very pleasantly surprised, Paul," he said, "because people were being very, very respectful. They were telling the police we love you, too. We're human like you. We just want our voices heard."

He claimed to have spoken to many non-white rioters, and to Biden supporters who were primarily concerned not about the false claims of electoral fraud that drove the insurrection, but about the negative impacts of the COVID mitigation measures on their lives. He described a cheerful environment, with a lot of flag-waving and selfies. To Willis, the crush of bodies at the doorways were the result of people "leaning forward, as peacefully as that could possibly happen."

After his proud patriot speech, Willis told Chek, he went back to the Capitol and to the "very peaceful" scene. He was troubled by the broken windows, and by two troublemakers pushing at the front of the line. He told them quite sternly to stop.

"Liberals and conservatives are not really that far apart," Willis offered, as he groped for a New Age off-ramp for his account. He framed the siege as an unnecessary and antihuman conflict caused by right and left extremism— and as if *Plandemic* had nothing to do with the escalations that led to Washington. No, it couldn't have been him driving people apart by spiking a media fever in the spring, and then stepping back for an "objective" view in January.

"It's this very small group of people that they often refer to as the elite," Willis said. "They're very powerful and very wealthy. And they're playing us and dividing us so they can conquer."

FOR WILLIS, vaccines don't work. It doesn't really matter why. Rail against Big Pharma. Talk about a generations-long Deep State conspiracy. Shout the word "Tuskegee." Cite Andrew Wakefield's falsified study erroneously linking vaccines with autism. Blame Joe Biden.

In the spirit of unity, and definitely not playing anyone, Willis also teamed up with the COVID-minimizing doctor who first alerted Donald Trump to the pseudoscientific benefits of hydroxychloroquine, Dr. Vladimir Zelenko. Zelenko, a middle-aged Ukrainian American ultra-Orthodox Haredi Jew, had left the Upstate New York community where he'd practiced for years after elders accused him of lying about the COVID case rates in the village. In the months before he died of lung cancer on June 30, 2022, Zelenko began marketing Z-Stack, a supplement for "prevention/protection for the next pandemic." Willis joined the $151 billion global supplement industry by helping Zelenko sell it through newsletters and promotional videos.

What's in Z-stack? Mainly vitamin C, which can shorten the duration of the common cold by about a day, plus other ingredients that have not been proven effective in preventing or treating COVID-19. How much does it cost? Derek sourced the separate ingredients and did the math, using Zelenko's ratios. Including the veggie capsules, the thirty servings in one bottle cost $5.90 to make. That bottle sells for $55—or $52.25 if you use Willis's discount code.

CHAPTER 21

J. "PEPE" SEARS, MAGA LIFE COACH

As we edge closer to a completely groundless, too-online space, some prickly questions return. Is conspirituality a social movement or a grift? Are these people practicing a new and legitimate form of spirituality? Are they caught in the no-man's-land of audience capture? Are their hopes and fears in earnest? Are they high on their own supply?

These are all judgment calls that point to a spectrum of guesses. When Kelly Brogan quotes Tom Cowan quoting Rudolf Steiner on the spiritual delusion of the pandemic, she's working her angle. But her eyes genuinely seem to burn with quiet certainty. Charles Eisenstein's brain has gone smooth in the river of his own mythic poetry, but it appears he's committed to the flow. Christiane Northrup is a devotee, albeit of two masters: QAnon dog whistles on one hand and supplements on the other. A sales pitch always complicates sincerity. And Mikki Willis? He's a true believer—in himself.

But when we get to wellness-influencer-turned-right-wing shitposter JP Sears, all questions of intention and authenticity turn back on themselves and disappear into a black hole where we look in vain for a moral center. Because if there's one thing we can say for sure about Sears, it's that he makes it impossible to assess whether he believes in anything, even as he pushes his ragtag demographic toward right-wing extremism through a semiconscious alchemy of pranks and clout chasing.

In 2013, Sears is helping people with anger management via YouTube. In 2015, he's gently coaching men away from porn addiction. In 2017, he's flipped from life coach to comedian who makes fun of life coaches. In 2020, he's mocking people afraid of COVID-19 and doing tactical training with former Green Berets. In 2021, he's posing with his arm around Donald Trump under the palm fronds of Mar-a-Lago. The story of Sears is that of a man becoming more and more of a cartoon as he finds an increasingly monetizable identity. How does he find it? By climbing a ladder out of beta-male wellness into toxic alpha masculinity. He's someone with no discernible stake in politics beyond its ability to capture attention, who accidentally became a political spoiler.

Sears's public life began with aspirational videos. The content was harmless and fluffy, but also promised far more than his training as a life coach could deliver: "How To Be Happy and Increase Self Esteem!"; "Nurturing Your Inner Child"; "Healthy Sexuality"; "Lose Body Fat Through Emotional Healing." He had some culture-jamming hooks going for him: bright red hair flowing past his shoulders, a nasal Ohio accent, and the earnestness of a 1980s presenter on children's television. And he did okay, with the most popular video from this earnest period being "How To Thrive as an Introvert," clocking in at 182,000 views.

Sears 2.0 emerged in 2014. He started posting videos poking fun at his own gig, life coaching. He took swipes at yoga people, and then vegans, and then conspiracy theorists. Progressives in the wellness world regarded him as a clever—and bracing—breath of fresh air amidst a tyranny of pious consumerism and organic food porn. His "How to Be Ultra Spiritual" series, with each episode introduced with a New Age gong, was a smash hit. The pilot reached over two million views; the project eventually spun out into a book.

Why the pivot? "I needed it for self-therapy," he told the *Charleston City Paper* in 2018. "I was finding myself having egotistical agendas and judgments hiding within my new age and spiritual practices." The Ultra Spiritual brand "became a way for me to shine the light of awareness on the shadow side of me," he said.

But this paradoxical role of life coach and life coach satirist was gear grinding. Holly English describes it as an awkward time for Sears, dominated by his attempt to leap from wellness-world gig work to social media celebrity. They met in 2016 when he came to her hometown of Byron Bay, where she works as a photographer and illustrator. She calls Byron "the creepy spiritual capital of Australia."

Sears was slated as a guest speaker at a spiritual retreat. He and English had a two-week whirlwind romance that culminated in a commitment ceremony on Tallow Beach, complete with seaweed crowns and a whale breaching on the horizon. English had dated drug addicts, and had had spiritual boyfriends: "They're the worst, because they don't know they have a problem." But Sears was a different breed. Off stage, she remembers an impish dag who could be sweet, who expressed no strong spiritual or ideological ideas, and who wasn't dogmatic about working out or healthy eating. They never spoke about pharmaceuticals or vaccines. Or politics. His comedy was defensive, English said, and his focus was on approval. "You could feel it when you were with him," she said in an interview. "His drive to celebrity is because he's deeply insecure."

Sears found a way of sublimating insecurity into an extroverted method that attracted soaring view counts. As his life coaching content dwindled, Sears 3.0 emerged: a jackass who now parodied everything, and for whom nothing was sacred. If he lost followers by mocking gluten intolerance or Buddhism, they were replaced by a larger contingent who lapped up the smirk. By 2017, Sears's content was detached from any semblance of life coaching at all. That year he met his current wife, Amber, in Costa Rica, where she led shamanic retreats as a holistic nutritionist, organized through her robust online brand, Epic Self.

Until COVID-19 slammed into 2020, Sears's tone remained lighthearted. But COVID mitigation orders prompted his oppositional-defiant star to rise. He turned to vaccine-skeptical content, then made fun of people who wore masks. He swerved into straight-up COVID minimization, and then Big Lie content, and then videos laughing at trans people and the woke. He wore a purple wig and spoke in a lisp to own the lesbian libs. In March 2022, he covered himself in shit with a parody news report in which he implied that the war in Ukraine was fake.

The bizarre arc raises the question: Who is JP Sears, and what kind of world enables him? How has he possibly earned close to three million followers on YouTube, racking up nearly half a billion views?

IF YOU DIP into the content he was producing before meeting Holly English in Byron Bay and his turn toward celebrity, you find an earnest, almost childlike person who wants to be a caregiver. He's doing his best to help people, with a good webcam and a spotty education.

A video from 2015 called "Porn Addiction" presents Sears with a frank and open demeanor, talking about what he acknowledges can be a shameful issue. The vibe is a little retro. He refers to a letter from a "lovely lady" who describes feelings of betrayal over her partner's porn usage. He keeps the language modest and his eyes soft. He's fresh and young but comes off like a middle-aged youth counselor in a midwestern high school or church.

Sears has nothing to say about the neuroscience of porn addiction or gender politics and power. His framework depends on the ideas of psychological displacement and self-protection. Users are not addicted to pornography per se, he argues. They are addicted to anxiety. They are addicted to secrets, to not getting caught, to disappointing their partners. Pornography, Sears says, allows the user to fence off their intimacy from their biology and to serve their need for control over sexual encounters.

It's not a bad talk, until Sears revs up the New Age responsibilism. Without knowing much at all about the lovely lady, he challenges her to see how her partner's porn addiction is really a gift that helps expose her own feelings of inadequacy. "There is a reason," he says, "why your husband—both his light side and his shadow side—why he's been a perfect match for you. There's a perfect vibration there." This is how the New Age updates the old: "If you weren't such a nag, he wouldn't look elsewhere," reasoning of prior generations. Now it's more like: "If you would only deal with your own wounds, he wouldn't have to put salt on them."

This contemptuous argument, disguised in good intentions, is copy-and-pasted from any one of a number of New Age life coaching sources that make a virtue of victim blaming. Pioneering motivational speaker, author, and stadium seminar leader Tony Robbins—who has a net worth of $600 million, and who Sears has helped market—once told a San Jose audience that women came forward during #MeToo with claims they were sexually abused to gain "significance" in life. He later apologized for his comments and expressed support for the #MeToo movement. Best-selling self-help author and creator of The Work Byron Katie tells followers that every act of cruelty—including having one's child torn from one's arms at Auschwitz—is a pathway to God consciousness. Sears doesn't go that far here, settling instead for the basic technique of both inflating and reducing a complex issue so that it can be resolved with a pat generalization: "loving yourself," "seeking your truth," or "healing your wounds." The method is key for con-spiritualists who have single products and methods—be it yoga, essential oils, or Reiki—that must speak to every issue. But beneath the vagary and brain-melted logic, it's hard to deny that Sears's intention to help is earnest.

Since 2016, however, Sears has become increasingly two-dimensional—more so even than Mikki Willis, who despite always seeming to be on stage, at least tries to connect with followers in an unironic way. Sears now has a single vacuous persona that can fill up with aggression on a moment's notice. He does stand-up comedy, shills for supplements and T-shirts, mocks social justice warriors, and lampoons the media as corrupt, as though he's not part of it. Riding this emptiness, his content arc has mirrored and amplified a cultural drift toward right-wing cruelty. And why? For the clicks and lulz? It's a drift he came to symbolize as much as provoke.

Sears now presents as an empty shell: a cipher for an American culture yearning to enjoy its hypocrisies and tolerate its paradoxes. An America that wants to feel good but act bad, to eat organic and jet-set on spiritual vacays. To be kind but also an asshole. To be an outsider on the inside. "You crazy freedom-loving weirdos kept asking for it," he said on a post selling "Let's Go Brandon" T-shirts in November 2021. "So here it is." In MAGA land, the chant translates as "Fuck Joe Biden." Sears modeled the shirt with a smug tilt of his head.

A METAPHOR CAN HELP with this infuriating figure. JP Sears is like the Pepe the Frog of the New Age world: a viral cartoon that became a bell-wether of the times.

Drawn quietly for years by San Francisco artist Matt Furie, Pepe first appeared in Furie's *Boy's Club* comic in 2008, where he hung out with his three crusty housemates, getting high, playing video games, and taking pleasure in simple acts like dropping his pants and underwear all the way down to the floor to pee. "Feels good man," he told his friend when asked about his toilet kink. Pepe grins, accepting his weirdo self.

Through the lottery of the internet, the "feels good man" frog got scanned and uploaded and shared countless times, becoming the mascot of disaffected 4chan users. At first, they made him into a talisman of self-satisfaction. Over time, Pepe became a plasticine avatar they could shape and reshape, copy and paste, and post as an embodiment of their emotional range, without having to leave the safety of the cartoon-pixelated world.

Pepe the Frog, like JP Sears, spoke to a lost but impulsive demographic that knew it was ridiculous and insecure. Pepe rejected the world he wanted to belong to. He celebrated being stupid, but resented feeling ignorant. A bazillion iterations later, the Pepes of 4chan morphed to reflect the angst of the users and their time. His grin went flat, turned into a frown, and then a grimace of rage. Pepe could be drawn covered in Nazi symbols, or laughing as bombs fell on Syria, or wearing the Donald Trump blond toupee. No one could really take him seriously, yet he drew everyone's focus toward an increasingly cruel space.

Furie and his soft-spoken Bay Area friends watched in horror as the scene unfolded. The cartoon of the childlike gamer frog who laughed at fart jokes got listed as a hate symbol by the Anti-Defamation League. They were as mystified as the yoga people who watched the quirky JP Sears transform through countless social media engagements from a happy-go-lucky life coach with a "feels good man" vibe to a funny-not-funny puppet of right-wing populism.

"WHEN A LIBERAL FINALLY Becomes a Conservative" dropped on May 1, 2020. It's garnered 1.2 million views.

In it, Sears tried on the joke of comparing his political transition to a gender transition, while also literally coming out as a conservative in camo pants and a tactical T-shirt. He joked that society should stop discriminating against the trans-political who have discovered their true identity.

On May 19, it was the video "Blue Pill People," which mocked those complying with COVID-19 mitigation measures as sheep. "Keep sheltering in place, and enjoy the safety of peaceful slavery," Sears said, as he parodied a newscaster. "Peaceful slavery" is cribbed from a Thomas Jefferson quote that has since become popular in conspirituality circles: "I prefer dangerous freedom over peaceful slavery." (Jefferson was weighing up the costs of revolution against King George III of England, imagining complying with the crown to be a form of slavery, while downplaying his status as an owner of slaves.) As this book heads toward publication, this video is approaching one million views.

The following day, Sears hosted former UFC fighter and ex-Special Forces sniper Tim Kennedy on his podcast. He says Kennedy "stopped by to discuss the state of our freedoms during the pandemic." Episode title: "Peaceful Slavery or Dangerous Freedom?" They talked about working out, guns, Kennedy's exploits in the octagon and on the battlefield, how American pioneers were real men who had to fight bears, and how much they hate the COVID mitigation measures. Throughout the interview, Sears pandered to Kennedy's hypermasculinity, playing beta to his alpha. It's not a surprise to Holly English. "He's so wanting approval," she said, "he finds people like Mikki Willis, who's good looking. Or the guy with the guns."

In August, Tim Kennedy posted a photo of himself in fatigues beside an unmarked minivan packed with military gear. "If you are doing evil," read the caption, "you should fear the minivan. #tacticalminivan #streetsnatchers #dontriot #playstupidgameswinstupidprizes #letsride #letsroll #tactical #tacticalgear #tacticallife #tacticalminivans." Kennedy doesn't say he's on his way to Portland, Oregon. But multiple reports from George Floyd protests in that city that week document the presence of armed agents, wearing no official identification, shoving protestors into unmarked minivans.

In November, Sears attended tactical training through Kennedy's company, Sheepdog Response. Kennedy's teams run dozens of trainings every year throughout the United States, focused on shooting, hand-to-hand combat, situational awareness, field medicine, and urban warfare. The sheepdog theme comes from Lt. Col. Dave Grossman's 2004 book, *On Combat*, in which the sheepdog might frighten the sheep of the herd because he looks like the wolf, but who will hunt down and exterminate any threat. Grossman's Killology Research Group trains law enforcement officers across the US to be less hesitant about killing. He's been criticized for his emphasis on militarization, his conspiracy theorizing about malevolent forces gathering everywhere to attack the police, and telling trainees that the sex they will have the night they kill someone will be the best of their lives. (He has since walked back that statement, claiming his comments were taken out of context.)

AT SOME MOMENT NOW lost to the mists of 4chan, Pepe underwent the first of a series of transformations that freed his vibe from the moral universe altogether. Where once it had functioned as a flippant-reaction emoji for the alienated, it began appearing as an ironic but aggressive symbol of bloodlust. 4channers were starting to post about the beta uprising, by which disaffected, unemployed weirdos would seek real-world revenge against the normies. They started to draw Pepe holding hunting knives or automatic rifles. And when online tensions boiled over into incel assaults and mass shootings, yet another Pepe appeared. "Smug Pepe" gazed out of the screen, eyelids slightly raised, with a flipper hand stroking his chin. In 2015, Smug Pepe often appeared as Donald Trump, the shitposting candidate who would fulfill the online need for disruption and lulz.

Sears's arc—from earnestly feel-good to ironic to smugly nihilistic—followed Pepe's by a few years, as is usual per the relationship between the chan boards and mainstream social media. On December 20, 2020, Sears had his triumphant Smug Trump Pepe moment. He got a retweet from the lame duck President himself for a video that spread election fraud misinformation. Some identified it as parody, but it reinforced the Big Lie that drove the Capitol riot. It was viewed over 700,000 times.

When it came to the Capitol riot itself, Sears was ready to run interference for Trump. It took him just over twenty-four hours to write, record, edit, and upload a ten-minute satirical news report on the event, which he built on the common talking points the MAGA movement put out to frame it as a false flag. The Capitol Police let the rioters in, Sears said. The most violent of the protesters belonged to Antifa, he said—and the fact that Twitter had labeled that charge as misinformation was proof it was true.

"USERS WEREN'T DEBATING TOPICS to reach some sort of shared understanding or consensus," author Dale Beran wrote, describing the posting ethos on Something Awful, the message board that gave rise to 2chan, hosted Pepe on 4chan, and led to 8chan, where Q began to post in 2017—the year that JP Sears 1.0 seemed to die.

"They were elaborating on jokes, sharing files, or generating something that was unique to the web—inverted discussions where the point was not communication, but the performance of sliced-up gibberish, in which disaffected teenagers all tried collectively to derail the conversation."

This is the Sears vibe in a nutshell—plus mainstream appeal, but also something else. He wasn't content with the "irony poisoning" described by online hate-speech experts, whereby the reality status of any statement or seeming political commitment is eventually called into question. He wrapped that irony up in the bubble wrap of a New Age aphorism: "Don't outsource your truth." At the very moment he tells his followers that everyone is lying, he's claiming that truth can be internally generated. He's a hollow man, asking people to look inside. It's a phrase he uses to prioritize intuition over evidence, impulse over relationship, and the influence of people like Joe Rogan over public health officials.

How did this resonate with so many people? How are there tens of thousands cheering on every video and post? It's possible that Sears models an attractive orientation for his followers: He navigates a soulless landscape and meaningless discourse while asserting he's thinking for himself. He's a switchboard operator for every bad idea on the internet while claiming to retain internal integrity. It may be that he reassures people who feel they do not have a center that they can still act as if they do. By saying, "Don't outsource your truth," Sears is using quasi-yogic lingo to reanimate the zombie of extreme online culture: the isolated self. His ultimate life coach hook is to give his followers permission to disappear into selfishness while feeling something, anything—even if it's just smug.

CHAPTER 22

THE JESUS DOCTOR, FREED FROM EMPATHY

IN THE SUMMER of 2019, Dr. Zach Bush told a story about a spiritual epiphany to vacationers at a fancy foodie and yoga retreat in Tuscany.

Years before, he explained, he had been snorkeling off the coast of Tulum, a town on the Yucatán Peninsula. He was at a crossroads in life, not knowing whether to commit to his future wife or to a more monastic path of contemplation and clinical studies. It sounds like he was depressed. He swam, feeling for sense in the waves, peering for answers amid the coral reefs.

Suddenly, he was enveloped by a quarter-mile-long column of countless silvery sardines. The vastness of the school crushed his ego. They poured around and past him, opening a narrow space to birth him into what felt like a higher consciousness. He became, he explained, inseparable from the energy of Sardine.

After forty-five minutes in a trancelike sardine storm, Bush heard and saw sudden explosions of microbubbles all around. It was pelicans striking at the school, filling their bills with prey. For a moment he was mortified that his new friends were being eaten.

But then the sardines seemed to shout at him, saying he was wrong to feel frightened or sad. Because, in reality, they were elated to be dying. Merged with the swirling and dying sardines, Bush sensed that "transformation was happening at a very, very high, energetic level. There was zero empathy for the loss of their brethren."

Up to this point, Bush was skillfully reveling in a naturalistic mysticism where human morality and attachments melt away, along with modernity.

It's the realm of nineteenth-century romantics, who viewed themselves at the crossroads of nature and progress, and who opted to project their animal needs and longings onto the natural world. It's all pretty cool.

But then, Bush takes a skid into woo-woo territory, by suggesting that the sardine death drive is what human men feel, or should feel, as they face machine gun fire.

"You see that same thing when one million men march into war," he said, rhapsodic. "There's a loss of empathy for the individual. And there's only a sense of there's human suffering and there's human victory. And I want to be a part of that. And I'm just as willing to be part of the human suffering and loss of life as I am to be part of the victory."

There's no video of the talk, but in the audio you can hear what sounds like thirty-odd people in the room, sighing at the beauty of his self-reflection, sometimes chuckling at his self-deprecations. It's midafternoon, perhaps, with the sun streaming into the warm, engaged circle of seekers. We can imagine Bush sitting on a white couch, the listeners seated on cushions on the hardwood floor, some wrapped up in chadors or blankets. The villa waitstaff is cleaning up after an exquisitely healthy buffet. People are sipping herbal tea.

OurPlantPowerWorld, hosted yearly, runs about $8,000 to attend. Host One was vegan ultra-endurance athlete and New Age wellness podcaster Rich Roll, who had interviewed Bush six months prior to the Tuscany trip. Host Two was Rolls's business and life partner Julie Piatt, aka SriMati, a "mystic mother" and "wayshower" who sells SriMu, a vegan cheese made out of nuts. She also sells Zoom sessions that according to her website offer "powerful devotional prayer delivered from a compassionate mother, a clearing of energy residue from past and ancestral trauma and a facilitation of self initiation and empowerment into the divine mission of embodying the full blueprint of the being." The cost is $463 for either sixty or seventy-five minutes, "depending on what is mandated by the higher self."

"I think in warfare," Bush murmured in his higher-self voice, "we can reach this state of non-empathic presence. And so our challenge now as humans is I believe to reach non-empathic presence, without war. What if we can not-empathically witness loss of life?"

Bush has not been through war. But when COVID hit, he got his marching orders to embody the answer to his question. He downplayed the severity of the disease and cast doubt on the efficacy of vaccines. From 2020 onward, his contribution to conspirituality, overall, was a cruel form of mystical eugenics. A doctor preaching a religion of mystical surrender, dressed up in eco-poetry, a thinly veiled fascist-themed death wish, and a crucifixion-based understanding of the meaning of pain. There are also hints of the *Bhagavad Gita* wafting through the Tuscany villa—likely appealing to a yoga crowd drawn to Piatt and her pseudo-Sanskrit name. In the beloved poem, the faltering warrior Arjuna has a vision of countless soldiers devoured in the countless mouths of his god and master Krishna, the destroyer and redeemer of worlds. Arjuna's despondency is relieved by the knowledge that the meat-grinder war that is coming is an unavoidable sacrament that honors the divine.

Coming back to Earth, Bush ended his sardine talk by describing his hospice patients as if they were sardines. For instance, he disapproves of offering opiates to the dying, arguing that it's a selfish and fearful obstruction of the patient's spiritual transition, imposed out of misdirected empathy. He instructs his nurses to use Reiki instead. (Reiki is a modern Japanese pseudoscience of transferring "energy" between the practitioner and patient through touch or hovering hands. It has no mechanism of action, and there is no evidence that it does anything.)

"Touching them with energy and raising their vibration," he says, "pain goes down immediately. And so a non-empathic approach to pain and loss of life raises vibration." Just as the sardines realized, with joy, they were part of the cycle of life, Bush suggested his patients should have the same chance. "They were thrilled by the opportunity to be engaged in the cycle of life," he said, "which was death and rebirth."

So we've met Dr. Brogan and Dr. Cowan and Dr. Northrup. Dr. Bush is yet another fringe medic that hundreds of thousands turned to during COVID for vague advice and spiritual relief.

Somehow their followers overlooked (and they themselves obscured) the fact that none of them had ever treated a COVID patient. Followers also overlooked the narcissistic paradoxes in their reasoning. Because, with all the talk about letting the patient have their spiritual journey—up to and including sickness and death—there was no acknowledgment that said journey was only made meaningful through their version of reality. These are doctors pretending to give agency to their patients—but only if the patients accept certain beliefs about spiritual transformation.

Bush seems so confused about consent and boundaries that he believes opiates, which presumably a patient (or their legal representative authorized through the power of attorney) would be asking for, are obstructions to spiritual experience. The magic of Reiki, however—which he seems to believe is engaging the very soul of the patient—is perfectly fine.

The hypocrisy—and cruelty—reveal key contradictions in conspirituality-based health care. On one hand, conspiritualists claim that material facts like COVID aren't serious, or may not even be real. PCR tests tell us nothing, they might say, and vaccines are useless at best and poisonous at worst. Therefore, they argue, submitting to flawed treatments you can't understand is a violation of informed consent.

On the other hand, does relying on spiritual beliefs in the oneness of everything and the glory of death constitute informed consent? When Brogan, Cowan, Northrup, and Bush imply that epidemiologists are not following good evidence, how are they filling that gap? With peer-reviewed research on Kundalini Yoga, angel channeling, and Reiki? No. They are filling the epistemological gap with their charisma and speculations about God. In this position, it becomes plausible to believe that Reiki is simultaneously a powerful treatment and an intervention that doesn't require informed consent.

Conspirituality doctors do have a plausible critique to make of modern biomedicine. They are correct to note that its science and mechanisms are inaccessible to the understanding of laypeople. Research on COVID and vaccines is published in a language that requires expertise to decode. For that decoded knowledge to enter the public sphere, cultural trust in the expertise is required. In the medical sphere, this trust can easily be lost to highly visible abuses, such as when Merck concealed the cardiac risk of Vioxx. But it can also be lost through run-of-the-mill mistakes and neglect. The lab loses a test. The family doctor misses a key diagnostic moment. It is into these cracks that the conspiritualist answer leaps, offering a false sense of empowerment by pointing to spiritual solutions that, in fact, no one can understand in a scientific and replicable—this is also to say, democratic—way. These are solutions that no one has full access to, that cannot be tested or falsified.

No one can definitively understand what Bush is saying in the way that, say, vaccine manufacturers must understand COVID research in order to produce and test vaccines. Bush is using language in a poetic mode to point at metaphysical beliefs. What's dangerous about it is that the pleasure this provides to his followers can feel like understanding. And that feeling of understanding can in turn feel like consent. They are listening to a doctor from whom they would normally hear something they cannot understand. He is speaking a language of supposed universal tenderness. They can relax in the conflation of spiritual relief with medical competency. It feels like understanding, but it's probably more like parasocial attachment.

A funny thing happens when doctors pretend to be priests, and vice versa. Matthew recalls a hopeless confusion emerging while reporting on cultic dynamics in yoga groups, in which the leaders were lauded as both masters of the physical body and shamans of the spirit. In his book on Pattabhi Jois, the founder of Ashtanga Yoga, he showed how Jois's gurudom was based on a double promise. Many devotees regarded him as some kind of postural genius who was able to intuit and correct subtle misalignments in spines and joints that were signs of—or could lead to—chronic pain or spiritual darkness. Miracle stories circulated about how his physical interventions healed injuries. These stories also erased the reality that many of these interactions were actually physical or sexual assaults. In addition to his supposed brilliance as a physician, Jois was lauded as a spiritual master, able to lead devotees toward awakening.

The double promise is attractive and duplicitous. In Jois's case, it allowed the goalposts of practice to be moved so often that they eventually disappeared. If the intense postures and manhandling adjustments didn't bring about spiritual revelation, then at least they made the body healthy and strong. But if those very same postures and sacred assaults tore the devotee's joints apart or injured their spine, the pain was a spiritual opportunity to transcend the body. If Jois didn't enlighten you, he was just a doctor, and the awakening was your responsibility. If he injured you, he was your priest, conferring painful but essential lessons.

The bitter irony was that Jois was incompetent in both categories. Despite the idealizing projections of his non-Indian students, he never actually offered any lessons in yoga philosophy or the Hindu religious practices that seemed to wrap him in a glow of piety. Several of his survivors said outright that there was never anything spiritual about the man. At the same time, he had zero education in anatomy or biomechanics. He was allowed to strut around for decades, pretending to dole out physical therapy.

Somehow, a double incompetency, hidden by charisma, allowed Jois to fail upward. In the case of Zach Bush, an ignorance of COVID research and clinical practice combined with a cruel but alluring religious flare to make him a conspirituality celebrity.

On May 19, 2020, Bush went viral on Del Bigtree's anti-vax podcast *The HighWire*. Bush regaled the audience of over 170,000 followers with his life story of learning, and then doubting, evidence-based medicine. He described a path that took him from volunteering in a birthing center in the Philippines to med school, and then on to specializing in internal medicine and hospice care, and then private boutique nutritional services. He told Bigtree that COVID-19 is an environmental, not an epidemiological, problem.

Within two weeks, the video racked up over 1.4 million views. Bigtree's YouTube channel (210,000 subscribers) was deleted that July after a Media Matters investigation detailed how Bigtree labeled COVID-19 as "one of the most mild illnesses there is," that wearing a mask was unhealthy, that people should expose themselves to the virus in order to build herd immunity, and that the forthcoming vaccines would be dangerous. At the time of writing, Bush's appearance on Bigtree's show is still up on Bush's YouTube channel, and has been shared over 3,600 times on Facebook.

Bigtree, a former field producer for the TV show *Dr. Phil*, made his debut in anti-vax propaganda by producing a film lionizing Andrew Wakefield, the originator of the discredited theory that vaccines cause autism. Bigtree is the CEO of anti-vax lobby group Informed Consent Action Network, and drew a 2019 salary of $232,000. According to a report by the Center for Countering Digital Hate, Bigtree's anti-vax propaganda generates close to $3.5 million in yearly income.

The platform is lucrative, but not necessarily a grift. By all appearances, Bigtree is a true believer. A year after sitting down with Bush, he even risked his life for his anti-vax beliefs. Chronically bleeding hemorrhoids landed him in the hospital with dangerously low hemoglobin. Unwilling to receive transfusions from donors who might have been vaccinated, he set out on a harrowing journey to find "clean" blood, which followers reportedly located for him through a cancer clinic in Tijuana. He flew there in a private jet.

Bigtree asked Bush leading questions about whether COVID-19 was manufactured in a Chinese lab. Bush didn't commit to an opinion, but claimed, without evidence, that he'd predicted a pandemic emerging from Wuhan due to the region's high rates of air and soil pollution. He also speculated that COVID-19 treatment should be the same as for cyanide poisoning and that ventilators are of no use.

Bush cloaks his anti-vax and COVID-minimization attitudes behind plausible concerns about the human microbiome—the bacteriological milieu of gut and skin health. He argues that we humans have been weeding ourselves to death, externally and internally, depleting the biodiversity of our soils and bodies with pesticides and antibiotics, to the point at which robust immunity and holistic resilience are beyond our reach. He's also clear about climate danger—a topic typically missing from conspirituality discourse. Among our cast so far, Bush rocks the most holistic, internationally minded, and ecologically concerned look.

A key subtext of Zach Bush's COVID-19 content—coming from a doctor who never worked on the pandemic front lines—is that COVID researchers and health care workers are ignorant in a religious sense. He implies that the pandemic is revealing the spiritual illiteracy of conventional medicine while unmasking the toxicity of our environment. "There's something poetic about that," he stated in another interview, adding that social distancing and vaccines will make the pandemic worse because they won't address the underlying spiritual wounds.

Bush's job within the anti-vax movement, it seems, is to generate a surge of poetic oratory. In the closing minutes of the Bigtree interview, Bush launched into a Tuscany-style sermon about life and death. It poured out like a revelation, and again turned toward military metaphors.

"Marines are taught to never leave a soldier on the battlefield," he said. "Marines will literally charge into machine gun fire, into rocket fire, to go grab that injured soldier so that they don't die alone in enemy hands." But then he suggested that frontline COVID-19 workers were cowardly because they were not facing war, but a condition with mortality rates similar to flu.

Bush claims that crimes against humanity are being perpetrated in ICUs, where patients are dying alone, on a kind of battlefield. Doctors should be like

Marines, never abandoning their comrades. (Of course they never did. News reports of COVID-19 patients dying alone uniformly described the tragic absence of *family*, not medical staff.) He criticizes doctors for not acting like Marines (when in fact they are not fleeing the battlefield), but also argues that this kind of imitation is unnecessary, because COVID-19 isn't all that bad, certainly not like war. COVID-19 is a war when Bush needs a war to symbolize modern corruption. But it's a flu when he needs a flu to illuminate modern cowardice.

There's no way of making Bush make sense. And that's what makes Bush's next pivot really interesting. Out of the senseless mess he has made of the world and his own brain, a religious attitude shines forth as the only plausible answer. "What are we doing with this tyranny of fear?" he asked.

> We are tearing apart the very fabric of what it means to be human. There is an innate drive in us to stay connected, to stay in one another's presence. To have fellowship with one another, it's written into our constitution that you will not block public gatherings, you will not block the ability for us to get together and practice our spiritual faith, to practice our spiritual experience, and if anything is a hallowed ground of spiritual environment, it is the birthplace of a child and the birthplace of an elder person, about to transition to the other side. There are two births that happen to humankind.

IT IS NOT SURPRISING to learn that Bush's father was a preacher in Boulder, Colorado. The day before his Bigtree gig, Bush appeared on a Facebook livestream and told the story of his family's links to the Bush political dynasty, and his evangelical upbringing in a home church founded by a former union leader out of Detroit whose mission was to "save the hippies from their drug-infested culture." (The "home" or "house church" movement was an outgrowth of socially conservative 1960s "restorationism," which sought to re-create the small-scale religious communities imagined to exist in biblical times, free from clerical bureaucracy and state influence.)

"Their approach to evangelism," Bush said, "was to pick hippies up off the street and throw them against the wall and threaten to beat the crap out of them if they didn't come to church Sunday night." That's how they recruited his father, who went from down on his luck to church elder, and stayed for forty years.

Bigtree shares this part of Bush's background. His own father, Jack Gro-verland, has been a senior preacher at Unity of Boulder—also for over forty years—alongside Bigtree's mother, Norma Bigtree, who leads the choir. Unity of Boulder is affiliated with the Unity movement, which emerged in the late nineteenth century as part of the Christian New Thought movement. It was founded by Myrtle Fillmore, a former schoolteacher who believed she'd cured her chronic tuberculosis through the power of prayer. The faith's vibe is universalist, transcendentalist, and art-friendly in a sentimental way.

Jack and Norma met in the New York City theater scene in the 1960s, and the stagecraft at their Unity franchise in Boulder shows it. She wears feathers and beads honoring her Mohawk heritage; he wears linen-silk Nehru jackets. The sound and lights are sharp and the synthesizers drone during the breaks. The stage altar is layered with silks and curtains and festooned with a smorgasbord of iconography: Tibetan seed-syllable thang-kas, a menorah, a golden cross, a Tantric deity in bronze. On March 15, 2020, only four days after the WHO declared a pandemic, Groverland took to the stage to deliver a sermon called "Coronavirus and Truth," in which he quoted heavily from *A Course in Miracles* to remind his parishioners that sickness only happens to those who believe they are separate from each other, and from God.

Groverland's focus illuminates what's so intolerable about the pandemic from a New Age point of view: anything a person regards as fearful in the world is an illusory projection of one's own ignorance and fear. It is an abomination to think that we must hide ourselves from each other, for fear of making each other sick. This idea violates the most stubbornly hopeful belief of the demographic: that one's inner nature is wholly good, wholly pure, that it's inconceivable that the invisible part of oneself—especially the breath, upon which the soul rides—might be dangerous to others.

"If to love oneself is to heal oneself," Groverland intoned while a PowerPoint slide show projected quotes from *A Course in Miracles*, "therefore they are asking for the love that would heal them, but which they are denying to themselves. If they knew the truth about themselves they could not be sick."

To his credit, just days later, Groverland released an announcement with his daughter and son-in-law (both ministers) to say that Unity of Boulder would be closing its doors to comply with state and local COVID restrictions. They assured parishioners that they would remain connected by Spirit.

Del Bigtree isn't in the family church business, but he has appeared at Unity of Boulder to give talks on the dangers of vaccines. We were interested in finding out how much of Bigtree's content—which eschews the overtly spiritual for nonstop pseudoscience—was informed by his father's ministry. Neither returned our request for comment.

WELLNESS PUNDITS KRISTA Williams and Lindsey Simcik described getting tearful while interviewing Bush for their podcast, *Almost 30*, a project they say has netted seventy-five million downloads.

> KRISTA: He started speaking about, just like, the beauty of nature and the beauty of us as humans outside of things that make us feel separate from ourselves and wow I mean, so I was crying.... When I looked at you crying too, I was like, "Oh my god, dude."
>
> LINDSEY: And then you look at Zach and he's just Jesus Christ.
>
> KRISTA: Jesus Christ on screen. Fully Jesus Christ. He's literally come back after channeling Jesus Christ. You guys: this is us just saying it. He never said that he was channeling Jesus Christ, FYI. And it was like just fully holding his own energy of whatever was said, and just following the intuition of it.

Williams and Simcik weren't specific about when their waterworks started. It might have been during this typically Bushian ecstatic monologue, which they clipped and remixed for Instagram, adding gorgeous visuals:

> Go create with nature today. Don't buy something today. Go create something today. Plant a seed. Stack a stack of rocks in the river and see the river move those. Play with nature today. Go outside and revisit your beauty. You don't even know yourself yet. Society has not let you see it. You don't know what lies within you, because society has made sure you don't know your own power. You are a force to be reckoned with, and you are graceful, and you are beautiful. O my God you are so beautiful and you showed up right now. Thank you for the courage that it took to show up at the tipping point of all things. Thank you for being willing to listen to nature and see her and follow her into a different path

for humanity. Thank you for finding yourself behind the makeup, behind the products, behind the clothes. Find yourself. Love yourself. And through that, we will find our beauty and we will find the reverence for humanity as much as nature.

The rhapsody, delivered in Bush's signature drone, tinged by his gravelly vocal fry, is handcrafted for the "female-dominated New Age (with its positive focus on self)," described for us by Charlotte Ward and David Voas, way back in 2011. Its evangelicalism, laundered of explicitly Christian language, is catnip for a conspirituality world that views itself as nondenominational.

With Bush's *Almost 30* sermon, we can see some clear techniques emerge:

1. **Patronize.** Start from the guilt-inducing assumption that the listener has been ignoring nature, that they don't realize they live on a planet, amidst "nature." If the female audience is given to gender essentialism, the guilt is sharpened. Women, of all people, should not be ignoring nature.
2. **Exclude.** Pretend that everyone has access to a river on a lazy afternoon, and that playing there will solve all problems.
3. **Flatter.** Tell the two women you're sermonizing at how beautiful they are, knowing that they have millions of female listeners. As they tear up, press on.
4. **Subtly shame.** Thank two women who are wearing makeup and beauty products for radiating a beauty that transcends makeup and products. Subliminally note the wellness pornography they cosign, but also tell them they're better than all that.

Zach Bush is not on the alt-health glamor circuit because people understand or even need his pseudoscience hot takes. He's there to provide emotional and sensual stimulation. He's there to provide a contrast to the unsexy work of public health. Did we mention how extremely good-looking he is? He's a pseudoscience thirst trap, with a side order of Jesus.

CHAPTER 23

A KENNEDY SON SPIRALS

IN THE SUMMER of 2003, Matthew had been out of Endeavor Academy for only a few short months. He began his return into the real world and working life. He waited on tables, took a crash course in yoga teaching, then helped convert a vacant warehouse space in the small town of Baraboo, Wisconsin, into the area's first yoga studio. He also started to daydream about politics again. One Sunday afternoon in September he found himself sitting in the rickety grandstand of the Sauk County Fairgrounds, listening to Robert F. Kennedy Jr. bible-thump about environmental pollution.

The old-timey chautauqua-style event was called Fighting Bob Fest, named after Wisconsin's famed socialist governor Robert La Follette (1901–1906). Speaking alongside Kennedy was Jim Hightower, the anticorporatist from Texas with a ten-gallon cowboy hat, and a raft of pro-labor organizers. Kennedy was handsome and brash, speaking full paragraphs with only quick glances at dog-eared index cards. He touched lightly on an issue or two that might have predicted this anti-vax trajectory: the problem with GMOs and the dangers of fluoride in tap water and mercury in the rivers.

The air was brisk, the sun bright, the mood cheerful. There was a beer tent, a BBQ pit, and fiddle music. It was a thrilling day that started to re-awaken the activism of Matthew's pre-cult life. But he was still a long way from home, still alienated from old friends and family, still recovering. He had to make money, find some confidence, and get his feet on the ground. On Monday it was back to waiting tables.

Letting the inspiration of that day fizzle out might have been a blessing. With a different turn of the screw, Matthew could well have found himself following Kennedy into political organizing or lobbying work, and then unconsciously drifting from cult life into an anti-vax culture disguised as progressive idealism. The only pathway for Matthew into the anti-vax world would have been from the left, and that is exactly what this buttoned-down firebrand offered.

ON JUNE 7, 2020, Robert F. Kennedy Jr. led a protest on the steps of the Colorado Capitol in Denver that linked civil rights activism to anti-vax and COVID conspiracy theories. Alongside him were a Black Senate candidate, an NAACP leader, and a local Black Lives Matter leader.

Kennedy's alliance with Black leaders capitalizes on the civil rights legacy of his family, exploits the historical trauma of medical racism in the United States, and helps provide the largely white anti-vax movement with a veneer of diversity. But the pro-social vibe is complicated when the players include Tony Muhammad of the Nation of Islam, designated by the Southern Poverty Law Center as a Black supremacist hate group that promotes antisemitic and anti-LGBTQ rhetoric.

At the protest, Theo Wilson, the BLM leader, raised the ghost of the Tuskegee Syphilis Study. This medical atrocity, which ran from 1932 to 1972, recruited Black men afflicted with the disease so that government researchers, who were mostly white, could study its long-term effects. The researchers did not disclose the men's diagnosis to them and only treated their symptoms with placebos. The ghoulish aim was to document what would happen as the disease progressed. Twenty-eight of the 399 sick patients died directly from syphilis. A hundred died from complications related to syphilis, 40 of the men's wives were infected, and 19 children were born with the disease.

Black pro-vaccine activists reject the Tuskegee comparison, because it involved withholding medication without consent. In critiquing Kennedy's racial opportunism, they explain that whatever vaccine hesitancy exists in their communities stems from current structural racism, producing impacts such as unequal access to care—an issue that Kennedy and other white anti-vax activists do not highlight.

KENNEDY, THE SON of assassinated presidential candidate Bobby Kennedy, is best known as an environmental rights lawyer focused on industrial pollution and the excesses of agribusiness. His son, Conor, has an anaphylactic allergy to peanuts. In 1998, Kennedy and then-wife Mary Richardson co-founded the Food Allergy Initiative (now renamed Food Allergy Research and Education) to raise funds for scientific research seeking to understand and find cures for food allergies. But in 2005, Kennedy expanded his interests to vaccines when an activist mother showed up on his Cape Cod, Massachusetts, doorstep with piles of documents purporting to show a link between vaccines and autism. In 2016, he founded Children's Health Defense, one of the largest anti-vax nonprofits in the US. In addition to propagandizing against vaccines, the organization claims that pesticides, fluoride, and exposure to other chemicals have caused "an epidemic of chronic disease in children." Kennedy's main focus has been on the false idea that the mercury compound thimerosal makes vaccines unsafe, even though it has been phased out since 2001. Back in his environmentalist days, mercury poisoning in water and food chains was one of Kennedy's top concerns. In 2017 he wrote the foreword to *The Peanut Allergy Epidemic*, which falsely alleges that childhood vaccines cause food allergies, and whose cover bears a large image of a syringe needle.

In 2019, Kennedy's activism was implicated in a measles outbreak in Samoa that infected 5,700 and killed 83. Kennedy had personally visited Samoa earlier that year, and was pictured with local anti-vaccine advocates at the US embassy. This was followed by his Children's Health Defense organization sending a letter to the president of Samoa, urging him to question the safety of the MMR vaccine, which protects against measles, mumps, and rubella. This tragedy rhymed with measles outbreaks in Somali immigrant communities in Minnesota in 2011 and 2017. They had been specifically targeted by anti-vax propagandist Andrew Wakefield, whose falsified 1998 study started the still-lingering conspiracy theory that the MMR vaccine causes autism.

In March 2021, Children's Health Defense released a one-hour film titled *Medical Racism: The New Apartheid*. Again, it abused the valid critique of Tuskegee as a launchpad for anti-vax conspiracy theories and COVID-denial propaganda. It also misrepresented data on Somali immigrants and the rubella vaccine, and falsely claimed that vitamin D protects against COVID-19 and that Black people are naturally immune to the disease.

This propaganda film promoted the deadly belief that Blacks have stronger natural immunity. Kennedy's website lists Tony Muhammad, prominent leader in the Black separatist and openly antisemitic Nation of Islam, as a coproducer. Since 2015, Muhammad has been repeating the false claim that the CDC genetically modified MMR vaccines to harm Black and Latino boys.

KENNEDY'S POLITICAL HERITAGE and leftward lean make him unique among anti-vax sources. But his methods are not unique at all. They follow a conspirituality playbook in which experts in one area seize upon a presumed expertise in another. They weave a Russian-doll story, in which threats to the body are conflated with threats to the entire world, and in which the language of justice movements is turned inside out.

But let's back up a bit. So far, we've seen how medical doctors can deploy their credentials and legacies to disguise and advance conspirituality. To do it successfully, they typically convert credible clinical experience in some narrow aspect of physiology into grand pronouncements about global systems they do not understand.

Some examples we already know: Christiane Northrup mobilizes her iconic status as a women's reproductive health advocate to falsely warn about how vaccines cause widespread sterility—in the vaccinated and unvaccinated alike. Apparently not content with that, she gives podcast talks on "rebirthing the world." On a parallel track, Northrup's friend Kelly Brogan bounces from a focused critique of the bias of conventional psychiatry to pathologize reasonable stress responses—especially the anger of women in a misogynistic rise-and-grind culture—to becoming, in her words, a "doctor of the soul."

In the case of Robert F. Kennedy Jr., we see the workflow running in the opposite direction: from macro to micro. He's a big-picture environmentalist fluent in geopolitical intrigue and corporate malfeasance. But when Kennedy pivots to anti-vax content, these large-scale themes collapse into a single medical-sized issue. His expertise on the imperiled global environment shoehorns down to an obsession with the individual body—especially the child's body—as its symbolic victim.

But Kennedy also has a second reduction in play. Leaning on the iconic authority of his family's civil rights legacy, he conflates the repressions of structural racism with the best practices of public health. Kennedy deploys the dynastic trust his family has secured from Black communities to suggest that vaccination is a racially targeted poison—akin to unequal voting laws, the problem of food deserts, or police brutality.

Kennedy does find some contemporary Black allies who cosign his pitch, but this narrow and self-serving view of Black liberation efforts in the field of public health erases a nuanced history. We never hear from Kennedy, for example, about how in the 1970s the Black Panthers made access to free, evidence-based health care a pillar of their revolutionary vision. They established thirteen free health clinics in communities across the country, offering physicals, gynecological and dental exams, and cancer screenings. They sponsored pioneering research. They also provided...wait for it...free vaccinations.

This movement continues, albeit with less bombast than Kennedy's saviorism. Dr. Mary Bassett, former health commissioner for New York City, cut her teeth as a volunteer in the Black Panther clinic in Boston, where she set up a screening program for sickle cell anemia—a disease that mainly affects Black people, and that had long been neglected by mainly white research institutions. And in April 2020, Philadelphia-based pediatric surgeon Dr. Ala Stanford founded the Black Doctors COVID-19 Consortium, which went on to provide over twenty-six thousand COVID-19 tests and more than ten thousand COVID-19 vaccinations in Black community settings. Stanford cites her father's affinity with the Black Panthers as a guiding light in her work.

The urgent dread of Kennedy's rhetoric makes it sound like the full horror of environmental and racial injustice quivers at the tip of a syringe. When he speaks about the vaccine injected into the child's arm, you'd think he was watching countless bullets enter countless bodies in slow motion. Mass vaccination policy becomes a global grassy-knoll conspiracy that Kennedy seems compelled to unravel forever.

As Northrup, Brogan, Kennedy—and many more—toggle between nation and body, macro and micro, they invigorate the memory of an old axiom of hermetic, occult, and now New Age thought. "As above, so below," as the phrase goes—attributed by medieval alchemists to the mythic Greek Egyptian figure of Hermes Trismegistus. A similar thought shows up centuries earlier in Indian scripture: the Sanskrit phrase *yathā brahmāṇḍa tathā piṇḍāṇḍa* translates to "as is the individual, so is the universe."

This idea is at the root of holism. Disease in the body reflects disease in the land, which itself reflects imbalances in the cosmos, or even conflict among the gods. This is the foundation of astrology—a favorite conspirituality discipline—in which a lunar eclipse can portend the death of one's mother, tuberculosis, or drought. It is also the basis of premodern medicine, in which the body's illnesses are mirrored in the weather, and in which fever carries the blessing of the sun, and life force flows like a river.

Resurrected from a time in which medicine and religion were inseparable, holism pushes back against scientific compartmentalization, and speaks to the common disillusionment with the fifteen-minute doctor's visit—that feeling that the person in the white coat isn't really seeing the whole you. Kelly Brogan wields influence to the extent that she has been trained in the brain chemistry of depression. She can wear a white lab coat with authority. But she can also don the white pajamas of the Kundalini cult and behold a vision of your soul. She can prescribe the pills if she must, but her greater gift is to empower you with yoga.

The tropes of holism can soothe the fragmented modern mind. But the salve can come with the high price of category confusion, false equivalency, and therapeutic vagueness. When Northrup links vaccination drives to rape culture, when Brogan calls masking submission signaling vis-à-vis the state, and when Kennedy links environmental degradation and structural racism to vaccination, their rhetoric might be in the black, but their solution game is in the red.

When it comes down to it, conspirituality influencers never seem to have the resources or skills to upgrade their products as they scale their profiles to the task of public health. Northrup is still selling the same herbal remedies she was promoting before the pandemic hit. Brogan is still advocating that people meditate to enhance their immunity. And when Kennedy flips from the global environment to vaccines, he's still talking about mercury poisoning—a problem in the Hudson River, but not in vaccines.

In more than two years of watching Robert F. Kennedy Jr. bluster about imagined vaccine aggression against Black Americans—in the midst of a pandemic that disproportionately killed them—we didn't once see him offer anything of concrete benefit to the demographic he fetishizes and co-opts. He never came close to echoing the rhetoric of his uncle standing on the stage of Madison Square Garden in 1962, arguing for the same universal health care that the Black Panthers enshrined as a policy objective.

The vacuum of real-world solutions is a conspirituality dilemma. After rejecting consensus reality on viruses and vaccines, what's the actual plan? It's a mystery, which is why it's not surprising that the pandemic marathon led Kennedy toward God. By Labor Day of 2021, he was giving the keynote address at Godspeak Calvary Chapel in Thousand Oaks, California. It was part of a conference that braided COVID-contrarianism with false claims about vaccines and autism.

Kennedy used some pretty extreme language in his speech. "We are in the last battle. This is the apocalypse. We are fighting for the salvation of all humanity."

ON JANUARY 23, 2022, Kennedy enjoyed top billing at the Defeat the Mandates march that gathered at the Lincoln Memorial.

The master of ceremonies was none other than JP Sears, who tossed red meat to the MAGA crowd. "Freedom wins," he shouted, "and God's plan wins—the only question is, what's the timeline? You and I are here together to accelerate the timeline of freedom, and we're not here to ask permission."

Sears invoked Martin Luther King Jr.'s axiom that "one has a moral responsibility to disobey unjust laws," continuing that "MLK wasn't such a mandate guy as it turns out, he was very pro-freedom."

Kennedy took the stage and said that over the past two years they had "witnessed a coup d'état of democracy and a controlled demolition of the Constitution and the Bill of Rights." He railed against the censorship of free speech while speaking to thousands through a microphone on the steps of the Lincoln Memorial.

When in their flow, conspiritualists never really know when to stop. "What we're seeing today," Kennedy bellowed, "is what I call turnkey totalitarianism." Every totalitarian state, he claimed, has sought to control every aspect of life, and been unsuccessful, until now. "None of them have been able to do it," Kennedy said. "They didn't have the technological capacity. Even in Hitler's Germany you could cross the Alps into Switzerland, you could hide in an attic like Anne Frank did." He must have meant Holland. Kennedy quickly apologized for the comment in response to a flood of criticism.

While Kennedy made an ass of himself at the Lincoln Memorial, news reports showed that his Children's Health Defense had doubled their income to $6.8 million in 2020. His payout that year as chairman was $345,561, up from $90,000 in 2019. Currently, Kennedy has an Amazon-ranked bestseller targeting the alleged corruption of Anthony Fauci. Sales are estimated to bring in between $2.5 and $3.8 million.

In May 2020, Kennedy's Children's Health Defense took a PPP loan worth $146,685. The PPP, or Paycheck Protection Program, is a federal government aid program that provided forgivable loans to small businesses and nonprofits to pay their employees during the COVID pandemic. Kennedy's personal net worth (according to the website Celebrity Net Worth) currently stands at $50 million, but that didn't stop him from taking out an additional PPP loan on April 30, 2020, of $20,000, for himself.

These government-sponsored COVID-relief loans turn out to have been quite popular among those decrying pandemic public health measures and spreading conspiracy theories about government tyranny. JP Sears, for example, received $58,488 on February 8, 2021. The *Washington Post* reported that in addition to Children's Health Defense, four other prominent anti-vaccine organizations combined for a shared haul of over $850,000—all most likely plowed back into prolonging the pandemic with misinformation that risked the lives of the most vulnerable.

The Center for Countering Digital Hate ranked Kennedy in second place on their list of the twelve influencers responsible for up to 73 percent of all anti-vax content on Facebook, and 65 percent of all digital anti-vax content overall. Kennedy had already been identified in 2019 as the leading buyer of anti-vax ads on Facebook.

CHAPTER 24

5D FEMME

To walk into the RA MA Institute in Venice Beach, California, is like walking into an intergenerational cult vortex. The walls are plastered with images of 1970s yoga leaders instructing huge classes on the beach. But those walls lead to a shrine room tricked out with top-shelf AV gear pointed at a teaching dais where white-turbanned instructors can stream live classes around the world. If you arrive at the right time, you'll encounter a radiant ruckus: students twisting, sighing, laughing, hyperventilating, and singing endless chants. What you won't encounter, these days at least, is the eccentric force behind it all. Guru Jagat's outsized personality, her fabulous fashion, her reactionary pseudo-feminism, her dreadful behavior, and the dangerous misinformation she pumped out during the pandemic were all stopped short by her early death.

She was born as Katie Griggs in Colorado in 1979. For a short while, she was a top dog in the land of Kundalini Yoga—a pastiche of contrived esoteric yoga practices, faux Sikh devotionalism, and alternative health woo. As she rose in the ranks, she drifted between aliases: Athena Day, Katie Day, and Kundalini Katie. Before her sudden passing in November 2021, Griggs headed up an extremely online franchise of Kundalini called the RA MA Institute. The flagship studio has been blessed by the glow of celebrities like Alicia Keys, Kate Hudson, and Kelly Rutherford. Griggs claimed that she'd received the name Guru Jagat from Kundalini founder Yogi Bhajan before he died in 2004, but there's no evidence that they actually met. It's now widely known that Bhajan was a serial rapist and fraudster.

Griggs's business partner was Steven Hartzell, known as Harijiwan, a direct disciple of Bhajan. Now sixty-eight, Hartzell served jail time in 2000 for defrauding customers of his office supply business. He earned the nickname "Toner Bandit" after a scam involving billing companies for printer toner that he never shipped. Investigative reports quoted former RA MA students saying that Hartzell was pulling all the strings, with one calling him the "puppet master" in relation to Griggs's business and content choices. Another former student of Hartzell's called him "the man behind the curtain."

As this book goes to press, we know of two documentary teams working on the Griggs story for competing streaming services. It makes sense: Griggs's estate brings terabytes of archival footage and orphaned social media accounts to the editing room. There are music videos and eulogies. Her fashion line now haunts the charity shops of LA, and hundreds of former followers remember her through hundreds of differing lenses. There's also been an entire academic history written about her so-called lineage, painting a detailed picture of the machine she both fell into and supercharged.

Yoga scholar Philip Deslippe, who used to be a follower of Bhajan, meticulously researched all of Bhajan's claims of authenticity, and turned up no evidence to confirm any of them. The guru that Bhajan said he was inspired by may never have existed. The practices that he claimed came from a venerable tradition have no known antecedent. The Indian Sikhs with whom he shared heritage generally loathe his usage of Sikhism to authenticate his charlatanry. Bhajan was a bullshitter and cult leader in the classic post-1960s mold, and Griggs inherited his bag. Deslippe likens her next-generation content to a photocopy of a counterfeit bill.

Bingeable Netflix subjects can easily become two-dimensional cartoons, especially when the underwear beneath the cultic robes is on full display. To see Katie Griggs—and Guru Jagat—clearly and humanely requires walking a tightrope similar to the ones she teetered across. We have to be clear about how she hurt people, and also how she was hurting. About how she made choices, but often under the pressure of cultic predetermination.

IN CULTIC TERMS, Griggs is an intergenerational cipher who inherited the authority, the grandiosity, and the shame of a monster. She got swept up into a decades-old organization in which the founder's cruelty and assaults and racism were rationalized—if they were acknowledged at all. Her mentors were compromised by this legacy, which gave her a complicated pathway to power, and perhaps even the sense that she could do better, that the twenty-first century would be different. When she found power in that network, she seized it, blurring the line between victim and perpetrator.

If we zoom out, we also see that Griggs walked another line, between the misogyny of her spiritual heritage and her desire to be a feminist icon. Yogi Bhajan held women in utter contempt. He kept an inner circle of "secretaries" responsible for administrative duties and providing him with sex. He would call women prostitutes if they displeased him or indicated the desire to leave. He said that being gay, lesbian, or divorced was a sign of spiritual weakness that invited a person to be exploited.

On the idealizing side, Bhajan gushed a firehose of spiritualized gender binaries in which men were kings and women were queens, but never the twain should be equal. In Bhajan's world, a woman could be a leader if she accepted her divine role in a binary universe, defined by her sexual allure and reproductive enthusiasm. Griggs took all of that on, but also chopped and tossed it with sass, fashion, and tech for a new generation hooked on social media.

LA-based journalist Stacie Stukin summed up Griggs on a podcast panel shortly after her death. "Funny, appealing, a good yoga teacher who owned her sexuality, her business acumen, her distinctive style—all in a very positive way. And as she ascended to her stature before her death… That idiosyncratic, girl-boss style became an attractive characteristic. It was appealing and relatable."

With her theater background, Instagram wizardry, and a finger on the pulse of Los Angeles fashion, Griggs was the ideal millennial reformer of a boomer cult in decline. She updated Yogi Bhajan's manic hodgepodge of stretches, breathing exercises, fruit fasts, and all-night meditation sessions with a tightly run media operation, clothing line, and starlet clientele. On the fashion front, she loosened up Bhajan's unironic uniform of white Punjabis, kurtas, and bejeweled turbans with a sense of untidy bohemian vogue and an eye for cultural echoes.

Griggs's appeal, Stukin explained, won out with "a creative class of mostly white women who wanted successful relationships, prosperous businesses, spiritual enlightenment, and health." Her pastiche lifestyle brand was accessorized with competing eras, cultures, and feminisms.

"She very skillfully managed her image," Stukin told us. She described reviewing Griggs's headshots, and finding one in which she mimicked the look of Gloria Steinem, with a black turtleneck and oversized glasses. "It's the iconic second-wave feminist image," Stukin said, "and Guru Jagat had never worn black." For Stukin, it couldn't have been a coincidence. "She was purposely taking on the mantle of feminism and building upon it, and asserting her place, as the modern representative of what she called '5D femme.'"

But the slick term, Stukin concluded, "is a RA MA–ism that has no relevance outside that rape-apologist bubble."

Griggs's feminist veneer and style upgrades worked for the New Age Los Angeles set, but they disgusted the global Sikh community, which already despised Kundalini Yoga's lazy appropriations of Sikhism. "Guru" is a blasphemous honorific for a religion that reserves the title for its ten core saints. And Griggs was famous for styling her loosened turban into a Burning Man headscarf that let her dreadlocks zigzag free. To Sikhs, Griggs's sloppy turban was akin to showing up on the gym floor in a sports bra with one breast hanging out.

When COVID struck, Griggs's RA MA operation was shuttered, until she decided to disobey masking mandates in LA County. But overall, the pandemic was a boon to Griggs. Her brand was in crisis and the pandemic offered a prime opportunity for her to change the channel, expand online operations, and offer rich new veins of conspiratorial content.

Cults are built on conspiracy theorizing, and history is filled with paranoid cult leaders who use persecution complexes to sharpen their edges: Osho—whose story was told in the Netflix blockbuster *Wild Wild Country*—was so on edge he aided and abetted a biowarfare attack on his Oregonian neighbors. Jim Jones fled to Guyana, convinced that the CIA had a price on his head. Matthew's cult leader, Charles Anderson, offered the pronoia version of the pattern. Every day, Anderson predicted that CNN would show up with a satellite truck to broadcast his sermons on prime time.

Anything dangerous in the outside world that can bolster a conspiratorial mindset will also confirm the myth of in-group safety. It's gold to the savvy leader. When Yogi Bhajan would drone on about how the FBI was out to get him, he became at once the target of danger, and the source of safety from it. So the question of how much Griggs really believed in the COVID conspiracism and Q-adjacent content that eventually ate her brain is obscured by the problem of how useful it was for her at any given moment and how much it allowed her to play the role of protector for her followers.

* * *

GRIGGS FOUNDED RA MA in 2013—nine years after Yogi Bhajan's death of heart failure. In cult years, this is a reasonable time frame for a leadership transition. It took another seven years for Griggs's inheritance to really be tested—as the full extent of Yogi Bhajan's abuses were revealed, and as COVID provided a once-in-a-lifetime opportunity to circle the wagons.

In January 2020, Pamela Dyson, formerly known as Premka, published a memoir about her time as a "secretary" for Yogi Bhajan. She described meeting him in 1968 at the age of twenty-five, and quickly being swept up into decades of emotional and sexual exploitation. Her renown within the group gave weight and volume to whispers that had circulated for years. Within weeks, a Facebook group formed to study and support Dyson's book, and soon attracted dozens of similar testimonies of abuse—including from those who as children had been separated from their families by Bhajan and sent to ashram schools in India that were poorly organized and rife with abuse.

The spotlight brought renewed attention to Bhajan's odious record, with recordings of his lectures recovered and circulated on Facebook. "Rape is always invited," he told followers in 1978. "A person who is raped is always providing subconsciously the environments and the arrangements. If you do not provide the circumstances and the arrangements, it is impossible."

Griggs could have found a new direction in this spotlit moment—perhaps one that would have given her feminist branding some substance. Instead, she cast her lot in with the patriarchs by promoting a video by Hartzell that implied Dyson was lying, and by sermonizing on Instagram: "This tale is no truer than any other tale—the Truth as always lies in the eye of the Beholder."

As the pandemic kicked into high gear, Griggs rode the cultic victim blaming for all it was worth. This allowed her to bundle the revelations about Bhajan and mainstream reporting on the pandemic under the same banner of fake news. By the summer of 2020, Griggs accelerated into more extreme content by starting to interview QAnon boosters.

GRIGGS MAY NOT HAVE had a choice but to go fully red-pilled. That July, an anonymous Instagram account called @ramawrong began publishing anonymous allegations of abusive behavior at RA MA Institute. Griggs was accused of verbally and emotionally abusing volunteers who were expected to attend to her capricious needs at all hours. A year later, an investigative piece in *VICE* verified the stories. "According to her former followers," wrote journalist Cassidy George,

> several of whom said that they are currently in therapy and reported increased feelings of anxiety and depression, as well as symptoms of PTSD, due to the time they spent under her tutelage, Griggs is merely modifying an age-old cycle of abuse, this time, for the Instagram generation. Under the veil of her fashionable facade and feminist discourse, she's repackaged Bhajan's tactics for spiritual indoctrination in a cloud of millennial pink.

George's investigation also uncovered a lawsuit launched in 2016 against Griggs by former business partners at a RA MA franchise in Boulder, Colorado. The suit, which was settled out of court, alleged financial fraud and breach of contract.

WhatsApp exchanges between Griggs and her inner circle reveal her sharing Mikki Willis's *Plandemic* and other conspiracy theory videos from YouTube. Griggs's stepfather participated in a *Vanity Fair* investigation and said that she had yelled at the family, warning them not to watch CNN, "because they were part of the deep state and George Soros was behind this thing, Pizzagate stuff. Crazy bullshit."

By the fall of 2020, she was speculating on alien wars, how spirit guides can be infiltrated and compromised, and suggesting the California forest fires were being started by space lasers.

"I AM SO HONORED to be able to sit down with a woman who is on a quest for truth," said Griggs as she introduced guest Kerry Cassidy for an hourlong podcast on July 21, 2020. Cassidy is a veteran YouTuber who focuses on UFO conspiracy theories.

The episode was released five days after the publication of a *Los Angeles Magazine* investigative report by Stacie Stukin that catalogued generations of abuse within Kundalini Yoga.

"[Bhajan] will be remembered like a Harvey Weinstein or a Jerry Sandusky of yoga," Kundalini Yoga historian Philip Deslippe told Stukin. "I believe his teachings will be tainted in a way that will make it very hard to rebrand or salvage them."

On the podcast, Cassidy helped Griggs shift attention away from the bad press.

"We're under a lot of attack right now," she warned,

> from the dark magicians, as I call them…the Illuminati, the committee of three hundred, if you want to call them that. There's a lot of families that are part of this particular group of bloodlines that are basically trying to rule the Earth and go back to the days of the Anunnaki in Egypt and before that to Atlantis.

Griggs gazed into the middle distance of her webcam and nodded with grave concern. Cassidy went on to improvise on a series of themes about alien races and giants from the inner Earth collaborating to control humanity. She implied that COVID-19 is a strategy to prevent human ascension, and that the murder of George Floyd as the instigating incident of the then-incendiary BLM protests was questionable.

"As an investigative journalist," Cassidy said, "I use my intuition, I'm a psychic, and I've activated my kundalini." Griggs smiled knowingly.

Griggs's amplification of conspiracy theory content accelerated as the pandemic wore on. On January 21, 2021, she published an interview with David Icke.

"We're in this global lockdown," Griggs said as she opened the discussion with Icke.

> We know there's other reasons for it besides what they're telling us. I would love to just kind of go into where you think the layers of other agendas, in terms of extraterrestrial invasions, secret space, if there's some sort of connection between China and some extraterrestrials. Where are you going with deconstructing the bigger narrative of what's happening?

In a rambling series of anecdotes and deepities, Icke obliged, explaining that human perception was hijacked a very long time ago, and had been accelerated by technology, resulting in billions of people tricked into complying with COVID-19 house arrest. He predicted that Jupiter outshining Saturn in the heavens would soon bring an end to "this global cult that I've been exposing for thirty years," which he described as a spider's web.

Icke offered no citations for any of his claims, and attributed his expertise to mystical experiences he had in the 1990s, which led him to believe that changes in human perception change human reality. "This is a basis of all spiritual teachings," Griggs agreed, warning that spiritual communities hijacked by woke ideology were moving in the wrong direction.

We don't know if Griggs ever met Yogi Bhajan in the flesh, but there's something about Icke that fills out the silhouette left by the absent guru. Icke, like Bhajan, is burly, ruddy, wheezy, imperious, and speaks a slow, deliberate slurry of bullshit and ultra-certainty. Big drunken patriarch energy exudes from both of them. Plus: crypto-fascism. Icke goes on about how the Cabal must be destroyed, and Bhajan had his fetish for Adolf Hitler.

In the library of lectures Bhajan's students have maintained online, "Hitler" turns up forty times. In several lectures, he coached students through a made-up yoga exercise that looks like a Sieg heil, executed while hyperventilating. In one, Bhajan claimed that Hitler was really teaching the Germans a form of sun salutation. In another lecture from 1982, he made weird, insensitive, antisemitic remarks that held out Hitler as some kind of flawed hero. A great vegetarian, no enemy of the Jews, a humanitarian who loved all people. Bhajan was clearly fascinated by power and domination, so long as he could put a spiritual spin on it, which must have generated paralyzing levels of cognitive dissonance for his devotees. This is the scene Griggs and Cassidy were obscuring, days after the most damning account of Bhajan's abuse dropped in their hometown magazine.

"EVERY DAY WE SHOULD remember that our inner peace is what's going to create world peace." Champ Parinya, the digital artist who created the QAnon "Great Awakening Map," was speaking quietly on Griggs's podcast. It was April 2021. "And world peace creates cosmic peace." At this moment, Griggs had four months to live.

The "Map," created in 2018 when Parinya was thirty-six, is an apophenic, mandala-like depiction of the QAnon universe, framed through Parinya's brain-melted understanding of the same branch of Tibetan Buddhism that Griggs and Hartzell laid claim to. On his marketplace website, Parinya describes the map as "the supreme red-pill navigational chart for Escaping the Matrix and Returning to Source."

After Parinya described for Griggs the mystical intuitions and psychedelic substances that allowed him to visualize each map element, she homed in on the Buddhist theme. QAnon and conspiracy theory data points, she noted, are like *terma*, using the old Tibetan word that came to describe purported secret teachings of the Buddha, unlocked by adepts from their hiding places in split river stones, or whorls of a knot in an oak tree.

By platforming the soft-spoken, equanimous Parinya, Griggs reached a peak of QAnon mainstreaming through a seamless merging with a new, post–Yogi Bhajan brand.

"There are thousands of extraterrestrial groups surrounding our Earth right now," Parinya said. "And they're waiting for us to make that next small leap in consciousness that will allow them to come and visit us and bring cosmic Peace."

GRIGGS DIED ON AUGUST 1, 2021, at the age of forty-one. According to her followers, the cause of death was pulmonary embolism following surgery on an ankle she injured during a teaching tour of Germany.

Her followers gathered every day for several weeks to mourn her passing. True to her memory, livestreams showed dozens of attendees sitting shoulder to shoulder, without masks, in violation of the mask mandates for indoor spaces at the time. On August 8, the LA County Department of Public Health reported over three thousand new COVID cases. Griggs was an outspoken anti-masker, and believed that mask ordinances were unconstitutional. She also refused to be vaccinated against COVID-19.

The celebrations of her life involved chanting, rhythmic hyperventilation, and forced laughing.

CHAPTER 25

A CHORUS OF CHANNELERS AND LIGHTWORKERS

So far, our gallery is populated with figures who are enthralled by conspirituality as a heady blend of paranoia and hope, enacted through a behavioral divide: they terrify followers and then soothe them. These are figures who have adopted an orientation toward reality that they are using to explain—or disrupt—the world. Katie Griggs was a theater kid who latched on to conspirituality as she cult-jacked Kundalini Yoga infrastructure. RFK Jr., an heir to a political dynasty, weaponized conspirituality against vaccine science. They found a compelling worldview, and they've used it to manipulate their worlds.

But, dear reader, this instrumentalism is a very crude form of conspirituality. Low vibration, we might say. There is a higher, *purer* expression in which the practice is not learned or performed by regular people. This is a conspirituality that is fully embodied by gifted persons whose status as human is in a kind of sacred flux. They are, as the early twentieth-century Jesuit paleontologist and mystic Teilhard de Chardin famously put it, "spiritual beings having a human experience."

These are the channelers who, empty of all material taint, allow raw truth to shine through them without the corruptions of ego. In fact, they are so egoless that they are free to parody each other endlessly. While our other rogues stand tall in their individualism, and at least try to brand themselves uniquely, the channelers sing together like a Greek chorus.

And they do not need conspirituality to validate their pseudomedicine, like Kelly Brogan, Christiane Northrup, or Zach Bush. All they need to do is to speak in the tongue of their guides. These days, they do it for hours at a time, into the memory holes of Instagram and YouTube.

"THIS IS A MESSAGE from higher-dimensional beings," New Age channeler Lorie Ladd says quietly, intensely. It's August 12, 2020. The video is called "Is Trump a Lightworker."

In most of her videos, Ladd is open, relaxed, and looks like she's taking a break from housework. This video, however, is "the most challenging" she's ever put out there, she claims. So challenging, viewers might be triggered. If they can, she advises, they should try to settle into their bodies, and "release the labels, the duality, right and wrong, good and bad, Left, Right, Democrat, Republican, and just tap into the message, the information, the words. Try to release what you have been programmed to believe and just see what resonates." According to Ladd, any preexisting Democrat loyalty, or aversion to Trump, may in fact be a kind of brainwashing out of which she can lead her 228,000 Instagram followers.

But who are these beings transmitting this message that you're not really supposed to listen to in any detail, but rather let the message wash over you? On Facebook (where Christiane Northrup bumps her repeatedly) Ladd runs it down. "The Galactic Federation is a cooperative group of advanced spiritual beings watching over the collective evolution of Gaia and sentient life. It is made up of these four star nations: Pleiadians, Andromedans, Arcturians, and Sirians." Ladd is one of many channelers who confer starseed status on their followers, meaning that they are emissaries of these nations, waking up to their true identities. This positions Ladd as a kind of elder sibling in a family constellation of aliens, separated by misfortune, and now living on Earth as refugees. Ladd is no different from her followers, as she will remind them often. She's just more aware of where they all come from, and so a step ahead on the way back home.

"Trump is a massive lightworker," Ladd announces in the flagship video, which now has over fifteen thousand Facebook shares, and close to a half-million views.

LIGHTWORKER IS NEW AGE–ESE for a hero who transforms lower and denser forms of consciousness to higher, lighter forms. The idea goes back to time out of mind, but became a New Age focal point beginning, roughly, with Helena Blavatsky. The founder of Theosophy was inspired by Indo-Tibetan descriptions of the bodies of saints dissolving into rainbows.

"Light does not attack darkness, but it does shine it away," says *A Course in Miracles*, in which "light" appears 738 times in 1,333 pages. The inner circle of Endeavor Academy described themselves as lightworkers. When Matthew suffered severe headaches from a combination of existential dread, social pressure, and protein-poor food, he was told the light was simply moving through him. When a fellow group member dropped dead from a massive stroke during an ecstatic prayer session, the official explanation was that the light was too much for her.

The lightworker concept collides with New Age conspiracism most loudly in Barbara Marciniak's 1992 book *Bringers of the Dawn*—the first in a series of four, which have collectively sold over 500,000 copies and been translated into twenty languages. Born in 1948, Marciniak claims to have been contacted by the Pleiadians the year she turned forty. They spoke through her, she says, to help humanity in the time of a great transition. It's a vision that places humanity and planet Earth within an imaginative cosmic history, roiled by a battle between the good aliens who chose to speak through her and evil reptilian aliens who have gained control of our planet and feed on the energy of human fear from an invisible hidden dimension. Readers are called to recognize their spiritual identity as lightworkers who can inspire and save the free-will zone of Earth.

None other than David Icke popularized the reptilian alien theme with the 1999 release of *The Biggest Secret*, which claimed, naturally, that shapeshifting, blood-drinking reptilian aliens live in underground bases and are genetically interbred with the ruling political elites and royal families of our planet.

BUT LADD WAS TALKING about Trump, and we interrupted her trance state. "This man," she continued,

> is a third-dimensional human with a personality that was required for him to have in order to do what he came onto the earthplane to do, which is dismantling systems so ingrained into the human collective that it is almost impossible. Corruption, greed, sexual misconduct in satanic rituals, mind control—these are all things he is standing in the middle of and breaking apart. He's one of

the most prolific wayshowers of our time. This is not about voting, it's about ascension.

It's common within the broader channeling demographic to assess the spiritual development of a person according to a hierarchy of dimensions. The 3D space is conventional to humans, with typical subject-object relations. The person is distinct, encapsulated within a body, and believes they are separated from other people, objects in the world, and the world itself. Graduating into the 4D world demands a lessening of attachment to self-identity and a softening of boundaries, a process said to usher in a 5D state of nondual union with everything. This is called ascension, and it's said to be harrowing. Christiane Northrup focuses a portion of her Great Awakening content on giving meaning to the physical and mental symptoms of ascending to 5D consciousness. Part of her harp playing is about soothing those supposed symptoms.

Trump's misogyny, racism, contempt, and history of assault allegations are an optics challenge that conspiritualists have to be equipped to deal with. When Ladd coyly gestures that his personality is required for breaking apart the very things he is guilty of—with the exception of satanic rituals—she is drawing on the theme of crazy wisdom, a kind of spiritual hazing that has an ancient pedigree in many religio-philosophical cultures. The premise is that spiritual enlightenment shatters the conventional order, and so we should expect that certain gifted teachers will bestow it in transgressive forms. In ancient Greece, Diogenes expressed his commitment to Cynicism by acting like a dog (the Greek for "doglike" is *kunikos*)—urinating on those who disputed him, defecating in the theater, and masturbating in the public square. In medieval Tibet, the hermit Marpa drank himself shitfaced and battered his enslaved star student, Milarepa, with his sandals.

But the concept of crazy wisdom is also deployed to resolve the cognitive dissonance experienced by followers of the abusive leaders they must frame as loving. All manner of corrupt behavior is explained as a kind of divine play, engineered to expose the hypocritical pieties of disciples. When Osho, who moved his ill-fated cult from Pune, India, to rural Oregon in 1981, collected a fleet of Rolls Royces bought via the unpaid labor of his sannyasin devotees, the cult explained that he was deconstructing their hang-ups around status and money.

When Chögyam Trungpa, the founder of Shambhala Buddhism, committed clerical sexual misconduct with married students, he was framed as stress-testing their maudlin relationships. When he drank to such excess he slurred his sermons, devotees were taught to think that he was mimicking both Marpa and the debauchery of his unenlightened students in order to endear himself to them. And not only that! He was *also* purifying their conflictual guilt over addictive behaviors. When he had thugs drag a literary celebrity and his partner into a drunken party in the Boulder temple and forcibly strip them so they could be beaten and humiliated, Trungpa wasn't ordering assault and battery and intimidating his followers. Not at all. He was challenging their egotism and pride.

What should communities do with their crazy wise men? Ladd's advice to release labels and moral responses is on-brand for the conspirituality movement's rigorous apolitical stance. Things don't happen or change because you do something, or because you react to your world. Things change when you release your preconceptions, surrender your boundaries, and allow everything in to work its beneficent magic. Trump's personality isn't an issue to vote on. It's a force that can rearrange your perception of reality. For the better, of course.

Is Trump a crazy wisdom teacher, according to Ladd? She doesn't spell it out explicitly. But all the elements are there: a presumed wisdom or nobility or bravery that must be concealed and even inverted in order to both attract and challenge corruption directly. The more crass and abusive Trump is, the more his skill for rooting out hypocrisy is on display. The more he transgresses social norms, the more awareness he generates of the hidden transgressions that fuel the global Cabal.

THE ORACULAR ROOTS of channeling persist in noncommercial forms in Indigenous and post-colonial cultures, as when the Dalai Lama consults the Nechung oracle, or Hindu nationalist politicians consult astrologers on propitious dates. Its premises and techniques have been mainstays of alt-spirituality since the time of Ouija boards and table-turning séances, and ostensibly reconnect a fallen modern world with an enchanted past.

As we saw in Chapter 9, channeling was a forte of late nineteenth-century spirit mediums like Helena Blavatsky, who says she found ancient scriptures written in languages only she could translate. The Akashic Records informed Rudolf Steiner about the mysteries of Atlantis, the fascist hierarchy of races, and the danger of vaccines. Edgar Cayce (1877–1945), dubbed "The Sleeping Prophet" for his practice of giving clairvoyant readings while in a trancelike state, blended his channeling with New Age fascinations that are still going strong: past lives, mind-over-matter healing, astral projection, and seeing auras. While all of this can sound exotic and fringe, it's not that different from the channeled origins of Mormonism—as believed by former candidate for American president Mitt Romney.

In 1965, Helen Schucman, a depressed research psychologist at Columbia University, began taking dictation from an inner voice claiming to be Jesus. Her colleague, Dr. William Thetford, helped with the transcription of Schucman's channeling sessions, and later with editing out Jesus's homophobia and general sex negativity, while sharpening his apparent love for iambic pentameter. In 1975, the resulting text was published as *A Course in Miracles*. The following year, Marianne Williamson started reading it, initiating an arc that brought it into mainstream awareness with the publication of her 1992 *Course*-inspired self-help book, *A Return to Love*, which was boosted to bestseller status by Oprah Winfrey, who considers Williamson to be a spiritual advisor.

Winfrey really deserves her own book as an enabler of dodgy channeled wisdom. She played a key role in boosting the American psychic and Amway superstar Esther Hicks and her "Law of Attraction," a thoughts-change-reality concept. Hicks claims that the "Law" emerged from channeling a gaggle of entities she calls Abraham.

Abraham offers garden variety self-help bromides, such as "When you change the way you look at things, the things you look at change." But Abraham also spiced it up with some truly disgusting claims, such as only 1 percent of rape allegations being true violations, with the rest being attractions. Abraham also believes that for Black people in America, slavery was "the beginning of a journey that was better" and part of an "overall improvement in humanity." Like the New Age celebrity publisher of Hicks's bestsellers, Louise Hay of Hay House, Abraham also thinks that people contract AIDS when they don't love themselves.

Winfrey is also largely responsible for the globalized popularity of spirit medium João Teixeira de Faria, known to followers as John of God. For four decades, De Faria lorded over a rural Brazilian empire by pretending to be the meat suit of a collection of divine entities, who would allegedly guide him through trance states during which he would perform fake surgeries on hundreds of pilgrims per day. With unsterilized kitchen knives and surgical scissors, De Faria joined a long line of psychic surgeons from the region who pretended to extract tumors or bloody lumps of bad karma. What he was really channeling was a fortune in cash and gems as he ran supply and protection rackets throughout the region, and assaulted and raped women under the cover of healing.

João Teixeira de Faria is now serving multiple life sentences, but at home, on account of fragile health and COVID burning through the prisons of Brazil. Oprah Winfrey has deleted the two episodes of her show in which she boosted him. But her interviews with Abraham Hicks are still posted. So are her multiple appearances with Marianne Williamson.

Williamson doesn't claim to channel Jesus. But her favorite book, *A Course in Miracles*, does. She still teaches out of it, via recorded lectures that are posted online. This hasn't hampered her mainstream appeal. The fact that she's been able to integrate the wisdom of New Age Jesus into a persona that can mount a plausible run for the Democratic presidential ticket tells us that the normalization and acceptability of channeling as a means of knowing the world has legs beyond Oprah's studio, and can stride into the realm of virtual politics.

LADD WASN'T ALONE AMONG channelers who found inspiration in QAnon jargon, and then spread it far and wide. Elizabeth April also squared off against the Deep State.

April is a Zoomer channeler with a Coachella glamor vibe. In her bio, she describes what sounds like a neuroatypical childhood. By the age of three, she was talking with God. At eighteen, she was abducted by aliens. Now, she hangs with the very same Galactic Federation, which might account for her beta-testing of one of Ladd's key themes in July 2019 with a Facebook live called "The Donald is a Lightworker," which got forty-two thousand views. In the COVID era, she appeared on Katie Griggs's podcast to discuss her Galactic Federation School in April 2020, and then went full-bore on QAnon during the #savethechildren scare of July.

"I was told by the Galactic Federation of Light back in 2011," April posted to Instagram, "about Reptilians torturing children in order to drink their blood. Since then I have seen at least hundreds of past lifetimes from my clients where they were a part of these blood and sex rituals…this trauma scars your SOUL…not just your body." The hashtags convened all of the key QAnon threads: #childtrafficking #stopchildabuse #wakeup #children-rightsarehumanrights #childrights #thegreatawakening #reptillian #illu-minati #spiritualawakening #5D #ascension #empowerment. The following day, April, who is white, announced that her guides told her that the Black Lives Matter protests were actually Plan B, and that the more direct show of solidarity with the oppressed of the Earth would be to protest the collection of adrenochrome from those who still suffered from slavery: children.

British starseeds found a powerful guide through the jolly channeling of Magenta Pixie, who could be April's aunt. Pixie is *not* affiliated with the Galactic Federation, as her About page wants you to know. Her guides are from the White Winged Collective Consciousness of Nine. Like April, Pixie also describes a psychic childhood, albeit from a more bucolic, pre-digital era, in which she daydreamed and devoured the colonial adventure stories of Enid Blyton. Pixie describes herself as a fairie, has 138,000 subscribers on YouTube, and is fond of using coded language. Donald Trump (of course a world savior battling a global Cabal) is Mr. Tea Tree, and the Capitol Po-lice are gnomes. The COVID-19 vaccines are poison apple juice that will obstruct the ascension process. The White Winged Collective also guides her to shower QAnon congressperson Marjorie Taylor Greene with rainbow heart emojis, while going all-in on saving the children with her own tagline, Kids Lives Matter.

In the fall of 2021, Pixie fell ill with COVID, became short of breath with a suspected pulmonary embolism, and developed a deep vein thrombosis that swelled her leg to five times its normal size. After a perilous hospitaliza-tion, during which followers posted prayers of intercession to her Telegram channel, Pixie recovered. After Christmas, she was back in Telegram, post-ing about the stamina it would require to see the spiritual war through to its end. "Bringing down the cabal and exposing everything is going to take time," she posted. "We are strong, we are ready."

MOST NEW AGE CHANNELING—ESPECIALLY in the era of social media—is quite unmysterious when you look carefully at its moral content. While channelers often affect a whistleblowing, transgressive persona, it is almost impossible to find a message from *A Course in Miracles*, Abraham Hicks, the Galactic Federation, or the White Winged Collective that challenges any social or political status quo or that adds anything unique to any literature at all.

What is this secret New Age knowledge all about? It carries none of the existential dread of ancient oracles or Old Testament prophets. No wisdom of the ancestors about the land or the cycles of life. It's about raising your vibration and alchemizing (Ladd's favorite word) whatever conflict you find in your world. It's about finding your Source, imagining a 5D consciousness, believing you are ascending toward it, and talking about how it feels to be on the journey. The content is an endless laundry list of vague aspirations that rarely make reference to real-world problems or basic human paradoxes.

Researching this material means scrubbing through hours of audio and video content, looking, often in vain, for any kind of solid idea about anything. At a certain point it seems that the endless channeling isn't about information at all. It's about soothing anxieties. Listening to Ladd, Swan, April, and Pixie can feel like being a very small child, rocked to sleep by a humming parent. Occasionally, they will make a foggy prediction about something that might be happening sometime soon, or maybe not. But it seems the main function of their predictions is for the follower to imagine a future together with the channeler, regardless of what may come. A future where the rocking and humming will continue.

But the lack of solid content in these sources is a kind of content in itself, and its angle is reactionary. It never discusses poverty or inequality, or holding the powerful to account. The overwhelming instruction doled out by the New Age source is that we should learn to accept things as they are, as perfect expressions of a divine plan. That we should accept our circumstances as both divinely ordained and chosen by us through the Law of Attraction—if we're listening to Abraham Hicks. This depends on never questioning those circumstances, but rather, implicitly validating them. When Hicks recycles self-help bromides blended with prosperity gospel promises, for instance, what she really seems to be channeling is a subconscious yearning to win at capitalism—or at least for capitalism to feel like it can be manageable.

Sometimes these New Age shills for the status quo let the mask fully slip, as when Hicks channels the idea that slavery was the starting point of a better history for Black people. In these cases, what they're really channeling, apologizing for, and spiritualizing is structural brutality. And when Elizabeth April and Lorie Ladd channel messages from their guides that Donald Trump is a lightworker, laboring to redeem the world, we bear witness to a form of spiritualized fawn response.

New Age cultural critic and gonzo guru buster Be Scofield sums up the empty and craven messaging in a 2012 article.

"Why can't this divine evolutionary impulse awaken us to the reality of things that actually matter," she asks, "like deforestation, pollution, racism, homophobia or imperialism? Why couldn't experiencing Being and connecting to our divine source actually provide us with tangible knowledge and concern about the ravages of industrial capitalism instead of disembodied, abstract and politically neutral states of presence?"

THE CONTENT OF CHANNELING is often banal. Its techniques are clichéd. Its politics are reactionary, in the sense that they mainly serve to absolve the moral and social disasters du jour. But isn't it all just harmless fun? Does anyone take Lorie Ladd seriously? Magenta Pixie? Elizabeth April? Are they not entertainers, first and foremost?

Quantifying the toxicity of channelers is not really about measuring their engagement or sales numbers. It's about how they normalize epistemological chaos and throw kerosene on the sparks of social tension.

"I was lying on my floor listening to music," Ladd says, gazing at her webcam with deadeye radiance. "The Galactic Federation jolted me out of my chill state and said 'Do you want us to share with you what's going on with humanity right now—really powerful important message?' And I was like, 'Sure.'"

It was December 27, 2020, and the tone hints at New Year's predictions. She waxes about "an uprising in which warriors of light take action to dismantle the consciousnesses that are not shifting with us." But she warns about a difficult road ahead.

"What they showed me tonight is that there are many, many of us who've been standing back behind the scene, behind the gate, just watching to see what's going to unravel, not wanting to go in and touch that evil and that dark. We're going to touch that evil and that dark. We're going to stand up to it in a way we never thought we would have to, and never thought we would."

As this book goes to publication, this Ladd superhit is heading toward a half-million views, and logging more than three thousand comments, making it by far Ladd's most popular content.

About the epistemological chaos: once a follower believes Ladd is in contact with intergalactic sages who give her insights into the destiny of humanity, a row of dominoes is poised to fall. Their political, psychological, cultural, and medical sources of authority, or ways of establishing knowledge, can now be filtered through an archetypally authoritarian style. It's like the followers are hearing the voice of a prophet, or the cult leader who claims to be God.

It's not me and my limited ego, the typical channeler says. *It is this thing that comes through me that is a source of ultimate, absolute truth beyond question, beyond evidence, beyond reason. If it doesn't make sense, that's because your ego is resisting or is still limited to 4D consciousness.*

The epistemology of channeling makes pseudoscience and conspiracism much more likely to take hold. It offers a frictionless pathway into valuing dramatic intuitions above all else. Was there anything in place to hinder Ladd's slide from milquetoast homilies about living your best life to shoveling out red-pilled content? The medium favors the implausible and the extreme. And it also covers its tracks: the light and love and crystals and rainbows of the digital channeler deftly obscure the radical, insidious nature of their authoritarian fantasies.

What about that splashing kerosene? We don't have access to Ladd's search history, but given her red-pill power level at the time, it's reasonable to guess that by December 27, 2020, she was aware that the Stop the Steal movement was gearing up for heavy action on January 6, 2021. Conspirituality and QAnon channels were jammed with insurrection chatter from at least December 23 onward.

So was Ladd really predicting anything in late December? Or was she really just "channeling" her own simplistic take on a plan already in motion, but wording it vaguely enough to sound at once topical and prophetic? When psychics pull this trick, it's called cold reading. They make generalized statements about the client's life until they hit on something that resonates, that they can pursue and follow up on with a kind of predatory attention that can be mistaken, by the enthralled client, for empathy and insight. Channelers like Ladd basically offer cold readings to the public at large. Unlike the psychic examining the client's face for signs of vulnerability, the extremely online channeler gazes at the social feeds to test the wind, and see if they can make it howl.

"Many of you are going to be asked to play very different roles as we move forward into 2021," Ladd says in her December 27 post. She had been talking about direct confrontation with the Cabal. "So don't make it wrong, don't make it right. Just remember that this is why you're here. Do it with an open heart."

The language is militant, but aspirational. "We charge forward, arm-in-arm, hand in hand, saying I'm ready to level-up." Ladd seemed to be basking in the quiet ecstasy of a New Age holy war. "There is no right or wrong. We all have free will. But many of us in 2021 are going to rise up, and I am so excited to rise up with you."

It's unclear how Ladd rose up with anyone, except via algorithm. She did not communicate any transmissions from the Galactic Federation on January 6, 2021. But the following morning, she took to Facebook from her car to assure her followers that however things appear in the world, "there is a divine design and perfection in how the human collective shifts consciousness." The sermon goes on for five minutes, avoiding all mention of warriorship, the Cabal, or stepping out from behind the gate to touch evil.

"If you put out a call to arms and then people are killed," wrote one commenter who noticed the hypocrisy, "you need to reexamine your conscience. Spreading this message entraps many innocent Lightworkers in your dark web of manipulation."

CHAPTER 26

PLACEBO JOE

LOUIS, A LIFE COACH from San Diego, was dying of late-stage pancreatic cancer in 2020. His wife, Mary, tended to him with worried love. He was only forty-four years old. Mary told us how she helped him with medications, food, and appointments. She admired and supported his resilience and good nature. But she also grew increasingly irked by Louis's fascination with Joe Dispenza, a former chiropractor who allows himself to be called a neuroscientist by the many alt-med platforms that host him, and promises followers they can cure their diseases through breathwork and meditation. Mary had always loved Louis's credulity, his willingness to think the best of people. She trusted that he was getting some kind of relief she couldn't quite name from this influencer she described as having a God complex. But it didn't sit right.

Louis had introduced Dispenza to Mary before his cancer diagnosis upended their lives. They used his recorded meditations to help them fall asleep. As Dispenza droned on in what Mary described as a megachurch style, she got creeped out, and asked Louis to shut him off. Now that he was ill, she worried that this newfound obsession could hurt Louis while he navigated the perils to come. By her lights, Dispenza was camped out in Louis's mind at a vulnerable time, offering garbage in the form of hope.

Mary (we're withholding surnames for privacy) told us she had always had a science brain, but she wasn't completely closed off to spirituality. She'd taken a yoga teacher training course. As a certified applied psychologist, she was clear on the researched value of positive thinking. Louis, on the other hand, had always placed New Age spirituality and far-out health ideas at the center of his life. She used to joke that he had a real master's degree—an

MBA from Duke that made her a proud girlfriend and wife—and then his fake master's in spiritual psychology, from a New Age degree mill called University of Santa Monica, which gave her a permanent case of side-eye.

At USM, which was founded in 1978 by a notoriously paranoid cult leader named John-Roger Hinkins, Louis learned a little about Freud and Jung, and a lot about Akashic Records, the tarot, yoga and meditation, and how to recall past lives. He also completed a certification program in Conscious, Radiant Health and Healing, which he believed had helped him heal an injured knee without surgery. On their first date, Mary snooped through his bookshelf and spotted *Psychology for Dummies*. "Was that your course textbook?" she asked. The ribbing didn't kill the date—at all. Within months, like a positive and negative charge of mystic rationalism, they married. But they only had a few months together before Louis started quickly losing weight.

Pancreatic cancer has a tragically low survival rate. Initially, Louis fared well with his conventional treatment. The labs were encouraging and the specialists urged him to stay the course. But the advice he was really hooked on came from people like Dispenza and the meditations he taught, based in part on his 2014 book, *You Are the Placebo*, in which he describes healing his six vertebrae that were shattered in a bicycle crash by refusing surgery and spending hours a day using a higher intelligence to visualize his spine knitting itself back together. According to Dispenza, accessing this quantum field of matter allowed him to dispense with medical advice, and think his bones back into wholeness. He dubs the process "becoming your own placebo." It's a nonsense phrase that translates to "You can become an inert substance that has no medical effect, but could fool you temporarily into feeling relief from symptoms." It seems impossible that Dispenza could mean this, let alone understand it. But we're not in the realm of understanding here. After all, the first book endorsement after the title page comes from our very own Christiane Northrup. "*You Are the Placebo* is the instruction manual for how to produce miracles in your body, with your health, and in your life," she writes. "This may be the only prescription you'll ever require."

"I was able to heal my knee," Mary remembers Louis saying about the meditations, "so I should be able to heal this."

IN THE MIDST OF this cancer storm, everything that Mary knew about Joe Dispenza came through the eyes of Louis, who felt he needed him. That aspirational view chafed against Mary's knowledge that if he was going to make any miraculous recovery, it would be by focusing on the very worldly plan laid out by his oncologist. What Mary didn't know was that that content came from a whole ecosystem of cultic faith healing that tracks back to the late 1980s, when Dispenza was the chiropractor for JZ Knight—and possibly her channeled spirit, Ramtha, who she says is 35,000 years old.

Knight, a former rodeo queen and cable TV saleswoman, became famous through a 1985 appearance on *The Merv Griffin Show*, where she apparently fell into a trance and then woke up as Ramtha to ask Griffin: "Thees ees that wheech is called teleeveesion?"

In 1989, Knight founded the Ramtha's School of Enlightenment in Yelm, Washington, where her group has hosted thousands of pilgrims seeking the wisdom of her channeling. Notable graduates include filmmaker Mark Vicente, who while at RSE produced the 2004 pseudoscience movie *What the Bleep Do We Know?* Dispenza was a leading talking head in the film. Word-of-mouth marketing got *What the Bleep* into 146 theaters across the United States and brought in almost $16 million in earnings worldwide. Vicente went on to become a lieutenant of Keith Raniere in the NXIVM cult, but more recently has become an anti-cult crusader.

In 2012, ex-members of Knight's school outed her channeling as being lubricated by a steady supply of red wine. They leaked video footage of her drunkenly hurling antisemitic and racist abuse during prayer gatherings. The Southern Poverty Law Center reviewed the tapes. "Fuck God's chosen people!" Knight said. "I think they have earned enough cash to have paid their way out of the goddamned gas chambers by now." The SPLC reported that Knight declared that "Mexicans 'breed like rabbits' and are 'poison,' that all gay men were once Catholic priests, and that organic farmers have questionable hygiene." Knight claimed that the quotes were taken out of context. And to be fair, it wasn't really Knight speaking, was it?

The differences between Dispenza's content and the principles of Ramtha's School of Enlightenment are a matter of framing rather than ideology. Ramtha's four axioms are boilerplate-vague New Ageisms. RSE adepts must internalize the saying "You are God." They must "make known the unknown," and pledge allegiance to the "concept that consciousness and energy creates the nature of reality." They must also accept "the challenge to conquer" themselves. What Dispenza's Gen X branding adds to Ramtha's boomer schtick is the veneer of scientific sense-making.

In December of 2020, Dispenza visited Aubrey Marcus's podcast studio, and summed up why he thinks his magic works.

"Science has become the contemporary language of mysticism," he said. "And if you can combine a little quantum physics with a little neuroscience with neuroendocrinology with psychoneuroimmunology, the mind body connection, epigenetics—all of those sciences point the finger at possibility."

They might. Unfortunately, Dispenza has no clinical training or experience in any of these subjects to be able to say for sure. He graduated from Life University in Marietta, Georgia, in the mid-1980s with a degree in chiropractic. In 2002, Life University lost its accreditation with the governing chiropractic regulators, which is quite a feat. A report from the time said that "Life students were not being taught how to detect and deal with problems that require medical attention." Students were taught that all underlying causes of illness come from subluxations, a term used by "straight" chiropractors (those who focus solely on skeletal adjustments) to denote a partial or full dislocation of a joint or organ—and which, they say, cannot necessarily be observed by X-rays. It's a bunk theory.

"If you talk about religion," Dispenza continued, "if you talk about culture, if you talk about tradition, even spirituality, I notice that you divide the audience. But science in that sense creates community."

It's a sneaky argument, given the popular impression—exaggerated by alt-health players—that science culture is cold and inhumane. It's a way for Dispenza's scientific pretensions to be validated by the good vibes of a charismatic event. Science that feels that good must be science done correctly, right?

Dispenza's abuse of scientific language conceals the fact that his in-person events play out like tent-revival faith healing, where he practices laying on hands, promises women his meditations can cure their infertility, and participants weep and praise God. The mirage of science and respectability also made it difficult for someone like Mary to completely dismiss him when Louis was in his hour of need. So when he wanted to go to one of Dispenza's intensive healing events, during a peak wave of COVID—in Florida no less, which at the time had some of the most lax protections in place for the immunocompromised—Mary gave him her blessing, and hoped that participants would be masked and that he would keep track of his medications.

Louis went for a week. Mary managed waves of anxiety as she imagined the participants unmasked and hugging each other in faith-healing ecstasies. While we don't know exactly what Louis's week looked like, her fears were reasonable.

Aubrey Marcus opened his December 2020 podcast episode featuring Dispenza with an account of how much he'd enjoyed a recent Dispenza retreat in Cancún, which at the time didn't have COVID travel barriers in place. Dispenza corroborated Marcus's praise by describing the altar calls at his events where people testify to being instantly healed of cancer. "We bring children in at the end of the event and we heal them of really serious health conditions," he said.

"Our community gets closer," he said. "You get people opening their heart. Love bonds; you can't not bond in love. You have to hug, you have to connect, you have to bond." He told a story of a woman spontaneously cured of Parkinson's disease in front of 1,500 people. (Attendance fees for similar events run at around $2,299 per person, before accommodation.)

"When you see that person," Dispenza said, "stand on the stage and tell that story—just like an infection can spread amongst the community and create disease, all of a sudden health and wellness are as infectious as disease." He described one woman who arrived at the event with severe allergies. At the beginning, she was wearing a mask and a ventilator.

"In the middle of the event, she's in the front of the room, dancing around with no mask, no nothing. You start seeing people freeing themselves from their own limitations."

Louis's return home wasn't smooth. He told Mary that he was considering freeing himself from the limitations of chemotherapy. He had his meditations from Joe, and he was feeling better. Ironically, feeling better was most likely the result of having had to delay a chemotherapy treatment while he'd been away.

"Outside of him actually dying," Mary told us, "it was the most devastation I've ever felt."

On one hand, Mary said, it was like Louis was giving up. But giving up on what? "I think that there was a mixed feeling," Mary said. "I think he wanted to believe that this meditation was working, because he didn't want to be sick anymore."

Louis was definitely ready to give up on chemotherapy nausea. Mary knew that the meditation was less painful, more hopeful. That it offered some kind of existential relief, even though, she said, he could beat himself up about not doing it for long enough. When he did manage to meditate, however, it might have allowed him to give up on living in a way that limited shame and demoralization.

If Dispenza's meditation had simply been religious in nature, if it had been about accepting death or gratitude or setting one's moral affairs in order, that would have been one thing. But pseudoscience isn't honest in that way. It's one thing pretending to be another. Dispenza was promising healing, spontaneous remission. The former chiropractor, who calls himself a doctor, was giving Louis cover for giving up on real doctors.

Dispenza was also giving Louis permission to pretend he was healing himself, with some kind of dignity, even while he was saying goodbye.

JOE DISPENZA IS NOT the capstone for this part of the book because he's been a big COVID disruptor. He's not even a good conspiritualist, given how singular his focus is. His content is heavily weighted toward the New Age and aspirational side of the equation. You won't hear Dispenza talking about microchips in vaccines or pedophiles in Washington, DC. To his credit, he keeps things upbeat.

But the upbeat has a downside when we see that Dispenza's affable vibe and hopeful content make him an open-armed gateway into more paranoid and brain-melted worlds. We're ending this part with him because he's playing a major role in the normalization and domestication of a spiritual pseudoscience that looms large on mainstream platforms like Facebook, and makes money through cross-promotion with straight-up QAnon materials. Unlike Katie Griggs, Dispenza doesn't have to platform David Icke directly to make money. But Dispenza benefits from being platformed right beside Icke on Gaia, the Netflix of conspirituality.

In a way, Dispenza merging with Gaia is a kind of homecoming. But there's something paradigmatic going on as well: an expansion and streamlining of content that signifies the almost complete digitization of conspirituality.

Dispenza builds an effective bridge between the 1980s cult world and the parasocial clusterfuck of today. He's not quite a boomer. He's a middle-class Italian American Gen X boy who, according to his own account, got along with his mom and dad. He wears nice tailored shirts. He can speak to the Northrup crowd as a favored son and to millennials as an inspiring uncle. And he can do it all with an efficiency unknown to boomer cult leaders, who always had the pressures of brick and mortar overhead. For decades, Knight's eighty-acre ranch and pilgrimage site has needed constant upkeep and an inflow of pilgrims shedding cash. All Dispenza needs—along with Teal Swan, Lorie Ladd, Mikki Willis, and nearly every other conspiritualist we profile in this book—is an inflow of attention that drives up subscriptions.

Max Weber, the founder of modern sociology, said that a primary organizational challenge for a group that orbits around charismatic leadership is succession. For instance: whether by state murder or not, Jesus was always going to die. The question is how that inspiration will continue. What happens to all that juice? Weber said that the solution for succession is found through a process of routinization, in which inspiration is systematized and codified into a series of rituals that can be sustained through time and throughout a less and less centralized network.

Dispenza is not running JZ Knight's church. The internet means he doesn't have to. But in terms of the continuity of content, we can see that Dispenza has routinized the magic of Ramtha. He's made it normal, everyday, consumerist, regulated by subscriptions and affiliate links instead of prophecies and initiations. Joe Dispenza, through Gaia, is now just another part of a Facebook experience.

IN THE END, LOUIS didn't give up on either the chemotherapy treatment or the teachings of Joe Dispenza. In line with the probabilities, his condition worsened.

Amid the pain and sorrow of knowing his time was near, Mary noticed something that reveals just how complex conspirituality can be as an influence in alternative medicine. She saw that Louis's concentration on meditation was working in an off-label way, despite the promises of Dispenza.

"I saw how at peace he was at the end of his life," she told us. "He was okay. He was content. He wasn't angry." Mary felt that he knew he was saved.

Looking back, Mary's sorrow at Louis's death has become layered with another mourning.

"All of these beliefs carried him to that place," she said, referring to a spiritual imagination she could never sustain. "I wish I believed the things that he believed. I wish I believed that he was sitting here next to me. I wish I believed those things, because it's really hard to know that you're never going to see someone again."

During the emotional peak of our interview, snow started to fall outside Mary's window. She joked that her rational mind would never allow her to interpret a sight like that as a sign that Louis was listening. Skepticism has a price.

"If there was something that would bring me to believe," she said, remembering how Louis faded away into grace, "I would think it would be this. And it didn't."

THIS IS A GOOD place to stop this train. We've looked at a lot of contemptuous behavior from conspiritualists with brain-melted beliefs. But it's through absorbing how it impacts the life and death of regular people in tangled ways that we gain the real clues. We learn how attractive conspirituality is, how human its believers are, and how it can both guide them toward and away from existential honesty. In this case, Joe Dispenza's lies may even have prompted Louis to find some kind of personal peace.

We know for sure that Mary stands where many people stand now, and will stand in the future, as they negotiate with friends and family members who get drawn into the sphere of the Dispenzas and the Northrups. Mary loved a person she knew intimately, but didn't entirely understand. She loved a person whose framework for reality became an island he could not leave, and she could not visit. She accepted his unstable beliefs because she knew that giving up those beliefs would have hollowed Louis out in his time of need.

Through the chaos of a year dominated by cancer, Mary improvised a wisdom, by the skin of her teeth, that has taken seasoned therapists in the cult recovery movement decades to distill. No matter what a person believes, the wisdom goes, nor how harmful it might be to them, the best thing you can do is to love them in a way that an influencer or cult leader never could. To love them without expectation or false promises.

If there's some universal source of pain that conspirituality pretends to soothe, it is loneliness. That loneliness can curdle into isolation, and slowly deprive a person of the ability to trust in medicine, governments, the democratic process, and fellow citizens. If Joe Dispenza accelerates that process for people like Louis, they have to be shown that there are more stable forms of love and care.

Joe Dispenza can't keep his promises, but a real friend and partner can, and that's where rebuilding social trust might begin.

PART FOUR

BEYOND CONSPIRITUALITY

CHAPTER 27

LEARNING FROM LISTENERS

I T'S EASY TO TRACK the number of Facebook followers on Christiane Northrup's page. YouTube tells us instantly how many times a Zach Bush sermon has been viewed. Book sale totals for Charles Eisenstein, Robert F. Kennedy Jr., and Joe Dispenza are only a few clicks away. Mikki Willis claims *Plandemic* has been viewed "a billion" times, and that's bullshit, but eight-million-plus verified views are nothing to sniff at.

We can make good guesses at the kind of money Aubrey Marcus makes in supplement sales and coaching schemes. (We do know that he likely brought in nine figures from his sale of Onnit to Unilever.) We know that Kelly Brogan first pitched her COVID lunacy to over two thousand paying subscribers to her online mental health program. And we can use Crowd-Tangle to track social shares of conspirituality content packets as they either vanish into the ether or cross a certain threshold of virality to attain the status of online scripture.

But nerding out on the internet artifacts of conspirituality influencers isn't ultimately satisfying. It can start to feel like reading stock reports and consumer indexes. It's a decent place to start, given that most gateways into the movement are digital and economic. But the numbers can ring hollow when we try to measure them against the lived experience of those who become absorbed in conspirituality's anxious promises to solve existential problems.

We imagine that the most data-savvy sociologists of religion will struggle for years to assess basic impacts of conspirituality. They would want to know how conspirituality affects people's physical and mental health, their community engagement, and their relationships. Finding answers would only come after the tricky task of designing survey questions that define membership and levels of buy-in.

Political scientists may have it easier, in the sense that the influence of a party or leadership style can be measured through elections and policy initiatives. These techniques can be used to track the spread of QAnon as a political reality. Major media outlets reported that QAnon was becoming a minor religion in May 2021. One in five survey respondents who identified as Anons said that pedophiles control the levers of political power—and may have to be removed by violence. By fall the percentage had ticked up three points. For the 2020 election, CNN reported that nearly two dozen down-ballot candidates who had expressed support for QAnon were running for office. Sitting congressional representatives Marjorie Taylor Greene and Lauren Boebert repeated QAnon tropes and, along with GOP rank and file, endorsed the Big Lie. Twenty-six QAnon candidates were on the ballot in the 2022 midterms—most notably those attempting a "coalition of secretaries of state" to wrest control of future presidential elections at the state level. Three hundred and forty-five candidates for office were found by the Brookings Institution to have endorsed Donald Trump's discredited claims of 2020 election fraud. Over 170 of those candidates won. Luckily, twelve of thirteen Big Lie candidates for governor, secretary of state, or attorney general—roles that could interfere with election integrity in key battleground states—lost. For now it seems, disaster has been averted. But some of those races came down to a single percentage point difference. With conspiracy propaganda still everywhere, campaigns that work to subvert democracy may be with us for the foreseeable future.

Early in our research, we wondered whether a clear impact of conspirituality could be gleaned from a well-tracked public health metric. In particular, how many people in a given country are vaccine hesitant? We knew, for example, that almost half of the influencers we profile in this book were identified in May 2021 as qualifying for an infamous club of disinformation mongers that collectively produces about 65 percent of the anti-vax content available on the internet. That material must raise levels of vaccine hesitancy. We can surmise that in areas most affected by these conspiritualists, COVID mitigation compliance falls, while cases, hospitalizations, and deaths rise. Suddenly, we look at Christiane Northrup, strumming her harp gently in Maine, and have a gut feeling that she's actually got blood on her hands.

We spoke to experts far above our pay grade who said our gut feeling was plausible. But they were cagey as to how it could be tested and verified. Too many variables at play, too much information to crunch. So we left that question hanging and turned to the qualitative data that has flooded our channels for more than two years: many hundreds of emails, direct messages, and disclosures in comment threads. People talking about how long they were under the spell of a yoga school that suddenly went anti-mask or about how much money they dropped on a breathwork course or psychedelic plant medicine retreat, where the instructor simply recycled whatever red-pilled material they were into that month. We heard stories about chiropractors and naturopaths telling patients that vaccines are poison and chemotherapy doesn't work.

There was another category that struck deeper chords. After reporting on Stephanie Sibbio wailing and weeping at that Toronto anti-vax rally, we heard from a group of her old friends. They came on the show to describe what it was like to watch their friend seem to lose her mind. That was the episode that prompted Mary to reach out to tell us about her husband, Louis.

"The broad discussion of conspirituality," Mary wrote in an email, "doesn't always cover that there are real people who experience real trauma." She said that we need to pay attention to the quieter stories. "I'm not a cult survivor, I'm not a former anti-vaxxer who discovered science, and I'm not a QAnon survivor. I am simply a wife caring for her husband, trying to be open-minded and as neutral as possible to honor the suffering of everyone else who loved him."

We leaned in to this stream with more specific callouts for stories. We asked listeners to write about their experiences with conspirituality, and how they survived it, or didn't. We received almost a hundred detailed narratives that all taught us a lot about the networked impacts of conspirituality. We've chosen three for the end of this book. The first is about how Cortney and Shana grew up and grew out of a New Age cult. The second is about how Gavin nursed his wife, Fey, through the ravages of breast cancer, which she might have survived if she hadn't been red-pilled by conspirituality health influencers. Last, we listen to Ishi Dinim discuss how the red-pilling of his father Joseph, a left-wing activist, has impacted their relationship. These stories illuminate the human dimension of our beat, and frame some of the lessons we've learned. We've withheld some surnames for privacy reasons.

The story of how Cortney and Shana's mother brought them to the Ramtha's School of Enlightenment in the late 1980s, when they were only teens, presents a microcosm of how the yoga and wellness worlds were thrown into the conspiracy theory whirlpool in March 2020. They had no idea where they were going or how it was going to work out. Their world was fractured into believers and the condemned, set against each other in an ominous but transformational conflict. They watched grown-ass adults try to bend spoons with their minds and heal tumors with magic spells. They feared the Days to Come but also craved ascension out of their bodies.

Thirty years after Cortney and Shana left the Ramtha cult, its leader, JZ Knight, became the first prominent New Age icon to boost QAnon, and one of their old cult-mates, Joe Dispenza, was gaining clout. Cortney and Shana reached out to us with their story of déjà vu. It was as if their 1980s VHS tapes were suddenly being livestreamed around the world.

After we reported on the fake quantum medicisms of Placebo Joe, Gavin wrote in from Australia with a stark memory about his late partner, Fey. "My wife was full of this stuff when she stopped taking all the treatments that had finally turned her breast cancer around," he wrote. "Right up to the day she died of it, still fully convinced she was going to heal herself by sheer force of wishful thinking."

Gavin is still mourning Fey. Cortney and Shana love their mother, though they've had to set boundaries. Mom has left the Ramtha group, but her mind is still chock-full of conspirituality, and the sisters can't process it all.

But each of them, in different ways, has acquired some kind of wisdom. Conspirituality, as a social movement, an ideology, and an industry, has mangled core relationships in their lives. But they have figured out something that a lot of us will have to learn in the post-QAnon, post-pandemic world. How to live in one world while caring for someone in another in a way that keeps the door open. We believe this is a position that more and more of us will have to confront.

CHAPTER 28

LEAVING ENLIGHTENMENT

CORTNEY AND SHANA can't remember exactly how they first became aware of the New Age promises and anxieties that would come to dominate every aspect of their lives. Mom brought it into the house bit by bit. It just felt like part of growing up.

As kids in the early 1980s, they would fall asleep to visualizations by Wayne Dyer, the self-help guru, on audiocassette. Mom would read passages from Paramahansa Yogananda's *Autobiography of a Yogi* after tucking them into bed. Cortney remembers an eerie photograph of the yogi's corpse in a glass coffin in a mortuary. The lore was that he just wouldn't decay. "Mom had a real fascination with beating death," she told us.

When the girls were still in elementary school, Mom took them to an attunement, which must have made them the youngest Reiki masters in Green Bay, Wisconsin—if not the whole Midwest. "She was on a search," Shana told us.

At some point, the local massage training, the health food store flyers, and the mail-order books weren't enough. Mom started traveling to events all the way out in Washington. She came home with a VHS tape that showed a woman named JZ Knight transform into someone she called Ramtha, who she said was 35,000 years old and carried the wisdom of the ages. She also bought audiocassettes of Ramtha, which they played in the car.

This was their introduction to channeling. As young teens, they didn't know what to think. Was it magic? Funny? Ramtha sounded like the Great Gazoo. They'd show the tape to their friends and giggle when Mom was away. But they also felt strange about it. Embarrassed.

267

* * *

"I REMEMBER YELLING at my mom, 'Why can't you be normal?'" Shana said. What they understand now is how much she desperately needed to find something meaningful.

"She was really struggling in the Catholic religion," Shana said. "And her marriage," Cortney added. "And midlife. It was the perfect storm."

Soon their mother was away more often and for longer stretches. When Cortney was seventeen and Shana was fourteen, she announced her plans to permanently move to the Ramtha's School of Enlightenment. She pitched the school as a great place for teens: fewer rules, lots of freedom. A horse ranch on eighty acres! But there was an anxious undertone to their discussions, as Mom began to talk about the Days to Come. "The entertainment value," Shana said, "suddenly became much more serious."

The family therapist tried to put a good spin on it, making it sound like the sisters were free to decide whether they wanted to go. But they were closer to their mom than to their dad, so it didn't really feel like a choice. They started helping her pack. Mom was obsessed with canning and drying food. She instructed the girls to say goodbye to their friends forever.

The notion that everyone they knew was going to die, while they ascended to some enlightened plane, was never made explicit. But the girls could feel it in the shifting ground beneath their feet.

CORTNEY AND SHANA ARRIVED with their mom (and younger sister, who didn't feel ready to speak about it all quite yet) in Yelm, Washington, homeless. As they couch-surfed for a year, they made friends with *other* teenage girls who had *also* moved from all over the country with *their* single mothers to be close to the great Ramtha.

It was a mixed bag. They bonded with their fellow "Ramsters." But they couldn't really get close to the kids at the local high school. Not only because it would have been embarrassing to fess up to what they and their crazy parents were up to, but because those kids, like their old friends back in Green Bay, were not preparing for the Days to Come. It was best not to form attachments that would only be snuffed out.

Their status as the elect was also a mixed bag. On one hand they were constantly reminded how lucky and special they were to be living in the glow of Ramtha. "You guys are so lucky," their mom would say. "You're so young! I wish I knew this when I was younger. You can do anything!"

But "you can do anything" for the young Ramsters often meant a general ethos of parental neglect. The adults had brought their children to the end point of human possibility. They had done their job. The kids couldn't be in a better place—why should they worry? This is not uncommon for groups like this, in which parent-members are infantilized by the leader to the point they stop seeing themselves as being responsible for anything beyond their own minds.

"You can do anything" also meant "You're responsible for everything." They were told that they had chosen their own journey. Suffering was a lesson they invited onto themselves. Everything that happened was for their ultimate benefit. As for things that went wrong, or the Days to Come? There was a disconnect, Cortney said. "All this bad stuff is going to happen, but you can do something about it. You are responsible for saving yourself."

Ramtha taught the standard New Age axiom, the law that governs conspirituality: *thoughts create reality.* Therefore, thoughts had to be controlled and reprogrammed. "As a kid going through this process," Shana said, remembering the terrible responsibility, "we were terrified of our thoughts." They were an anxious family to begin with, the sisters explained, laughing. They didn't need the added burden of worrying that their thoughts could be deadly. Or make them sick. They took it on because they had no choice, and learned the mindset of magical healing that eventually made its way to Fey's computer through people like Ramtha's most famous graduate, Joe Dispenza.

"There was a big emphasis on energy healing," Cortney said. Healing circles were a regular thing, she explained. The circles featured breathing exercises and visualizations not unlike those that Mary's husband, Louis, was hoping would beat back his cancer. Conventional medical care was thought to be crude and ineffective. "What that meant," Cortney said, "is that as kids we knew a lot of people who died. We knew a lot of people who got very sick, and tried very hard in these healing circles to get well. And ultimately didn't."

To grow up around adults in denial and refusing medical care increased the urgency of controlling their thoughts. Because it wasn't just that the sick person was thinking incorrectly—it was that if you did not believe they could be healed—by themselves or you—you were contributing to their illness. "We were getting all of these fears of cancer," Shana said, describing the feedback loop. "There were all of these things we were watching people die from, and terrified that we were going to create them for ourselves."

Cortney remembered a friend of their mother who lived with them as she died of cancer. They tried to heal the woman with their mind-power tricks—even though they believed that she had created the cancer herself. Cortney confessed that she wanted the keys to avoiding the same fate. "I even asked her at one point," she said, "how do you think you created this?"

Knight's world had locked them into a narcissistic house of mirrors. Everyone was on their own spiritual journey. They chose their parents, their circumstances, their struggles, and their fate. If the Days to Come bring terror, this will awaken you from your mundane perceptions of life. If Ramtha yells and swears at you, it is a teaching. If you suffer because your friend is sick, this is part of your chosen journey as well.

But because anything is possible—nothing is solid, nothing is real, everything is energy—you could work to reverse the perception of them dying by attempting to heal them with your thoughts and prayers. There was no limit to how hard you could work at turning things around, through the sheer power of intention. But if the person died, you could also cut them loose immediately. They had chosen to move on, after all.

It's a world in which people are given tools that let them pretend that they care for each other. But secretly, in the end, you never really have to love or mourn anyone, or do any concrete work to figure out how to make life better. Consciously or not, this is what cults tend to do: place members in an impossible situation with no one to turn to but a charismatic leader and their promises of transcendence.

How DID IT ALL come apart? Through public schools and broadening friend networks, Cortney and Shana became more connected with the reality-based world. And they also were the witnesses and recipients of real material care at a crucial moment in their lives.

Cortney was in her late twenties, married to a fellow Ramster. (All three sisters married within the group; all six have exited and recovered.) Cortney's husband was in a near-fatal car accident. They had been out of the group for years, but it wasn't until she and Shana were standing at his bedside in the trauma center that they realized the utter bankruptcy of the group's beliefs. "Nothing was going to save him except for that medicine," Cortney said. "It didn't matter what we were doing." No hands-on healing or power of prayer was going to stabilize his vitals. "That really was the beginning of the unraveling." Cortney could feel that the entire teaching of Ramtha stood on the illusion of personal control, instead of the project of careful, cooperative help the hospital was now providing.

While her son-in-law was in intensive care, Cortney's mom traveled back to Yelm to organize a prayer group. Another Ramtha elder showed up and started pontificating about what was happening and what they all needed to do.

"I was just like, fuck that," Cortney said. "I'm talking to surgeons. I'm talking to people who are actively trying to save his life."

CORTNEY AND SHANA were horrified—but not surprised—to learn that the first A-list New Age cult leader to publicly take up QAnon was their one and only JZ Knight. What is QAnon, after all, if not a movement of channelers, tuning in to the ethers to catch each Q-drop for translation and interpretation?

In 2019, Knight planted her flag against the Deep State when she invited QAnon rocker J. T. Wilde to open a revival-type event at her eighty-acre farm in Yelm, Washington, with his hit song "WWG1WGA." Attendees wore QAnon-themed T-shirts at the event. A spokesperson for Knight's Ramtha's School of Enlightenment told QAnon investigator Will Sommer that Ramtha declared that the person behind QAnon "is divine intelligence."

Cortney and Shana can't help but to finish each other's sentences. They laugh a lot, and talk about how important it has been to process their childhood trauma together. It feels lucky, because in many ways, they are otherwise orphaned. They still feel close to their mom, although they say she still lives in another world.

They need each other even more, given how hard it is to relate to the folks back in Green Bay. When they left all those decades ago, the town whispered that they had gone mad, that they were joining a nudist colony—which was about the worst thing they could imagine at the time. They were ostracized, which made it easier for Cortney and Shana to cut bait.

Now, the tables are turned. Over the past few years, they've realized that many in the old crowd have turned hard-core MAGA. Some are even red-pilled.

Part of Cortney's exit from the Ramtha's School of Enlightenment involved going to chiropractic school. Ironically, part of her decision was prompted by encouragement from Joe Dispenza, the cult chiropractor. Looking back, she says the move was both brave and obvious. Brave because she had to leave a cult to do it. Obvious because going to medical school would have been too much of a paradigm leap into a reality-based world.

"There is a lot of cult-like thinking and wellness garbage baked into chiropractic philosophy," she said. "So it made sense at the time." But after a few years of cracking backs and raising two small children, she burned out. She moved with her husband to a small island close to Seattle, and turned her pottery hobby into a small business, in a home studio. She loves working with clay.

While Cortney throws pots and mixes glaze, Shana is completing her training to become a marriage and family therapist. She wants to specialize in helping people recover from the stress of cults and the New Age. We bet she's going to be very busy.

CHAPTER 29

REMEMBERING FEY

GAVIN RYAN IS AN ARTIST from Australia who works in sculpture, installations, and giant paintings. He completed an eleven-foot by seven-foot acrylic called *The Tipping Point* in 2008. The stark, mural-sized canvas uses a War-in-Iraq color palette to depict all of humanity packed into a shopping cart, teetering on a cliff at the edge of an immiserated desert. In the handle section of the cart, where toddlers sit, a Donald Trump–type king lords over the wealthy, who hobnob with their luxurious distractions of food and fashion and pornography. A line of soldiers with machine guns separates them from the main carriage, where the hoi polloi battle over scarce resources or zone out in front of a television.

Some of the poors have turned away from the television to petition the gods in the sky. People from the Global South squat among barrels of toxic waste. One worker cuts down a potted apple tree with a chainsaw, while others drag boxes of sticks from the landscape to feed into a smoking furnace at the center of the crowd. A view of the side of the cart shows that the madding crowd is standing on layers of history in the form of generations of corpses. The whole shopping cart is about to fall into the abyss. No one is pushing it. No one is in control.

It's a depiction of late capitalist hell, worthy of Hieronymus Bosch. And there is no lie. Generously understood, conspirituality can be a good-faith answer to similar lucid, catastrophic visions. But like a New Age cult, it can only offer a yin to the yang. A heaven in which there are no shopping carts, no desert or edge of the world, no conflict, and certainly no death. What's missing is the panel in the middle, showing all the hard, uncertain work between the reality and the dream. The places where we can take hold of the cart.

* * *

ACCORDING TO GAVIN, FEY would have liked to have told everyone that she and Gavin had met in one of the yoga classes she taught in the Balinese resort town of Ubud. The more sheepish truth was that they'd met on Indonesia's version of OkCupid. But that story didn't seem to fit how star-crossed their journey felt. It was one of the things they laughed about.

Gavin had come to Bali from Queensland in search of hand carvers to collaborate with on his sculpture projects. Aged fifty-one, with two children from a previous relationship, he was looking for a new start. There were artists on his father's side, and scientists and academics on his mother's side, in prewar England. They were Theosophists who had hobnobbed with Jiddu Krishnamurti and Robert Oppenheimer. Gavin was working on a system for helping people create personal altar spaces centered on symbols derived from their dreams.

Fey was forty. She had recently fled a terrible relationship in Jakarta, where her close-knit extended family remained. Surviving the chaos of Borneo during the Suharto years, they had toiled their way into middle-class stability. In this new chapter, Fey had taken a yoga teacher training and quickly found work leading Ubud's steady influx of spirituality tourists through stretches, breathing, and dreaming of new worlds.

Gavin told us that everyone who met Fey loved her within ten minutes. She radiated kindness. A real people pleaser—"a heart of gold," as he put it. He sent us photos, several from her yoga portfolio. She stands in tree pose in a banyan forest at the foot of stone temple steps, carved Balinese dragons on either side. Another photo shows her in warrior pose, balanced on a black earth ridge in a verdant rice paddy. Another one: sitting cross-legged at the front of a class with one hand on her heart and the other on her belly. In one candid dinner shot, she tilts her head and gazes into Gavin's lens with what seems like a sense of inner peace.

When they met, they were both reading *The Power of Now.* They appreciated Eckhart Tolle's gentle encouragement to leave the past behind and give up on shortsighted desires. The ideas were helping Fey deal with panic attacks. Her main focus was compassion, Gavin said. People felt it in her yoga classes. They didn't come for yoga, he said. They came for her.

They had a happy year together before Fey found the lump in her breast. The triple-positive diagnosis was delivered by a top-tier oncologist, but they found him abrasive and the proposed treatment plan harrowing. Double mastectomy, all lymph nodes excised, full rounds of chemotherapy. Fey left the office feeling shell-shocked, as well as patronized and unheard.

Back at home, they made an appointment with Dr. Google, where Fey's yogaland algorithms led her into a world of hope, hype, and unproven therapies no insurance or governmental scheme would cover. Dismayed by the cold conventions of Western medicine, their journey into conspirituality began.

GAVIN SUPPORTED FEY'S SKEPTICISM of mainstream medicine—which he shared, to an extent. He also worried that the childlike radiance he loved in Fey might include a naive streak, especially when it came to medical or scientific information. Back in Jakarta, her family supported her interest in herbs, but expressed the hope that whatever alternative treatments she pursued would not conflict with the best available care. They knew she could be stubborn in her beliefs, and so they took a soft approach.

It wasn't lost on Gavin that the same internet that brought them together was selling them on miracle stories. A chorus of online voices claimed there was no need to listen to doctors who didn't understand the power of spiritual healing. Cancer could be easily—easily!—beaten with essiac tea, bloodroot, kitchen spices, coffee enemas, graviola, and intravenous vitamin C. They drank alkaline water purchased through an MLM scheme called Kangan. Their friends were supportive. Ubud society was bonded by anti–Big Pharma views that could also hint at other forms of alternative knowledge, like 9/11 trutherism.

Gavin found that cancer-cure Facebook favored the wishful and those who would monetize wishes. Whenever he heard about a promising alternative treatment, he'd go looking for personal testimonials—both for and against. The miracle stories were easy to find; strangely, failures were nowhere to be seen. If you got forensic about it, you could follow a person's progress over months through various groups to track how their supposed miracle panned out. And if they weren't too embarrassed to post it, you might find the full reality check, where the winning message ultimately lost out to the cold light of day.

Fey tried all the treatments. She also read voraciously. *You Can Heal Your Life* by Louise Hay, blog posts on miracle mushrooms and herbs by

David "Avocado" Wolfe (who went full QAnon in 2020). *You Are the Placebo* by Joe Dispenza. There was content by Joe Mercola, named in 2021 as a top spreader of vaccine disinformation. And the docsploitation videos by Ty and Charlene Bollinger, *The Truth About Cancer.* They subscribed to Gaia for a while. Fey also read books by the boomer cult leader Osho, famous for deepities like "Life begins where fear ends."

Her physical health went up and down, but the alternative medicine content was like a life jacket for her spirit. She wanted to keep teaching yoga and keep inspiring people to live their best lives even as her own became more fragile. She was up for anything, including a radical treatment involving something called black salve. They found an American herbalist who ran several clinics in Bali offering the treatment. Gavin thought he was a real cowboy, but had to admit that the dramatic results were impressive. Black salve is highly corrosive. Cancer specialists have been warning against using it for over a hundred years.

"It eats a fucking hole in your flesh," Gavin said as he described the blackened blood clots that oozed out of Fey's breast. The cowboy told them *that* was the cancer. She was being healed in real time. It was extremely painful, which gave Fey the sense that something powerful was happening. It didn't take long for the adrenaline rush of the catharsis to subside, and for the illness to make itself known again.

Something we can virtually guarantee that Fey did not learn during her yoga teacher training was how to evaluate critical health information propagated through Facebook yoga groups. While her career change offered her a new lease on life, it also led her into an information network that likely shortened it. Had she survived, the cycle would have surely repeated with COVID—with the same influencers.

Gaining scientific literacy while on the run from cancer is no easy task. Just a few pointers could have helped her make the leap from social media to Google Scholar. After searching for "breast cancer treatment" and finding an interesting paper, Gavin and Fey could have assessed the quality of the journal it was published in by looking up its ranking, which measures impact in the field. She could have looked for conflict-of-interest disclosures, to see whether the authors were working off of grants.

At a low point, it became clear that Fey had to get the help she'd been delaying. Gavin sponsored her naturalization to Australia so that she could sign up for treatment under the country's universal health care scheme. He had the sense that the doctors were rolling their eyes behind their backs after hearing the stories of Fey's prior treatments. But they were respectful and kind, and their best practices helped Fey achieve a remission. She was relieved, but she also downplayed the medical success, and turned her focus back to the alternative influencers who spoke to her soul.

When a six-month check-in found a lesion on her rib, Fey doubled down on alternative medicine after waving away the clinical recommendations. It was hard for Gavin to remember what the real doctors had suggested. In our interview he used the plural grammar of the caregiver. He said "we" when referring to what had happened to Fey. They were almost merged; it felt as though the disease was in his body as well. It made sense that it was hard for him to remember ideas and proposals that she rejected.

After Fey weakened, slipping to eighty-two pounds and beginning to rely on a wheelchair, she conceded to another round of medical care. Scans showed that a tumor was growing on her liver. She didn't want to believe it was cancer. She submitted to the palliative chemotherapy prescribed to her and used medical cannabis to ease the nausea. When she made an unlikely rally, she declared she was cured and wanted to return to Ubud. She was upbeat about restarting her yoga business. After she left, she never saw her cancer doctors again.

Gavin remembers that the more frail she became, the more she seemed to radiate confidence and grace. Her yoga friends praised her bravery. She reciprocated by inspiring them. There were also dark nights of the soul. One night she woke up to tell Gavin about a harrowing near-death experience, not unlike the one she had read in a favorite book, *Dying to Be Me*, by Anita Moorjani, who believed that she willed herself back from the brink of a cancer death through realizing her divine nature. "That's what she'd been primed for," he said, "with Anita Moorjani's experience. And so she took it right on."

When they left Australia, Gavin knew Fey wouldn't return. They went on a bucket list holiday to Vietnam and Malaysia. He continued to support her beliefs. As she weakened, he felt the stakes were rising—that supporting her was not quite enough. Fey needed Gavin to believe in the miracles she was expecting, or else they wouldn't come true. Even as she faded away, she told her yoga friends that she was absolutely healed. Gavin wondered who they were looking at when they affirmed her claim. She was clearly dying. No one wanted to say it. Something about maintaining this paradox made her glow even brighter. Gavin held these things with confused awe.

Fey died at the age of forty-seven in the backyard of her home in Ubud with Gavin at her side. It was just down the road from where they'd met. From her bed she could look up and see the stars through the coconut palms. "This too will pass," she told him.

What didn't pass, Gavin noticed while grieving, was the wave of contrarian spirituality that had carried Fey off too soon. She didn't live to see the beginning of the pandemic, but she would have been right in the thick of it. The same influencers who had told her that cancer was an illusion would be telling her that the real virus was fear. While she wasn't a political person, her willingness to favor magic over evidence may have made her vulnerable to the pseudopolitics of conspirituality.

FOR GAVIN, WATCHING his artistic and New Age communities in Ubud and Australia implode with conspirituality in 2020 was like a terrible echo. It was as if an entire culture was following his wife into the same radiant but anxious denial. Vulnerable people all over the world, in the midst of life changes, wanted something better for themselves, something more complete. "Partial measures avail us nothing" was the vibe. They were turning away from institutional actors toward influencers who presented as more humane. They were drawn to transgressive therapies presented as authentic, but with as much substance as the data streams they traveled on.

For Fey it all accelerated when a man in a white coat saw only her cancer, not her spirit. He didn't know *her*. Others heard the call of #savethechildren and felt that their governments would never protect the innocent. Still others heard warnings about the transhuman agenda and knew from the bottom of their hearts that the answer was not just political or material. Rather, they must transform themselves and transcend this worldly plane.

Caregiving for Fey prepared Gavin for a broader form of consideration. He learned about and managed the cognitive dissonance of loving a good person consumed by beliefs that did not serve her.

"There was a schism between what I had to give to the person I adored," he said. "Between what she wanted and what she needed. Two such completely different things, opposite to each other. Is there a way around that? I don't know. I tried to reach inside her head and find the switch to get her to open up to some other ways of looking at things.

"We've just been through it all again with COVID," Gavin said. "So many people I know are lost into the things they think. Just believing what they want to believe. And they'll say the same about me. So which one of us is right? Maybe there isn't an answer. Maybe there's just some things that don't have answers."

WHICH ONE OF ANY of us is right? There seem to be concentric circles within which that question zips and echoes. In the outermost rim, the space of social reproduction, it's possible for influencers to be emotionally right at a key moment in a person's life while being morally lazy at that same moment. Paradoxically, Eckhart Tolle's *Power of Now* is only powerful sometimes.

Joe Dispenza can be right about the zeitgeist of the moment when he tells Aubrey Marcus that scientific language—or in his case, pseudoscientific language—can function as a kind of modern liturgical prayer. Then he can also be disastrously, negligently wrong in his grift of "being your own placebo." Anita Moorjani can write a wonderful story about her near-death experience, but also be absolutely wrong that her private revelation provides some kind of blueprint for humanity.

Often we are asked: "Who are the good people in the New Age world? Where are the good teachers, the honest content providers?" We get the impulse and longing, but endorsements are not our lane, and they're not consistent with a critical project pushing back against a torrent of aspirational advertising. What we can say is that when we look for moral and spiritual consistency in this landscape, we find it in those who have survived it with eyes wide open and have tended others within it. What the stories of Gavin (and Mary, in Chapter 26) show is that a future surviving partner can end up living in two worlds on behalf of the dying lover. On the one hand, they must remain anchored in the evidence-based world and advocate for the best care possible. On the other hand, they also must accept and even celebrate pathways they may doubt or even resent—or even feel jealous of, if they represent ways in which a personal bond with kin has been diminished in favor of a parasocial bond with an influencer.

The people who know how to deal with conspirituality intimately have learned to walk a tightrope between consensus reality and the inner world of the person they love. Their task is to try to get these two worlds to communicate, which is almost impossible. In the end, they might end up living alone in a world from which their partner has fled like a refugee.

They also have to reckon with the failures of both worlds. When the oncologist says, "This is fourth stage and terminal," but offers no spiritual support, the partner has to fill in the gap. When the miracle healer says, "This is a dream and you can wake up," the partner has to provide a reality check, but not one that is so sharp that they wake up into despair. In both instances, the priority is to maintain and even strengthen the relationship as it hangs across a chasm of scrambled information and heightened emotion. Ultimately, they have to learn the art of displacing skepticism with love at the right moment.

They do this, perhaps instinctively, because they know that the crisis in conspirituality—this tangle of conspiracy theories and empty spiritual hopes—is largely a crisis in interpersonal and social trust. What Mary and Gavin went through with Louis and Fey is microcosmic to what many of us are going through in relation to the culture and these times. We think their gift is showing us that a crisis in trust can indeed be answered through the hard work of practicing trust, one relationship at a time.

CHAPTER 30

O FATHER, WHERE ART THOU?

MANY, MANY STORIES REMAIN unresolved.

By the spring of 2021, Ishi Dinim was accustomed to getting strange texts and emails about COVID-19 from his father, Joseph. The links to stories about medical lies and government conspiracies had begun trickling into Ishi's phone at the beginning of the pandemic, building up to a steady flow. Every story was a bit different, but the angle and tone were familiar.

Since 1982, when Ishi was three, Joseph had been the one-man publishing army behind *Common Ground*, a scrappy monthly newspaper based in the old hippy neighborhood of Kitsilano in Vancouver. A newsrack mainstay in vegan restaurants, health food shops, and indie bookstores, *Common Ground* served up a West Coast blend of progressive muckraking, paid for by advertisements for shamanic healers, healing crystals, and spiritual retreat centers.

Every issue was a potpourri of critical topics: environmentalism, antimilitarism, mercury in rivers and vaccines, the surveillance state. Also included were monthly columns that came in from Dr. David Suzuki (Canada's David Attenborough), primatologist Dr. Jane Goodall, and Oprah-level New Age celebrity Eckhart Tolle that extolled the "power of now" and egolessness. The magazine's copy was righteous and vigilant, with an urgency that sometimes crossed an invisible line into paranoia. This cast a veil between Joseph and those who needed him emotionally.

Joseph's favorite phrase was "To thine own self be true." His second favorite phrase was "Seize the day." He had a conviction that things mattered enough to act. Ishi admired this energy. He shared his father's progressive, anti-authoritarian values—even if some of his other beliefs seemed bizarre. But he also wished his dad would occasionally let the world save itself, and pay more attention to his family.

Amidst his feverish work, Joseph was no stranger to stillness and reflection. He loved music. He'd scribble out polemics all morning before melting into his beloved piano playing in the afternoons. With Joseph, it was either revolution or transcendence. Ishi longed to meet him somewhere in between.

One bright day, mid-pandemic, Ishi spotted his dad across the street, through his driver's side window. Ishi was heading to the library with his wife and two daughters, aged ten and thirteen. They watched Joseph stride along, carrying books under his arm, on a mission, as usual. He was wearing a navy blue T-shirt in an odd way—over a rumpled green button-down. There was a large rectangular iron-on decal on the front. It featured a drawing of a huge syringe surrounded by green cartoon virus particles and framed with all-caps text: COVID CULT BAPTISM.

So here's Joseph, father and grandfather, walking down the street in a T-shirt fit for an internet troll. Ishi and his family—all vaccinated—felt uncomfortable, but waved him to come over. Ishi tried to ignore the shirt and did his best to keep the conversation casual. Before they parted, Ishi asked to take his father's picture, so he could remember the shirt. Joseph obliged.

In the photo, Joseph proudly shows off his T-shirt. He's standing in a parking lot, yellow buttercups poking out of the traffic island behind him. He's holding two books in his right hand. One is *No Logo*, Naomi Klein's influential examination of global corporatization. The other is an anthology of the writings of I. F. Stone, the famed radical journalist who kept center-liberal politicians in the United States on their toes for over four decades. Two lefty classics, brandished by a self-described progressive activist who's wearing a shirt that looks like it was printed in a MAGA sweatshop.

What was happening?

Two months later, Joseph's editorial for the August-September issue of *Common Ground* featured a famous quote from Stone: "All governments lie." Ironically, the issue, with a print run of 300,000, was itself chock-full of lies: anti-mask propaganda, complaints about medical apartheid, misinformation about vaccine injuries, and warnings about the elite and The Great Reset. Joseph's main article tiptoed right up to QAnon land by calling the Canadian prime minister, Justin Trudeau, a pimp for the pharmaceutical industry. He was, Joseph claimed, herding Canadians toward the unparalleled catastrophe of institutional fascism. The cover was a parody of a Penguin paperback cover for George Orwell's most famous book, with *COVID NINETEEN EIGHTY-FOUR* as the new title. The community pages featured listings for channeled angel readers and organic diapers.

Ishi tried to reason with his father. He brought up the problem of how the conspiracism *Common Ground* was publishing relied on antisemitic tropes as dog whistles. Ishi said he should be more sensitive. His mother's family—Joseph's ex-wife's family—were Holocaust survivors after all. Joseph got agitated. "Oh yeah? Who are you going to report me to? What are you, a brownshirt?" he said.

"I don't believe he's a happy person," Ishi told Matthew in one of several interviews over a number of months, "when so much of his energy and so much of his brain space is taken up with seeing all the bad in the world."

By the spring of 2022, Ishi was distanced from his father, who had escalated to speaking at QAnon-sponsored protests and organizing blockades connected to the so-called Freedom Convoy that had terrorized downtown Ottawa for nearly a month with parked rigs blowing air horns at all hours. In the middle of Ishi's birthday dinner, Joseph called, not to wish him a happy birthday—evidently he'd forgotten—but to monologue about the COVID hoax. He also missed the birthday of one of his granddaughters. Instead of coming to the party or dropping off a card, he left three copies of *Common Ground*, each folded back to reveal a different, specific article, on the family's porch.

Then, Joseph made national news when the Canadian Broadcasting Corporation called him out in an investigation into how he used federal arts grant money to publish COVID denialism materials. He pivoted quickly to living on cash donations from his longtime readers, dropped off in person at his bungalow.

We reached out to Joseph for comment, and a possible interview.

"Because my son, who I love dearly, is discussing this with you, I gave your request consideration," he wrote by email.

But after reviewing the online footprint of the podcast, he determined "there is not a good fit," and declined to respond to specific questions.

Joseph's email sign-off quoted Samuel Butler from the 1872 novel *Erewhon*: "Reason uncorrected by instinct is as bad as instinct uncorrected by reason."

WHY DID ISHI REACH out to a journalist—a stranger—about his father?

"I wanted to counteract some of the misinformation he's been putting out there," Ishi said. "I don't have a magazine. I'm not going to start my own podcast. But at the same time, I don't want to harm him."

In fact, Ishi feels protective of Joseph, who is increasingly vulnerable to backlash. There have been death threats from activists on the other side of the COVID divide. Ominous phone calls, and warnings that his computer systems will be hacked and destroyed. Ishi has taken a number of panicked calls from Joseph, asking what he should do.

"I've told him he should contact the police. And also—that he should take ownership for the reaction. That he's spreading lies while people are dying. I'm not condoning violence. The threats are not excusable. But the reaction is understandable."

Ishi has always known that his father's universe of progressive activism and alternative spirituality was vulnerable to curdling. Behind the facade of the charismatic networker stood a disheveled and paranoid man, twisting yards of yarn around pushpins stuck in a corkboard. The signs had been there for years. The volatility has demanded that the son, in many ways, has had to father himself.

But those signs never pushed Ishi out of his father's world entirely. Ishi remains active in political life—arguably with more commitment than Joseph has ever risked. Over the years, they've laughed together that Ishi has been arrested twice at environmental protests while Joseph has somehow steered clear of the cops.

On the spiritual front, Ishi never bought into what he calls the "snake oil" his father advertised. Rather, he happened upon something more seemingly sustainable than the three of us authors have ever known.

THE SALT SPRING CENTRE of Yoga is several car ferry stops west from Vancouver, in the Gulf Islands. It was founded by a Hindu monk named

Baba Hari Dass, who taught a quiet blend of philosophy and meditation to pilgrims like Ishi, who could trade room and board for work in the kitchens and gardens. "Quiet" is the operative word here, as Dass had taken a vow of silence as a young adult, and communicated with students by writing concise answers to their questions on a small chalkboard that hung from a rope around his neck. It's about as far away from internet culture as quill and ink.

In Dass, Ishi found a leader who couldn't have been more different from his father. A patient listener who didn't give in to snap judgments or easy answers. Dass nurtured a quiet place in the world of alternative spirituality where the careful observation of life could ease anxiety. Ishi found the baby in the bathwater, and is still nurturing it.

Conspirituality has deep roots. But some of them may wind back to—or remain connected to—nourishing places. This suggests it is something the generations can recover from, if the disillusionment isn't total. We asked Ishi how he thought things would turn out between him and his father.

"COVID will end someday," he said. "And at that point, we're just going to be people who need to live with each other again."

Ishi would prefer that his father could admit that there's a chance he was wrong about COVID. That there is no shame in being wrong. Humility is a form of spirituality, too. It costs less than a yoga retreat, and is more practical than New Age bromides.

"I want him to put down that burden a little bit and just play music, and enjoy his grandkids," Ishi said. "In this present reality. Not in this externalized need to save the world. Because it hasn't worked."

Ishi's response to his dad hints at values absorbed from his yoga years—including some of the universalism and nonattachment that made this whole subculture so appealing. He spoke about leaving the door open for some kind of magic to happen. He offered that healing our common domestic wounds—or at least trying to—is at the root of addressing other immediate issues, like climate change and global conflicts. Even if reconciliation with his father doesn't happen, he said, leaving the door open would still be his best choice. He tries to be present with that value. "It might be less than twenty years left that we have each other. It might be less than five."

It's an old lesson. A yogi acts with love and compassion not because they are attached to being rewarded, but because those actions are joyful in themselves. At the same time, Ishi is also very attached to what he calls the continuum of life: the sense that he must work toward a better future, to honor the unlikely miracle of being born, and the responsibility he feels for his part of the web.

"I want this story to continue," he said.

CHAPTER 31

WHAT WE'VE BEEN GIVEN

THIS IS DEFINITELY NOT a self-help book, and we're a long way out from the days in which, as yoga and wellness gig workers, we presumed to give advice. More than that, we're painfully aware that conspirituality has strong roots in the cringey instinct to tell people what to think from a morally superior position.

But discussions with listeners (and our editors) made it clear it would be fruitful to end this book by sharing some of what we've learned about living in the era of conspirituality, which we predict will be with us for some time to come. Neither spirituality nor conspiracy theories are going anywhere in an age of increasing worldly disillusionment and accelerating uncertainty. Conspirituality hacks the zeitgeist because it offers high-calorie, low-nutritional food to a hungry world.

Spirituality—at any level of integrity—speaks to deep human needs for meaning, purpose, and community. When people gather in these orbits, they bond through emotive rituals that create flow states and give access to neuroplastic changes in habits, beliefs, and priorities. The process can be beautiful and beneficial. But it can also amplify vulnerabilities and exploit good intentions.

Ungrounded spirituality can engender a fetish for transcendence that devalues everyday life and worldly concerns. Intense bonds within an in-group can create cult-like dependence and mistrust of the "outside" world. Ritual ecstasies that can be healing in the context of mind-body practices also make people highly suggestible to outlandish interpretations of what those states mean. *We are awake. We are invulnerable. We can see the Truth.* The history of spiritual excess is littered with the wreckage of individuals and groups high on their own grandiose supply. Indoctrinated into beliefs that *feel so right* in the moment, they believe they have attained superior consciousness. The irony is that their hubris rises in tandem with their disconnection from reality. As the spiritually deluded person becomes more enchanted with their sense of internal power, their real-world agency can decline.

Healthy spirituality, in our view, should be balanced by healthy skepticism. Healthy spirituality wouldn't promise quick and categorical transformation. It wouldn't revolve around narcissists with messiah complexes making outlandish promises. It would accept and welcome doubt and agnosticism as part of the general learning process and the human condition. But immature spirituality attempts to eliminate the instinct to doubt, toward the goal of nurturing a uniformly pure and positive outlook. The problem is that all of that doubt has to go somewhere—and conspirituality tells you where to put it. In order to keep your spiritual life unquestionably pure, your doubt must be deflected onto institutions, governments, scholarly disciplines, and the media.

So: some strains of spirituality give a false impression of personal growth and empowerment. Meanwhile, conspiracy theories give the false impression of healthy skepticism and control. As we've discussed from the start, both spirituality and conspiracism demand that devotees awaken to a hidden reality. Both rely on a magical connecting-of-the-dots that values the rush of apophenia (perceiving patterns where they don't exist) over a more careful attitude of inquiry. The dot-connecting becomes even more manic when that spirituality is embedded within quasi-material ideas about the body and world. Most of the influencers we covered in Part Three have apophenic views of the body, expressed through giddy tangles of meridians and chakras and hierarchies of higher and lower selves. They mirror the Corkboard Guy, who solves political intrigues by tracking obscure connections with his pushpins and yarn.

When immature spirituality takes on Corkboard Guy energy, the result is a premature and anxious certainty about the nature of the world. Just as conspiracism generalizes a paranoid mistrust of all authorities and institutions and scientific inquiries, cursed spirituality can seed a worldview so committed to the revelation of spiritual knowingness, heart wisdom, or intuitive guidance that it comes to reject science, psychology, and critical examination of its own core beliefs. When personal growth is defined as an ever-increasing commitment to this solipsism, it ironically makes adherents more closed-minded, narcissistic, and convinced of beliefs that can be mortally dangerous.

BUT THAT'S ENOUGH from us. We'd like to leave you with a montage of key bits of insight and advice we've gathered from the many experts we've been honored to interview over the years on the *Conspirituality* podcast. The topics are diverse, but the message is consistent: there are real, empathetic ways of navigating life in the era of conspirituality.

Jivana Heyman (episode 9) founded the nonprofit Accessible Yoga Association, and is a leading voice in the disability rights movement in wellness spaces. His vocation was born during the height of the AIDS epidemic in the 1980s. Stretching and mindfulness were sometimes all his dying friends in San Francisco had, and all he could give them as a young yoga teacher. In the midst of this tragedy, yoga could never have been about the implausible and self-centered aims of purifying the body or perfecting the immune system. In Heyman's view, the purpose of yoga in difficult times is not about hoarding or selling secret knowledge, or waking up into a superior state. It's about feeling your way into a shared vulnerability that seeks neither scapegoats nor magical pills, and is always ready to listen and learn.

Imran Ahmed (episodes 10 and 100) is the most driven and uncompromising digital ethicist we know. He founded the Center for Countering Digital Hate, which conducts forensic audits into the extent and effects of online extremism. Their pre-pandemic work in countering online misogyny and bigotry against Muslims put them in pole position in the race to fight COVID misinformation. He took us aback with a single evidence-based rule: Never feed the algorithm. Because any engagement with misinformation—even to disagree or debunk—boosts the visibility of the content. Before speaking with Ahmed, we didn't fully understand the technological jet fuel of conspirituality: that social media is built to monetize controversy, contrarianism, and outrage. What makes it so addictive is what makes it so lucrative. The answer? Block, ignore, and then go create your own post sharing accurate information.

Regan Williams (episode 12) founded the nonprofit Seen&Heard, which helps marginalized youth through performing arts training. She delivered the painful news that some of her clients got red-pilled by the sex-trafficking moral panic driven by QAnon. The story made enough sense to those clients to co-opt their lived experience of institutional betrayal. We learned a new consequence of conspiracy-driven clicktivism, but also how important it is to both acknowledge and repair wounded social trust—something that involves sensitivity and skill.

Dr. Theodora Wildcroft (episodes 12 and 13) is a teacher, trainer, writer, and scholar whose research considers the democratization of yoga "post-lineage," and the evolving practice of teaching yoga for community health. Her scholarship is informed by and embedded in the yoga #MeToo movement. She illuminated for us a crucial connection between the psychology of survivorship and the gamification of QAnon. Survivors of institutional abuse, she explained, can spend years or even decades without ever feeling as though they are able to speak, let alone be heard. Perhaps the most important thing QAnon offered its members was a sense of agency in relation to disclosing a terrible secret. More than being heard, Wildcroft suggested, they could be centered. QAnon may have provided a flawed but compelling framework in which a survivor could feel acknowledged as the detective of their own tragedy, and the hero of their recovery. In that light, it is more than a conspiracy theory to be debunked. It is a Rorschach test for how a society negotiates unprocessed trauma, and a potentially important part of understanding how and why people fall under its spell.

Jared Yates Sexton (episode 17) is a political analyst and writing professor. He told us that one antidote to conspiratorial world-making might be a solid education in history. He helped us see how the myths of American exceptionalism and Manifest Destiny still cast their shadow over a conspirituality world rife with colonialist and domineering attitudes. That many wellness influencers fail to empathize with the poor and dispossessed is not some random artifact of this history. It's a feature, which means that conspirituality is part of a larger geopolitical story.

Dr. Dan Wilson (episode 29) is a molecular biologist who fights misinformation and conspiracy theories in the medical world through his *Debunk* *the Funk* YouTube channel. His deadpan delivery and meticulous sourcing consistently eviscerate the pseudoscience of COVID contrarians. But there's something humble and approachable about his presentation—and that has to do with what he told us about his youth. Years before graduate studies sharpened his filters, he was a 9/11 truther. He bought it all: it was an inside job, a controlled demolition, a massive cover-up. He remembers the exhilaration of feeling like he was on the inside of a secret, that he understood the deep truth about globalized American corruption. He knows that the conspiratorial drive seeks justice, even though it finds chaos. And this has given him an empathy and vulnerability that seem to only increase his patience and stamina for a job that's unlikely to end.

Dr. Annie Kelly (episode 61) researches digital antifeminism. Her work shows how the violence of QAnon found roots in virtual soil manured by years of online misogyny and shitposting. She coined the term "subversion anxiety" to describe a core driver of the conspiracy sphere. Patriarchy—goes the fear—will be replaced by social justice autocrats. Feminism will destroy heterosexual freedoms and pleasures. Human bodies will become genderless cyborgs. Collectivism will replace capitalism. Kelly also applied this listening-based scholarship to a brilliant podcast series that detailed the centuries-long history of anti-vax protests against the smallpox vaccine, and how, in the end, public health won the day. It modeled for us—and all extremism researchers—that understanding social grievances is at the root of imagining better ways of communicating the common good.

Dale Beran (episode 62) came of age online in the chan-world in the early aughts. His auto-ethnography of years spent on anonymous message boards pulled back yet another veil on the isolation and alienation of virtual life in late capitalism. Until we read his book *It Came From Something Awful*, we didn't grasp that the online spaces that incubate conspiracy chaos are not ideological so much as depressive and despairing. Before QAnon red-pilled conspiritualists, the chan boards "black-pilled" unemployed, immiserated Anons. Understanding this more clearly made the political amorality of JP Sears—and the appeal of his irony poisoning—make sense. It also gave us insight into how the raw, aggressive emotions of grievance, especially among young men, are very easy to convert into the affects and aesthetics of fascism.

Beran's work is descriptive, not prescriptive. But listening to him made it clear that discussions about online disruption are empty if they do not point to the nuts and bolts of social and communal support in the real world.

Lee McIntyre (episode 75) is a philosophy professor who joined us to talk about his book, *How to Talk to a Science Denier*. In it, he steps outside of the ivory tower of speculation and the Twitterverse of dunks to chronicle his real-world experiments in interacting with conspiracy theorists on their own turf. He visited flat-Earth, anti-vaccine, and 9/11-truther conventions. And he just talked to people. He concluded that all science denial relies on the same set of fallacies: cherry-picking data, expecting science to be perfect, fake experts, and bad reasoning. But he also found that the pop psychology view that people with false beliefs only dig their heels in more when contradicted with facts and evidence is in fact a cliché, disproven by more recent research. His suggestions? Approach people with respect and kindness. Don't be a dick. Build genuine trust by listening to their ideas with empathy and curiosity. Stick with it. Recognize that every little bit helps.

Dr. Danielle Belardo (episode 112) is a cardiologist and science communicator who hits Instagram hard. She talked to us about the danger of keeping medicine locked away in academic texts and clinical files. People want to know what's going on in their bodies, and if qualified practitioners don't make that possible in accessible ways, charlatans will. Cholesterol, heart disease, vaccines—there's a lot out there to debunk and clarify. Belardo makes it part of her rounds in a way that shows that actual doctors can step into the gap between institutional knowledge and popular online culture that conspiritualists have exploited.

Rina Raphael (episode 121) is a journalist who came on to discuss *The Gospel of Wellness*, her book that focuses on how the wellness industry markets itself, pseudo-religiously, to women. She examines the politics of clean beauty, the unnatural vs. the natural, and the promises of community and support that wellness businesses struggle to keep. The transactional and superficial nature of wellness spirituality became clear to Raphael when her father died. She realized the emptiness of working on her body while grieving, and that it wouldn't occur to her spin instructor to bring her a casserole.

But Raphael left us on a hopeful note. The buzz she'd been hearing from wellness publicists was that Zoomers are not buying in. "Wellness may be over," she said. TikTok might be chock-full of pseudoscience and MLMs selling essential oils. But it's also bristling with rebellion against healthist preciousness. Yes, it's dodgy when kids video themselves cooking chicken in NyQuil or gorging themselves on a mukbang. But a little recklessness and contrarianism might just push back against body fascism.

Christina Flinders (bonus episode, September 2022) answered our callout for listener stories by sharing her rollercoaster bio. She grew up in an uber-intellectual neo-Hindu cult, where the leader abused girls and women, including her mother, starting when her mother was fourteen. Her rebellion threw her into the strangely parallel world of strip clubs, where dancing gave her partial autonomy, but also sharpened her understanding of coercive misogyny. Her pivot to teaching yoga in Phoenix sounds like the climax of a New Age redemption story worthy of *Yoga Journal*. But it wasn't that simple. When 2020 hit, she watched her community get red-pilled. Her undergrad degree in hard knocks told her it was time to cut bait.

She's in grad school now studying political science, and writing short stories about her nights in the clubs. In one story, she describes the parallel between her mom not being protected from her abuser and how floor managers would force her to continue dancing for abusive clients. When we asked her about her takeaways from a life in cursed yogaland, she expanded our definition of "bypassing." People can use any sort of defense or presumed credential to obscure the real pain of their lives, she explained. These can include meditation or academic study, or confusing exploitation for empowerment.

Tim McKee is the publisher of North Atlantic Books. He has not been a guest on our show, but he has shown us a big W that we'll end with. Remember that essay he published, disowning the COVID misinformation of one of his top authors, Charles Eisenstein? As of October 2022, his company has made good on the promise to mitigate the harm of Eisenstein's influence. North Atlantic has donated over $34,000 from the sales of Eisenstein's books to three nonprofits:

Frontline Workers Counseling Project, which connects essential and frontline workers with free psychotherapy services and support groups in the San Francisco Bay Area.

Disability Visibility Project, which creates and amplifies disability media online.

Facing History and Ourselves, which is an anti-hate civics organization in Boston.

ONE LAST THING, for now.

We want to acknowledge that for many of you, the events of 2020 and beyond, and the stories in this book, may lead to a sense of spiritual despair. The weight of our reporting seems to suggest that personal growth, health and wellness pursuits, and tending to our inner lives are hopelessly corrupted by cultish beliefs, conspiracism, and New Age pseudoscience libertarianism.

It does seem inevitable that if what we call "spirituality" continues to be colonized by an absence of critical thinking and the politics of bodily purity, spiritual tourism, and the self project—toxic dynamics will result.

We believe, however, that spirituality can be informed by an enthusiasm for the hard work of research, a basic honesty about injustice and trauma, a desire for the common good, and a deep respect for the psychological, cultural, and political complexity of being human.

We're often asked what we believe in now, given all these stories, all this disillusionment. It's a tough question for all of us. But we do know that working on this book, and learning through the discussions that arise from it, has been and will continue to be something like a spiritual practice.

ACKNOWLEDGMENTS

We would like to thank our agent, Rebecca Gradinger, for her vision and enthusiasm, and our editors Colleen Lawrie, Pamela Murray, and Lauren Park for helping us find the statue in the boulder.

Over the past three years, over 2000 listeners have supported us through Patreon. This financial and moral support has been crucial in bringing this book to light. Thank you.

Finally, we'd like to thank the guests, colleagues, friends and family members who have helped us professionally and personally as we've struggled to make sense of these volatile times:

Beatrice Adler-Bolton
Imran Ahmed
Dr. Taslim Alani-Verjee
Dr. Amarnath Amarasingam
Sara Aniano
Dr. Jacqueline Antonovich
Rick Archer
Dr. Marc-André Argentino
Brenna Artinger
Alex Auder
Devendra Banhart
Danielle Belardo
John Bemrose
Dr. Kathleen Belew
Ruth Ben-Ghiat
Dale Beran
Amy Berg
Jonathan Berman

Rebekah Borucki
Chris Boutté
Beau Brink
Jennings Brown
Dr. Matthew Brown
Kathryn Bruni-Young
Kiera Butler
Alessia Caputo
Dr. Rebecca Carter-Chand
Dr. Timothy Caulfield
Dan Collen
Seane Corn
Susannah Crockford
Lisa Braun Dübels
Mallory DeMille
Angela Denker
Philip Deslippe
EJ Dickson
Alex Ebert
RP Eddy
Jill Etteinger
Jules Evans
Patrick Farnsworth
Julian Feeld
Andy Fleming
Aoife Gallagher
dapper gander
Sarah Garden
Anand Giriharadas
Dr. Ann Glenn
Aubrey Gordon
Philip Gorski
Jack Graham
Lydia Greene
Emily Guerin
Kyra Haglund

Ali Haider
Anna Halafoff
Kathleen Hale
Colin Hall
Kim Hall
Melissa Harris-Perry
Virginia Heffernan
Britt Hermes
Jivana Heyman
Sarah Hightower
Michael Hobbes
Jessica Hopper
Cathleen Hoskins
Håkon F. Høydal
Jitarth Jadeja
Jonathan Jarry
Michelle Cassandra Johnson
Nitai Joseph
Dr. Chris Kavanagh
Dr. Annie Kelly
Kerri Kelly
Sam Kestenbaum
Stephan Kesting
Hala Khouri
Kevin Klatt
Jordan Klepper
Daniel Latorre
Thomas Lecaque
Ben Lee
Maggie Levantovskaya
Alan Levinovitz
Lorna Liana
Paola Marino
Lee McIntyre
Anna Merlan
Jill Miller

Jude Mills
Dr. Jay Mohan
George Monbiot
Mooncat
David Morris
Alexi Mostrous
Brian Muraresku
Jason Nagata
Dr. C. Thi Nguyen
Andy O'Brien
Dr. Jonathan O'Donnell
Alyce Ornella
India Oxenberg
Samual Perry
Natalia Petrzela
Jayme Poisson
Sean Prophet
Dr. Aaron Rabinowitz
Dr. Shyam Raganathan
Mike Rains
Rina Raphael
Dr. Lissa Rankin
David Remski
Abbie Richards
Anke Richter
Jessica Malaty Rivera
Caolan Robertson
Jake Rockatansky
Chelsea Roff
Dr. Mark Roseman
Dax-Devlon Ross
Mike Rothschild
Gavin Ryan
Jennifer Sapio
Jared Yates Sexton
Daniel Sherrell

Elizabeth Simons
Heather Simpson
Dr. Izzy Smith
Cam Smith
Sheena Sood
Will Sommer
Thenmozhi Soundararajan
Dr. Peter Staudenmaier
Mary Steffenhagen
Tara Stiles
Will Storr
Stacie Stukin
Benjamin Teitelbaum
Joe Trinder
Francesca Tripodi
Antonio Valladeres
Travis View
Tamara Venit-Shelton
Mirna Wabi-Sabi
Melody Walker
Enqi Weng
Dr. Theodora Wildcroft
Regan Williams
Dr. Dan Wilson
Morgan Yew

NOTES

INTRODUCTION

6 **At first he advised the public not to wear masks:** Grace Panetta, "Fauci Says He Doesn't Regret Telling Americans Not to Wear Masks at the Beginning of the Pandemic," *Business Insider*, July 16, 2020, https://www.businessinsider.com/fauci -doesnt-regret-advising-against-masks-early-in-pandemic-2020-7.

6 **a highbrow resentment on spring break beach partiers:** Zeynep Tufekci, "Scolding Beachgoers Isn't Helping," *The Atlantic*, July 4, 2020, https://www.theatlantic .com/health/archive/2020/07/it-okay-go-beach/613849/.

6 **turned away thousands of doses of the Johnson & Johnson vaccine:** Ganesh Setty, "Detroit mayor declines Johnson & Johnson allotment, saying the other vaccines are better," CNN, March 5, 2021, https://www.cnn.com/2021/03/04/health/detroit -mayor-johnson-and-johnson-vaccine/index.

6 **Pfizer released a flawed report on vaccine injuries:** Junaid Naibi, "What the Pandemic Has Taught Us About Science Communication," World Economic Forum, June 16, 2021, https://www.weforum.org/agenda/2021/06/lessons-for-science -communication-from-the-covid-19-pandemic/.

15 **Derek published an explainer piece:** Derek Beres, "Why Are Conspiracy Theories Rampant in the 'Wellness' Industry? Welcome to Conspirituality," Big Think, April 19, 2022, https://bigthink.com/the-present/conspirituality/.

15 **prompting Julian to publish a viral piece:** Julian Walker, "The Red Pill Overlap," Medium, May 20, 2020, https://julianwalker111.medium.com/the-red-pill-overlap -19ad346c62f0.

CHAPTER 1. CHARLOTTE'S WEB

19 **"to act in accordance with an awakened 'new paradigm' worldview":** Charlotte Ward and David Voas, "The Emergence of Conspirituality," *Journal of Contemporary Religion* 26, no. 1 (2011): 103–21, doi:10.1080/13537903.2011.539846.

21 **rising interest in what she termed "A Global Awakening":** Conspirituality.org, Tracking the Global Awakening, About page, archived, accessed November 17, 2021, https://web.archive.org/web/20150102074524/http://conspirituality.org/about/.

21 **a meticulous archive of research on religious movements:** UCL faculty page for David Voas, accessed November 17, 2021, https://iris.ucl.ac.uk/iris/browse/pro file?upi=DVOAS54.

22 **As "clients seek to expose—depose—a shadow government":** Charlotte Ward and David Voas, "The Emergence of Conspirituality," *Journal of Contemporary Religion* 26, no. 1 (2011): 103–21, doi:10.1080/13537903.2011.539846, 103.

22 **the British conspiracy mongerer David Icke:** Will Offley, "Selected Quotes of David Icke," accessed November 18, 2021, http://www.publiceye.org/Icke/Icke quotes.htm.

23 **"there is simply injustice":** David Icke, "Time to Tell the Truth About Israel without Fear of the Mind Police," accessed March 30, 2009, https://web.archive.org/web/20150110215459/http://www.davidicke.com/headlines/19027-time-to-tell-the-truth-about-israel-without-fear-of-the-mind-police/.

23 **in a passage that links to Icke:** David Icke, "BBC in the Service of Israeli Propaganda," accessed November 17, 2021, https://web.archive.org/web/20150112010521/http://www.davidicke.com/headlines/bbc-in-the-service-of-israeli-propaganda/.

23 **the British conspiracy website thetruthseeker.co.uk:** Gilad Atzmon, "Roger Waters, the Pig and the Star of David," accessed November 17, 2021, http://www.thetruthseeker.co.uk/?p=75992.

23 **Illuminati tracker David Wilcock:** David Wilcock, "FINANCIAL TYRANNY: Defeating the Greatest Cover-Up of All Time," accessed November 17, 2021, http://divinecosmos.com/start-here/davids-blog/1023-financial-tyrannyOST?font style=f-smaller&start=2.

23 **Wilcock, a QAnon booster:** MJ Banias, "Popular UFO Conspiracy Theorists Are Cashing in on the COVID-19 Pandemic," *VICE*, May 13, 2020, https://www.vice.com/en/article/4ayyqw/david-wilcock-ufo-conspiracy-theorist-covid-19-deep-state-ascension.

23 **who hints he may be the reincarnation of famed nineteenth-century clairvoyant Edgar Cayce:** Wynn Free and David Wilcock, *The Reincarnation of Edgar Cayce? Interdimensional Communication and Global Transformation* (Berkeley, CA: Frog Books, 2004).

23 **secret human contact with aliens is about to usher in a global spiritual transformation:** Will Sommer, "Inside the War Between a UFO Influencer and Alien-Friendly Streaming Company," *Daily Beast*, May 16, 2021, https://www.thedailybeast.com/ufo-community-explodes-in-lawsuit-drama-accusations-of-luciferianism.

23 **As the eventual court judgment described:** Royal Courts of Justice, "Re P and Q (Children: Care Proceedings: Fact Finding)," accessed November 18, 2021, https://www.judiciary.uk/wp-content/uploads/2015/03/gareeva-dearman-2015.pdf.

23 **it saw 175 adults subjected to mob allegations of Satanic Ritual Abuse (SRA):** Eloise Whitmore et al., "Episode 1: Secrets and Lies," Tortoise, *Hoaxed*, September 22, 2022, https://www.tortoisemedia.com/audio/hoaxed-alexi-mostrous-secrets-and-lies/

23 **a lurid tale about him and fellow teachers at Christ Church Primary School:** Paul Wright, "Mum 'Who Tortured Kids' to Invent Hampstead Satanic Abuse Fantasy Loses Appeal." Ham & High, August 7, 2015, https://www.hamhigh.co.uk/news/crime/mum-who-tortured-kids-to-invent-hampstead-satanic-abuse-fantasy-3500232; Jon King, "Man Jailed Over Hampstead 'Satanic Abuse' Hoax," Ham & High, September 7, 2015, https://www.hamhigh.co.uk/news/crime/jail-for-rupert-wilson-quaintance-over-hampstead-satanic-abuse-hoax-3570176.

24 **The children's mother was a Bikram Yoga teacher, and her new partner was a raw food fanatic:** Eloise Whitmore et al., "Episode 1: Secrets and Lies," Tortoise, *Hoaxed*, September 22, 2022, https://www.tortoisemedia.com/audio/hoaxed-alexi-mostrous-secrets-and-lies/.

24 **Two of the rumormongers who spread the Hampstead allegations online to a global audience of an estimated four million were jailed:** Connor Boyd and Joel Adams, "Pensioner, 74, Who Claimed Parents Were Abusing Their Children as Part of a Satanic Cult which Drank Babies' Blood and Cooked Youngsters in Secret Room in McDonald's Is Jailed for Nine Years," *Daily Mail*, October 26, 2022, https://www.dailymail.co.uk/news/article-6577369/Hampstead-pensioner-74-claimed-parents-satanic-cult-jailed-nine-years.html.

24 **a screenshot maze of email addresses and YouTube accounts:** "Mel and Charlotte: When in Doubt, Blame Hackers," accessed November 17, 2021, https://hoaxteadresearch.wordpress.com/2016/11/10/mel-and-charlotte-when-in-doubt-blame-hackers/, full dossier archived on authors' website: https://www.conspirituality.net/book-resources.

24 **the HTML link for her author's page pointing to Charlotte in the address line:** "Author Jacqui," accessed November 17 2021, https://web.archive.org/web/20150108093648/http://conspirituality.org/author/Charlotte/.

24 **She signed the email "Charlotte Ward aka Jacqui Farmer":** El Coyote, "Charlotte Ward Denounces 'Hampstead Psy Op,'" Hoaxtead Research, May 27, 2018, https://hoaxteadresearch.wordpress.com/2018/05/27/charlotte-ward-denounces-hampstead-psy-op/.

24 **authored by Jacqui Farmer:** Jacqui Farmer, *Illuminati Party!—Reasons Not to Be Scared of the Illuminati* (self-pub. 2014), accessed November 19, 2021, https://books.google.ca/books/about/Illuminati_Party_Reasons_Not_to_Be_Scare.html?id=aUtfCAAAQBAJ&redir_esc=y.

CHAPTER 2. THE MYSTIC AND PARANOID TRIFECTA

28 **The world is terrible, but the terror has a purpose:** Michael Barkun, *Culture of Conspiracy: Apocalyptic Visions in Contemporary America* (Oakland: University of California Press, 2003), 3–4.

28 **"a powerful method to eradicate the virus and suffering from the world":** "Love in the Time of the Virus: Online Retreat & Course with Geshe Michael Roach August 1–September 5, 2020," Asian Classics Institute, https://www.asianclassicsinstitute.org/insights-online-love-in-the-time-of-the-virus.

28 **quasi-Buddhist self-help books:** "Geshe Michael Roach: Penguin Random House," PenguinRandomhouse.com, https://www.penguinrandomhouse.com/authors/25686/geshe-michael-roach/.

28 **recruitment forays into yogaworld:** "Geshe Michael Roach's Advice to Yoga Teachers, Part Two: Get Them to Practice," YouTube, November 12, 2014, https://www.youtube.com/watch?v=nGkf0e0ykhg.

28 **a corporate coaching business:** Brian Mendoza, "DCI Global: We Take You Deeper," Diamond Cutter Institute, January 11, 2019, https://diamondcutterinstitute.com/.

31 **gold fringe on US flags in the White House:** Reuters staff, "Fact Check: No Evidence to Support QAnon Claims of Mass Arrests, Military Takeover, Illegitimacy of Biden's Presidency or Trump's Return to Power," https://www.reuters.com/article/uk-factcheck-qanon-military-theories-idUSKBN29R1ZA.

31 **his verbal tics:** Travis M. Andrews, "He's a Former QAnon Believer. He Doesn't Want to Tell His Story, but Thinks It Might Help," https://www.washingtonpost.com/technology/2020/10/24/qanon-believer-conspiracy-theory/.

31 **"QAnon Map":** Dylan Louis Munroe, "QAnon Map," accessed November 25, 2021, https://www.vaultofculture.com/vault/nst/2020/07/27/qanon.

31 **"Great Awakening Map":** Champ Parinya, "Great Awakening Map," accessed November 25, 2021, https://static1.squarespace.com/static/53c4798be4b07557fac30898/t/601bb948d076a03f48c35d36/1612429673341/GreatAwakeningMap_11x14_V10_Lotus_Hi-Res_Web.jpg.

CHAPTER 3. SECRET PRETEND KNOWLEDGE, FOR SURVIVAL AND COMMUNITY

33 **"because they have a storm brewing inside them":** Ana T. Forrest, *Fierce Medicine: Discovering the Healing Power of Your Body's Wisdom* (New York: HarperOne, 2011), 2.

34 **Forrest is not an overt "pretendian":** Melissa Ridgen, "Pretendians and What to Do with People Who Falsely Say They're Indigenous," January 28, 2021, https://www.aptnnews.ca/infocus/pretendians-and-what-to-do-with-people-who-falsely-say-theyre-indigenous-put-infocus/.

34 **clients for his rings and medallions:** Heyoka Merrifield, "Heyoka Merrifield," accessed November 25, 2021, https://www.heyokamerrifield.com/.

34 **"Mending the Hoop of the People":** Ana T. Forrest, *Fierce Medicine: Discovering the Healing Power of Your Body's Wisdom* (New York: HarperOne, 2011), 2.

34 **former Forrest students have asked her to clarify whether she secured consent from the Zia:** "Our Statement on Diversity and Inclusion," Forrest Yoga New York, accessed November 23, 2022, https://www.forrestyoganewyork.com/new-page-1.

35 **"to conceal its complicity with often brutal domination":** Renato Rosaldo, "Imperialist Nostalgia," *Representations* 26 (1989): 107–122, https://doi.org/10.2307/2928525, 108. PDF available here: https://www.sas.upenn.edu/~cavitch/pdf-library/Rosaldo_Imperialist.pdf.

35 **Appropriation can be used against the marginalized people it lionizes:** Joseph Pierce, "The Capitol Rioter Dressed Up as a Native American Is Part of a Long Cultural History of 'Playing Indian.' We Ignore It at Our Peril," Artnet News, January 18, 2021, https://news.artnet.com/opinion/native-capitol-rioter-1937684.

36 **"an active practitioner of yoga, and eats only organic food":** Ashley Cole, "St. Louis Lawyer Representing Capitol Rioter Seen in Viral Photos Says Trump Should Pardon Him," Ksdk.com, January 15, 2021, https://www.ksdk.com/article/news/local/al-watkins-representing-jake-angeli-capitol-riot/63-e0b65042-b133-464a-a3a3-d32a0a0cd0af.

CHAPTER 4. DISASTER SPIRITUALITY

37 **"to keep them alive and available until the politically impossible becomes politically inevitable":** Milton Friedman, *Capitalism and Freedom* (Chicago: University of Chicago Press, 2002), xiv.

38 **"the tendency to use spiritual ideas and practices as a way to sidestep or avoid facing unresolved emotional issues":** Tina Fossella, "Human Nature, Buddha Nature: An Interview with John Welwood," *Tricycle*, May 2011, https://tricycle.org/magazine/human-nature-buddha-nature/.

39 **a golden opportunity to accelerate the march toward privatizing everything:** Naomi Klein, *The Shock Doctrine* (New York: Henry Holt, 2010), 5–7.

39 **For example, Klein noted that New Orleans's public school system ran 123 schools at the time Katrina hit:** Naomi Klein, *The Shock Doctrine* (New York: Henry Holt, 2010), 6.

40 **a "wonder drug with miraculous effectiveness" against COVID:** Beatrice Dupuy, "No Evidence Ivermectin Is a Miracle Drug against Covid-19," *AP News*, December 11, 2020, https://apnews.com/article/fact-checking-afs:Content:9768999400.

40 **the efficacy of ivermectin was being suppressed by Big Pharma:** Jonathan Jarry, "Science vs. Joe Rogan," Office for Science and Society, November 20, 2021, https://www.mcgill.ca/oss/article/covid-19-health-and-nutrition-pseudoscience/science-vs-joe-rogan.

40 **pseudomedical combinations of dodgy drugs:** Christina Szalinski, "Fringe Doctors' Groups Promote Ivermectin for Covid Despite a Lack of Evidence," *Scientific American*, September 29, 2021, https://www.scientificamerican.com/article/fringe-doctors-groups-promote-ivermectin-for-covid-despite-a-lack-of-evidence/.

40 **a supposed COVID-preventative to his extensive email list:** Matthew Remski, "Mikki Willis to Sell Pills Against Next P(l)andemic," Medium, September 15, 2021, https://matthewremski.medium.com/mikki-willis-to-sell-pills-against-next-p-l-andemic-d8b66cceebd8.

40 **pet collar for your cat or dog to create a force field against the supposed dangers of 5G radiation:** Shubham Agarwal, "Inside the Strange and Scammy World of Anti-5G Accessories," *Digital Trends*, September 19, 2021, https://www.digitaltrends.com/mobile/anti-5g-devices-scams-online/.

41 **a twenty-four-thousand-word essay exploring the spiritual implications of QAnon:** Bernhard Guenther, "Qanon—The Great Awakening: PsyOp or the Real Deal?," Piercing the Veil of Reality, June 20, 2020, https://veilofreality.com/2020/06/20/qanon-the-great-awakening-psyop-or-the-real-deal/.

42 **"the potential for awakening has never been greater":** Bernhard Guenther, "Time of Transition: Embodied Soul Awakening," Piercing the Veil of Reality, October 28, 2021, https://veilofreality.com/time-of-transition-embodied-soul-awakening/.

CHAPTER 5. CONSPIRITUALITY VS. QANON

44 *Illuminati Party!—Reasons Not to Be Scared of the Illuminati:* Jacqui Farmer, *Illuminati Party!—Reasons Not to Be Scared of the Illuminati* (self-pub. 2014), accessed November 25, 2021, p. 32.

44 **4chan incubates nasty humor, online mobbing, competitive transgressions, and a whole lot of shitposting:** Mike Wendling, "QAnon: What Is It and Where Did It Come From?," *BBC News*, January 6, 2021, https://www.bbc.com/news/53498434.

45 **Donald Trump's use of the term the "Calm Before the Storm":** Mark Landler, "What Did President Trump Mean by 'Calm Before the Storm'?," *New York Times*, October 6, 2017, https://www.nytimes.com/2017/10/06/us/politics/trump-calls-meeting-with-military-leaders-the-calm-before-the-storm.html.

45 **A number were able to monetize their offerings on YouTube or hawk merchandise on Amazon:** Mike Rothschild, "You Can Now Buy QAnon Swag to Take Down the Deep State," *Daily Dot*, July 23, 2020, https://www.dailydot.com/debug/q-anon-merchandise/.

45 **save the children sex-trafficked by the evil Cabal:** "QAnon," ADL, September 24, 2020, https://www.adl.org/resources/backgrounder/qanon.

45 **to usher in humanity's ascent into a new fifth-dimensional enlightened reality:** Nicole Karlis, "Why Some New Age Influencers Believe Trump Is a 'Lightworker,'" *Salon*, March 6, 2021, https://www.salon.com/2021/03/04/why-some-new-age-in fluencers-believe-trump-is-a-lightworker/.

45 **Jews kidnapped and murdered Christian children to then use their blood for Passover rituals, such as baking matzo:** "QAnon's Antisemitism and What Comes Next," ADL, September 24, 2020, https://www.adl.org/resources/reports /qanons-antisemitism-and-what-comes-next.

45 **inspiring a string of strange, violent crimes:** Lois Beckett, "QAnon: A Timeline of Violence Linked to the Conspiracy Theory," *Guardian*, October 16, 2020, https:// www.theguardian.com/us-news/2020/oct/15/qanon-violence-crimes-timeline.

47 **celebrated the birth of his son by trolling trans people:** JP Sears, "Because There's No Biological Difference between Men and Women, I Decided to Start Breastfeeding Wilder," Facebook, December 25, 2020, https://www.facebook.com /961065217242674/photos/pb.100044526485662.-2207520000../4204951486187348 /?type=3.

47 **how easy it would be for real men with military training to kill wokes, who have nothing but pronouns to hide behind:** Archived on authors' website: https:// www.conspirituality.net /book-resources.

47 **boosted by failed QAnon congressional candidate Deanna Lorraine:** Maggie Baska and Lily Wakefield, "Right-wingers Are Spreading Rumours That Michelle Obama Is Transgender—Again," PinkNews, May 18, 2020, https://www.pinknews .co.uk/2020/05/18/michelle-obama-transgender-man-video-trans-woman/.

47 **then by Alex Jones:** Chloe Farand, "Michelle Obama Is Secretly a Man, Claims Trump's Favourite Conspiracy Theorist," *Independent*, August 24, 2020, https:// www.independent.co.uk/news/world/americas/alex-jones-michelle-obama-man -proof-infowars-conspiracy-theorist-sandy-hook-a7911996.html.

47 **Being "red-pilled" later became a phrase used by MAGA influencers like Candace Owens:** Nick Fouriezos, "This Conservative Convert Dishes out 'Red Pills' Online," OZY, April 5, 2018, https://www.ozy.com/news-and-politics/this-conser vative-convert-dishes-out-red-pills-online/85410/.

47 **a metaphor for their own journey into transgender identity:** James Crowley, "'The Matrix' Creator Explains What the Red Pill Really Is and Men's Rights Activists Aren't Going to Be Happy," *Newsweek*, August 7, 2020, https://www.news week.com/matrix-creator-red-pill-trans-allegory-mens-rights-activists-1523669.

47 **Ji also reposted a meme with the hashtag #pizzagateisreal:** Matthew Remski, "Inside Kelly Brogan's Covid-Denying, VAX-Resistant Conspiracy Machine," Medium, September 17, 2020, https://gen.medium.com/inside-kelly-brogans-covid -denying-vax-resistant-conspiracy-machine-28342e6369b1.

47 **a preposterous fiction that led to a potentially dangerous vigilante shooting:** Matthew Haag and Maya Salam, "Gunman in 'Pizzagate' Shooting Is Sentenced to 4 Years in Prison," *New York Times*, June 23, 2017, https://www.nytimes.com/2017 /06/22/us/pizzagate-attack-sentence.html.

48 **unwilling to even acknowledge their prior boosting of QAnon content:** Matthew Remski, "When QAnon Came to Canada," *Walrus*, December 3, 2020, accessed November 27, 2021, https://thewalrus.ca/when-qanon-came-to-canada/.

48 **Devotees suffering these gifts were definitely undergoing a vibrational shift:**
Harris Terri, "5D Ascension Symptoms: 31 Clear Signs You Are Ascending," Spirit
Nomad, December 15, 2021, https://thespiritnomad.com/blog/5d-ascension/.

49 **an herb from Thailand, which has not been shown to have any significant benefit for the conditions stated on her website:** Posted by Dr. Christiane Northrup,
"Vaginosis," Christiane Northrup, MD, March 27, 2015, https://www.drnorthrup
.com/vaginosis/; Amatalife, "Menopause Relief," Amatalife, accessed September
27, 2022, https://amatalife.com/pages/menopause-relief. "Pueraria Mirifica Health
Benefits, Dosage, Safety, Side-Effects, and More: Supplements," *Examine*, January
21, 2022, https://examine.com/supplements/pueraria-mirifica.

49 **"recruitment and radicalisation pipelines into female dominated ecosystems":**
Marc-André Argentino, "Pastel QAnon," *GNET*, March 17, 2021, https://gnet-re
search.org/2021/03/17/pastel-qanon/.

50 **"Avoid GMOs where you can":** Jacqui Farmer, *Illuminati Party!—Reasons Not to
Be Scared of the Illuminati* (self-pub. 2014), 32.

50 **"grow cannabis, refuse vaccination":** Jacqui Farmer, *Illuminati Party!—Reasons
Not to Be Scared of the Illuminati* (self-pub. 2014), 138.

CHAPTER 6. CONSPIRITUALISTS ARE NOT WRONG

52 **the billionaire class padded their net worth by $1 trillion:** Michael Sainato, "Bil-
lionaires Add $1tn to Net worth During Pandemic as Their Workers Struggle,"
Guardian, January 15, 2021, https://www.theguardian.com/world/2021/jan/15/bil
lionaires-net-worth-coronavirus-pandemic-jeff-bezos-elon-musk.

54 **the scar left by the smallpox vaccine was "the mark of the beast":** Eula Biss, *On
Immunity: An Inoculation* (London: Fitzcarraldo Editions, 2016), 18.

54 **"We are entitled to as much survival as we can purchase":** *Conspirituality* podcast, "101: Eugenic Pandemic (w/Beatrice Adler-Bolton)," *Conspirituality*, October
27, 2022, https://www.conspirituality.net/episodes/101-eugenic-pandemic-wbeatrice
-adler-bolton.

54 **Organization of Economic Co-operation and Development:** "U.S. Health Care
from a Global Perspective, 2019: Higher Spending, Worse Outcomes?," Common-
wealth Fund, January 30, 2020, https://www.commonwealthfund.org/publications
/issue-briefs/2020/jan/us-health-care-global-perspective-2019.

55 **doctors interrupt their patients within eleven seconds:** Naykky Singh Ospina,
Kari A. Phillips, Rene Rodriguez-Gutierrez, Ana Castaneda-Guarderas, Michael
R. Gionfriddo, Megan E. Branda, and Victor M. Montori, "Eliciting the Patient's
Agenda—Secondary Analysis of Recorded Clinical Encounters," *Journal of Gen-
eral Internal Medicine* 34, no. 1 (2018): 36–40, https://doi.org/10.1007/s11606-018
-4540-5.

57 **through the power of the #savethechildren hashtag:** Kevin Roose, "How 'Save the
Children' Is Keeping QAnon Alive," *New York Times*, September 28, 2020, https://
www.nytimes.com/2020/09/28/technology/save-the-children-qanon.html.

57 **a statement distancing themselves from QAnon:** "Save the Children Statement
on Use of Its Name in Unaffiliated Campaigns," Save the Children, August 7, 2020,
https://www.savethechildren.org/us/about-us/media-and-news/2020-press-re
leases/save-the-children-statement-on-use-of-its-name-in-unaffiliated-c.

57 **A spokeswoman for Wayfair denied the absurd theory:** Geoff Herbert, "Wayfair Responds to Human Sex Trafficking Conspiracy Theory over Cabinets with

Human Names," Syracuse, July 13, 2020, https://www.syracuse.com/business /2020/07/wayfair-responds-to-sex-trafficking-conspiracy-theory-over-cabinets -with-human-names.html.

57 **at least 300,000 are sex trafficked:** Kaitlyn Tiffany, "The Great (Fake) Child-Sex -Trafficking Epidemic," *Atlantic*, February 14, 2022, https://www.theatlantic.com /magazine/archive/2022/01/children-sex-trafficking-conspiracy-epidemic/620845/.

58 **combating real-world sex trafficking:** *Conspirituality* podcast, "12: So You Want to Stop Child Abuse (w/Regan Williams & Dr Theo Wildcroft)," *Conspirituality*, October 21, 2022, https://www.conspirituality.net/episodes/12-so-you-want-to-stop -child-abuse-regan-williams-amp-dr-theo-wildcroft.

58 **QAnon talking points in his many media appearances:** Kevin Roose, "QAnon Followers Are Hijacking the #Savethechildren Movement," *New York Times*, August 12, 2020, https://www.nytimes.com/2020/08/12/technology/qanon-save-the -children-trafficking.html.

58 **led by a young LA influencer:** Brandy Zadrozny and Ben Collins, "QAnon Looms behind Nationwide Rallies and Viral #SavetheChildren Hashtags," NBCNews .com, August 22, 2020, https://www.nbcnews.com/tech/tech-news/qanon-looms -behind-nationwide-rallies-viral-hashtags-n1237722.

58 **who presents as Native American on Facebook:** Scotty Rojas, Scotty the Kid Music—Facebook, March 29, 2017, accessed November 29, 2021, https://www.face book.com/photo/?fbid=10158304802245618&set=a.10150201328625618.430039 .472070320617.

58 **red face paint in the shape of a hand, which covered his mouth:** Donie Sullivan, "QAnon Has Hijacked the Name of Save the Children, a Real Children's Charity— CNN Video," *CNN*, October 19, 2020, time cue: 2:22, https://www.cnn.com/videos /tech/2020/10/19/save-the-children-qanon-conspiracy-gr-orig.cnn. Image: https:// www.conspirituality.net/book-resources.

58 **as she ran the 2019 Boston Marathon:** Alaa Abdeldaiem, "Jordan Daniel on Native American Awareness, Activism," *Sports Illustrated*, April 29, 2019, https:// www.si.com/edge/2019/04/29/jordan-daniel-native-american-rights-awareness -running-boston-marathon-2019.

58 **"According to Statistics Canada," writes Commissioner Michèle Audette of the National Inquiry into Missing and Murdered Indigenous Women and Girls:** "Final Report," MMIWG, May 29, 2019, https://www.mmiwg-ffada.ca/fi nal-report/.

58 **the US Department of Justice's federal missing persons database, NamUs, only logged 116 cases:** "Missing and Murdered Indigenous Women & Girls," Urban Indian Health Institute, November 27, 2019, https://www.uihi.org/wp-content /uploads/2018/11/Missing-and-Murdered-Indigenous-Women-and-Girls-Report .pdf/.

59 **"Make New Zealand Great Again":** Tina Ngata, "The Rise of Māori MAGA— E-Tangata," *E-Tangata*, September 8, 2020, https://e-tangata.co.nz/comment-and -analysis/the-rise-of-maori-maga/.

59 **supporting the Standing Rock pipeline protests of 2016:** Ali Katz, "'This Is the First Time Our History Will Reflect the Truth' Mikki Willis about the Importance of On…" Medium, December 2, 2016, https://medium.com/reports-from-stand ing-rock/this-is-the-first-time-our-history-will-reflect-the-truth-mikki-willis -about-the-importance-of-on-5df3d7e6d9d7.

59 **aggrieved citizens seeking to be heard:** Matthew Remski, *"Plandemic's* Mikki Willis Joins, Praises Violent Capitol Mob," *Conspirituality,* January 11, 2021, https:// conspirituality.net/transmissions/plandemics-mikki-willis-joins-praises-violent -capitol-mob/.

59 **to stoke anti-state fears:** Canadian Tire Fire, "Canadian Anti-Semites and Far-Right Conspiracy Theorists Try New Tactic: Aligning with Indigenous Communities," It's Going Down, November 24, 2021, https://itsgoingdown.org/cana dian-anti-semites-and-far-right-conspiracy-theorists-try-new-tactic-aligning -with-indigenous-communities/.

59 **Morgan Yew, a video journalist who covered anti-lockdown protests in Toronto:** *Conspirituality* podcast, "79: Anti-Hate Work in Canada (w/Dan Collen, Elizabeth Simons, & Morgan Yew)," *Conspirituality,* October 26, 2022, https://www.conspir ituality.net/episodes/79-anti-hate-work-in-canada-dan-collen-elizabeth-simons -morgan-yew.

59 **in an attempt to forcibly vaccinate them:** Mack Lamoureux and Anya Zoledzio-wski, "An Anti-Vax Conspiracy Theory Went Viral. An Indigenous Community Paid the Price," *VICE,* October 20, 2021, https://www.vice.com/en/article/akvwep /conspiracy-black-lake-pat-king.

59 **a condemnation of King's misinformation:** Michael Bramadat-Willcock, "No 'Dire Situation' as False 'Forced' Vaccine Claims Target Black Lake," *Prince Albert Daily Herald,* October 20, 2021, https://paherald.sk.ca/2021/10/18/no-dire-situa tion-as-false-forced-vaccine-claims-target-black-lake/.

60 **what philosophy and religion scholar Alan Levinovitz calls "empowerment epistemology":** *Conspirituality* podcast, "114: Guns, Germs & Fear (w/Alan Levi-novitz)," *Conspirituality,* October 27, 2022, https://www.conspirituality.net/epi sodes/114-guns-germs-amp-fear-alan-levinovitz.

CHAPTER 7. DID NAZIS LOVE YOGA?

65 **conspired to make us ill so that it can sell us medicine:** Marianne Williamson, "We don't have a healthcare system, we have a sickness care system. Why are Americans so sick to begin with—with higher rates of chronic disease than in other wealthy countries? We have to treat the cause, not just symptom. It starts with the food we eat," Twitter, May 13, 2020, https://twitter.com/marwilliamson /status/1260615484057235460.

67 **herbs from Thailand that she blends into vaginal moisturizers:** Amatalife, "Vag-inal Moisturizer," accessed December 1, 2021, https://amatalife.com/pages/vagi nal-moisturizer.

67 **No Nut November:** EJ Dickson, "How a New Meme Exposes the Far-Right Roots of #NoNutNovember," *Rolling Stone,* November 8, 2019, https://www.rollingstone .com/culture/culture-features/coomer-meme-no-nut-november-nofap-908676/.

67 **a golden age of fascist junk science:** Derek Beres, "What's with the Far-Right's Interest in Ball Tanning?" *Rolling Stone,* April 20, 2022, https://www.rolling stone.com/culture/culture-news/ball-testicle-tanning-far-right-tucker-carlson -1339809/.

CHAPTER 8. A MAN NAMED EUGENICS

69 ***Strength and How to Obtain It,* 1897:** Eugen Sandow, *Strength and How to Obtain It with Anatomical Charts, Illustrating the Exercises for the Physical Development*

(London: Gale & Polden, 1897), 7, accessed November 30, 2021, https://www.guten
berg.org/files/65987/65987-h/65987-h.htm.

69 **"fully agreed with the warning I gave the boy":** Eugen Sandow, *Strength and How to Obtain It with Anatomical Charts, Illustrating the Exercises for the Physical Development* (London: Gale & Polden, 1897), 121, accessed December 1, 2021, https://www.gutenberg.org/files/65987/65987-h/65987-h.htm.

70 **the reproductive dominance of white women:** Laura L. Lovett, *Conceiving the Future: Pronatalism, Reproduction, and the Family in the United States, 1890–1938* (Chapel Hill: University of North Carolina Press, 2009), 77–78.

70 **performing weightlifting feats:** Caroline Daley, "The Strongman of Eugenics, Eugen Sandow," *Australian Historical Studies* 33, no. 120 (2002): 233–48, doi: 10.1080/10314610208596217, p. 234.

70 **Sir Arthur Conan Doyle gushed over his perfect physique:** Vike Martina Plock, "A Feat of Strength in 'Ithaca': Eugen Sandow and Physical Culture in Joyce's Ulysses," *Journal of Modern Literature* 30, no. 1 (2007): 129–39, doi:10.1353/jml.2006.0064, p. 130.

70 **got rid of his birth name and adopted "Eugen":** Vike Martina Plock, "A Feat of Strength in 'Ithaca': Eugen Sandow and Physical Culture in Joyce's Ulysses," *Journal of Modern Literature* 30, no. 1 (2007): 129–39, doi:10.1353/jml.2006.0064.

70 **"Eugen"—for eugenics:** Vike Martina Plock, "A Feat of Strength in 'Ithaca': Eugen Sandow and Physical Culture in Joyce's Ulysses," *Journal of Modern Literature* 30, no. 1 (2007): 129–39, doi:10.1353/jml.2006.0064.

70 **"life was a mere race for money":** Caroline Daley, "The Strongman of Eugenics, Eugen Sandow," *Australian Historical Studies* 33, no. 120 (2002): 240, https://doi.org/10.1080/10314610208596217.

71 **an almost-forgotten exercise, the sun salutation:** Elliott Goldberg, *The Path of Modern Yoga: The History of an Embodied Spiritual Practice* (Rochester, VT: Inner Traditions, 2016), 180–84.

71 **slang for any fit man:** Elliott Goldberg, *The Path of Modern Yoga: The History of an Embodied Spiritual Practice* (Rochester, VT: Inner Traditions, 2016), 271.

71 **more of an influence on the development of modern Indian yoga than any Indian figure:** Joseph S Alter, *Yoga in Modern India: The Body between Science and Philosophy* (Princeton and Oxford: Princeton University Press, 2004), 28; Mark Singleton, *Yoga Body: The Origins of Modern Posture Practice* (Oxford: Oxford University Press, 2010), 89.

71 **his nine-year-old daughter asked him if he had brought her any "n***** boys" to play with:** Michael Anton Budd, *The Sculpture Machine: Physical Culture and Body Politics in the Age of Empire* (Basingstoke, UK: Macmillan, 1998), 90–92.

72 **not being granted a monopoly over marketing homespun clothes nationwide:** Kaushik Deka, "From BFFs to Frenemies, Ramdev's Fickle Relationship with Narendra Modi," *Quartz*, May 2, 2017, https://qz.com/india/972480/from-bffs-to-frenemies-patanjali-founder-yoga-guru-ramdevs-fickle-relationship-with-narendra-modi/.

73 **he's teaching that yoga can cure homosexuality:** Andrea Jain and Michael Schulson, "The World's Most Influential Yoga Teacher Is a Homophobic Right-Wing Activist," *Religion Dispatches*, June 7, 2018, https://religiondispatches.org/baba-ramdev/.

73 **Hindu nationalism is also big on pseudoscience and pseudohistory:** Meera Nanda, *Prophets Facing Backwards: Postmodern Critiques of Science and New Social Movements in India* (New Brunswick, NJ: Rutgers University Press, 2000).

73 **riots that slaughtered over a thousand Muslims in 2002:** "Timeline of the Riots in Modi's Gujarat," *New York Times*, April 6, 2014, https://www.nytimes.com/interactive/2014/04/06/world/asia/modi-gujarat-riots-timeline.html#/#time287_8535.

73 **"[yoga] can help us deal with climate change":** Narendra Modi, "Text of the PM's Statement at the United Nations General Assembly," September 27, 2014, https://www.narendramodi.in/text-of-the-pms-statement-at-the-united-nations-general-assembly-6660.

73 **that would tie yoga to India, as Champagne is tied to France:** Annie Gowen, "India's New Prime Minister, Narendra Modi, Aims to Rebrand and Promote Yoga in India," *Washington Post*, December 2, 2014, https://www.washingtonpost.com/world/asia_pacific/indias-new-prime-minister-narendra-modi-wants-to-rebrand-and-promote-yoga-in-india/2014/12/02/7c5291de-7006-11e4-a2c2-478179fd0489_story.html.

73 **"used yoga to treat their patients":** Al Jazeera, "Free Covid Jabs for All Indian Adults as Modi Hails Yoga 'Shield'." *Al Jazeera*, June 21, 2021, https://www.aljazeera.com/news/2021/6/21/free-covid-vaccine-india-adults-modi-yoga-day.

73 **case numbers surged toward seven million in November 2020:** Hannah Ritchie, Edouard Mathieu, Lucas Rodés-Guirao, Cameron Appel, Charlie Giattino, Esteban Ortiz-Ospina, Joe Hasell, Bobbie Macdonald, Diana Beltekian, and Max Roser, "Coronavirus Pandemic (COVID-19)—the Data—Statistics and Research," Our World in Data, March 5, 2020, accessed December 6, 2021, https://ourworldindata.org/coronavirus-data?country=~IND.

73 **a grainy 1938 video of B. K. S. Iyengar:** Unnati Sharma, "1938 Clip of BKS Iyengar Is Being Shared as 'rare' Video of PM Modi Doing Yoga," ThePrint, November 25, 2020, https://theprint.in/hoaxposed/1938-clip-of-bks-iyengar-is-being-shared-as-rare-video-of-pm-modi-doing-yoga/551548/.

74 **Modi himself performing "high level yoga practice":** Adv Shruti Desai, "A rare amazing video of Narendra Modiji.... You too will be surprised, High Level Yoga Practice @PMOIndia #Yog," Twitter, November 24, 2020, https://twitter.com/AdvShrutidesai/status/1331080037823516674?s=20.

74 **a 99 percent infection rate among the returning pilgrims:** Matthew Remski, "Modi's Covid Constellations," Medium, May 12, 2021, https://matthewremski.medium.com/modis-covid-constellations-a914f519427b.

74 **as oxygen canisters sold out:** Ian Christopher Rocha, Mary Grace Pelayo, and Sudhan Rackimuthu, "Kumbh Mela Religious Gathering as a Massive Superspreading Event: Potential Culprit for the Exponential Surge of COVID-19 Cases in India," *The American Journal of Tropical Medicine and Hygiene* 105, no. 4 (2021): 868–71, https://doi.org/10.4269/ajtmh.21-0601.

75 **"the discovery of lasting happiness":** "The Jivamukti Method," Jivamukti Yoga, July 29, 2021, https://jivamuktiyoga.com/the-jivamukti-method/.

75 **in the broader world of Tibetan Buddhism:** Nina Burleigh, "Sex and Death on the Road to Nirvana," *Rolling Stone*, June 25, 2018, https://www.rollingstone.com/culture/culture-news/sex-and-death-on-the-road-to-nirvana-86995/.

76 **"then only will you see the light":** B. K. S. Iyengar and Noëlle Perez-Christiaens, *Sparks of Divinity: The Teachings of B. K. S. Iyengar from 1959 to 1975* (Berkeley, CA: Rodmell Press, 2012), loc. 1979 of 5970, Kindle.

76 **"What is pain if it enables you to see God?":** B. K. S. Iyengar and Noëlle Perez-Christiaens, *Sparks of Divinity: The Teachings of B. K. S. Iyengar from 1959 to 1975* (Berkeley, CA: Rodmell Press, 2012), loc. 1545 of 5970, Kindle.

76 **"Pain is your guru":** B. K. S. Iyengar and Noëlle Perez-Christiaens, *Sparks of Divinity: The Teachings of B. K. S. Iyengar from 1959 to 1975* (Berkeley, CA: Rodmell Press, 2012), loc. 2061 of 5970, Kindle.

77 **and conceived of the SS as a yogic monastic order:** Palash Ghosh, "Heinrich7 Himmler: The Nazi Hindu," *International Business Times*, November 9, 2012, https://www.ibtimes.com/heinrich-himmler-nazi-hindu-214444; Jules Evans, "Nazi Hippies: When the New Age and Far Right Overlap," Medium, November 29, 2020, https://gen.medium.com/nazi-hippies-when-the-new-age-and-far-right-overlap -d1a6ddcd7.

77 **it became a national bestseller:** Natasha Noman, "The Strange History of How Hitler's 'Mein Kampf' Became a Bestseller in India," *Mic*, June 11, 2015, https://www.mic.com/articles/120411/how-hitler-s-mein-kampf-became-a-bestseller-in-india.

77 **Iyengar's first international demonstration and teaching tour in Switzerland, France, and England:** Iyengar Yoga UK—Practice Yoga in the UK, "TIMELINE," Iyengar Yoga UK, May 26, 2021, https://iyengaryoga.org.uk/timeline/.

77 **he played a concert at the newly liberated Bergen-Belsen concentration camp and was thereafter haunted:** Tom Huizenga, "Yehudi Menuhin's Potent Blend of Music, Humanism and Politics," *NPR*, April 22, 2016, https://www.npr.org/sections/deceptivecadence/2016/04/22/474824320/yehudi-menuhins-potent-blend-of -music-humanism-and-politics.

77 **when asked if he was or ever had been a member of the Rashtriya Swayamsevak Sangh:** Elizabeth Kadetsky, *First There Is a Mountain: A Yoga Romance* (Boston: Little, Brown and Company, 2004).

78 **Jois sexually and physically assaulted his students on a near-daily basis:** Matthew Remski, *Practice and All Is Coming: Abuse, Cult Dynamics, and Healing in Yoga and Beyond* (Rangiora, NZ: Embodied Wisdom Publishing, 2019).

78 **Mark Singleton, a British religious studies scholar, popularized his PhD thesis on the real history of modern yoga:** Mark Singleton, *Yoga Body: The Origins of Modern Posture Practice* (Oxford: University Press, 2010).

79 **Victor Van Kooten told Matthew in an interview in 2004:** Archived on authors' website: https://www.conspirituality.net/book-resources.

CHAPTER 9. EVOLVING THE SOULS OF CHILDREN

80 **thousand-plus Waldorf schools in more than sixty countries worldwide:** "Waldorf World List," Freunde Waldorf, accessed September 27, 2022, https://www.freunde-waldorf.de/en/waldorf-worldwide/waldorf-education/waldorf-world-list/.

80 **all events, thoughts, and desires that have ever existed:** "Theosophy," *Encyclopædia Britannica*, https://www.britannica.com/topic/theosophy.

81 **When we interviewed her for the podcast:** *Conspirituality* podcast, "Conspirituality: 59: Is Rudolf Steiner Dead Yet? (w/Jennifer Sapio)," July 8, 2021, Conspirituality, https://www.conspirituality.net/episodes/59-is-rudolf-steiner-dead-yet-jennifer-sapio.

81 **parents pay up to $20,000 per year in tuition:** "Tuitions & Fees," Austin Waldorf School, September 3, 2021, https://austinwaldorf.org/admissions/tuitions-fees/.

82 **"tendency to delete racist and antisemitic passages from translated editions of Steiner's publications":** Peter Staudenmaier, "Anthroposophy and Ecofascism," Institute for Social Ecology, September 17, 2010, https://social-ecology.org/wp/2009/01/anthroposophy-and-ecofascism-2/.

82 **the 1999 English translation of the book it appeared in:** Rudolf Steiner, *The Fall of the Spirits of Darkness: Fourteen Lectures Given in Dornach 29 September–28 October 1917* (Bristol, UK: Rudolf Steiner Press, 1993), 199–200, 33.

83 **they purged impurities that manifested as disabilities and diseases:** Peter Staudenmaier, "Anthroposophy and Ecofascism," Institute for Social Ecology, September 17, 2010, accessed December 2, 2021, https://social-ecology.org/wp/2009/01/anthroposophy-and-ecofascism-2/.

83 **the more spiritually mature Aryans:** Julie Chajes, "Blavatsky and Monotheism: Towards the Historicisation of a Critical Category," *Journal of Religion in Europe* 9, nos. 2–3 (2016): 24–75, doi:10.1163/18748929-00902008.

83 **"atavistic powers are present that do not allow the spirit to achieve complete harmony with the flesh":** Peter Staudenmaier, "Race and Redemption: Racial and Ethnic Evolution in Rudolf Steiner's Anthroposophy," *Nova Religio* 11, no. 3 (2008): 4–36, doi:10.1525/nr.2008.11.3.4.

83 **sharing her experience since then to warn others:** Jennifer Sapio, PhD, "Waldorf Schools Are Inherently Racist Cults," Medium, June 29, 2020, https://medium.com/age-of-awareness/waldorf-schools-are-inherently-racist-cults-91193d1fbef6.

84 **His 1911 pseudohistory of *The Submerged Continents of Atlantis and Lemuria, Their History and Civilization*:** Rudolf Steiner, *The Submerged Continents of Atlantis and Lemuria, Their History and Civilization: Being Chapters from the Âkâshic Records* (London: Theosophical Publishing Society, 1911).

84 **legitimate journalism that would push back against the Third Reich:** Timothy Snyder, "How Hitler Pioneered 'Fake News,'" *New York Times*, October 16, 2019, https://www.nytimes.com/2019/10/16/opinion/hitler-speech-1919.html.

84 **"the Nazis' rejection of a rational, factual world":** Benjamin Carter Hett, *The Death of Democracy: Hitler's Rise to Power and the Downfall of the Weimar Republic* (London: Windmill Books, 2019), 13.

84 **granted him a sense that he was clairvoyant:** Rudolf Steiner and Marie Steiner, *Correspondence and Documents 1901–1925* (London: Rudolf Steiner Press, 1988), 9.

85 **"But you have to then figure out the details":** Katie Nicholson, Jason Ho, and Jeff Yates, "Viral Video Claiming 5G Caused Pandemic Easily Debunked," *CBC News*, March 23, 2020, https://www.cbc.ca/news/science/fact-check-viral-video-coronavirus-1.5506595.

85 **"They are not the cause of anything":** Archived on authors' website: https://www.conspirituality.net/book-resources.

85 **he prescribed an unapproved quack cancer treatment to a patient he'd never met:** Barbara Feder Ostrov, "Conspiracy Theory Doctor Surrenders Medical License," *CalMatters*, February 6, 2021, https://calmatters.org/health/2021/02/conspiracy-theory-doctor-surrenders-medical-license/.

86 **"in the eyes of materialists":** Rudolf Steiner, *The Fall of the Spirits of Darkness: Fourteen Lectures Given in Dornach 29 September–28 October 1917* (Bristol, UK: Rudolf Steiner Press, 1993), 199–200.

86 **with 46.25 percent of parents refusing to vaccinate their children:** Steve Levine, "Austin Schools Top Vaccine Exemption List," Texmed, August 30, 2019, https://www.texmed.org/Template.aspx?id=51403.

CHAPTER 10. CLEANSING AND THE SACRED FIRE

87 **"improve your immune system to fight flus, colds, bacteria and viruses":** Bethany Lindsay, "Licence Pulled from Delta Yoga Studio after False COVID-19 Claims," *CBC News*, March 20, 2020, https://www.cbc.ca/news/canada/british-columbia/licence-pulled-from-delta-yoga-studio-after-false-covid-19-claims-1.5504014.

87 **He'd been posting videos, coughing and rambling about an illness:** "Covid-19 Denier and Conspiracy Theorist Mak Parhar Dead at 48," *CBC News*, November 6, 2021, https://www.cbc.ca/news/canada/british-columbia/mak-parhar-dead-at-48-1.6238751.

87 **Currently fleeing US prosecution related to allegations of sexual assault:** Richard Godwin, "'He Said He Could Do What He Wanted': The Scandal That Rocked Bikram Yoga," *Guardian*, February 18, 2017, https://www.theguardian.com/lifeandstyle/2017/feb/18/bikram-hot-yoga-scandal-choudhury-what-he-wanted.

87 **the temperatures in his native Calcutta:** Colin Hall, "Hot and Bothered: The Hype, History, and Science of Hot Yoga," *Yoga International*, February 4, 2016, https://yogainternational.com/article/view/hot-and-bothered-the-hype-history-and-science-of-hot-yoga/.

88 **participants were clocking internal temperatures of up to 104°F:** Emily Quandt, John Porcari, Jeff Stephen, Manny Felix, Carl Foster, and Daniel Green, "Pro-Source™: May 2015—ACE Study Examines Effects of Bikram Yoga on Core Body Temps," ACE, May 2015, https://www.acefitness.org/education-and-resources/professional/prosource/may-2015/5355/ace-study-examines-effects-of-bikram-yoga-on-core-body-temps/.

88 **"it is not necessary to spend a single cent on a doctor in your whole life":** Jerome Armstrong, *Calcutta Yoga: How Modern Yoga Travelled to the World from the Streets of Calcutta* (New Delhi: Macmillan, 2020), 508.

88 **help the elderly have multiple orgasms:** Loraine Despres, "Yoga's Bad Boy: Bikram Choudhury," *Yoga Journal*, September 2, 2021, https://www.yogajournal.com/yoga-101/yoga-s-bad-boy-bikram-choudhury/.

88 **after paying tuition and fees of over $10,000:** Clancy Martin, "The Overheated, Oversexed Cult of Bikram Choudhury," *GQ*, February 1, 2011, https://www.gq.com/story/yoga-guru-bikram-choudhury.

88 **"mental stress and strain is the cause of all the diseases—even the infectious ones":** Bikram Choudhury, "Bikram Dialogue © 1997 Oct 2 2018 7 31 PM: Archive-mistress: Free Download, Borrow, and Streaming," Internet Archive, October 3, 2018, https://archive.org/details/BikramDialogueC1997Oct22018731PM_201810.

88 **Bishnu Ghosh, who counted none other than Eugen Sandow as a primary influence:** "Lock the Knee—The Influence of Weightlifting on Yoga," Ghosh Yoga, May 25, 2017, https://www.ghoshyoga.org/blogs/lock-the-knee-the-influence-of-weightlifting-on-yoga.

88 **personally familiar with the virus he thought was a hoax** Mak Parhar, "Truther Ostriches," Facebook Watch, November 4, 2021, https://www.facebook.com/mak.parhar/videos/420894549611626.

88 **while denying he had "Convid":** "COVID-19 Denier and Conspiracy Theorist Mak Parhar Dead at 48," *CBC News*, November 6, 2021, accessed December 5, 2021, https://www.cbc.ca/news/canada/british-columbia/mak-parhar-dead-at-48-1 .6238751.

88 **died of ethanol, fentanyl, and cocaine poisoning:** "COVID-19 Denier Mak Parhar Died from Drugs, Not the Coronavirus, B.C. Coroner Confirms," *CBC News*, February 6, 2023, accessed March 12,2023, https://www.cbc.ca/news/canada /british-columbia/mak-parhar-coroners-report-1.6739167.

88 **"NASA is nothing but liars...do the research":** Mak Parhar, "Time to Wake Up...... Earth Is FLAT," Facebook, January 26, 2017, https://www.facebook.com /mak.parhar/posts/10154807884447481.

89 **to claim he wasn't subject to Canadian law:** Bethany Lindsay, "B.C. COVID-19 Conspiracy Theorist Charged with Breaking Quarantine Law," *CBC News*, November 7, 2020, https://www.cbc.ca/news/canada/british-columbia/bc-covid-con spiracy-theorist-charged-1.5790376.

89 **found no statute under which they could issue tickets:** Bethany Lindsay, "Delta Police Have 'No Powers' to Stop Meetings of COVID-19 Conspiracy Theorists, Chief Says," *CBC News*, April 12, 2020, https://www.cbc.ca/news/canada/british -columbia/delta-police-have-no-powers-to-stop-meetings-of-covid-19-conspiracy -theorists-chief-says-1.5525849.

89 **claiming that the heat could help one's immune system fight off COVID-19:** "FDA Warning Letter," Thomas N. Dahdouh to Enlighten Sauna, 1395 Martsen Rd. Unit A, Burlingame, CA 94010, December 21, 2020, https://www.ftc.gov/system /files/warning-letters/covid-19-letter-enlighten-sauna.pdf.

89 **the worst of his symptoms were caused by eating a teaspoon of sugar:** Matthew Remski, "'Master Coach' Preston Smiles, Gets COVID, Takes Ivermectin, Finds Jesus," Medium, August 27, 2021, https://matthewremski.medium.com/master -coach-preston-smiles-gets-covid-takes-ivermectin-finds-jesus-8be57f690e21.

90 **the xenophobic mythos of neo-Hinduism:** Kaveree Bamzai, "David Frawley Is the American Hippy Who Became RSS's Favourite Western Intellectual," *ThePrint*, November 17, 2018, https://theprint.in/opinion/david-frawley-is-the-american-hippy -who-became-rsss-favourite-western-intellectual/150759/.

90 **"taking our life-force beyond the boundaries of the skin":** David Frawley, *Yoga and the Sacred Fire: Self Realization and Planetary Transformation* (Delhi: Motilal Banarsidass, 2006), 164.

91 **"to drown themselves in the sea or live in a dark room for the rest of their lives":** Mohammad Ali, "Those Who Want to Avoid Yoga Can Leave India: Yogi Adityanath," *The Hindu*, April 2, 2016, https://www.thehindu.com/news/national /other-states/yogi-adityanath-says-those-who-avoid-yoga-can-leave-india/arti cle7297946.ece.

91 **believed to clear the liver and gallbladder of gallstones:** A. R. Gaby, "Nutritional Approaches to Prevention and Treatment of Gallstones," *Alternative Medicine Review: A Journal of Clinical Therapeutic*, September 14, 2009, https://pubmed.ncbi .nlm.nih.gov/19803550/.

94 **His primary obsession is with the power of celery juice:** Anthony William, "Medical Medium Celery Juice," Penguin Random House Canada, https://www .penguinrandomhouse.ca/books/609906/medical-medium-celery-juice-by -anthony-william/9781401957650.

94 **with a COVID-style microscopic viral graphic on the cover:** Jonathan Jarry, "Cracked Science 25: Is the Medical Medium Practicing Medicine?," Office for Science and Society, January 18, 2019, https://www.mcgill.ca/oss/article/videos -quackery/medical-medium-practicing-medicine-cs25.

94 **spiritual rationalization for disordered eating:** Chelsea Roff, "The Truth About Yoga and Eating Disorders," *Yoga Journal*, September 8, 2014, https://www.yoga journal.com/lifestyle/health/truth-yoga-eating-disorders/.

94 **forcing people to stay in overheated, white-cultist-run "sweat lodges" until they die:** Matt Stroud, "The Death Dealer," *The Verge*, December 4, 2013, https://www .theverge.com/2013/12/4/5038930/the-death-dealer-james-arthur-sweat-lodge -deaths-in-sedona.

CHAPTER 11. ANXIETY OF THE PUREBLOODS

95 **Eula Biss, *On Immunity: An Inoculation*, 2015:** Eula Biss, *On Immunity: An Inoculation* (Minneapolis: Graywolf, 2015), 76.

95 **considered scams by actual qualified medical experts and nutritionists:** Dara Mohammadi, "You Can't Detox Your Body. It's a Myth. So How Do You Get Healthy?," *Guardian*, December 5, 2014, https://www.theguardian.com/lifeand style/2014/dec/05/detox-myth-health-diet-science-ignorance.

96 **to sell unvaccinated sperm in online bazaars:** Samantha Cole, "Antivaxers Think Their 'Pure' Semen Will Skyrocket in Value," *VICE*, August 13, 2021, https://www .vice.com/en/article/epn8j4/antivax-semen-fertility-covid-vaccine-safe.

96 **dating apps that promise to connect people for sweet unvaccinated love:** "Pure Friendships, Pure Hearts, Pure Love," Pure, accessed November 28, 2022, https:// web.archive.org/web/20221102015332/https://www.purematch.com.au/pre-regis tration/.

96 **an obsession with genitals and the anxious desire to protect the right kind of semen:** Khaleda Rahman, "'This Is So Gay': Tucker Carlson's 'End of Men' Doc Mocked as Homoerotic," *Newsweek*, April 17, 2022, https://www.newsweek.com /tucker-carlson-end-men-doc-mocked-homoerotic-1698482.

97 **Modi is a lifelong RSS soapbox preacher:** Christophe Jaffrelot, "How Narendra Modi Transformed from an RSS Pracharak to a Full-Fledged Politician and Hindu Hridaysamrat," *The Wire*, August 24, 2021, https://thewire.in/politics/narendra -modi-rss-pracharak-politician.

97 **The group advocates celibacy for its senior leaders:** Ashok K. Singh, "What RSS Can Learn About Sex from Hindu Gods," *dailyO*, March 15, 2016, https://www .dailyo.in/politics/celibacy-rss-sevika-samiti-hinduism-khaki-shorts-hinduism -fascism-reich-9548.

97 **tasked with protecting the purity and vitality of the nation:** James Tapper, "Indians Prefer Politicians Who Refuse to Have Sex or Get Married," *The World*, April 21, 2014, https://theworld.org/stories/2014-04-21/indians-prefer-politicians-who -refuse-have-sex-or-get-married.

97 **"we will take one hundred Muslim girls":** Gulam Jeelani, "From Love Jihad, Conversion to SRK: 10 Controversial Comments by UP's New CM Yogi Adityanath," *Hindustan Times*, April 6, 2017, https://www.hindustantimes.com /assembly-elections/from-love-jihad-conversion-to-srk-10-controversial-com ments-by-up-s-new-cm-yogi-adityanath/story-5JW2ZFGZzAdIZeIcjcZCNM .html.

97 *"like an infection they continue to spread and poison the country"*: David Frawley, *Arise Arjuna: Hinduism Resurgent in a New Century* (New Delhi: Voice of India, 1994). 13.

97 **"Yoga and Ayurveda is very helpful with the long term issues," he writes:** David Frawley, "Vaccination is necessary to deal with the immediate and acute problem of the virus. Strengthening physical and psychological immunity through Yoga and Ayurveda is very helpful with the long term issues. Govt. of India is promoting both approaches," Twitter, May 19, 2021, https://twitter.com/davidfrawleyved/status/1395012490023641089.

97 **the great wisdom of the ages carries the antidote to the root causes of all disease:** David Frawley, "Along with vaccines, which are mainly for acute conditions, we can still benefit from right lifestyle factors of diet, herbs, exercise, massage, and meditation as per Yoga and Ayurveda. These have preventative value for many diseases, particularly of a chronic nature," Twitter, December 14, 2020, https://twitter.com/davidfrawleyved/status/1338555589417447424.

98 **"so too with immunity, which is a common trust as much as it is a private account":** Eula Biss, *On Immunity: An Inoculation* (Minneapolis: Graywolf, 2015), 19–20.

98 **she explained she was making a Harry Potter joke:** Sabine Joseph, "Anti-vaxxers Are Now Identifying Themselves as 'Pure Bloods,' " *Daily Dot*, September 21, 2021, https://www.dailydot.com/debug/anti-vaxxers-pure-bloods/.

98 **right-wing influencer Lyndsey Marie:** Tess Owen, "Unvaccinated TikTokers Are Calling Themselves 'Purebloods,' " *VICE*, September 15, 2021, https://www.vice.com/en/article/7kvywd/unvaccinated-tiktok-purebloods-covid.

98 **who goes by @patriot_lydnz:** TikTok, accessed November 24, 2021, https://www.tiktok.com/@patriot_lyndz.

99 **aspiring wizards with no Muggle (non-magic normie) blood:** "Pure-blood," Harry Potter Wiki, https://harrypotter.fandom.com/wiki/Pure-blood.

99 **"There are quite consciously overtones of Nazi Germany," she told** *Dateline***:** Meredith Veira, "Harry Potter: The Final Chapter," TODAYshow.com, July 30, 2007, https://web.archive.org/web/20071014014450/http://today.msnbc.msn.com/id/20001720/page/4/.

99 **Angeline rhymes:** Matthew Remski, "Anti-Vax Reverse Contagion Anxiety," Medium, April 24, 2021, https://matthewremski.medium.com/anti-vax-reverse-contagion-anxiety-81724ea216e0.

100 **withhold sex from partners who were considering getting the vaccine:** Matthew Remski, "Christiane Northrup Encourages Anti-Vaxxers to Shun Pro-Vax Partners," Medium, April 19, 2021, https://matthewremski.medium.com/christiane-northrup-encourages-anti-vaxxers-to-shun-pro-vax-partners-1ee1021a870.

100 **Lin Wood, who took to the stage to call for the execution of all political enemies:** Michael Foust, " 'Q Is the Truth': Lin Wood Promotes QAnon at Bible College to Cheering Crowds," Christian Headlines, April 19, 2021, https://www.christianheadlines.com/contributors/michael-foust/q-is-the-truth-lin-wood-promotes-qanon-at-bible-college-to-cheering-crowds.html; Patriot Takes, " 'Every lie will be revealed. They are killing our children, send them to jail. Put them in front of the firing squad. They are committing acts against humanity. The penalty for an act against humanity is death. Take them out.' -Lin Wood," Twitter, April 18, 2021, https:// twitter.com /patriottakes /status /1383709884114341892.

100 **Mike Pence could "face execution by firing squad" for "treason":** Adam Rawnsley, "Trump Team Backs Away from Lin Wood After Pence Tweets," *Daily Beast*,

January 2, 2021, https://www.thedailybeast.com/trump-team-runs-away-from-lin-wood-after-pence-tweets.

100 **"Pledge your lives, your fortunes & your sacred honor":** Ryan Mac, "Trump-Supporting Lawyer Lin Wood Has Been Permanently Banned from Twitter," *BuzzFeed News*, January 7, 2021, https://www.buzzfeednews.com/article/ryanmac/twitter-bans-lin-wood.

100 **make women infertile, and poison the sperm of men:** Christiane Northrup, "Don't Let the Lemmings Trample You on the Way to the Cliff [2021-04-17]—Dr. Christiane Northrup," BitChute, April 29, 2021, https://www.bitchute.com/video/IGHDFADrA1Wi/.

100 **"This is an evil agenda by bloodline families that's been going on for two thousand years":** "An Evil Agenda by Bloodline Families—Dr. Christiane Northrup," Video Banned, August 19, 2021, https://videobanned.nl/aiovg_videos/an-evil-agenda-by-bloodline-families-dr-christiane-northrup/.

100 **"if you're drinking the blood of little children, watch out":** PatriotTakes, "Lin Wood warning people who are killing, sacrificing, and drinking the blood of little children," Twitter, April 19, 2021, https://twitter.com/patriottakes/status/1384242708529631236.

101 **to harvest their blood to bake into Passover matzo:** "Blood Libel: A False, Incendiary Claim Against Jews," Anti-Defamation League, https://www.adl.org/education/resources/glossary-terms/blood-libel.

101 **a substance that Anons believe the Elites extract from kidnapped children to ingest as a youth elixir:** Brian Friedberg, "The Dark Virality of a Hollywood Blood-Harvesting Conspiracy," Wired, July 31, 2020, https://www.wired.com/story/opinion-the-dark-virality-of-a-hollywood-blood-harvesting-conspiracy/.

101 **panda eyes are striking on the mostly white faces:** Kristina Gildejeva, "Conspiracy Theorists Without Borders: How QAnon Mutated in Europe," *Logically*, September 24, 2020, https://www.logically.ai/articles/conspiracy-theorists-without-borders-how-qanon-mutated-in-europe.

101 **"where a single needle penetrates both":** Eula Biss, *On Immunity: An Inoculation* (Minneapolis: Graywolf, 2015), 133.

102 **until it was resurrected in 1896 and became a root text of modern antisemitism:** Tal Lavin, "QAnon, Blood Libel, and the Satanic Panic," *New Republic*, September 29, 2020, https://newrepublic.com/article/159529/qanon-blood-libel-satanic-panic.

CHAPTER 12. THE BARBARA SNOW JOB

104 **following the publication of *Michelle Remembers*:** Michelle Smith and Lawrence Pazder, *Michelle Remembers* (London: Sphere, 1981).

104 **in what became a viral movement to identify and prosecute allegedly rampant Satanism:** Megan Goodwin, "They Couldn't Get My Soul," *Studies in Religion/Sciences Religieuses* 47, no. 2 (2018): 280–98, https://doi.org/10.1177/0008429817748138.

104 **no forensic or corroborated evidence that it was a reality:** Daniel Goleman, "Proof Lacking for Ritual Abuse by Satanists," *New York Times*, October 31, 1994, https://www.nytimes.com/1994/10/31/us/proof-lacking-for-ritual-abuse-by-satanists.html?sq=satanic%2Britual%2Babuse&scp=1&st=nyt.

105 **pressure children into producing fictitious memories:** Emily Pasiuk, "Satanic Panic: How a Tiny Town Was Swept up in a Wave of Accusations," *CBC News*, March 15, 2020, https://newsinteractives.cbc.ca/longform/satanic-panic.

105 **"the terrible acts that were perpetrated upon them":** Jacqui Farmer, *Illuminati Party!—Reasons Not to Be Scared of the Illuminati* (self-pub. 2014), 52.

106 **"an upgraded blueprint of humanity" that will save the world, according to the New Age clearinghouse Gaia.com:** Andye Murphy, "13 Indigo Children Traits & Signs of a New Age Revolutionary," Gaia, September 17, 2020, https://www.gaia .com/article/13-signs-you-are-an-indigo-child.

106 **Teal Swan, born in 1984:** "About Teal Swan," Teal Swan, https://tealswan.com /about-teal/.

106 **"In time we will know how much of it can be validated":** Michelle Smith and Lawrence Pazder, *Michelle Remembers* (London: Sphere, 1981), ix.

107 **failed to validate a single detail of Smith's account:** Paul Grescoe, "Things That Go Bump in Victoria," *Maclean's*, October 27, 1980, https://archive.macleans.ca /article/1980/10/27/things-that-go-bump-in-victoria; Debbie Nathan and Michael R. Snedeker, *Satan's Silence: Ritual Abuse and the Making of a Modern American Witch Hunt* (New York: Authors Choice Press, 2001), 45–50.

107 **Pazder worked there as a doctor in the early 1960s:** Nicholas P. Spanos, *Multiple Identities & False Memories: A Sociocognitive Perspective* (Washington, DC: American Psychological Association, 2001), 269.

107 **On May 16, 1985, Pazder was a featured talking head:** "'20/20' The Devil Worshippers—May 16, 1985," YouTube, March 5, 2015, https://www.youtube.com /watch?v=_UQuwxBgpAg.

107 **led to "ritual abuse" being codified and institutionalized in their diagnostic manual:** Megan Goodwin, "They Couldn't Get My Soul," *Studies in Religion /Sciences Religieuses* 47, no. 2 (2018): 280–98, https://doi.org/10.1177/000842981774 8138.

107 **"Why Are Victims Alleging Things That Seem Not To Be True?":** "Investigator's Guide to Allegations of 'Ritual' Child Abuse," Office of Justice Programs (National Center for the Analysis of Violent Crime), January 1992, https://www.ojp.gov/pdf files1/Digitization/136592NCJRS.pdf.

107 **gave Pazder's and others' claims about SRA great cultural impact:** "Research Update | Winter 1989–1990," Office of Justice Programs, https://www.ojp.gov/pdf files1/Digitization/124094NCJRS.pdf.

107 **discussed the topic with more critical skepticism:** "Investigator's Guide to Allegations of 'Ritual' Child Abuse," Office of Justice Programs (National Center for the Analysis of Violent Crime), https://www.ojp.gov/pdffiles1/Digitization/136592NC JRS.pdf.

108 **the less spectacular but very real problem—abuse committed by family members:** Paul M. Renfro, "QAnon Misdirects Our Attention Away from the Real Threats to Children," *Washington Post*, August 27, 2020, https://www.washington post.com/outlook/2020/08/27/qanon-misdirects-our-attention-away-real-threats -children/.

108 **"even—as some parents came to believe—members of the Anaheim Angels baseball team":** Debbie Nathan and Michael R. Snedeker, *Satan's Silence: Ritual Abuse and the Making of a Modern American Witch Hunt* (New York: Authors Choice Press, 2001), 89.

108 **what to do if a child recanted their disclosure:** Debbie Nathan and Michael R. Snedeker, *Satan's Silence: Ritual Abuse and the Making of a Modern American Witch Hunt* (New York: Authors Choice Press, 2001), 128–30.

108 **having treated over one hundred cases each:** Jeffrey S. Victor, *Satanic Panic: The Creation of a Contemporary Legend* (Chicago: Open Court, 1994), 257–58.

108 **a minor bible among Satanic Panic therapists:** Barbara Snow and Teena Sorensen, "Ritualistic Child Abuse in a Neighborhood Setting," *Journal of Interpersonal Violence* 5, no. 4 (1990): 474–87, https://doi.org/10.1177/088626090005004004.

109 **Snow admitted that she never took notes:** "Arden Brett Bullock, Petitioner-Appellant, v. Scott Carver, Warden, Utah State Prison, Respondent-Appellee. No. 00-4023. Decided: July 23, 2002," Findlaw (United States Court of Appeals, Tenth Circuit), https://caselaw.findlaw.com/us-10th-circuit/1260586.html.

109 **" 'I didn't believe any of those kids when they told me it didn't happen' ":** Kamala London et al., "Disclosure of Child Sexual Abuse: What Does the Research Tell Us About the Ways That Children Tell?," *Psychology, Public Policy, and Law* 11, no. 1 (2005): 194–226, https://doi.org/10.1037/1076-8971.11.1.194.

109 **He described Snow pressuring children into disclosing abuse that they originally denied:** Massimo Introvigne, "A Rumor of Devils: Allegations of Satanic Child Abuse and Mormonism, 1985–1994," Center for Studies on New Religions (Annual Conference of The Mormon History Association), https://www.cesnur.org/2001/archive/mi_mormons.htm.

109 **Snow would not let her leave until she made an accusation of ritual abuse:** "A Rumor of Devils: Allegations of Satanic Child Abuse and Mormonism, 1985–1994," Center for Studies on New Religions (Annual Conference of The Mormon History Association), 2022, https://www.cesnur.org/2001/archive/mi_mormons.htm.

109 **"Disclosure became a process, not an event":** Barbara Snow and Teena Sorensen, "Ritualistic Child Abuse in a Neighborhood Setting," *Journal of Interpersonal Violence* 5, no. 4 (1990): 485, https://doi.org/10.1177/088626090005004004.

109 **and battered family members she accused of enabling ritual abuse:** Lisa Rosetta, "Therapist Under Investigation," *Salt Lake Tribune*, January 20, 2007, https://archive.sltrib.com/story.php?ref=%2Fnews%2Fci_5051155.

110 **a well-researched podcast series with journalist Jennings Brown:** Jennings Brown, "Gizmodo Launches 'the Gateway,' an Investigative Podcast about a Controversial Internet Spiritual Guru," *Gizmodo*, May 30, 2018, https://gizmodo.com/weve-launched-an-investigative-podcast-about-a-controve-1826416613.

110 **a highly sensationalistic streaming docu series on Hulu:** *The Deep End*, TV miniseries 2022, IMDB, https://www.imdb.com/title/tt19387554/.

110 **and once spent twelve hours sewn into a corpse:** Be Scofield, "The Gucci Guru: Inside Teal Swan's Posh Cult," *Guru Magazine*, December 26, 2018, https://gurumag.com/the-gucci-guru-inside-teal-swans-posh-cult/.

110 **a $5,000 weeklong retreat at her casa in Costa Rica:** Teal Swan, https://tealswan.com/.

110 **will help people to manifest what they want in their lives:** "Frequencies by Teal Swan," Teal Swan Shop, https://shop.tealswan.com/.

110 **describing suicide as a reset button:** "Teal Swan's Preoccupation with Death & Suicide," Teal Swan Exposed, May 21, 2018, https://tealswanblog.wordpress.com/suicide/.

110 **one had succeeded, after exposure to Swan's views on the subject:** Lebo Diseko, "Teal Swan: The Woman Encouraging Her Followers to Visualise Death," *BBC News*, November 23, 2019, https://www.bbc.com/news/world-us-canada-50478821.

111 **she had been writing in a secret language:** "Teal Swan Allegations Documents," MuckRock, accessed March 30, 2022, https://www.muckrock.com/foi/north-logan -31630/teal-swan-allegations-documents-55988/#file-212621.

111 **over three hundred submissions in response to a callout:** Rachel Brathen, "#MeToo— the Yoga Stories (Part 1)," Yoga Girl, https://www.yogagirl.com/read/metoo/me-too -the-yoga-stories-part-1.

111 **yoga superstars like Bikram Choudhury:** Julia Lowrie Henderson, "Bikram," *30 for 30 Podcasts*, May 22, 2018, https://30for30podcasts.com/bikram/.

111 **Manouso Manos:** Miranda Leitsinger, "#MeToo Unmasks the Open Secret of Sexual Abuse in Yoga," *KQED*, September 7, 2018, https://www.kqed.org/news /11690316/metoo-unmasks-the-open-secret-of-sexual-abuse-in-yoga.

111 **Matthew's book on Pattabhi Jois's abusive practices:** Matthew Remski, *Practice and All Is Coming: Abuse, Cult Dynamics, and Healing in Yoga and Beyond* (Rangiora, NZ: Embodied Wisdom Publishing, 2019).

111 **a multinational organization that claims to have trained fifty thousand yoga teachers since the late 1960s:** Matthew Remski, "How a #MeToo Facebook Post Toppled a Yoga Icon," Medium, January 27, 2020, https://gen.medium.com/how -a-metoo-facebook-post-toppled-a-yoga-icon-c25577185e40.

113 **"appealing to people's interest in alternative health practices and mistrust of the government":** Seane Corn, "Wellness Community Statement," Facebook, September 12, 2020, https://www.facebook.com/permalink.php?story_fbid=34249124 20885720&id=131305493579779.

113 **sparking coverage in the *New York Times*:** Kevin Roose, "Yoga Teachers Take On QAnon," *New York Times*, September 15, 2020, https://www.nytimes.com/2020/09 /15/technology/yoga-teachers-take-on-qanon.html.

113 **and *Rolling Stone*:** EJ Dickson, "Wellness Influencers Are Calling Out QAnon Conspiracy Theorists for Spreading Lies," *Rolling Stone*, September 15, 2020, https://www.rollingstone.com/culture/culture-news/qanon-wellness-influencers -seane-corn-yoga-1059856/.

113 **"This isn't happening. Please use more discernment":** "This Yoga Instructor Is Fighting the Rise of QAnon in the Wellness Community," CBC/Radio Canada, September 17, 2020, https://www.cbc.ca/radio/asithappens/as-it-happens-thurs day-edition-1.5728151/this-yoga-instructor-is-fighting-the-rise-of-qanon-in-the -wellness-community-1.5728153.

CHAPTER 13. CURSED YOGA NETWORKS

115 **The year is 1936:** Elliott Goldberg, *The Path of Modern Yoga: The History of an Embodied Spiritual Practice* (Rochester, VT: Inner Traditions, 2016), 364–73.

115 **"He broke my back," Iyengar recalled:** Eric Shaw, "Introduction to: Seizing the Whip: B. K. S. Iyengar and the Making of Modern Yoga," Scribd, accessed November 23, 2022, https://www.scribd.com/document/329896486/Introduction-to-Seiz ing-the-Whip-B-K-S-Iyengar-and-the-Making-of-Modern-Yoga-by-Eric-Shaw.

116 **"I used to give the demonstrations," he told *Yoga Journal*:** Anne Cushman, "Iyengar Looks Back," *Yoga Journal*, November/December, 1997, https://annecush man.com/pdf-essays/AnneCushman-interviews-Iyengar-1997.pdf.

117 **in which he would purport to treat people with heart conditions, infertility, and cancer:** Lemiod, "Medical Class, BKS Iyengar in Australia '92," YouTube, May 7, 2015, https://www.youtube.com/watch?v=G2dPWoKaUYI.

117 **has sold three million copies worldwide:** Nirmala George, "Obituary: B. K. S. Iyengar, 95; Was Known Worldwide as Creator of Iyengar Yoga," *Washington Post*, August 23, 2014, https://www.washingtonpost.com/lifestyle/wellness/obituary-bks -iyengar-95-was-known-worldwide-as-creator-of-iyengar-yoga/2014/08/22/fe0f 4548-28b5-11e4-86ca-6f03cbd15c1a_story.html.

117 **with over six hundred images of Iyengar himself posing against a white back-drop, like a specimen:** B. K. S. Iyengar, *Light on Yoga* (New Delhi: HarperCollins Publishers, 2006).

118 **fueling what is now an over $88 billion hub for the wellness economy:** "Yoga Industry Growth, Market Trends & Analysis 2021/22," Wellness Creative Co., December 3, 2021, https://www.wellnesscreatives.com/yoga-industry-trends/.

119 **hyped through the release of preprint papers—studies not yet verified by other researchers:** Rachel Schraer and Jack Goodman, "Ivermectin: How False Science Created a Covid 'Miracle' Drug," *BBC News*, October 6, 2021, https://www.bbc .com/news/health-58170809.

119 **they wound up in the hands of people like Joe Rogan:** Kieran Press-Reynolds, "Spotify Airs Joe Rogan Podcast Touting Ivermectin as Part of His COVID-19 Treatment, despite the FDA Calling It 'Dangerous,'" *Business Insider*, September 8, 2021, https://www.businessinsider.com/joe-rogan-experience-ivermectin-spotify -covid19-treatment-19-2021-9.

120 **diagnoses like feeble-mindedness in the early days of clinical psychology:** Rudolf Pintner and Donald G. Paterson, "A Psychological Basis for the Diagnosis of Feeble-Mindedness," *Journal of the American Institute of Criminal Law and Criminology* 7, no. 1 (1916): 32, https://doi.org/10.2307/1133610.

121 **a landmark publication on the state of medical education in North America:** Thomas P. Duffy, "The Flexner Report—100 Years Later," *The Yale Journal of Biology and Medicine*, September 2011, https://www.ncbi.nlm.nih.gov/pmc/articles /PMC3178858/.

121 **Abraham Flexner was bigoted toward women and non-white doctors:** Gabrielle Redford, "AAMC Renames Prestigious Abraham Flexner Award in Light of Racist and Sexist Writings," AAMC, November 17, 2020, https://www.aamc.org/news-in sights/aamc-renames-prestigious-abraham-flexner-award-light-racist-and-sexist -writings.

121 **"alternative medicine"—a term that first appeared in a medical journal in 1975:** Pekka Louhiala, "Alternative, Complementary, Integrative—Conceptual Problems in Marketing Healthcare Ideologies and Services," *Focus on Alternative and Complementary Therapies* 17, no. 3, September 2012, https://www.researchgate.net /publication/264647120. DOI:10.1111/j.2042-7166.2012.01147.x.

122 **a new term appeared in the medical literature: "complementary medicine":** Pekka Louhiala, "Alternative, Complementary, Integrative—Conceptual Problems in Marketing…," *Focus on Alternative and Complementary Therapies* 17, no. 3, September 2012, https://www.researchgate.net/publication/264647120_Al ternative_complementary_integrative_-_Conceptual_problems_in_marketing _healthcare_ideologies_and_services. DOI: 10.1111/j.2042-7166.2012.01147.x.

122 **a US federal agency called the Office of Alternative Medicine was established:** "NIH Complementary and Integrative Health Agency Gets New Name," National Institutes of Health, December 17, 2014, https://www.nih.gov/news-events/news -releases/nih-complementary-integrative-health-agency-gets-new-name.

122 **the agency was renamed as the National Institute for Complementary and Alternative Medicine:** "NIH Complementary and Integrative Health Agency Gets New Name," National Institutes of Health, December 17, 2014, https://www.nih.gov/news-events/news-releases/nih-complementary-integrative-health-agency-gets-new-name.

122 **In 2014, it became the National Center for Complementary and Integrative Health:** "NIH Complementary and Integrative Health Agency Gets New Name," National Institutes of Health, December 17, 2014, https://www.nih.gov/news-events/news-releases/nih-complementary-integrative-health-agency-gets-new-name.

122 **a total of $2.5 billion to study irregular, alternative, complementary, or integrative treatments:** Susan Perry, "Is Taxpayer Money Well Spent or Wasted on Alternative-Medicine Research?," *MinnPost*, May 3, 2012, https://www.minnpost.com/second-opinion/2012/05/taxpayer-money-well-spent-or-wasted-alternative-medicine-research/; *Associated Press*, "$2.5 Billion Spent, No Alternative Cures Found," NBC News, June 10, 2009, https://www.nbcnews.com/id/wbna31190909.

123 **They pointed out that the agency spent $250,000:** Susan Perry, "Is Taxpayer Money Well Spent or Wasted on Alternative-Medicine Research?," *MinnPost*, May 3, 2012, https://www.minnpost.com/second-opinion/2012/05/taxpayer-money-well-spent-or-wasted-alternative-medicine-research/.

123 **Podcast guest Britt Hermes gave us a number of clues:** *Conspirituality* podcast, "7: Doctoring Covid: Christiane Northrup's Great Truther Awakening (w/Britt Hermes)," *Conspirituality*, July 9, 2020, https://www.conspirituality.net/episodes/7-doctoring-covid-christiane-northrups-great-truther-awakening-britt-hermes.

124 **the first truly integrative health sciences complex for training, research, and patient care:** Julianna LeMieux, "In Exchange for $200 Million, UC Irvine Legitimizes Pseudoscience," American Council on Science and Health, May 27, 2020, https://www.acsh.org/news/2017/09/22/exchange-200-million-uc-irvine-legitimizes-pseudoscience-11858.

124 **Sivananda Yoga claims to have graduated fifty thousand people:** "Teachers' Training," Sivananda International, https://sivananda.org/teachers-training/.

124 **a cultish leader who sexually abused many students—including his personal assistant—for decades:** Matthew Remski, "How a #MeToo Facebook Post Toppled a Yoga Icon," Medium, January 27, 2020, https://gen.medium.com/how-a-metoo-facebook-post-toppled-a-yoga-icon-c25577185e40.

124 **Hindu gods, riding through time in spaceships crafted in the Iron Age:** Lise McKean, *Divine Enterprise: Gurus and the Hindu Nationalist Movement* (Chicago: University of Chicago Press, 1996), 237–39.

124 **registering over 6,600 schools worldwide:** "Directory-Registrants | Registered Yoga Schools," Yoga Alliance, accessed November 23, 2022, https://www.yogaalliance.org/Directory-Registrants?type=School&designation=1.

126 **On the first page of the 156-page, ring-bound photocopied manual:** "Jivamukti Yoga: Jivamukti 300 Hour Teacher Training at Omega Institute" (Rhinebeck, NY, April 22—May 17, 2007, Jivamukti Inc.), 2007.

127 **levels of confidence on specific topics were inversely correlated with actual knowledge or education:** Kendra Cherry, "Dunning-Kruger Effect: Why Incompetent People Think They Are Superior," *Verywell Mind*, August 9, 2022, https://www.verywellmind.com/an-overview-of-the-dunning-kruger-effect-4160740.

129 **less than 1 percent of participants make any profit at all:** Jon M. Taylor, "Chapter 7: MLM's Abysmal Numbers," Federal Trade Commission, https://www.ftc.gov/sites/default/files/documents/public_comments/trade-regulation-rule-disclosure-requirements-and-prohibitions-concerning-business-opportunities-ftc.r511993-00008%C2%A0/00008-57281.pdf.

129 **prosperity gospel megachurches where sales data paves the road to a holy land:** Nea Logan, "How MLM Schemes like LuLaRoe Target Women and Moms," *Evie*, September 23, 2021, https://www.eviemagazine.com/post/how-mlm-schemes-like-lularoe-target-women-and-moms.

130 **In one investigation we did for the podcast, we found that Elena Brower:** *Conspirituality* podcast, "74: Elena Brower Could Stop Selling doTerra," *Conspirituality*, October 26, 2021, https://www.conspirituality.net/episodes/74-elena-brower-could-stop-selling-doterra.

CHAPTER 14. THAT'S US IN A HEADSTAND, LOSING OUR COGNITION

135 **ecumenical Hinduism, sweetened by yoga, could put an end to "sectarianism, bigotry, and its horrible descendant, fanaticism":** Swami Vivekananda, "Swami Vivekananda and His 1893 Speech," The Art Institute of Chicago, https://www.artic.edu/swami-vivekananda-and-his-1893-speech.

135 **the alleged sex abuser Swami Satchidananda:** Eliza Griswold, "Yoga Reconsiders the Role of the Guru in the Age of #MeToo," *New Yorker*, July 23, 2019, https://www.newyorker.com/news/news-desk/yoga-reconsiders-the-role-of-the-guru-in-the-age-of-metoo.

135 **when he took the stage in white robes to open the Woodstock Festival in 1969:** Sri Swami Satchidananda, "Swami Satchidananda's Woodstock Address," Sri Swami Satchidananda, March 17, 2019, https://swamisatchidananda.org/life/woodstock-guru/swami-satchidanandas-woodstock-address/.

136 **they destroyed a centuries-old mosque in Ayodhya, Uttar Pradesh, with iron pipes, clubs, and their bare hands:** Edward A. Gargan, "Hindu Militants Destroy Mosque, Setting Off a New Crisis in India," *New York Times*, December 7, 1992, https://www.nytimes.com/1992/12/07/world/hindu-militants-destroy-mosque-setting-off-a-new-crisis-in-india.html.

136 **the postmodern rise of the nationalist BJP and its sun-saluting paramilitary, the RSS:** Vidya Subrahmaniam, "Babri Masjid's Destruction Laid the Foundation of Modi's New India of Today," *The Wire*, December 6, 2018, https://thewire.in/politics/babri-masjid-narendra-modi-bjp.

136 **"and instead reflected the self-developmental desires that dominated consumer culture":** Andrea R. Jain, *Selling Yoga: From Counterculture to Pop Culture* (Oxford: Oxford University Press, 2015), 46.

136 **Getting loose meant stretching, breathing, and relaxing from two paradigms:** Sam Binkley, *Getting Loose: Lifestyle Consumption in the 1970s* (Durham, NC: Duke University Press, 2007).

136 **"the lifestyle adviser whose prescriptions were always available in the latest journal, book, or magazine on the New Life":** Sam Binkley, *Getting Loose: Lifestyle Consumption in the 1970s* (Durham, NC: Duke University Press, 2007), 5.

136 **it was the only publication of its kind for more than a decade:** "Yoga Journal Number 1, May 1975," Google Books, accessed December 10, 2021, https://

books.google.ca/books?id=9-sDAAAAMBAJ&printsec=frontcover&rview=1&
source=gbs_ge_summary_r&cad=0#v=onepage&q&f=false.

137 **reaching 1 million readers by 2010:** "The Yoga Journal Story," *Yoga Journal*, January 24, 2010, https://web.archive.org/web/20100124085914/http://www.yogajournal.com/global/34.

137 **The print edition is currently published internationally in eleven languages:** "International Editions," *Yoga Journal*, accessed November 23, 2022, https://www.yogajournal.com/yoga-journal-international-editions/.

137 **Another discussed yoga and the endocrine system:** "Yoga Journal July–August 1975," Google Books, accessed December 10, 2021, https://books.google.ca/books?id=xesDAAAAMBAJ&printsec=frontcover&rview=1&source=gbs_ge_summary_r&cad=0#v=onepage&q&f=false.

137 **readers should be concerned about aluminum and plastics in food:** Yoga Journal November–December 1975, Google Books, accessed December 10, 2021, https://books.google.ca/books?id=x-sDAAAAMBAJ&printsec=frontcover&rview=1&source=gbs_ge_summary_r&cad=0#v=onepage&q&f=false.

137 **"serious minded persons who felt deeply committed to a vaguely perceived goal":** John Amodeo, "The Developing Political Awareness in the Growth Movement," *Yoga Journal* (July–August 1977): 14–18.

138 **Joanna Macy, beloved for her therapeutic reflections on global crises:** Stephan Bodian, "Despair and Personal Power in the Nuclear Age: A Conversation with Joanna Macy," *Yoga Journal* (January and February 1985): 22.

139 **The open, receptive—and very naive—vibe was perfectly captured in 2008:** Simha, "YogaVOTES | Voting from the Mat," transform, October 15, 2012, https://transform.transformativechange.org/2012/10/yogavotes-voting-from-the-mat/.

139 **For the 2012 cycle, they expanded their wellness services:** Arianna Huffington, "The Social and Political Implications of Downward-Facing Dog," *HuffPost*, November 3, 2012, https://www.huffpost.com/entry/huffpost-oasis_b_1852703.

139 **a yoga teachers' unionization drive gathering speed in Manhattan:** Sacha Pfeiffer, "Yoga Instructors Are Unionizing," *NPR*, October 12, 2019, https://www.npr.org/2019/10/12/769783749/yoga-instructors-are-unionizing.

CHAPTER 15. ALIENS KILLED THE LOVE AND LIGHT VIBE

141 **the sexual abuse committed by Swami Rama, the guru-founder of the Himalayan Institute of Honesdale, Pennsylvania:** Katharine Webster, "The Case against Swami Rama of the Himalayas," accessed September 27, 2022, http://prem-rawat-bio.org/nrms/info/rama1.htm.

142 **he was alleged to have violated the California Yoga Teachers Code of Ethics by having sex with two of his students:** Charlie Goodyear and Rona Marech, "Yoga Guru in Compromising Position / Celebrity Instructor Rodney Yee Faces Allegations of Misconduct with Students," *San Francisco Chronicle*, January 30, 2012, https://www.sfgate.com/bayarea/article/Yoga-guru-in-compromising-position-Celebrity-2836809.php.

142 **demanding he reinstate the no-misconduct policy and install an ethics board:** Archived on authors' website: https://www.conspirituality.net/book-resources.

142 **"It is not our place or business to rule on moral and ethical issues":** Archived on authors' website: https://www.conspirituality.net/book-resources.

143 **the largest conspiracy theory and fake-documentary platform in the world, Gaia:** Gaia, Inc., "Gaia Acquires Yoga International, a Leading Digital Yoga Service," GlobeNewswire News Room, December 22, 2021, https://www.globe newswire.com/news-release/2021/12/22/2357066/0/en/Gaia-Acquires-Yoga-Inter national-a-Leading-Digital-Yoga-Service.html.

143 **selling the mail order side of the business for $167 million:** "Gaiam Sells Consumer Products to Sequential Brands for $167 Million," FDRA, July 8, 1970, https://fdra.org/latest-news/gaiam-sells-consumer-products-to-sequential-brands-for -167-million/.

144 **Shining brightest in their firmament are figures like Gregg Braden:** Gregg Braden, "The God Code—Message Encoded as the DNA of Life," Gregg Braden, accessed November 23, 2022, https://greggbraden.com/press/the-god-code-mes sage-encoded-as-the-dna-of-life-science-to-sage-2014/.

144 **Caroline Myss, who has said that AIDS was caused by "victim consciousness":** "Stress and AIDS: Potential Connections," *The Wellspring*, accessed November 23, 2022, https://www.thewellspring.com/flex/the-wellness-paradigm/2226/stress-and -aids-potential-connections.cfm.html.

144 **Bruce Lipton, who claims that the new science of epigenetics proves:** "Bruce Lipton on Epigenetics," Gaia, accessed November 23, 2022, https://www.gaia.com /video/bruce-lipton-epigenetics.

144 **Lynne McTaggart, a passionate anti-vaccine activist:** Maia, "The Vaccination Bible, Lynne McTaggart," Touchingly Naive Books, March 26, 2007, https://touching lynaivebooks.wordpress.com/2006/02/26/the-vaccination-bible-lynne-mctaggart/.

144 **McTaggart coordinated thousands of participants in a weeklong meditation intention experiment:** Lynne McTaggart, "The Results of the Peace Intention Experiment," Lynne McTaggart, January 9, 2009, https://lynnemctaggart.com/the-re sults-of-the-peace-intention-experiment/.

144 **Facebook actually used them as a case study:** Grace O'Connell-Joshua, "How Reporter Rob Price Got an Inside Look into Gaia and Its World of Conspiracy Theories and Alternative Media," *Business Insider*, February 17, 2021, https://www .businessinsider.com/rob-price-interview-gaia-conspiracy-theories-alternative -media-2021-2.

144 **"How to Respond to Sexual Abuse Within a Yoga or Spiritual Community":** Karen Rain and Jubilee Cooke, "How to Respond to Sexual Abuse Within a Yoga or Spiritual Community," *Yoga International*, April 10, 2019, https://yogainterna tional.com/article/view/how-to-respond-to-sexual-abuse-within-a-yoga-or-spiri tual-community.

145 **signaled that the magazine's editorial independence would remain intact:** Gaia, Inc., "Gaia Acquires Yoga International, a Leading Digital Yoga Service," *Bakersfield Californian*, December 22, 2021, https://web.archive.org/web/20211222235310 /https://www.bakersfield.com/ap/news/gaia-acquires-yoga-international-a-lead ing-digital-yoga-service/article_b4621f50-d9c0-5a30-b68d-97520bc77d49.html.

145 **interviewed thirty existing or former employees at Gaia:** Rob Price, "Gaia Was a Wildly Popular Yoga Brand. Now It's a Publicly Traded Netflix Rival Pushing Conspiracy Theories While Employees Fear the CEO Is Invading Their Dreams," *Business Insider*, February 14, 2021, https://www.businessinsider.com/inside-gaia -video-streaming-website-conspiracy-theories-2021-1.

146 **"a pile of old art, cartoons, ads, video games, movies, TV shows, comic books, and toys":** Dale Beran, *It Came from Something Awful: How a New Generation of Trolls Accidentally Memed Donald Trump into the White House* (New York: St. Martin's Press, 2019), 149–54.

147 **"they fashioned their own context out of absurd medieval power fantasies":** Dale Beran, *It Came from Something Awful: How a New Generation of Trolls Accidentally Memed Donald Trump into the White House* (St. Martin's Press, 2019), 171.

148 **Secrets & Cover-Ups—a category with twelve different subcategories, including The Cabal:** "Topics," Gaia, accessed November 23, 2022, https://www.gaia.com /topics.

CHAPTER 16. CHARISMA, BELIEF, BULLSHIT, AND LONGING

149 **magnified by a mirror house of social validation:** Paul Joosse, "Becoming a God: Max Weber and the Social Construction of Charisma," *Journal of Classical Sociology* 14, no. 3 (2014): 266–83, doi: 10.1177/1468795x14536652.

149 **the aura of prophets, saints, mythic warriors:** Max Weber, A. M. Henderson, and Talcott Parsons, *The Theory of Social and Economic Organization* (New York: Oxford University Press, 1947), 358–59.

150 **the fear of COVID as symbolized by masks and social distancing:** Fatherflot, "'Blutkitt' ('Blood Cement')—Ernest Becker on the Psycho-Dynamics of the Trump Cult," *Daily Kos*, February 17, 2020, https://www.dailykos.com/stories /2020/1/17/1912155/-Blutkitt-Blood-Cement-Ernest-Becker-on-the-Psycho-dy namics-of-the-Trump-Cult.

150 **Louis Farrakhan built an antisemitic UFO-cult of lackies dedicated to carrying out his authoritarian whims:** "Louis Farrakhan," Southern Poverty Law Center, accessed November 23, 2022, https://www.splcenter.org/fighting-hate/extremist -files/individual/louis-farrakhan.

150 **Janja Lalich lists charismatic authority as one of four pillars of a cult:** Janja Lalich and Madeleine Tobias, *Take Back Your Life: Recovering from Cults and Abusive Relationships* (Berkeley, CA: Bay Tree Publishing, 2006), 210.

152 **preferred pronouns was a slippery slope toward Marxist-inspired mass murder:** Jordan Peterson, "Jordan Peterson: The Right to Be Politically Incorrect," *National Post*, November 8, 2016, https://nationalpost.com/opinion/jordan-peterson-the-right -to-be-politically-incorrect.

153 **he took time to pitch these products in court, while on the stand:** Bevan Hurley, "Alex Jones Tried to Hawk Supplements as He Took the Stand in $150M Defamation Trial," *Independent*, August 3, 2022, https://www.independent.co.uk/news/world /americas/alex-jones-trial-sandy-hook-vitamins-b2136841.html.

153 **He hosted firebrand progressive Dr. Cornel West:** "Joe Rogan Experience #1325— Dr. Cornel West," JRE Podcast, July 24, 2019, https://www.jrepodcast.com/episode /joe-rogan-experience-1325-dr-cornel-west/.

153 **Rogan also hosted Gavin McInnes:** "Joe Rogan Experience #920—Gavin McInnes," JRE Podcast, February 23, 2017, https://www.jrepodcast.com/episode /joe-rogan-experience-920-gavin-mcinnes/.

154 **hosting epidemiologist Michael Osterholm:** "Joe Rogan Experience #1779— Michael Osterholm," JRE Podcast, February 18, 2022, https://www.jrepodcast.com /episode/joe-rogan-experience-1779-michael-osterholm/.

154 **holy trinity of discredited doctors and anti-vaccine COVID-profiteers:** Kristina Fiore, "Misinformation Docs See Their Political Stars Rise," *Medical News*, May 19, 2022, https://www.medpagetoday.com/special-reports/exclusives/98810.

154 **similar to what Germans went through during the rise of Nazism:** Alex Paterson, "Spotify's Joe Rogan Promotes Anti-Vaccine Rally with Serial Misinformer Robert Malone," *Media Matters for America*, January 6, 2022, https://www.mediamatters .org/joe-rogan-experience/spotifys-joe-rogan-promotes-anti-vaccine-rally-serial -misinformer-robert.

154 **Kory (who has the biggest networked ivermectin sales website in the world) and his fellow guest Bret Weinstein:** Kelsey Piper, "The Dubious Rise of Ivermectin as a Covid-19 Treatment, Explained," *Vox*, September 17, 2021, https://www.vox.com /future-perfect/22663127/ivermectin-covid-treatments-vaccines-evidence.

154 **Sports celebrities like UFC president Dana White:** Pavel Ibarra Merda, "UFC Boss Dana White Thanks 'Doctor' Joe Rogan for Beating Covid," *MARCA*, December 5, 2021, https://www.marca.com/en/ufc/2021/12/05/61ac587b268e3ea5718 b45d5.html.

154 **Rogan advised healthy people who were twenty-one and younger and who work out not to get vaccinated against COVID:** Ashley Carman, "Spotify Is Okay with Joe Rogan Telling 21-Year-Olds Not to Get Vaccinated," *The Verge*, April 27, 2021, https://www.theverge.com/2021/4/27/22406315/joe-rogan-vaccine-spotify-podcast -covid-19.

154 **he recovered using an expensive cocktail of treatments that included the ineffective drug ivermectin:** Vanessa Romo, "Joe Rogan Says He Has Covid-19 and Has Taken the Drug Ivermectin," *NPR*, September 2, 2021, https://www.npr.org/2021 /09/01/1033485152/joe-rogan-covid-ivermectin.

155 **"I moved to Texas because I want fucking freedom":** Deepak Kumar, "Joe Rogan Finally Reveals the Real Reason He Left California for Texas in $14.4 Million Decision," *EssentiallySports*, July 28, 2022, https://www.essentiallysports.com /ufc-mma-news-joe-rogan-finally-reveals-the-real-reason-he-left-california-for -texas-in-14-4-million-decision/.

155 **In 2022, *Forbes* estimated his net worth to be $190 million:** Steve Bennett, "Joe Rogan Net Worth 2022 (Forbes): Assets Loans Spotify," *CAKnowledge*, June 9, 2022, https://caknowledge.com/joe-rogan-net-worth-forbes/.

CHAPTER 17. UPSCALE BONNIE AND CLYDE OF COVID DENIAL

159 **Their whirlwind story has it all:** "'Our Spiral Path,' Brogan's blog post and wedding video position her partnership with Ji as personally and politically transformative," accessed November 16, 2021, https://www.kellybroganmd.com/blog/celebration-of-love.

159 **yogic superpowers:** Brogan has long employed yoga as a supportive therapy to psychiatric treatment, but often in oversold ways, as in "Change Your Life in 12 Minutes a Day," accessed November 16, 2021, https://www.kellybroganmd.com /blog/change-your-life-in-12-minutes-a-day.

159 **three hours on Joe Rogan's podcast:** Steven Asarch, "Joe Rogan Experience with Kelly Brogan#968," May 31, 2017. The episode was deleted following Rogan's move to Spotify, presumably as part of this content purge, *Business Insider*, https:// www.businessinsider.com/joe-rogan-experience-podcast-episodes-removed-spo tify-2021-4. Brogan has preserved the episode here, accessed November 28, 2022: https://odysee.com/@kellybroganmd:a/joe-rogan-experience:9.

159 **Satanic Panic:** Matthew Remski, "Deplatformed for Anti-Vax Propaganda, Sayer Ji Turns to Satanic Panic Content," Medium, December 17, 2021, https://matthewremski.medium.com/deplatformed-for-anti-vax-propaganda-sayer-ji-turns-to-satanic-panic-content-fef783aedf68.

159 **their main site reaching one million views per month:** Jonathan Jarry, "Popular Health Guru Sayer Ji Curates the Scientific Literature with His Bachelor's Degree in Philosophy," Office for Science and Society, July 14, 2019, https://www.mcgill.ca/oss/article/pseudoscience/popular-health-guru-sayer-ji-curates-scientific-literature-his-bachelors-degree-philosophy.

159 **an online workshop group with over two thousand members who each paid up to $1,000 to sign up:** Matthew Remski, "Inside Kelly Brogan's Covid-Denying, VAX-Resistant Conspiracy Machine," Medium, September 17, 2020, https://gen.medium.com/inside-kelly-brogans-covid-denying-vax-resistant-conspiracy-machine-28342e6369b1.

159 **the pastel skies of Miami:** Florida Department of Health, License Verification for Practitioner Details, Kelly Brogan, accessed November 23, 2022, https://apps.mqa.doh.state.fl.us/MQASearchServices/HealthCareProviders/LicenseVerification?LicInd=136497&ProCde=1501&org=+.

159 **the WHO declared a global pandemic:** "WHO Director-General's Opening Remarks at the Media Briefing on COVID-19—11 March 2020," accessed November 16, 2021, https://www.who.int/director-general/speeches/detail/who-director-general-s-opening-remarks-at-the-media-briefing-on-covid-19—11-march-2020.

159 **a video selfie-sermon called "A Message to Dispel Fear" to a private online therapy group:** Kelly Brogan, "A Message to Dispel Fear," accessed November 16, 2021, https://web.archive.org/web/20210606030125/https://kellybroganmd.com/message-to-dispel-fear/. View source line 31 shows that the web post was March 11, 2020; line 32 says date modified to May 15, 2020.

159 **"dehumanization agendas that preceded the Holocaust":** Kelly Brogan, "What's Going On?," transcript, archived on authors' website, https://www.conspirituality.net/book-resources.

160 **She refers to herself as a "doctor of the soul," pinging the Greek etymology of the word *psychiatrist*:** Kelly Brogan and Nancy Marriott, *Own Your Self* (Carlsbad, CA: Hay House, 2019), 95–99.

160 **a spell of fear manipulated by Big Pharma to sell pills:** Kelly Brogan and Nancy Marriott, *Own Your Self* (Carlsbad, CA: Hay House, 2019), 80.

160 **patriarchal and controlling attitudes:** Kelly Brogan, "Homebirth: The Opportunity of a Lifetime," Kelly Brogan, MD, April 26, 2017, https://web.archive.org/web/20170610131150/https://www.kellybroganmd.com/homebirth-the-opportunity-of-a-lifetime/.

160 **her initial consultation fee set patients back $4,187. Subsequent forty-five-minute appointments cost $570:** Matthew Remski, "Inside Kelly Brogan's Covid-Denying, VAX-Resistant Conspiracy Machine," Medium, September 17, 2020, https://gen.medium.com/inside-kelly-brogans-covid-denying-vax-resistant-conspiracy-machine-28342e6369b1.

161 **a Madison Avenue lewk:** "Kelly v Brogan MD in New York, NY," WebMD, accessed November 23, 2022, https://doctor.webmd.com/practice/kelly-v-brogan-md-3ab73137-fc9f-e311-9e77-001f29e3eb44-overview.

161 **holding court at pricey events:** Dr. Jen Gunther, "What Was the Point of In Goop Health?," https://drjengunter.com/2018/02/08/what-was-the-point-of-in-goop -health/.

161 **articles about depression being caused by inflammation:** Kelly Brogan, "The Roots of Mental Health—Maybe They're Not in Our Heads," *Goop*, May 25, 2020, https://web.archive.org/web/20200813204233/https://goop.com/wellness/health /the-roots-of-mental-health-maybe-theyre-not-in-our-heads/.

161 **emotional pain being eased through Kundalini Yoga:** Kelly Brogan, "How We Can Learn to Tolerate Emotional Pain," *Goop*, October 17, 2019, https:// web.archive.org/web/20200401234946/https://goop.com/wellness/mindfulness /how-to-tolerate-emotional-pain/.

161 **a platform built on couture pseudoscience:** Dr. Timothy Caulfield, "Gwyneth Paltrow's New Goop Lab is an Infomercial for Her Pseudoscience Business," *The Conversation*, https://theconversation.com/gwyneth-paltrows-new-goop-lab-is-an -infomercial-for-her-pseudoscience-business-129674.

161 **managing a health food store in Naples, Florida:** Jonna Rubin, "Share Your Story: Health Food Store Manager Finds Career by Accident," *Naples News*, September 16, 2006, https://archive.naplesnews.com/community/share-your-story-health-food -store-manager-finds-career-by-accident-ep-405746795-331400321.html/.

161 **draws up to 440,000 visitors per month:** As per https://www.similarweb.com /website/greenmedinfo.com/, accessed November 16, 2021. It's worth noting that this is less than half of the monthly traffic Remski reported using the same tool in September 2020, indicating the effectiveness of the CCDH's deplatforming campaign.

161 **reach over 300,000 subscribers:** GreenMedInfo, "About Us," accessed November 17, 2021, https://web.archive.org/web/20211114151511/https://www.greenmedinfo .com/page/about-us.

161 **affiliate agreements he'd forged over years throughout the alt-health world:** As an example, affiliate deals to promote fellow Disinformation Dozen members Ty and Charlene Bollinger's anti-vax materials have paid out $12 million. "Inside one network cashing in on vaccine disinformation," *AP News*, May 13, 2021, https:// apnews.com/article/anti-vaccine-bollinger-coronavirus-disinformation-a7b8e 1f33990670563b4c469b462c9bf. Related reporting shows Sayer Ji at the top of an earnings pyramid for promoting the anti-vax propaganda film *The Truth about Vaccines*, "Facebook Is Finally Doing Something About the Biggest Spreaders of Anti-Vax Lies," *VICE*, accessed November 17, 2021, https://www.vice.com/en/arti cle/m7evpn/bill-gates-anti-vax-covid-lies-facebook-banned.

161 **she collaborated with Ji on launching the website questioningcovid.com:** Launch date was April 19, 2021, per webarchive.org, accessed November 16, 2021, http:// web.archive.org/web/20200501000000*/questioningcovid.com.

161 **some new websites, including one advertising an (anti-) 5G Summit:** Debra Greene, "5G—The Global Human Experiment without Consent & Most Censored Topic of Our Time," Green Med Info, May 3, 2020, https://www.greenmedinfo .com/blog/5g-global-human-experiment-without-consent-1.

161 **The video was called "Love in the Time of Covid":** Kelly Brogan, "Love in the Time of Covid," accessed November 17, 2021, https://kellybroganmd.mykajabi .com/livecast-love-in-the-time-of-covid.

163 **She dubbed their union Our Spiral Path:** Kelly Brogan, MD, "Our Spiral Path," YouTube video, accessed January 10, 2022, https://www.kellybroganmd.com/blog /celebration-of-love.

163 **their Community Is Immunity campaign:** Kelly Brogan, "Livecast: Community Is Immunity," YouTube, July 8, 2020, https://www.youtube.com/watch?v=pzq3P GUAsJw.

163 **vaginal kung fu:** Archived on authors' website: https://www.conspirituality.net /book-resources.

163 **cryptocurrency:** Archived on authors' website: https://www.conspirituality.net /book-resources.

163 **the pseudolaw of the sovereign citizen movement:** Archived on authors' website: https://www.conspirituality.net/book-resources.

163 **a high-end video documentary of her wedding day with Ji in November of the previous year:** KellyBroganMD, "Our Spiral Path [Updated]," YouTube, May 5, 2020, https://www.youtube.com/watch?v=Ye1qWcAanRM.

164 **to forget about the negative outcomes of fashionable wellness consumption:** Matthew Remski, "The Wellness Pornographers," Medium, August 3, 2021, https:// matthewremski.medium.com/the-wellness-pornographers-4805318bf271.

164 **glamping tents for $400 per night:** "Spring Equinox Gathering with Modern ŌM," Chozen Retreat, accessed January 11, 2022, https://chozenretreat.secure.re treat.guru/program/spring-equinox-gathering/?lang=en.

165 **shutdown orders issued by Idaho governor Brad Little:** "Order to Self-Isolate for the State of Idaho," Dave Jesperson to All Citizens of the State of Idaho, Elected and Appointed Officials, March 25, 2020, accessed December 29, 2021, https:// coronavirus.idaho.gov/wp-content/uploads/2020/06/statewide-stay-home-or der_032520.pdf.

165 **the shelter-in-place provisions were authoritarian and genocidal:** Chad Sokol, "Idaho Rep. Heather Scott Calls Governor 'Little Hitler,' Compares Nonessential Workers to Holocaust Victims," *The Spokesman-Review*, April 16, 2020, https:// www.spokesman.com/stories/2020/apr/16/idaho-rep-heather-scott-calls-gover nor-little-hitl/.

165 **"it is historically insupportable and morally reprehensible":** "Statement on Comparisons of COVID-19 Regulations to Hitler and Nazis," Dallas Holocaust and Human Rights Museum, April 21, 2020, https://www.dhhrm.org/public-state ments/statement-on-comparisons-of-covid-19-regulations-to-hitler-and-nazis/.

165 **baby onesies printed with the words "Freedom Fighter":** "Products," 100million-moms, accessed January 2, 2022, https://100millionmoms.ca/collections/all.

165 **We're not allowed to use the toilet:** Matthew Remski, "Oppression Fantasies of White Anti-Vax Moms," Medium, June 1, 2021, https://matthewremski.medium .com/oppression-fantasies-of-white-anti-vax-moms-9992728a8fcc.

166 **"the probability of a comparison involving Nazis or Hitler approaches one":** Mike Godwin, "Meme, Counter-meme," Wired, October 1, 1994, https://www .wired.com/1994/10/godwin-if-2/.

166 **QAnon recruitment phrase "Take the red pill":** Matthew Remski, "Inside Kelly Brogan's Covid-Denying, VAX-Resistant Conspiracy Machine," Medium, September 17, 2020, https://gen.medium.com/inside-kelly-brogans-covid-denying-vax-res istant-conspiracy-machine-28342e6369b1.

166 **Dr. Judy Mikovits, had served on the GreenMedInfo advisory board:** Archived on authors' website: https://www.conspirituality.net/book-resources. Ji's accompanying blog post: "Must See Documentary: *Plandemic: InDOCTORnation—*The Most Censored Documentary of All Time," accessed November 17, 2021, https://web.archive.org/web/20210302203649/https://greenmedinfo.com/blog/must-see-documentary-plandemic-indoctornation-most-censored-documentary-all-time.

166 **responsible for up to 65 percent of all anti-vax propaganda online:** The Center for Countering Digital Hate report, March 24, 2021, https://252f2edd-1c8b-49f5-9bb2-cb57bb47e4ba.filesusr.com/ugd/f4d9b9_b7cedc0553604720b7137f8663366ee5.pdf.

166 **a life-or-death issue that tech platforms must address:** "Press Briefing by Press Secretary Jen Psaki," July 16, 2021, https://www.whitehouse.gov/briefing-room/press-briefings/2021/07/16/press-briefing-by-press-secretary-jen-psaki-july-16-2021/.

166 **where they retain a small percentage of their former Facebook follower count:** Ji's Telegram, accessed November 17, 2021, https://t.me/s/sayeregengmi; "Facebook Deletes Greenmedinfo.com's Page with Half a Million Followers," accessed November 17, 2021, https://web.archive.org/web/20210812153225/https://www.greenmedinfo.com/blog/facebook-deletes-greenmedinfocoms-page-half-million-followers5.

167 **Ji has been promoting cryptocurrency:** "Getting Started with Cryptocurrencies," accessed November 17, 2021, https://www.kellybroganmd.com/getting-started-with-cryptocurrencies; "The Dangers of the Centralized Internet.... and A SOLUTION You've Never Heard About," accessed November 17, 2021, https://stream.greenmedinfo.com/video/182/the-dangers-of-the-centralized-internet....and-a-solution-you-ve-never-heard-about?channelName=5ea5e05b3851e.

167 **Bill, who she describes as constantly snorting cocaine:** Cathy O'Brien, *TRANCE-formation of America* (self-pub. 1995), accessed November 17, 2021, https://cdn.preterhuman.net/texts/conspiracy/Trance%20Formation%20of%20America.pdf/.

167 **a beacon of courage for both himself and Brogan:** Matthew Remski, "Deplatformed for Anti-Vax Propaganda, Sayer Ji Turns to Satanic Panic Content," *Medium*, May 19, 2021, https://matthewremski.medium.com/deplatformed-for-anti-vax-propaganda-sayer-ji-turns-to-satanic-panic-content-fef783aedf68.

167 **the center of a new enlightened society, in which community is immunity:** "Livecast: Community Is Immunity," YouTube, accessed November 17, 2021, https://www.youtube.com/watch?v=pzq3PGUAsJw&t=209s/.

167 **the authoritarianism of daddy government and mommy medicine:** Kelly Brogan, "Masks: Have You Been Captured by This Psyop?," accessed November 17, 2021, https://web.archive.org/web/20200720230050/https://www.kellybroganmd.com/masks-have-you-been-captured-by-this-psyop/.

168 **"we are now in a spiritual war, and your body is the battlefield":** Kelly Brogan, "Health as Spiritual Warfare," accessed November 17, 2021, https://www.kellybroganmd.com/blog/health-as-spritual-warfare.

168 **Followers should stay tuned, she suggested, for brand new content:** Kelly Brogan, "Kelly Brogan MD on Instagram: 'as you begin to recollect the parts of yourself that were hiding beneath shame and fear…'" Instagram, December 16, 2021, https://www.instagram.com/p/CXit_h3LWbj/.

CHAPTER 18. NEW AGE Q

169 **published an essay with a punny coronavirus title:** Charles Eisenstein, "The Coronation," Charles Eisenstein, March 15, 2020, https://charleseisenstein.org/essays /the-coronation/.

169 **a single-word endorsement: "Remarkable":** Jack Dorsey, "Remarkable," Twitter, April 7, 2020, https://twitter.com/jack/status/1247343782279839744.

169 **quarantine measures as being fascist during the 2016 Zika outbreak:** Charles Eisenstein, "Zika and the Mentality of Control," Charles Eisenstein, March 2, 2016, https://charleseisenstein.org/essays/zika-and-the-mentality-of-control/.

170 **conspiracy theories are truths that haven't yet been accepted:** Charles Eisenstein, "The Conspiracy Myth," Charles Eisenstein, May 21, 2020, https://charleseisenstein.org/essays/the-conspiracy-myth/.

170 **after an initial period of COVID devastation in their communities:** Joanne Silberner, "Covid-19: How Native Americans Led the Way in the US Vaccination Effort," *BMJ*, September 17, 2021, https://doi.org/10.1136/bmj.n2168.

170 **respect for elders, community, and a desire to maintain tribal sovereignty:** Jackie Powder, "Keys to the Navajo Nation's COVID-19 Vaccination Success," Johns Hopkins Bloomberg School of Public Health, August 5, 2021, https://publichealth.jhu .edu/2021/keys-to-the-navajo-nations-covid-19-vaccination-success.

170 **QAnon stories have meaning even if they aren't true:** Charles Eisenstein, "From QAnon's Dark Mirror, Hope," Charles Eisenstein, December 5, 2020, https:// charleseisenstein.org/essays/from-qanons-dark-mirror-hope/.

170 **he praised a French commune that follows the teachings of 1970s-era New Age cult leader Adi Da and *A Course in Miracles*:** Charles Eisenstein, "Source Temple and the Great Reset," Charles Eisenstein, March 16, 2021, https://charleseisenstein .org/essays/source-temple-and-the-great-reset/.

171 **"In the inner reality of wholeness, the miracles happen":** Sayer Ji, "The More Beautiful World Our Hearts Know Is Possible," BeSovereign, April 13, 2022, https://besovereign.com/greenmedinfo/greenmedinfo/13-apr-11-00-the-more -beautiful-world-our-hearts-know-is-possible-938?video_id=330.

171 **Eisenstein wondered aloud whether the pedophile elite would ever be punished:** "Charles Eisenstein at Resonance NYE," YouTube, January 3, 2022, https://www .youtube.com/watch?v=-bQHYx0Zw5k.

171 **He's not a nutritionist, economist, anthropologist, or environmental scientist:** Charles Eisenstein, "About Charles," Charles Eisenstein, accessed January 2, 2022, https://charleseisenstein.org/about/.

171 **introduced as a "scholar" by Oprah Winfrey on her *Super Soul* podcast:** "Charles Eisenstein: A More Beautiful World Is Possible," Oprah, December 19, 2018, https://www.oprah.com/own-podcasts/charles-eisenstein-a-more-beautiful -world-is-possible.

172 **a self-described digital soldier who hosts a battery of QAnon, evangelical, and sovereign citizen guests:** Sean Morgan, "Sean Morgan Report," IHeart, accessed January 3, 2022, https://www.iheart.com/podcast/269-qanon-faq-63077230 /; Sean Morgan, "Charles Eisenstein on CoronaVirus, Conspiracy, and Diverging Timelines," IHeart, June 1, 2020, https://www.iheart.com/podcast/269-qanon -faq-63077230/episode/charles-eisenstein-on-coronavirus-conspiracy-and-6329 4897/.

172 **"QAnon, Covid-19, BLM, Riots, Lockdowns, Masks, Vaccines and Election Integrity":** Sean Morgan, "Sean Morgan Report—A Leading Voice in the Great Awakening," October 19, 2021, https://seanmorganreport.com/.

172 **an episode with the chilling title of "How to Redpill Your Mom #QAnon":** Sean Morgan, "How to Redpill Your Mom #QAnon—The Sean Morgan Report," IHeart, May 7, 2020, https://www.iheart.com/podcast/269-qanon-faq-63077230/episode /how-to-redpill-your-mom-qanon-63100516/.

172 **His response was a conspirituality primer:** "Charles Eisenstein on Coronavirus, Conspiracy, and Diverging Timelines," Buzzsprout, June 1, 2020, https://www .buzzsprout.com/1067875/4004843-charles-eisenstein-on-coronavirus-conspir acy-and-diverging-timelines.

173 **"we need them to flesh out conspiracy theories and give expression to the psychological energies driving those theories":** Charles Eisenstein, "Synchronicity, Myth, and the New World Order," Charles Eisenstein, December 1, 2013, https:// charleseisenstein.org/essays/synchronicity-myth-and-the-new-world-order/.

173 **(which was ultimately never played due to student backlash):** "Ivanka Trump's Graduation Speech to Class of 2020," YouTube, June 6, 2020, https://www.youtube.com /watch?v=pROPc1L93hc; Elizabeth Redden, "WSU Tech Cancels Ivanka Trump Commencement Speech," *Inside Higher Ed*, June 8, 2020, https://www.insidehighered.com /quicktakes/2020/06/08/wsu-tech-cancels-ivanka-trump-commencement-speech.

174 **which might be better than the Clinton alternative:** Charles Eisenstein, "The Election: Of Hate, Grief, and a New Story," November 1, 2016, https://charleseisen stein.org/essays/hategriefandanewstory/.

174 **a fable he first published in blog form in 2009:** Charles Eisenstein, "A Gathering of the Tribe," Charles Eisenstein, December 7, 2009, https://charleseisenstein.org /essays/a-gathering-of-the-tribe/.

174 **an animation that followed the story with ethereal figures making their descent:** Aubrey Marcus, "A Gathering of the Tribe | Powerful Short Film by Charles Eisenstein W/ Jon Hopkins & Aubrey Marcus," YouTube, December 7, 2021, https:// www.youtube.com/watch?v=XinVOpdcbVc.

174 **an anime artist whose other illustration work features a lot of very young nude women:** "Aldous Massie (See Pala) (@Aldousmassie)—Instagram," accessed November 23, 2022, https://www.instagram.com/aldousmassie/.

175 **His book sales total over eighty thousand copies:** Archived on authors' website: https://www.conspirituality.net/book-resources.

175 **an essay called "Mob Morality and the Unvaxxed":** Charles Eisenstein, "Mob Morality and the Unvaxxed," Charles Eisenstein, August 2, 2021, https://charleseisen stein.substack.com/p/mob-morality-and-the-unvaxxed.

175 **North Atlantic would thereafter donate 100 percent of the net sales of Eisenstein's books to three social justice organizations:** Tim McKee, "Disavowing Disinformation," North Atlantic Books, August 13, 2021, https://www.northatlan ticbooks.com/blog/disavowing-disinformation/.

175 **he had migrated all of his writing over to the subscription-based platform:** Charles Eisenstein, "What I'm Doing Here," Charles Eisenstein, August 20, 2021, https://charleseisenstein.substack.com/p/what-im-doing-here?s=r.

177 **"*Bought and sold...because they are moist*":** Aubrey Marcus, "The Forgotten Voices of the Pandemic Will Have You in Tears," YouTube, January 17, 2021, https://www.youtube.com/watch?v=EUZ0vTbpJcU.

178 **his wife gazing into his eyes, tapping his chest, and saying "Put it in your heart":** Aubrey Marcus on Instagram: "Announcement: Tomorrow morning I release the most emotional video I have ever created…," Instagram, January 16, 2021, https://www.instagram.com/p/CKIFeRoHgQD/.

178 **$80 million of it on his father's side:** Martin Schwartz, Dave Morine, and Paul Flint, *Pit Bull: Lessons from Wall Street's Champion Trader* (New York: Harper, 2010), 176.

178 **peaking with his CrossFit and fitness supplement:** Brian Heffernan, "How Is Joe Rogan Related to Health and Fitness Brand 'Onnit,'" *Sportskeeda*, October 26, 2022, https://www.sportskeeda.com/mma/news-how-joe-rogan-related-health-fitness-brand-onnit.

178 **Onnit was sold to Unilever in 2021:** Capitalism.com, "He Had One Product, $80K in Funding, and One Influencer—and Unilever Just Acquired His Company for 9 Figures," Capitalism.com, September 26, 2022, https://www.capitalism.com/onnit/.

178 **Eisenstein's breakout moment as the Marcus court philosopher came in 2021:** *Conspirituality* podcast, "87: The Aubrey Marcus Spectacle," *Conspirituality*, January 20, 2022, https://www.conspirituality.net/episodes/87-the-aubrey-marcus-spectacle.

178 **who pay up to $20,000 per year:** Max Hug, "Aubrey Marcus—Fit for Service Mastermind—Review," Max Hug, December 27, 2019, https://www.maxhug.com/aubrey-marcus-mastermind/.

CHAPTER 19. THE CURSED GOLDEN GIRL

179 **she earns at least $1 million in yearly sales:** Theresa Haney, "Usana Health and Freedom Newspaper," *Issuu*, January 5, 2011, https://issuu.com/theresahaney/docs/us-ennewspaper.

179 **starting with Christiane's mother Edna:** Usana Health Products, "Usana Living the Dream: Edna Northrup," YouTube, February 27, 2014, https://www.youtube.com/watch?v=Hq04pfEkTEY.

179 **telling women how to earn more while working less through changing their thought patterns:** Kate Northrup, "An Intimate Look behind the Scenes of My Business Model," Kate Northrup, May 7, 2015, https://katenorthrup.com/an-intimate-look-behind-the-scenes-of-my-business-model/.

179 **"Oprah makes you a household name and PBS makes people believe you have been vetted by academia":** Dr. Jen Gunter, "The Pandemic's Worst Woman: Dr. Christiane Northrup," *The Vajenda*, September 9, 2021, https://vajenda.substack.com/p/the-pandemics-worst-woman-dr-christiane?s=r.

182 **repurposed by QAnon in 2019, if not earlier, to predict a mass conversion or red-pilling event:** Adrienne LaFrance, "The Prophecies of Q," *Atlantic*, September 24, 2020, https://www.theatlantic.com/magazine/archive/2020/06/qanon-nothing-can-stop-what-is-coming/610567/.

182 **In the caption to the video, she linked to a newsletter:** "Urgent Call for 1 Million Meditators to Liberate and Reclaim Our World on April 4, 2020 at Precisely 10:45 PM EST When a Celestial Stargate Opens!" Global Peace Meditation, April 2020, https://mailchi.mp/dfb4970313b3/global-unity-and-peace-meditation-3-more-days-1301429.

182 **from a "global decentralised group of Lightworkers working on World Peace":** "Join Global Peace Meditation Network," Global Peace Meditation, accessed December 12, 2021, https://www.globalpeacemeditation.com/about-us.html.

183 **Alexandra Stein is the pioneer in the field of applying disorganized attachment theory to cultic bonds:** Alexandra Stein, "Attachment Theory and Post-Cult Recovery," Alexandra Stein, accessed January 20, 2022, http://www.alexandrastein .com/uploads/2/8/0/1/28010027/cults_final_ttsep16.pdf.

183 **"a folksy writing style that makes the reader believe she is advocating for you against medical misogyny":** Dr. Jen Gunter, "The Pandemic's Worst Woman: Dr. Christiane Northrup," *The Vajenda*, September 9, 2021, https://vajenda.substack .com/p/the-pandemics-worst-woman-dr-christiane?s=r.

184 **"this man was divinely guided to release it on Good Friday, and as I speak to you now, it's had nearly two million views":** Archived on authors' website: https:// www.conspirituality.net/book-resources.

185 *Hollywood* **is named for the poisonous holly plant, sacred to Druids:** Tarpley Hitt, "The Bonkers Hollywood-Pedophilia 'Documentary' QAnon Loves," *Daily Beast*, August 6, 2020, https://www.thedailybeast.com/inside-out-of-shadows-the -bonkers-hollywood-pedophilia-documentary-qanon-loves.

185 **Mike Donnelly published a report on the viral spread of the Smith film:** Mike Donnelly, "Far-Right Communities Are Pushing a Q-Anon Film," RPubs, April 15, 2020, https://rpubs.com/alexbnewhouse/outofshadows.

185 **Prior to that, the largest vector:** Sheera Frenkel, Ben Decker, and Davey Alba, "How the 'Plandemic' Movie and Its Falsehoods Spread Widely Online," *New York Times*, May 20, 2020, https://www.nytimes.com/2020/05/20/technology/plandemic -movie-youtube-facebook-coronavirus.html.

185 *Women's Bodies, Women's Wisdom*—**her bestselling magnum opus on women's alternative health:** Dr. Christiane Northrup, "My Newly Revised Edition of *Women's Bodies, Women's Wisdom* Is Available Today! I'm Here to Talk About How You Can Confidently Take Charge of Your Health Using the Information in My Book," Facebook, May 12, 2020, https://www.facebook.com/DrChristianeNorthrup/vid eos/243075257032548.

186 **she appeared on Sean Morgan's** *QAnon FAQ* **platform:** The Sean Morgan Report, "Dr. Christiane Northrup on Standing in Your Sovereignty during the Plandemic," Deezer, May 15, 2020, https://deezer.page.link/xSn6zoYtHZVHGe8C9.

186 **"Nor did I know that the term 'Great Awakening' was also associated with that movement," she said:** Dr. Christiane Northrup, "Dr. Christiane Northrup Great Awakening, October 17, 2020," Facebook, November, 5, 2020, https://www.face book.com/watch/?v=395678411591775.

186 **"sharing with family and friends, research, and emotional support":** Sean Morgan, "Dr. Christiane Northrup on Standing in Your Sovereignty during the Plandemic," IHeart, May 15, 2020, https://www.iheart.com/podcast/269-qanon-faq -63077230/episode/dr-christiane-northrup-on-standing-in-63100503/.

187 **in September 2020 alone:** Julian Walker, "Christiane Northrup's Campaign Contributions to Trump," *Conspirituality*, November 8, 2020, https://conspirituality .net/transmissions/christiane-northrups-campaign-contributions-to-trump/.

188 **she got tagged by the UK think tank Center for Countering Digital Hate as one of the Disinformation Dozen:** "The Disinformation Dozen: Why Platforms Must Act on Twelve Leading Online Anti-vaxxers," Center for Countering Digital Hate, March 24, 2021, https://counterhate.com/research/the-disinformation-dozen/.

188 **She called the report a smear campaign and compared it to Republicans chanting "Lock her up" at Trump rallies:** Dr. Christiane Northrup, "My Rebuttal to Being

Included in the Disinformation Dozen," Facebook, March 27, 2021, https://www
.facebook.com/permalink.php?story_fbid=10164903162225029&id=118912795028.

188 **tagged this argument with the phrase "Reverse Contagion Anxiety":** Matthew
Remski, "Anti-Vax Reverse Contagion Anxiety," Medium, April 24, 2021, https://
matthewremski.medium.com/anti-vax-reverse-contagion-anxiety-81724ea216e0.

188 **former Trump lawyer Lin Wood, who resurrected Q in a speech:** Will Sommer,
"OAN rapidly cuts away from Lin Wood after he starts making QAnon Q's in the Air,"
Twitter, April 17, 2021, https://twitter.com/willsommer/status/1383277740233687048.

188 **in which he called for the execution of political enemies:** PatriotTakes, "Every lie
will be revealed. They are killing our children, send them to jail. Put them in front
of the firing squad. They are committing acts against humanity. The penalty for an
act against humanity is death. Take them out, Lin Wood," Twitter, April 18, 2021,
https://twitter.com/patriottakes/status/1383709884114341892.

189 **their sexual relationships would end if the partner were to be vaccinated:** Matthew Remski, "Christiane Northrup Encourages Anti-Vaxxers to Shun Pro-Vax
Partners," Medium, April 19, 2021, https://matthewremski.medium.com/christiane
-northrup-encourages-anti-vaxxers-to-shun-pro-vax-partners-1ee1021a870.

189 **"This is a Medusa and we need to take it out altogether":** Derek Beres, Matthew
Remski, and Julian Walker, "Letter to Sacha Stone Regarding Inciting Political Violence," *Conspirituality*, November 10, 2020, https://conspirituality.net/transmis
sions/letter-to-sacha-stone-regarding-inciting-political-violence/.

189 **the pseudolegal framework of the Constitutional Sheriffs and Peace Officers
Association:** Dr. Christiane Northrup, "The Great Awakening October 15, 2020
Letter to My Local Sheriff, Being Banned on Twitter, Time for a Private Platform.
In the Meantime, Gratitude," Facebook, October 15, 2020, https://www.facebook
.com/watch/?v=349121439690249.

189 **a far-right organization headed up by a former Oath Keepers board member:**
Kimberly Kindy, "Boosted by the Pandemic, 'Constitutional Sheriffs' Are a Political Force," *Washington Post*, November 3, 2021, https://www.washingtonpost.com
/politics/constitutional-sheriffs-elections-trump-pandemic/2021/11/01/4c14c764
-368b-11ec-91dc-551d44733e2d_story.html.

189 **The Sheriffs went on to play a pivotal role in organizing the Capitol siege of
January 6:** Jessica Pishko, "Sheriffs Helped Lead This Insurrection," *Slate*, January
15, 2021, https://slate.com/news-and-politics/2021/01/constitutional-sheriffs-white
-supremacists-capitol-riot-insurrection.html.

190 **she was getting news from her colleagues in Washington:** Dr. Christiane
Northrup, "The Great Awakening. Jan 6, 2021 Hold the Vibration of What You
Want. Many Things Will Be Revealed Now," Facebook, January 6, 2021, https://
www.facebook.com/watch/?v=443317960023643.

190 **Northrup let the bloodlust fully rip:** Jeff Witzeman, "Signposts on the Road to
Ascension Trailer #1," YouTube, February 24, 2022, https://www.youtube.com
/watch?v=iX2pugomycY.

CHAPTER 20. NEW AGE ZELIG

192 **"Having been inside the twin towers just hours before they fell":** "Our Team,"
Elevate Films, September 17, 2015, http://elevate.us/team/.

192 **he recalls watching the towers collapse from the uptown apartment of a friend,
and then immediately running downtown to help:** decidecommitsucceed,

"Mikki Willis Share His 9/11 Experience," YouTube, September 11, 2011, https://www.youtube.com/watch?v=HUWgSYhqszw.

192 **he told the reporter, he slept for a few hours in an abandoned hotel:** Archived on authors' website: https://www.conspirituality.net/book-resources.

192 **"And it was all one big body of God":** "Mikki Willis Share His 9/11 Experience," YouTube, September 11, 2011, https://www.youtube.com/watch?v=HUWgSYhqszw.

193 **a torrent of false claims about COVID-19 and vaccines:** Scott Neuman, "Seen 'Plandemic'? We Take a Close Look at the Viral Conspiracy Video's Claims," *NPR*, May 8, 2020, https://www.npr.org/2020/05/08/852451652/seen-plandemic-we-take-a-close-look-at-the-viral-conspiracy-video-s-claims.

193 **The film gathered eight million views in a week:** Sheera Frenkel, Ben Decker, and Davey Alba, "How the 'Plandemic' Movie and Its Falsehoods Spread Widely Online," *New York Times*, May 20, 2020, https://www.nytimes.com/2020/05/20/technology/plandemic-movie-youtube-facebook-coronavirus.html.

194 **after alleging she'd stolen proprietary materials from the lab:** David Mikkelson, "'Plandemic': Was Judy Mikovits Arrested Without a Warrant and Jailed Without Charges?," *Snopes*, May 8, 2020, https://www.snopes.com/fact-check/plandemic-mikovits-arrest/.

194 **Within a week, Facebook and YouTube had deleted *Plandemic*:** Josh Rottenberg and Stacy Perman, "Meet the Ojai Dad Who Made the Most Notorious Piece of Coronavirus Disinformation Yet," *Los Angeles Times*, May 13, 2020, https://www.latimes.com/entertainment-arts/movies/story/2020-05-13/plandemic-coronavirus-documentary-director-mikki-willis-mikovits.

194 **Bill Gates was personally responsible for this cancellation:** "76. Mikki Willis | Remembering Our Innate Benevolence in the Midst of Contrasting Beliefs," The Great Unlearn, December 20, 2021, https://www.youtube.com/watch?v=vhV-TWpC6zI.

194 **Willis's sequel gathered no viral momentum:** Daniel Funke, "Politifact—Fact-Checking 'Plandemic 2': Another Video Full of Conspiracy Theories About COVID-19," *Politifact*, August 18, 2020, https://www.politifact.com/article/2020/aug/18/fact-checking-plandemic-2-video-recycles-inaccurat/.

194 **hit pieces driven by rage at anyone who goes against their narrative:** "76. Mikki Willis | Remembering Our Innate Benevolence in the Midst of Contrasting Beliefs," The Great Unlearn, December 20, 2021, https://www.youtube.com/watch?v=vhV-TWpC6zI.

194 **a globe-trotting mystic who died of leukemia in 2009, at the age of twenty-nine:** unusualadventure, "Daniel Thomas Northcott January 23, 1980—June 20, 2009," Dan's Unusual Adventure, July 2, 2009, https://dansunusualadventure.wordpress.com/2009/06/21/daniel-thomas-northcott-january-23-1980-june-20-2009/.

194 **Elevate helped crowdfund $184,000 for the project, which was never released:** Erin Northcott, "Be Brave—The True Story of Daniel Northcott," Indiegogo, December 1, 2012, https://www.indiegogo.com/projects/be-brave-the-true-story-of-daniel-northcott-2#/.

194 **Elevate crowdfunded $40,000 for a proposed-but-never-released doc called *From Neurons to Nirvana*:** "Neurons to Nirvana: Understanding Psychedelic Medicines," Kickstarter, June 26, 2014, https://www.kickstarter.com/projects/1055048000/neurons-to-nirvana-understanding-psychedelic-medic-0.

194 **in order to replace drones that had been shot out of the sky and buy winter camp-
ing gear:** Ali Katz, "'This Is the First Time Our History Will Reflect the Truth'
Mikki Willis about the Importance of on...," Medium, December 2, 2016, https://
medium.com/reports-from-standing-rock/this-is-the-first-time-our-history-will
-reflect-the-truth-mikki-willis-about-the-importance-of-on-5df3d7e6d9d7.

194 **one six-minute interview shot in a studio with a lawyer advocating for the protestors is currently available:** "It's Not Over—Daniel Sheehan on Standing Rock,"
YouTube, Elevate Films, August 5, 2017, https://www.youtube.com/watch?v=ifN-
2jkG7Jts&t=207s.

195 **A 2014 production reel for Elevate sums up the company vibe:** Willis has removed
it from both his Elevate website (https://elevate.us/) and YouTube channel. Still ex-
tant is the 2018 promo video: https://www.youtube.com/watch?v=7P5GWLVPgsc.

195 **"God sent me Mikki Willis":** Live Free or Die, "Dr. Judy Mikovitz—Defeat the
Mandates April 10, 2022," Rumble, April 18, 2022, https://rumble.com/v11f521
-april-18-2022.html.

196 **"up until now, our society has been ruled by a belief system known as patriarchy—
the rule of the fathers":** Dr. Christiane Northrup, *Women's Bodies, Women's Wisdom: Creating Physical and Emotional Health and Healing* (New York: Bantam
Books, 2020), xii.

196 **approximately 65 percent of those diagnosed are women:** Ashley R. Valdez et al.,
"Estimating Prevalence, Demographics, and Costs of ME/CFS Using Large Scale
Medical Claims Data and Machine Learning," *Frontiers in Pediatrics*, January 8,
2019, https://www.ncbi.nlm.nih.gov/labs/pmc/articles/PMC6331450/.

196 **"women internalize this message and become our own worst enemies":** Dr.
Christiane Northrup, *Women's Bodies, Women's Wisdom: Creating Physical and
Emotional Health and Healing* (New York: Bantam Books, 2020), 5.

196 **He took to Facebook to stream himself lit with a honey-yellow filter:** Matthew
Remski, "Terror and Salvation from *Plandemic* Director Mikki Willis," Medium,
April 1, 2021, https://matthewremski.medium.com/terror-and-salvation-from-plan
demic-director-mikki-willis-a0acbf67e523.

197 **contradictory impulses of terror and love that can only be resolved through devotion:** Alexandra Stein, *Terror, Love and Brainwashing: Attachment in Cults and
Totalitarian Systems* (New York: Routledge, 2021).

198 **Stewart Rhodes:** "Live Stream & Replay—2020 Jekyll Island 'Truthrising,'" Red
Pill Expo, February 22, 2021, https://redpillexpo.org/truthrising/.

199 **now convicted of seditious conspiracy over his January 6 activities:** "Elmer Stewart Rhodes," Southern Poverty Law Center, accessed March 17, 2022, https://www
.splcenter.org/fighting-hate/extremist-files/individual/elmer-stewart-rhodes.

199 **"How I Became a Recovering Socialist":** "How I Became a Recovering Socialist—
Mikki Willis—RPE2020," accessed March 17, 2022, https://www.brighteon.com
/embed/95cd8028-c36c-46e7-b2bc-737f6c49bb19.

199 **a life coach named Joyous Heart, led two prayers for Donald Trump:** Matthew
Remski, "*Plandemic*'s Mikki Willis Joins, Praises Violent Capitol Mob," *Conspirituality*, January 11, 2021, https://conspirituality.net/transmissions/plandemics
-mikki-willis-joins-praises-violent-capitol-mob/.

199 **Home Ranch and Gold Star Oasis, registered that month with plans to build on
Lake Travis:** Anna Merlan, "Leading New Age Conspiracy Influencers Plan Their
Retreat to Utopian Lagoon," *VICE*, January 28, 2021, https://www.vice.com/en/ar

ticle/n7vkdq/leading-new-age-conspiracy-influencers-plan-their-retreat-to-uto
pian-lagoon.

200 **and anti-vax propagandists**: Tarpley Hitt, "The Bonkers Hollywood-Pedophilia
'Documentary' QAnon Loves," *Daily Beast*, August 6, 2020, https://www.thedaily
beast.com/inside-out-of-shadows-the-bonkers-hollywood-pedophilia-documen
tary-qanon-loves.

200 **Roger Stone, the Trump-pardoned felon, was also on the initial billing**: *Conspirituality* podcast, "Plandemic's Mikki Willis Joins, Praises Violent Capitol Mob,"
Conspirituality, May 28, 2021, https://www.conspirituality.net/transmissions/plan
demics-mikki-willis-joins-praises-violent-capitol-mob/.

200 **who built her fame along with her husband Ty on marketing quack cancer cures**:
"The Disinformation Dozen: Why Platforms Must Act on Twelve Leading Online
Anti-Vaxxers," Center for Countering Digital Hate, March 24, 2021, https://www
.counterhate.com/_files/ugd/f4d9b9_b7cedc0553604720b7137f8663366ee5.pdf.

200 **Around him, the mob chants "Hang Mike Pence"**: "R/Publicfreakout—Trump
Supporters Chanting 'Hang Mike Pence' at the Capitol Building," Reddit, accessed
March 10, 2022, https://www.reddit.com/r/PublicFreakout/comments/krwqdm
/trump_supporters_chanting_hang_mike_pence_at_the/.

200 **Willis posted his account of his participation in the mob action to his Facebook page**: *Conspirituality* podcast, "Plandemic's Mikki Willis Joins, Praises Violent Capitol Mob," *Conspirituality*, May 28, 2021, https://www.conspirituality.net
/transmissions/plandemics-mikki-willis-joins-praises-violent-capitol-mob/.

201 **Chek grew up in the Self-Realization Fellowship**: Chris Shugart, "Deconstructing Paul Chek," *T Nation*, January 16, 2006, https://www.t-nation.com/training
/deconstructing-paul-chek/.

201 **"but your spiritual beliefs are your software by which you navigate life"**: Chris
Shugart, "Deconstructing Paul Chek," *T Nation*, January 16, 2006, https://www
.t-nation.com/training/deconstructing-paul-chek/.

201 **a strengthened immune system is all the protection one needs to fend off a novel
coronavirus**: Paul Chek, "Health & Fitness During the COVID-19 Pandemic,"
CHEK Institute, September 2, 2020, https://chekinstitute.com/blog/health-fitness
-during-the-covid-19-pandemic/.

201 **Stone was frantically throwing his fancy suits into black garbage bags in his
high-end suite at the Willard Hotel, plotting his exit**: Dalton Bennett and Jon
Swaine, "The Roger Stone Tapes," *Washington Post*, March 4, 2022, https://www
.washingtonpost.com/investigations/interactive/2022/roger-stone-documentary
-capitol-riot-trump-election/.

202 **"they're playing us and dividing us so they can conquer"**: Paul Chek, "Episode
141—Mikki Willis 2: What's Really Going on?," CHEK Institute, June 15, 2021,
https://chekinstitute.com/blog/podcast-episodes/episode-141-mikki-willis-2
-whats-really-going-on/.

202 **elders accused him of lying about the COVID case rates in the village**: Shira
Hanau, "Jewish MD Who Promoted Virus Cocktail Is Leaving Community Where
He Tested It," *Times of Israel*, May 21, 2020, https://www.timesofisrael.com/jew
ish-md-who-promoted-virus-cocktail-leaving-community-where-he-tested-it/.

202 **In the months before he died of lung cancer on June 30, 2022**: Clay Risen, "Vladimir Zelenko, 48, Dies; Promoted an Unfounded Covid Treatment," *New York Times*,
July 1, 2022, https://www.nytimes.com/2022/07/01/us/vladimir-zelenko-dead.html.

202 **if you use Willis's discount code:** Derek Beres, "The Endless Supplement Grift," *Trickle-Down Wellness*, November 3, 2021, https://derekberes.substack.com/p/the -endless-supplement-grift.

CHAPTER 21. J. "PEPE" SEARS, MAGA LIFE COACH

203 **Sears is helping people with anger management via YouTube:** JP Sears, "Anger Management Part 2—with JP Sears," YouTube, August 15, 2013, https://www.you tube.com/watch?v=gVL_YiBWKRo.

203 **he's gently coaching men away from porn addiction:** JP Sears, "Porn Addiction— with JP Sears," YouTube, January 2, 2015, https://www.youtube.com/watch?v=XB m5W8E9bYs.

203 **he's flipped from life coach to comedian who makes fun of life coaches:** JP Sears, "Dating Spiritual People—Ultra Spiritual Life…," YouTube, January 11, 2015, https://www.youtube.com/watch?v=g2nljqSMj9s.

204 **doing tactical training with former Green Berets:** JP Sears, "#84 Peaceful Slavery or Dangerous Freedom? With Tim Kennedy," *Awaken with JP Sears Show*, May 20, 2020, https://awakenwithjp.libsyn.com/84-peaceful-slavery-or-dangerous-freedom -with-tim-kennedy.

204 **he's posing with his arm around Donald Trump under the palm fronds of Mar-a-Lago:** JP Sears, "'It was an honor…and I have a…,'" Instagram, December 10, 2021, https://www.instagram.com/p/CXUInxMlNfw/.

204 **"a way for me to shine the light of awareness on the shadow side of me":** Heath Ellison, "Local Viral Video Star JP Sears Finds Success in Comedy and Sin-cerity," *Charleston City Paper*, January 24, 2018, https://web.archive.org/web /20210517225829/https://www.charlestoncitypaper.com/story/local-viral-video -star-jp-sears-finds-succes-in-comedy-and-sincerity?oid=14907268.

205 **organized through her robust online brand:** Ondina Hatvany, "The Shadow Side of Self-Proclaimed 'Light Leaders' or How I Got Scammed by Epic Academy," Ondina Wellness, July 2019, https://ondinawellness.com/the-shadow-side-of-self -proclaimed-light-leaders-or-how-i-got-scammed-by-epic-academy/.

205 **mitigation orders prompted his oppositional-defiant star to rise:** Jonathan Jarry, "The Clown Prince of Wellness," Office for Science and Society, November 19, 2020, https://www.mcgill.ca/oss/article/covid-19-critical-thinking-pseudoscience /clown-prince-wellness.

205 **laughing at trans people and the woke:** Eoin Higgins, "Comedian JP Sears Calls for Civil War, Killing of Trans People During Spokane Appearance," *The Flashpoint*, De-cember 10, 2021, https://eoinhiggins.substack.com/p/comedian-jp-sears-calls-for-civil.

205 **he implied that the war in Ukraine was fake:** AwakenWithJP, "Ukraine and Rus-sia: What the Media Wants You to Think!," YouTube, March 2, 2022, https://www .youtube.com/watch?v=q1W5o3Xz5OI.

206 **A video from 2015 called "Porn Addiction":** AwakenWithJP, "Porn Addiction— with JP Sears," YouTube, January 2, 2015, https://www.youtube.com/watch?v=XB m5W8E9bYs.

206 **who Sears has helped market:** AwakenWithJP, "The Tony Robbins Experience— Ultra Spiritual Life Episode 40," YouTube, September 14, 2016, https://www.you tube.com/watch?v=aPI5TexgiXA.

206 **claims they were sexually abused to gain "significance" in life:** Justin Caffier, "Tony Robbins Made Controversial #MeToo Comments, Angering His Own Fans,"

VICE, March 23, 2018, https://www.vice.com/en/article/d35897/tony-robbins-made
-controversial-metoo-comments-angering-his-own-fans.

207 **a post selling "Let's Go Brandon" T-shirts in November 2021:** AwakenWithJP,
"You Crazy Freedom Loving Weirdos Kept Asking for It, so Here It Is!," Face-
book, November 2, 2021, https://www.facebook.com/awakenwithjp/posts/pfbid0J
FAsePhR2xB2ot6A5LbcnCN5kUQbu7m4R2UydiJc5vzgt8tByankyz4tSY6tmBq9l.

207 **Pepe grins, accepting his weirdo self:** *Feels Good Man*: The Sundance Award-
Winning Documentary," Feels Good Man, accessed November 23, 2022, https://
www.feelsgoodmanfilm.com/.

208 **he drew everyone's focus toward an increasingly cruel space:** Dale Beran, *It Came
from Something Awful: How a New Generation of Trolls Accidentally Memed Donald Trump into the White House* (New York: St. Martin's Press, 2019), 114.

208 **a hate symbol by the Anti-Defamation League:** "Pepe the Frog," Anti-Defamation
League, accessed March 17, 2022, https://www.adl.org/education/references/hate
-symbols/pepe-the-frog.

208 **"When a Liberal Finally Becomes a Conservative":** AwakenWithJP, "When a Liberal Finally Becomes a Conservative," YouTube, May 1, 2021, https://www.youtube
.com/watch?v=b56Si3DY6cQ.

208 **the video "Blue Pill People":** AwakenWithJP, "Blue Pill People," YouTube, May 19,
2020, https://www.youtube.com/watch?v=dC_lZLzCrOI.

208 **"I prefer dangerous freedom over peaceful slavery":** "I Prefer Dangerous Freedom over Peaceful Slavery (Quotation)," Monticello, accessed December 13, 2021,
https://www.monticello.org/site/research-and-collections/i-prefer-dangerous
-freedom-over-peaceful-slavery-quotation.

209 **Sears hosted former UFC fighter and ex-Special Forces sniper Tim Kennedy on
his podcast:** JP Sears, "#84 Peaceful Slavery or Dangerous Freedom? With Tim
Kennedy," *Awaken with JP Sears Show*, May 20, 2020, https://awakenwithjp.libsyn
.com/84-peaceful-slavery-or-dangerous-freedom-with-tim-kennedy.

209 **#tactical #tacticalgear #tacticallife #tacticalminivans:** Tim Kennedy, "If You
Are Doing Evil, You Should Fear the Minivan," Facebook, August 15, 2020,
https://www.facebook.com/TimKennedyMMA/photos/if-you-are-doing-evil-you
-should-fear-the-minivan-tacticalminivan-streetsnatcher/3123432307694034/.

209 **Sears attended tactical training through Kennedy's company, Sheepdog Response:** JP Sears, "Warrior mode activated. Spent the past few days immersed in
@Timkennedymma's @sheepdogresponse training. It was extremely informative,
fun, painful, and humbling....," Facebook, November 22, 2020, https://www.face
book.com/permalink.php?story_fbid=4112704045412093&id=961065217242674.

209 **telling trainees that the sex they will have the night they kill someone will be
the best of their lives:** Radley Balko, "A Day with 'Killology' Police Trainer Dave
Grossman," *Washington Post*, October 26, 2021, https://www.washingtonpost.com
/news/the-watch/wp/2017/02/14/a-day-with-killology-police-trainer-dave-gross
man/.

210 **unemployed weirdos would seek real-world revenge:** Dale Beran, *It Came from
Something Awful: How a New Generation of Trolls Accidentally Memed Donald
Trump into the White House* (New York: St. Martin's Press, 2019), 119–120.

210 **Smug Pepe often appeared as Donald Trump:** Dale Beran, *It Came from Something Awful: How a New Generation of Trolls Accidentally Memed Donald Trump
into the White House* (New York: St. Martin's Press, 2019), 155.

210 **it reinforced the Big Lie that drove the Capitol riot:** "President Trump Retweeted a Video Clip Alleging Election Fraud from a Parody Comedian," Imgur, accessed December 12, 2021, https://imgur.com/gallery/rleqb7j.

210 **"in which disaffected teenagers all tried collectively to derail the conversation":** Dale Beran, *It Came from Something Awful: How a New Generation of Trolls Accidentally Memed Donald Trump into the White House* (New York: St. Martin's Press, 2019), 51.

211 **the reality status of any statement or seeming political commitment is eventually called into question:** S. I. Rosenbaum, "'Irony Poisoning': When Nasty Humor Spirals Downward into Something Far Worse," *Boston Globe*, August 24, 2018, https://www.bostonglobe.com/ideas/2018/08/24/irony-poisoning-when-nasty-humor-spirals-downward-into-something-far-worse/eykyPaE2jKsJIMwCZnfb3H/story.html.

CHAPTER 22. THE JESUS DOCTOR, FREED FROM EMPATHY

212 **peering for answers amid the coral reefs:** Rich Roll, "Transcend Your Story: Zach Bush, MD," YouTube, July 25, 2019, https://www.youtube.com/watch?v=5jjoZnUnT_s.

213 **OurPlantPowerWorld, hosted yearly, runs about $8,000 to attend:** "Italy," OurPlantPowerWorld, accessed March 21, 2022, https://www.ourplantpowerworld.com/schedule.

213 **a "mystic mother" and "wayshower" who sells SriMu, a vegan cheese made out of nuts:** "BIOS," OurPlantPowerWorld, accessed March 21, 2022, https://www.ourplantpowerworld.com/about-1.

213 **The cost is $463 for either sixty or seventy-five minutes, "depending on what is mandated by the higher self":** Julie Piatt, "Work with Me," Julie Piatt, accessed March 21, 2022, https://www.juliepiatt.com/workwithsri.

216 **In his book on Pattabhi Jois, the founder of Ashtanga Yoga:** Matthew Remski, *Practice and All Is Coming: Abuse, Cult Dynamics, and Healing in Yoga and Beyond* (Rangiora, NZ: Embodied Wisdom Publishing, 2019).

217 **He told Bigtree that COVID-19 is an environmental, not an epidemiological, problem:** Del Bigtree, "Doctor Who Predicted COVID-19 Answers All," BitChute, May 19, 2020, https://www.bitchute.com/video/88eP5o6Sns6r/.

217 **the forthcoming vaccines would be dangerous:** Timothy Johnson, "YouTube Terminates Anti-Vaccine Figure Del Bigtree's Account after He Pushed Dangerous Coronavirus and Vaccine Misinformation," *Media Matters for America*, July 30, 2020, https://www.mediamatters.org/coronavirus-covid-19/youtube-terminates-anti-vaccine-figure-del-bigtrees-account-after-he-pushed.

217 **and drew a 2019 salary of $232,000:** Ken Schwencke and Mike Tigas, "Informed Consent Action Network—Nonprofit Explorer," *ProPublica*, May 9, 2013, https://projects.propublica.org/nonprofits/organizations/814540235.

217 **Bigtree's anti-vax propaganda generates close to $3.5 million in yearly income:** *Pandemic Profiteers: The Business of Anti-Vax*, Center for Countering Digital Hate, June 1, 2021, https://252f2edd-1c8b-49f5-9bb2-cb57bb47e4ba.filesusr.com/ugd/f4d9b9_00b2ad56fe524d82b271a75e441cd06c.pdf.

218 **He flew there in a private jet:** Matthew Remski, "Do Anti-Vax Profiteers Believe Their Cultic Bullshit?," Medium, June 14, 2021, https://matthewremski.medium.com/do-anti-vax-profiteers-believe-their-cultic-bullshit-159bdf1907c.

218 **vaccines will make the pandemic worse because they won't address the underlying spiritual wounds:** "Zach Bush—Our COVID-19 Assumptions Are Wrong:

Why Social Distancing & Vaccines Will Make The Pandemic Worse," Digital Freedom Platform, July 31, 2020, https://freedomplatform.tv/zach-bush-our-covid-19-assumptions-are-wrong-why-social-distancing-vaccines-will-make-the-pandemic-worse/.

219 **small-scale religious communities imagined to exist in biblical times, free from clerical bureaucracy and state influence:** Michael Alison Chandler and Arianne Aryanpur, "Going to Church by Staying at Home," *Washington Post*, June 4, 2006, https://www.washingtonpost.com/wp-dyn/content/article/2006/06/03/AR2006060300225.html.

219 **whose mission was to "save the hippies from their drug-infested culture":** The-PachamamaAlliance, "Personal and Planetary Health Conversation with Zach Bush MD," YouTube, May 18, 2020, https://www.youtube.com/watch?v=Oy59Tf CKDXA.

220 **a senior preacher at Unity of Boulder:** "Jack Groverland," Unity of Boulder Church, September 25, 2020, https://unityofboulder.com/people/jack-groverland-4/.

220 **Norma Bigtree, who leads the choir:** "Norma Bigtree Groverland," Unity of Boulder Church, June 25, 2021, https://unityofboulder.com/people/norma-groverland-2/.

220 **a former schoolteacher who believed she'd cured her chronic tuberculosis through the power of prayer:** "Myrtle Page Fillmore," Encyclopædia Britannica, accessed November 23, 2022, https://www.britannica.com/biography/Myrtle-Page-Fillmore.

220 **a sermon called "Coronavirus and Truth":** Jack Groverland, "'The Coronavirus and Truth' by Rev. Jack—9 AM Service," YouTube, March 15, 2020, https://www.youtube.com/watch?v=wWxAUeDsF4Y.

221 **he has appeared at Unity of Boulder to give talks on the dangers of vaccines:** "Del Bigtree Will Be Speaking About 'The Vaccine Safety Project' at Unity of Boulder Spiritual Center on Saturday, November 25th at 6:00 P.M.," Facebook, November 21, 2017, https://www.facebook.com/unityboulder/posts/715404728659624.

221 **they say has netted seventy-five million downloads:** "Top 50 Podcast, Global Community & Inclusive Platform to Fuel Your Conscious Evolution," Almost 30, accessed November 23, 2022, https://almost30.com/.

221 **remixed for Instagram, adding gorgeous visuals:** "Creativity Is Our Only Pathway out of Disaster. If We Stay Curious About an Alternative World That We Live in Today, We Can Create That World—Dr. Zach Bush in This Eye-Opening Episode…," Almost 30 podcast, Instagram, August 17, 2021, https://www.instagram.com/p/CSr6BaUpSM4/.

222 **"we will find the reverence for humanity as much as nature":** "Dr. Zach Bush—Physician + Educator / Alternative Healing," Almost 30, September 10, 2021, https://almost30.com/health-wellness/2021/08/17/dr-zach-bush-on-fear-the-immune-system-and-the-real-meaning-of-life/.

CHAPTER 23. A KENNEDY SON SPIRALS

224 **a Black Senate candidate, an NAACP leader, and a local Black Lives Matter leader:** Peter Jamison, "Anti-vaccination Leaders Fuel Black Mistrust of Medical Establishment as Covid-19 Kills People of Color," *Washington Post*, July 21, 2020, https://www.washingtonpost.com/dc-md-va/2020/07/17/black-anti-vaccine-coronavirus-tuskegee-syphilis/.

224 **helps provide the largely white anti-vax movement with a veneer of diversity:** Paula Larsson, "The Inherent Racism of Anti-Vaxx Movements," *The Conversation*, October 14, 2021, https://theconversation.com/the-inherent-racism-of-anti-vaxx -movements-163456.

224 **a Black supremacist hate group that promotes antisemitic and anti-LGBTQ rhetoric:** "Nation of Islam," Southern Poverty Law Center, accessed February 3, 2022, https://www.splcenter.org/fighting-hate/extremist-files/group/nation-islam.

224 **19 children were born with the disease:** Ada McVean, "40 Years of Human Experimentation in America: The Tuskegee Study," Office for Science and Society, December 30, 2020, https://www.mcgill.ca/oss/article/history/40-years-human-ex perimentation-america-tuskegee-study.

224 **an issue that Kennedy and other white anti-vax activists do not highlight:** April Dembosky, "No, the Tuskegee Study Is Not the Top Reason Some Black Americans Question the COVID-19 Vaccine," *KQED*, February 25, 2021, https://www.kqed .org/news/11861810/no-the-tuskegee-study-is-not-the-top-reason-some-black -americans-question-the-covid-19-vaccine.

224 **His son, Conor, has an anaphylactic allergy to peanuts:** Page Six Team, "Conor Kennedy Has Nuts Allergy Scare," *Page Six*, December 30, 2013, https://pagesix .com/2013/12/30/conor-kennedy-has-nuts-allergy-scare/.

225 **to understand and find cures for food allergies:** "History of Fare," FoodAllergy.org, accessed November 23, 2022, https://www.foodallergy.org/about-us/history-fare.

225 **mercury poisoning in water and food chains was one of Kennedy's top concerns:** "The Anti-Vaxx Industry: How Big Tech Powers and Profits from Vaccine Misinformation," Center for Countering Digital Hate, 9–10, https://www.counterhate .com/_files/ugd/f4d9b9_6910f8ab94a241cfa088953dd5e60968.pdf.

225 **which falsely alleges that childhood vaccines cause food allergies:** "5 Myths about Peanuts," National Peanut Board, accessed November 23, 2022, https://www .nationalpeanutboard.org/wellness/5-myths-about-peanuts.htm.

225 **a measles outbreak in Samoa that infected 5,700 and killed 83:** Times Editorial Board, "Editorial: Samoa Measles Outbreak Shows What Happens When Antivaxxers Win," *Los Angeles Times*, December 7, 2019, https://www.latimes.com /opinion/story/2019-12-07/measles-outbreak-in-samoa-anti-vaccine-advocates -win.

225 **measles outbreaks in Somali immigrant communities in Minnesota in 2011 and 2017:** Helen Branswell May, "Measles Sweeps an Immigrant Community Targeted by Anti-vaccine Activists," *STAT*, May 8, 2017, https://www.statnews.com/2017/05 /08/measles-vaccines-somali/.

225 **falsified 1998 study started the still-lingering conspiracy theory that the MMR vaccine causes autism:** "Wakefield Paper Alleging Link Between MMR and Autism Fraudulent," History of Vaccines, accessed December 28, 2021, https://web .archive.org/web/20120511144607/http://www.historyofvaccines.org/content /blog/bmj-wakefield-paper-alleging-link-between-mmr-vaccine-and-autism-frau dulent.

225 **a one-hour film titled *Medical Racism: The New Apartheid*:** Brandy Zadrozny and Char Adams, "Covid's Devastation of Black Community Used as 'Marketing' in New Anti-vaccine Film," *NBC News*, March 12, 2021, https://www.nbcnews.com /news/nbcblk/covid-s-devastation-black-community-used-marketing-new-anti -vaxxer-n1260724.

225 **a launchpad for anti-vax conspiracy theories and COVID-denial propaganda:** Saranac Hale Spencer and Angelo Fichera, "RFK Jr. Video Pushes Known Vaccine Misrepresentations," FactCheck.org, April 28, 2021, https://www.factcheck.org /2021/03/scicheck-rfk-jr-video-pushes-known-vaccine-misrepresentations/.

225 **Black people are naturally immune to the disease:** Jonathan Jarry, "The Anti-Vaccine Propaganda of Robert F. Kennedy, Jr.," Office for Science and Society, April 19, 2021, https://www.mcgill.ca/oss/article/covid-19-health-pseudoscience /anti-vaccine-propaganda-robert-f-kennedy-jr.

226 **the false claim that the CDC genetically modified MMR vaccines to harm Black and Latino boys:** Anna Merlan, "The Anti-Vaccination Movement Is Working with the Nation of Islam to Scare Black Families," *Jezebel*, June 26, 2017, https://jezebel .com/the-anti-vaccination-movement-is-working-with-the-natio-1796021231.

226 **gives podcast talks on "rebirthing the world":** JJ Flizanes, "EP. 324: Rebirthing the Planet with Dr. Christiane Northrup on Apple Podcasts," *Spirit, Purpose & Energy*, December 6, 2021, https://podcasts.apple.com/us/podcast/ep-324-rebirth ing-the-planet-with-dr-christiane-northrup/id1163875124?i=1000544177117.

227 **They also provided ... wait for it ... free vaccinations:** Mary T. Bassett, "Beyond Berets: The Black Panthers as Health Activists," *American Journal of Public Health*, October 2016, https://www.ncbi.nlm.nih.gov/labs/pmc/articles/PMC5024403/.

227 **Stanford cites her father's affinity with the Black Panthers as a guiding light in her work:** Olivia B. Waxman, "What School Didn't Teach You about the Black Panthers," *Time*, February 25, 2021, https://time.com/5937647/black-panther-medical -clinics-history-school-covid-19/.

229 **arguing for the same universal health care:** "John F. Kennedy Argues for Universal Healthcare," Films For Action, accessed February 3, 2022, https://www.films foraction.org/watch/john-f-kennedy-argues-for-universal-healthcare/.

229 **"We are fighting for the salvation of all humanity":** Matthew Remski, "Deplatformed for Anti-Vax Content, R.F. Kennedy Jr. Predicts Apocalypse," Medium, June 17, 2021, https://matthewremski.medium.com/deplatformed-for-anti-vax-con tent-r-f-kennedy-jr-predicts-apocalypse-ea9f07d88c6b.

229 **top billing at the Defeat the Mandates march that gathered at the Lincoln Memorial:** Kara Voght, "'I'm a Full Anti-Vaxxer Now': How the Conspiracists Are Winning over Fresh Converts," *Rolling Stone*, January 24, 2022, https:// www.rollingstone.com/culture/culture-news/anti-vaccine-rfk-jr-rally-washing ton-dc-1289458/.

229 **"we're not here to ask permission":** JP Sears, "JP Sears Opening Speech @ March to Defeat the Mandates" YouTube, January 23, 2022, https://www.youtube.com /watch?v=7ng72hfB0Wc.

229 **Kennedy quickly apologized for the comment in response to a flood of criticism:** Associated Press in Washington, "Robert F. Kennedy Jr. Apologizes for Anne Frank Comparison in Anti-Vax Speech," *Guardian*, January 25, 2022, https:// www.theguardian.com/us-news/2022/jan/25/robert-f-kennedy-jr-vaccine-anne -frank.

230 **Sales are estimated to bring in between $2.5 and $3.8 million:** Isabel Vincent, "Robert F. Kennedy Jr. Is Making Millions off His Anti-Vax Crusade," *New York Post*, February 2, 2022, https://nypost.com/2022/02/02/robert-f-kennedy-jr-anti -vax-crusade-is-making-him-millions/.

230 **Children's Health Defense took a PPP loan worth $146,685:** "Children's Health Defense Co in Peachtree City, GA," FederalPay, accessed March 29, 2022, https://www.federalpay.org/paycheck-protection-program/childrens-health-defense-co-peachtree-city-ga.

230 **according to the website Celebrity Net Worth:** "Robert F. Kennedy, Jr. Net Worth," Celebrity Net Worth, June 30, 2021, https://www.celebritynetworth.com/richest-businessmen/lawyers/robert-f-kennedy-jr-net-worth/.

230 **an additional PPP loan on April 30, 2020, of $20,000, for himself:** Moiz Syed and Derek Willis, "Robert F. Kennedy Jr.," *ProPublica*, July 7, 2020, https://projects.propublica.org/coronavirus/bailouts/loans/robert-f-kennedy-jr-6063197304.

230 **JP Sears, for example, received $58,488 on February 8, 2021:** Moiz Syed and Derek Willis, "Awaken with JP LLC," *ProPublica*, July 7, 2020, https://projects.propublica.org/coronavirus/bailouts/loans/awaken-with-jp-llc-5409438402.

230 **misinformation that risked the lives of the most vulnerable:** Elizabeth Dwoskin and Aaron Gregg, "The Trump Administration Bailed Out Prominent Anti-Vaccine Groups during a Pandemic," *Washington Post*, January 20, 2021, https://www.washingtonpost.com/business/2021/01/18/ppp-loans-anti-vaccine/.

230 **the leading buyer of anti-vax ads on Facebook:** Beth Mole, "Robert F. Kennedy Jr. Is the Single Leading Source of Anti-Vax Ads on Facebook," *Ars Technica*, November 15, 2019, https://arstechnica.com/science/2019/11/robert-f-kennedy-jr-is-the-single-leading-source-of-anti-vax-ads-on-facebook/.

CHAPTER 24. 5D FEMME

231 **she drifted between aliases:** Hayley Phelan, "The Second Coming of Guru Jagat," *Vanity Fair*, December 1, 2021, https://www.vanityfair.com/style/2021/11/the-second-coming-of-guru-jagat.

231 **Bhajan was a serial rapist and fraudster:** Stacie Stukin, "Yogi Bhajan Turned an L.A. Yoga Studio into a Juggernaut, and Left Two Generations of Followers Reeling from Alleged Abuse," *Los Angeles*, July 15, 2020, https://www.lamag.com/citythinkblog/yogi-bhajan/.

232 **billing companies for printer toner that he never shipped:** Associated Press, "Toner Bandit Gets 2 Years in Prison," *Denver Post*, August 17, 2000, https://extras.denverpost.com/news/news0817r.htm.

232 **Another former student of Hartzell's called him "the man behind the curtain":** Cassidy George, "Inside the Dubious World of Ra Ma Yoga, and Its Girl Boss Guru to the Stars," *VICE*, July 13, 2021, https://www.vice.com/en/article/v7ey5b/inside-the-dubious-world-of-ra-ma-yoga-and-its-girl-boss-guru-jagat.

232 **turned up no evidence to confirm any of them:** Philip Deslippe, "From Maharaj to Mahan Tantric," *Sikh Formations* 8, no. 3 (2012): 369–87, https://doi.org/10.1080/17448727.2012.745303.

232 **a photocopy of a counterfeit bill:** *Conspirituality* podcast, "36: Guru Jagat's Pandemic Brandwash (W/Philip Deslippe & Stacie Stukin)," *Conspirituality*, January 28, 2021, https://www.conspirituality.net/episodes/36-guru-jagats-pandemic-brandwash-philip-deslippe-stacie-stukin.

233 **a sign of spiritual weakness that invited a person to be exploited:** "Los Angeles Lecture," The Yogi Bhajan Library of Teachings, accessed March 25, 2022, https://www.libraryofteachings.com/lecture.xqy?q=%22divorce+attorney

%22+sort%3Arelevance&id=c81367bd-646a-b917-c181-77ea94e35413&title=Los
-Angeles-Lecture.

233 **Stacie Stukin summed up Griggs on a podcast panel shortly after her death:**
Matthew Remski et al., "Remembering Guru Jagat," Medium, August 18, 2021,
https://matthewremski.medium.com/remembering-guru-jagat-567893fa7d6a.

235 **a memoir about her time as a "secretary" for Yogi Bhajan:** Pamela Saharah
Dyson, *Premka: White Bird in a Golden Cage: My Life with Yogi Bhajan* (London:
Eyes Wide Publishing, 2020).

235 **"If you do not provide the circumstances and the arrangements, it is impossible":** "Espanola Lecture," The Yogi Bhajan Library of Teachings, accessed March
25, 2022, https://www.libraryofteachings.com/lecture.xqy?q=rape+sort%3Arele
vance&id=1da5411e-933c-3391-e580-f08d1e359e15&title=Espanola-Lecture.

235 **"the Truth as always lies in the eye of the Beholder":** Hayley Phelan, "The Second Coming of Guru Jagat," *Vanity Fair*, December 1, 2021, https://www.vanityfair
.com/style/2021/11/the-second-coming-of-guru-jagat.

236 **"she's repackaged Bhajan's tactics for spiritual indoctrination in a cloud of
millennial pink":** Cassidy George, "Inside the Dubious World of Ra Ma Yoga,
and Its Girl Boss Guru to the Stars," *VICE*, July 13, 2021, https://www.vice.com/en
/article/v7ey5b/inside-the-dubious-world-of-ra-ma-yoga-and-its-girl-boss-guru
-jagat.

236 **"Crazy bullshit":** Hayley Phelan, "The Second Coming of Guru Jagat," *Vanity Fair*,
December 1, 2021, https://www.vanityfair.com/style/2021/11/the-second-coming
-of-guru-jagat.

236 **she was speculating on alien wars:** Wrong at Ra Ma, "#3 of 4 We've got some camp
grace highlights today! If you couldn't shell out the [money] this past weekend, no
worries—here's a little bit of what you missed," Instagram, September 16, 2020,
https://www.instagram.com/p/CFNNwcDhqKr/.

236 **spirit guides can be infiltrated and compromised:** Wrong at Ra Ma, "#2 of 4:
We've got some camp grace highlights today! If you couldn't shell out the [money]
this past weekend, no worries—here's a little bit of what you missed," Instagram,
September 16, 2020, https://www.instagram.com/p/CFM9-10hbkH/.

236 **the California forest fires were being started by space lasers:** Wrong at Ra Ma,
"#4 of 4: We've got some camp grace highlights today! If you couldn't shell out
the [money] this past weekend, no worries—here's a little bit of what you missed,"
Instagram, September 16, 2020, https://www.instagram.com/p/CFNh_jaBZz4/.

236 **she introduced guest Kerry Cassidy for an hour-long podcast on July 21, 2020:**
GuruJagat11, YouTube, July 21, 2020, accessed December 12, 2021, https://www
.youtube.com/watch?v=Gn3zh0KRbe4. (Video now deleted. Transcript is archived
on authors' website: https://www.conspirituality.net/book-resources.

237 **"tainted in a way that will make it very hard to rebrand or salvage them":** Stacie
Stukin, "Yogi Bhajan Turned an L.A. Yoga Studio into a Juggernaut, and Left Two
Generations of Followers Reeling from Alleged Abuse," *Los Angeles*, July 15, 2020,
https://www.lamag.com/citythinkblog/yogi-bhajan/.

238 **spiritual communities hijacked by woke ideology were moving in the wrong
direction:** fromahuman, "Perspective & Perception: Guru Jagat x David Icke,"
Odysee, January 31, 2021, https://odysee.com/@fromahuman:3/perspective-per
ception-guru-jagat-x-david-icke.

238 **speaking quietly on Griggs's podcast:** GuruJagat11, "The Great Awakening Map: Guru Jagat X Champ Parinya," YouTube, April 12, 2021, https://www.youtube.com /watch?v=0SvmqOjUfdk.

239 **"the supreme red-pill navigational chart for Escaping the Matrix and Returning to Source":** "The Great Awakening Will Not Be Televised," Art House 5D Shop, accessed March 1, 2022, https://www.greatawakeningmap.co/.

239 **LA County Department of Public Health reported over three thousand new COVID cases:** "LA County Daily Covid-19 Data," LA County Department of Public Health, accessed February 25, 2022, http://publichealth.lacounty.gov/media /coronavirus/data/index.htm#.

239 **believed that mask ordinances were unconstitutional:** Wrong at Ra Ma, "Katie Griggs = Your Paranoid Far-Right Uncle Who Lives on Facebook, Part 2/2," Instagram, October 2, 2020, https://www.instagram.com/p/CF2rAo9BSfn/.

239 **refused to be vaccinated against COVID-19:** Hayley Phelan, "The Second Coming of Guru Jagat," *Vanity Fair*, December 1, 2021, https://www.vanityfair.com /style/2021/11/the-second-coming-of-guru-jagat.

CHAPTER 25. A CHORUS OF CHANNELERS AND LIGHTWORKERS

241 **"Pleiadians, Andromedans, Arcturians, and Sirians":** "The Galactic Federation," Facebook, accessed March 21, 2022, https://www.facebook.com/groups/MYGA LACTICFEDERATION/about.

241 **fifteen thousand Facebook shares, and close to a half-million views:** Lorie Ladd, "Is Trump a Lightworker," YouTube, August 12, 2020, https://www.youtube.com /watch?v=Hju17fXIriQ.

242 **"Light does not attack darkness, but it does shine it away":** Helen Schucman and William Thetford, *A Course in Miracles* (Omaha, NE: Course in Miracles Society, 2009). 163.

242 **over 500,000 copies and been translated into twenty languages:** "The Pleiadians Channeled by Barbara Marciniak," Pleiadians, accessed November 29, 2022, https://www.pleiadians.com/.

242 **Marciniak claims to have been contacted by the Pleiadians the year she turned forty:** "Marciniak, Barbara (fl. Ca 1988)," Encyclopedia of Occultism and Parapsychology, Encyclopedia.com, accessed November 22, 2022, https://www.encyclopedia.com /science/encyclopedias-almanacs-transcripts-and-maps/marciniak-barbara-fl-ca-1988.

242 **The Biggest Secret:** David Icke, *The Biggest Secret: The Book That Will Change the World* (Bridge of Love Publications, USA, 1999).

243 **he was deconstructing their hang-ups around status and money:** Sam Wolleston, "Growing up in the Wild Wild Country Cult: 'You Heard People Having Sex All the Time, like Baboons,'" *Guardian*, April 24, 2018, https://www.theguardian.com /tv-and-radio/2018/apr/24/wild-wild-country-netflix-cult-sex-noa-maxwell-bhag wan-shree-rajneesh-commune-childhood.

243 **giving meaning to the physical and mental symptoms of ascending to 5D consciousness:** Dr. Christiane Northrup, "The Great Awakening Dec 12, 2020 Ascension Symptoms, Grieving the Past, What Are We Suffering from. Meditation with Lorie Ladd and Jason Shurka. My Hero Larry Palevsky, MD," Facebook, December 17, 2021, https://www.facebook.com/DrChristianeNorthrup/videos/69541 2064670521/.

244 **He was challenging their egotism and pride:** Matthew Remski, "Survivors of an International Buddhist Cult Share Their Stories," *Walrus*, September 28, 2020, https://thewalrus.ca/survivors-of-an-international-buddhist-cult-share-their-stories/.

245 **editing out Jesus's homophobia and general sex negativity:** Sean Reagan, "Sex and Acim Part Two," Sean Reagan, August 9, 2021, https://seanreagan.com/sex-and-acim-part-two/.

245 **boosted to bestseller status by Oprah Winfrey:** Amanda Fortini, "Marianne Williamson Is Campaigning for a Miracle," *Elle*, April 25, 2014, https://www.elle.com/culture/career-politics/interviews/a12708/marianne-williamson-profile/.

245 **Abraham also thinks that people contract AIDS when they don't love themselves:** Be Scofield, "A Critique of Abraham Hicks & the Law of Attraction," *Guru Magazine*, October 20, 2020, https://gurumag.com/a-critique-of-abraham-hicks-the-law-of-attraction/.

246 **assaulted and raped women under the cover of healing:** Matthew Remski, "John of Fraud," Medium, October 8, 2021, https://matthewremski.medium.com/john-of-fraud-c5e92acb786d.

246 **recorded lectures that are posted online:** Marianne Williamson, "365 Days of a Course in Miracles," accessed November 23, 2022, https://marianne.com/365-days-of-a-course-in-miracles/.

246 **At eighteen, she was abducted by aliens:** Elizabeth April, "My Story," Elizabeth April, March 19, 2022, https://elizabethapril.com/my-story/.

246 **she hangs with the very same Galactic Federation:** Katie Griggs, "Galactic Federation School: Guru Jagat X Elizabeth April," YouTube, April 6, 2020, https://www.youtube.com/watch?v=a36t73R5nrU.

246 **"The Donald is a Lightworker," which got forty-two thousand views:** Elizabeth April, "The Donald is a Lightworker," Facebook, December 25, 2021, https://www.facebook.com/PsychicElizabethApril/videos/885385755131222.

246 **she appeared on Katie Griggs's podcast to discuss her Galactic Federation School in April 2020:** Katie Griggs, "Galactic Federation School: Guru Jagat X Elizabeth April," YouTube, April 6, 2020, https://www.youtube.com/watch?v=a36t73R5nrU.

247 **#thegreatawakening #reptillian #illuminati #spiritualawakening #5D #ascension #empowerment:** Elizabeth April, "Would you protest for enslaved children?" Instagram, July 13, 2020, https://www.instagram.com/p/CCltn7-ACAG.

247 **of course a world savior battling a global Cabal:** Magenta Pixie, "Blog," Magenta Pixie, accessed March 22, 2022, https://www.magentapixie.com/blog.html.

247 **to shower QAnon congressperson Marjorie Taylor Greene with rainbow heart emojis:** Magenta Pixie, "If Marjorie Taylor Greene is kept in Congress after this vote then that is a massive win for the light. Let us collectively hold the energy for this brave lightwarrior who speaks for true patriots," Instagram, February 4, 2021, https://www.instagram.com/p/CK4c5WxnSe8.

247 **saving the children with her own tagline, Kids Lives Matter:** Magenta Pixie, "This is the real, organic call from humanity. It has not been drowned out or prevented even when using looking glass tech and Mandela effect manipulation for we hold the organic tech that is the true Ark of the Covenant," Instagram, August 10, 2020, https://www.instagram.com/p/CDt_pyonwkG.

247 **a deep vein thrombosis that swelled her leg to five times its normal size:** Anna Merlan, "'Lightworker' Who Said Covid Vaccines Harm the Spirit Hospitalized

with Covid," *VICE*, October 27, 2021, https://www.vice.com/en/article/v7dg49
/lightworker-who-said-covid-vaccines-harm-the-spirit-hospitalized-with-covid.

247 **"We are strong, we are ready"**: Archived on authors' website: https://www.con
spirituality.net/book-resources.

249 **"tangible knowledge and concern about the ravages of industrial capitalism
instead of disembodied, abstract and politically neutral states of presence?"**:
Be Scofield, "Why Eckhart Tolle's Evolutionary Activism Won't Save Us," *Tikkun
Daily Blog Archive*, July 8, 2012, https://www.tikkun.org/tikkundaily/2012/07/07
/why-eckhart-tolles-evolutionary-activism-wont-save-us/.

249 **gazing at her webcam with deadeye radiance**: Lorie Ladd, "Remember the Bigger
Picture: By Lorie Ladd," Facebook, accessed September 27, 2022, https://www.face
book.com/lorieladdofficial/videos/2493670010929546.

250 **making it by far Ladd's most popular content**: "Message from the Galactic Federation: Our Role in 2021: By Lorie Ladd," Facebook, accessed September 27, 2022,
https://www.facebook.com/watch/?v=1711558115685311.

250 **Conspirituality and QAnon channels were jammed with insurrection chatter
from at least December 23 onward**: Logan Jaffe, Lydia DePillis, Isaac Arnsdorf,
and J. David McSwane, "Capitol Rioters Planned for Weeks in Plain Sight. The
Police Weren't Ready," *ProPublica*, January 7, 2021, https://www.propublica.org
/article/capitol-rioters-planned-for-weeks-in-plain-sight-the-police-werent-ready.

CHAPTER 26. PLACEBO JOE

252 **Louis, a life coach from San Diego**: *Conspirituality* podcast, "89: Till Death Do Us
Part (w/Mary)," *Conspirituality*, February 3, 2022, https://www.conspirituality.net
/episodes/89-till-death-do-us-part-mary.

253 **based in part on his 2014 book**: Joe Dispenza, *You Are the Placebo* (Carlsbad, CA:
Hay House, 2014).

254 **Knight, a former rodeo queen and cable TV saleswoman**: Susy Buchanan,
"Ramtha, New Age Cult Leader, Unleashes Drunken, Racist, Homophobic Rants
to Large Following," *AlterNet*, June 6, 2014, https://www.alternet.org/2014/06
/ramtha-new-age-cult-leader-unleashes-drunken-racist-homophobic-rants-large
-following/.

254 **"Thees ees that wheech is called teleeveesion?"**: "Merv Griffin Show JZ Knight
As Ramtha—1985—14 Minutes," YouTube, June 9, 2019, https://www.youtube.com
/watch?v=w5stFb0mwfE.

254 **while at RSE produced the 2004 pseudoscience movie *What the Bleep Do We
Know?***: John Gorenfeld, "'Bleep' of Faith," *Salon*, September 16, 2004, https://www
.salon.com/2004/09/16/bleep_2/.

254 **brought in almost $16 million in earnings worldwide**: "What the #$*! Do We (K)
now!?," Box Office Mojo, accessed December 28, 2021, https://www.boxofficemojo
.com/release/rl3765995009/weekend/.

254 **more recently has become an anti-cult whistleblower**: Lauren Kranc, "Mark
Vicente and Bonnie Piesse Were Members of NXIVM. Now They're Helping Expose It," *Esquire*, August 31, 2020, https://www.esquire.com/entertainment/tv
/a33810813/nxivm-mark-vicente-bonnie-piesse-the-vow-today-now/.

254 **The Southern Poverty Law Center reviewed the tapes**: Susy Buchanan, "Ramtha,
New Age Cult Leader, Unleashes Drunken, Racist, Homophobic Rants to
Large Following," *Alternet*, June 6, 2014, https://www.alternet.org/2014/06/ramtha

-new-age-cult-leader-unleashes-drunken-racist-homophobic-rants-large-fol
lowing/.

254 **Ramtha's four axioms are boilerplate-vague New Ageisms:** "The Four Corner-
stones of Ramtha's Philosophy Are," Ramtha's School of Enlightenment, accessed
November 23, 2022, https://www.ramtha.com/content/learn.aspx.

255 **In December of 2020:** Aubrey Marcus, "Dr. Joe Dispenza—The Formula to Choose
Your Destiny: AMP #286," Aubrey Marcus, December 9, 2020, https://www.au
breymarcus.com/blogs/aubrey-marcus-podcast/the-formula-to-choose-your-des
tiny-with-dr-joe-dispenza-amp-286.

255 **He graduated from Life University:** "Life University Alumnus, Dr. Joe Dispenza,
Releases Newest Book...," Life University, November 3, 2017, https://www.life.edu
/wp-content/uploads/2016/02/11-3-17-Dr.-Joe-Dispenzas-Book-Release-Press-Re
lease.pdf.

255 **Life University lost its accreditation:** Courtney Lowery, "Life University Loses
Accreditation from Chiropractic Council," *The Chronicle of Higher Education*, July
23, 2020, https://www.chronicle.com/article/life-university-loses-accreditation-from
-chiropractic-council/.

255 **A report from the time:** Marc Kreidler, "Life University Loses CCE Accreditation,"
Quackwatch, November 6, 2002, https://quackwatch.org/chiropractic/edu/revocation/.

256 **Attendance fees for similar events:** "Week Long Advanced Retreats," Unlimited
with Dr Joe Dispenza, accessed November 23, 2022, https://drjoedispenza.com
/collections/week-long-advanced-retreats.

CHAPTER 27. LEARNING FROM LISTENERS

263 **We do know that he likely brought in nine figures from his sale of Onnit to
Unilever:** Capitalism.com, "He Had One Product, $80K in Funding, and One
Influencer—and Unilever Just Acquired His Company for 9 Figures," September
26, 2022, https://www.capitalism.com/onnit/.

264 **QAnon was becoming a minor religion in May 2021:** Giovanni Russonello, "QA-
non Now as Popular in U.S. as Some Major Religions, Poll Suggests," *New York
Times*, May 27, 2021, https://www.nytimes.com/2021/05/27/us/politics/qanon-re
publicans-trump.html.

264 **By fall the percentage had ticked up three points:** David Smith, "Belief in QA-
non Has Strengthened in US since Trump Was Voted out, Study Finds," *Guardian*,
February 24, 2022, https://www.theguardian.com/us-news/2022/feb/23/qanon-be
lievers-increased-america-study-finds.

264 **to wrest control of future presidential elections at the state level:** Em Steck, Nathan McDermott, and Christopher Hickey, "The Congressional Candidates Who
Have Engaged with the QAnon Conspiracy Theory," CNN, October 20, 2020,
https://www.cnn.com/interactive/2020/10/politics/qanon-cong-candidates/; Bill
McCarthy and Amy Sherman, "A Coalition of 'Stop the Steal' Republicans Aims to
Take Control of Us Elections. QAnon Is Helping," *Politifact*, June 7, 2022, https://
www.politifact.com/article/2022/jun/07/coalition-stop-steal-republicans-aims
-take-control/.

264 **Donald Trump's discredited claims of 2020 election fraud:** Elaine Kamarck and
Norman Eisen, "Democracy on the Ballot—How Many Election Deniers Are on
the Ballot in November and What Is Their Likelihood of Success?," Brookings
Institute, November 9, 2022, https://www.brookings.edu/blog/fixgov/2022/10/07

/democracy-on-the-ballot-how-many-election-deniers-are-on-the-ballot-in-no
vember-and-what-is-their-likelihood-of-success/.

264 **Over 170 of those candidates won:** Kayla Gallagher, "The Most Prominent Elec-
tion-Deniers Lost Their Races, but at Least 174 Have Won so Far," *Business Insider*,
November 16, 2022, https://www.businessinsider.com/election-deniers-whove-won
-and-lost-their-races-midterms-2022-11.

264 **roles that could interfere with election integrity in key battleground states:**
Adam Edelman, "Election Deniers Overwhelmingly Lost in Battleground States,"
NBC News, November 16, 2022, https://www.nbcnews.com/politics/2022-election
/election-deniers-overwhelmingly-lost-battleground-states-rcna57058.

264 **collectively produces about 65 percent of the anti-vax content available on the internet:** "Pandemic Profiteers: Center for Countering Digital Hate: United Kingdom,"
Center for Countering Digital Hate, https://www.counterhate.com/pandemicprofiteers.

CHAPTER 28. LEAVING ENLIGHTENMENT

267 **Cortney and Shana can't remember exactly how they first became aware of the
New Age:** *Conspirituality* podcast, "104: Leaving Ramtha's Ranch (w/Cortney &
Shana)," *Conspirituality*, May 19, 2022, https://www.conspirituality.net/episodes
/104-leaving-ramthas-ranch-cortney-shana.

271 **when she invited QAnon rocker J. T. Wilde:** The Young Turks, "The Conversation:
JT Wilde," The Young Turks, March 16, 2021, https://tyt.com/watch/7eJMbO6nI
jVFUK1ZNfNVdT/episodes/7E8OnlboB3KerZHSwy4RSo.

271 **his hit song "WWG1WGA":** *Genesis Retreat 3-9 March 2019 Music Playlist*,
Ramtha School of Enlightenment PDF, https://www.ramtha.com/content/pdf
/Genesis_2019.pdf.

271 **Attendees wore QAnon-themed T-shirts at the event:** Will Sommer, "QAnon
Teams Up with Alleged Cult Leader," *Daily Beast*, May 21, 2019, https://www.the
dailybeast.com/qanon-teams-up-with-alleged-cult-leader.

271 **Ramtha declared that the person behind QAnon "is divine intelligence":** Will
Sommer, "QAnon Teams Up with Alleged Cult Leader," *Daily Beast*, May 21, 2019,
https://www.thedailybeast.com/qanon-teams-up-with-alleged-cult-leader.

CHAPTER 29: REMEMBERING FEY

273 **an eleven-foot by seven-foot acrylic called *The Tipping Point* in 2008:** Gavin
Ryan, "Tipping Point," accessed May 10, 2022, https://www.personalshrine.com
/manifesto.

274 **According to Gavin:** *Conspirituality* podcast, "102: Conspirituality, Cancer, &
Compassion (w/Gavin Ryan)," *Conspirituality*, May 5, 2022, https://www.conspiri
tuality.net/episodes/102-conspirituality-cancer-amp-compassion-gavin-ryan.

CHAPTER 30: O FATHER, WHERE ART THOU?

282 **"All governments lie":** *Common Ground*, August/September 2021, *Issuu*, 2021,
https://issuu.com/commongroundmagazinecanada/docs/common_ground_aug
_sept_2021_for_iss_2e999ec9a3ce3b.

283 **the Canadian Broadcasting Corporation called him out in an investigation:**
Catherine Tunney, "Federal Department Gave Money to Magazine Publishing
Pandemic Misinformation," *CBC News*, March 11, 2022, https://www.cbc.ca/news
/politics/common-ground-heritage-misinformation-1.6379690.

INDEX

Derek Beres is a multifaceted author and media expert based in Portland, Oregon. He has served in senior editorial positions at a number of tech companies and has years of experience in health, science, and music writing. He has bylines at *Rolling Stone, National Geographic, Women's Health,* Big Think, and *Yoga Journal.* Derek taught group fitness at Equinox Fitness for seventeen years, where he also created Flow Play, an innovative program at the intersection of music, neuroscience, and movement. He is also one-half of the global music production team EarthRise SoundSystem. Derek received his degree in religion from Rutgers University in 1997.

Matthew Remski is an author and freelance journalist, with bylines in The Walrus and GEN by Medium. He's published eight books of poetry, fiction, and nonfiction, including *Threads of Yoga: A Remix of Patañjali-s Sūtra-s with Commentary and Reverie.* His most recent book, *Practice and All Is Coming: Abuse, Cult Dynamics, and Healing in Yoga and Beyond,* has earned international praise as a groundbreaking resource for critical thinking and community health. He lives in Toronto with his partner and their two sons.

Julian Walker grew up in South Africa and has been teaching yoga in Los Angeles for twenty-seven years. He also facilitates and DJs a weekly ecstatic dance event, runs a busy bodywork practice, and is a trained yoga instructor. Julian has taught at Esalen Institute and Kripalu, and co-created the Awakened Heart, Embodied Mind teacher training. He has been writing critically about New Age spirituality, gurus, and Western yoga culture since 2004. Julian has also made several appearances presenting his experiential synthesis of mindfulness, movement, neuroscience, and somatic psychology techniques at the UCLA Interpersonal Neurobiology conference.

PublicAffairs is a publishing house founded in 1997. It is a tribute to the standards, values, and flair of three persons who have served as mentors to countless reporters, writers, editors, and book people of all kinds, including me.

I. F. STONE, proprietor of *I. F. Stone's Weekly*, combined a commitment to the First Amendment with entrepreneurial zeal and reporting skill and became one of the great independent journalists in American history. At the age of eighty, Izzy published *The Trial of Socrates*, which was a national bestseller. He wrote the book after he taught himself ancient Greek.

BENJAMIN C. BRADLEE was for nearly thirty years the charismatic editorial leader of *The Washington Post*. It was Ben who gave the *Post* the range and courage to pursue such historic issues as Watergate. He supported his reporters with a tenacity that made them fearless and it is no accident that so many became authors of influential, best-selling books.

ROBERT L. BERNSTEIN, the chief executive of Random House for more than a quarter century, guided one of the nation's premier publishing houses. Bob was personally responsible for many books of political dissent and argument that challenged tyranny around the globe. He is also the founder and longtime chair of Human Rights Watch, one of the most respected human rights organizations in the world.

. . .

For fifty years, the banner of Public Affairs Press was carried by its owner Morris B. Schnapper, who published Gandhi, Nasser, Toynbee, Truman, and about 1,500 other authors. In 1983, Schnapper was described by *The Washington Post* as "a redoubtable gadfly." His legacy will endure in the books to come.

Peter Osnos, *Founder*